Second Edition

The Essentials of Business Research

Lawrence Silver

Robert E. Stevens

Courtney Kernek

David L. Loudon

Bruce Wrenn

Academic Media Solutions

Affordable - Quality Textbooks, Study Aids, & Custom Publishing

Cover photo: SFIO CRACHO/Shutterstock.com

Paperback (black/white):   ISBN–13: 978–1–942041–48–1
                              ISBN–10: 1–942041–48–9
Paperback (color):   ISBN–13: 978–1–942041–47–4
                              ISBN–10: 1–942041–47–0
Loose-leaf version (B/W): ISBN–13: 978–1–942041–49–8
                              ISBN–10: 1–942041–49–7
Online version: ISBN–13: 978–1–942041–50–4
                              ISBN–10: 1–942041–50–0

Printed in the United States of America by Academic Media Solutions.

Brief Contents

Contents

2 Ethics in Business Research 23

3 Secondary Data 43

APPENDIX A: Sample Proposals

APPENDIX B: Sample Questionnaires

Preface

The purpose in writing this book was to provide a concise treatment of the business research process. As the title implies, the essentials of research purpose, research ethics, research designs, data collection instruments development, data collection, analysis and report preparation are all covered in the text but without the detailed discussion of more theoretical concepts and more advanced data analysis techniques. We assume that readers of this book will probably have only one business research course but will also have had or will have courses in statistics and/or data analysis to complete their degree requirements.

The shorter length of the text, 14 chapters instead of 18–20 or more, also fits with the trend of offering shortened courses, 7–8 weeks, in MBA programs designed for working professionals. The material becomes much more manageable and allows for more emphasis on discussion boards and written assignments during the course.

The book also includes several research proposals and related questionnaires. The proposals cover statements of the problems/issues, related literature reviews, and the research methodology, including data collection and analysis. Also included is an estimate of the cost of the research project. The accompanying questionnaires demonstrate how the research project becomes the driver in the development of the questionnaire and thus the data that are collected to reach the research objectives. Because of the brevity of time in shortened online courses, some instructors may ask students to prepare a proposal and questionnaire on a work-related topic as a required assignment for the course.

PEDAGOGICAL FEATURES

The Essentials of Business Research, 2e, is a succinct, streamlined text that focuses on the core concepts and issues in the field while providing an approach to business research that balances theory with practice. It guides the student in designing, conducting, and interpreting research. This comprehensive textbook covers the full range of topics, including the following:

- Secondary research and data mining
- Business research ethics
- Internet research
- Qualitative and exploratory research
- Data collection tool design and deployment
- Qualitative data analysis
- Statistical analysis
- Research report preparation

This book offers a range of tools to help students develop and test their research and analytical skills.

- ***An accessible and relevant text that offers a unique narrative***—A natural and relaxed writing style promotes a sense of a conversation between the authors and student.
- ***Comprehensive coverage of current topics and scholarly research***—The text has been thoroughly updated to reflect recent research, theories, and scholarship from across the discipline.

- *Flexible format and organization*—The text provides the core theoretical foundations of business research while offering instructors the flexibility to incorporate a variety of outside course materials and cases.
- *Extensive use of real-world examples*—Each chapter contains a wide variety of real-world examples that illustrate text concepts and demonstrate the connection between theory and practice.
- *Student-friendly pedagogy and features*—Learning objectives, chapter outlines, key terms and on-page marginal key-term definitions, research project tips, research project assignments, chapter summaries, and discussion questions support student learning, retention, and critical analysis.
- *Complete Instructor's Support Package*—The support package includes the Instructor's Resource Manual, Test Item File, and PowerPoint Lecture Slides.

ONLINE AND IN PRINT

Student Options: Print and Online Versions

This second edition of *Essentials of Business Research* is available in multiple versions: online, in PDF, and in print as either a paperback or loose-leaf text. The content of each version is identical.

The most affordable version is the online book, with upgrade options including the online version bundled with a print version. What's nice about the print version is that it offers you the freedom of being unplugged—away from your computer. The people at Academic Media Solutions recognize that it's difficult to read from a screen at length and that most of us read much faster from a piece of paper. The print options are particularly useful when you have extended print passages to read.

The online edition allows you to take full advantage of embedded digital features, including search and notes. Use the search feature to locate and jump to discussions anywhere in the book. Use the notes feature to add personal comments or annotations. You can move out of the book to follow Web links. You can navigate within and between chapters using a clickable table of contents. These features allow you to work at your own pace and in your own style, as you read and surf your way through the material. (See "Harnessing the Online Version" for more tips on working with the online version.)

HARNESSING THE ONLINE VERSION

The online version of *Essentials of Business Research*/2e offers the following features to facilitate learning and to make using the book an easy, enjoyable experience:

- *Easy-to-navigate/clickable table of contents*—You can surf through the book quickly by clicking on chapter headings, or first- or second-level section headings. And the Table of Contents can be accessed from anywhere in the book.
- *Key terms search*—Type in a term, and a search engine will return every instance of that term in the book; then jump directly to the selection of your choice with one click.
- *Notes and highlighting*—The online version includes study apps such as notes and highlighting. Each of these apps can be found in the tools icon embedded in the Academic Media Solutions/Textbook Media's online eBook reading platform (http://www.academicmediasolutions.com).
- *Upgrades*—The online version includes the ability to purchase additional study apps and functionality that enhance the learning experience.

INSTRUCTOR SUPPLEMENTS

In addition to its student-friendly features and pedagogy, the variety of student formats available, and the uniquely affordable pricing options that are designed to provide students with a flexibility that fits any budget and/or learning style, *Essentials of Business Research*/2e comes with the following teaching and learning aids:

- ■ *Test Item File*—An extensive set of multiple-choice, short answer, and essay questions for every chapter for creating original quizzes and exams.
- ■ *Instructor's Manual*—An enhanced version of the book offering assistance in preparing lectures, identifying learning objectives, developing essay exams and assignments, and constructing course syllabi.
- ■ *PowerPoint Presentations*—Key points in each chapter are illustrated in a set of PowerPoint files designed to assist with instruction.

STUDENT SUPPLEMENTS AND UPGRADES (ADDITIONAL PURCHASE REQUIRED)

- ■ **Lecture Guide**—This printable lecture guide is designed for student use and is available as an in-class resource or study tool. Note: Instructors can request the PowerPoint version of these slides to use as developed or to customize.

ACKNOWLEDGMENTS

A book is seldom the work of the authors alone but includes the contributions of others. We would especially like to thank Stephanie Metts, Rhonda Richards, Bambi White and Emily Godfrey for their contributions to the instructors manual, sample proposals, and sample questionnaires. This book would not have been completed without their hard work to contribute to the final edition. We would also like to thank Dan Luciano for development of the concept of affordable college textbooks and his encouragement to write the book. And finally, Victoria Putman of Putman Productions for the production and editorial direction she provided to make this book a reality.

About the Authors

Dr. Lawrence S. Silver is the John Massey Endowed Chair and professor of marketing at Southeastern Oklahoma State University, Durant, OK. He has published numerous refereed articles and conference papers and has co-authored three books. Dr. Silver has extensive experience outside of academia. He served as an officer in the United States Navy, owned and operated an independent insurance agency, and served as an outside director for a community bank. In addition to his academic credentials, Dr. Silver holds the Chartered Property-Casualty Underwriter (CPCU) and Chartered Life Underwriter (CLU) designations. He is also active in the National Apartment Association and holds the Independent Rental Owner Professional (IROP) designation.

Dr. Robert E. Stevens is John Massey Professor of Business in the John Massey School of Business, Southeastern Oklahoma State University, Durant, Oklahoma. He has over 200 publications including 32 books, 128 articles, 25 cases and 14 other publications. Dr. Stevens taught at four other universities prior to joining the faculty at SOSU in 2006. Dr. Stevens has served as a consultant to local, regional, and national firms and has been an owner of 4 small businesses. He is co-editor of *Services Marketing Quarterly,* and *Health Marketing Quarterly*. He has served as program chair and president of Southwest Case Research Association and was named the McGraw-Hill Outstanding Educator by that group in 2017.

Dr. Courtney R. Kernek is an associate professor of marketing at Southeastern Oklahoma State University. She has also taught at Texas A&M University-Commerce. Dr. Kernek has published several refereed articles and conference papers and has co-authored two books. She has also been cited in a variety of academic and professional outlets. Dr. Kernek holds board positions in several professional organizations. She has been active in the field of marketing with over 15 years of industry experience. Dr. Kernek has been nationally recognized for her work in the profession of marketing. She is currently an active marketing consultant and her family owns and operates multiple small businesses.

Dr. Bruce Wrenn (retired) was the first recipient of the Colson Endowed Chair of Marketing at Andrews University. Prior to joining the Andrews faculty, he was Professor of Marketing at Indiana University South Bend where he taught for nineteen years. He received his Ph.D. in marketing from Northwestern University in 1989. Among the more than 100 scholarly and professional publications and presentations by Wrenn are a dozen books in marketing management, marketing research, marketing for religious organizations, and other marketing areas. Wrenn serves on the editorial review board of several scholarly journals, and has consulted with organizations in pharmaceutical, food, high-tech, bio-medical, and hospital industries as well as numerous religious organizations on marketing matters. He currently serves as a Subject Matter Expert in marketing to the American Management Association and a Marketing Mentor in the Harvard Business School's ManageMentor program. His current research and service interests are in assisting churches adopting marketing practices to achieve their goals.

Dr. David Loudon is Professor of Marketing in the Brock School of Business at Samford University and previously taught at Louisiana State University, University of Rhode Island, University of Louisiana at Monroe, and Hong Kong Shue Yan University. Dr. Loudon is the co-author of over twenty books ranging from textbooks used in college classrooms around the world to specialized books focused on organizations as varied as law firms and universities. His research has been published in a number of journals and in the proceedings of numerous professional conferences. Dr. Loudon serves as co-editor of two journals published by Taylor & Francis: *Services Marketing Quarterly* and *Health Marketing Quarterly*.

The Business Research Process and Decision Making

tonefotografia/Shutterstock.com

Introduction to Business Research

dizain/Shutterstock.com

Chapter Outline

Learning Objectives

Upon completing this chapter, you should understand:

- What is involved in the decision-making process.
- How research contributes to the decision-making process.
- The differences among the following: management problems and opportunities, decisional alternatives, and decisional criteria.
- How the research questions lead to formulating research hypotheses.

THE BUSINESS-DECISION ENVIRONMENT

Managers in contemporary organizations are required to make many important decisions. These decisions include what consumer segments to serve, where to locate retail outlets, and whether to hire or outsource salespeople and impact all areas of the firm. The decision to emphasize quality products, for example, affects decisions on procurement, production personnel, and quality control, among other areas.

Many companies are discovering that seemingly routine decisions involving management, marketing, human resources, and production have long-run implications for the organization and are being viewed as strategic in nature necessitating input from top managers. As some of these business decisions become strategic, they may involve commitments and directions that continue to guide efforts as long as they prove successful. A belief that future success requires the organization to become "market oriented"[1] or "market sensitive" has increased the importance of the intelligence function within organizations as they seek to make the right responses to an ever changing business environment. Right responses become increasingly important as competition heats up in markets. Firms are discovering that they must be market driven in order to make decisions that meet with market approval.

Developing an understanding of consumer needs, wants, and perceptions is a prerequisite to effective decision making. Consider the different results of marketing Pepsi AM in the United States and Cheetos in China. Pepsi AM was introduced without research, which would have revealed that the name suggested it to be drunk only in the morning, thereby restricting market size to specific-occasion usage. Frito-Lay did extensive research on the market for snack foods in China before introducing Cheetos there. They learned that cheese was not a common item in the Chinese diet. Thus, traditional Cheetos flavors did not appeal to consumers there, though other flavors such as American cream and zesty Japenese steak were found to be appealing. They also researched Chinese reaction to Chester Cheetah, the cartoon character on the bag, and the Chinese translation of "Cheetos" (luckily corresponding to Chinese characters *qu duo* or "new surprise"). Pepsi AM was a flop; Cheetos were such a success that Frito-Lay could not keep store shelves stocked.[2]

Business research is the specific management function relied upon to provide information for managerial decisions. However, it should be stressed at the outset that merely doing business research does not guarantee that better decisions will be made. The quality of each stage of a business research project will either contribute to better decision making or will make it an ever elusive goal. If research results are correctly analyzed and imaginatively applied, studies have shown that increased profitability is often the outcome.[3]

BUSINESS RESEARCH

Business research is the function that links the business to information and knowledge that can be used for determining, implementing, and evaluating the opportunities and goals for a firm. Business research specifies the information required to address management issues; designs the method for collecting information; manages and implements the data collection process; analyzes the results; and communicates the findings and their implications.

This rather lengthy definition suggests the connection between research and decision making in business organizations.

Research, in a business context, is defined as an organized, formal inquiry into an area to obtain information for use in decision making. There are generally two types of business research: **basic business research** and **applied business research**.

Business research the function that links the business to information and knowledge that can be used for determining, implementing, and evaluating the opportunities and goals for a firm.

Basic business research Business research that is exploratory in nature, and is not directly applicable to a specific business problem. Instead, basic research expands our knowledge and understanding of an issue.

Applied business research used to answer a specific question that has direct application to a particular business.

Applied business research is used to answer a specific question that has direct application to a particular business. Basic research, on the other hand, is more exploratory in nature, and is not directly applicable to a specific business **problem**. Instead, basic research expands our knowledge and understanding of an issue. The difference between the two types of research, then, is for what purposes each will be used.

An example of a basic research question is, "What are customer attitudes toward wait times at a fast food drive through?" Here we are expanding our knowledge about customer perceptions of service. Perhaps customers are generally satisfied with wait times. Or, perhaps customers feel the wait is too long. In the latter case, the manager of a fast food outlet may want to look at how to increase the speed of service as a competitive advantage.

Having conducted the basic research, the manager now as a specific question to investigate; how to decrease drive through wait time in her fast food outlet. In this case, she will use applied research to answer the question. She can experiment with having different windows for payment and food delivery, use two order call boxes, or reorganize the food production line. The point is that each type of research can be used to fit the particular decision-making environment with which management is faced.

BUSINESS RESEARCH AND DECISION MAKING

Although conducting the activities of business research requires using a variety of research techniques, the focus of the research *should not* be on the techniques. Business research should focus on decisions to be made rather than the collection techniques used to gather information to facilitate decision making. This focus is central to understanding the business research function in terms of what it should be, and to the effective and efficient use of research as an aid to decision making. Any user or provider of business research who loses sight of this central focus is likely to end up in one of two awkward and costly positions: (1) failing to collect the information actually needed to make a decision or (2) collecting information that is not needed in a given decision-making context.[4] The result of the first is ineffectiveness—not reaching a desired objective, and the result of the second is inefficiency—failing to reach an objective in the least costly manner. The chances of either of these occurring are greatly reduced when the decision to be made is the focus of the research effort.

To maintain this focal point, an understanding of the purpose and role of business research in decision making is necessary. The basic purpose of business research is to reduce uncertainty or error in decision making. It is the uncertainty of the outcome surrounding a decision that makes decision making difficult. If the outcome of choosing one alternative over another is known, then choosing the right alternative would be simple, given the decision-making criteria. If it were certain that alternative A would result in $100,000 in profit and that alternative B would result in $50,000 in profit, and the decision criterion was to maximize profits, then the choice of alternative A would be obvious. However, business decisions must be made under conditions of uncertainty—it is unknown if alternative A will produce $50,000 more than B. In fact, either or both alternatives may result in losses. It is the ability to reduce uncertainty that gives information its value.

Analyzing what is involved in making a decision will help in understanding how information aids decision making. Decision making is defined as a choice among alternative courses of action. For purposes of analysis, a decision can be broken down into four distinct steps (see Figure 1.1): (1) identify a problem or opportunity, (2) analyze the problem or opportunity, (3) identify alternative courses of action, and (4) select a specific course of action.

Identify a Problem or Opportunity

A **problem** or **opportunity** is the focus of management efforts to maintain or restore performance. A problem is anything that stands in the way of achieving an objective, whereas an opportunity is a chance to improve overall performance.

Problem anything that stands in the way of achieving an objective.

Opportunity a chance to improve overall performance.

Step 1	Step 2	Step 3	Step 4
Recognize the Existence of Problems and Opportunities	Analyze the Exact Nature of Problems and Opportunities	Identify Alternative Courses of Action	Select a Specific Course of Action

FIGURE 1.1 Steps in Decision Making

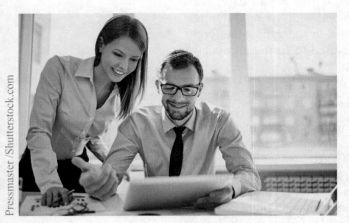

Managers need information to aid in recognizing problems and opportunities because before a problem can be defined and alternatives developed, it must be recognized. An example of this type of information is attitudinal data that compares attitudes toward competing brands. Since attitudes usually are predictive of sales behavior, if attitudes toward a company's product were less favorable than before, the attitudinal information would make the managers aware of the existence of a problem or potential problem. Opportunities may depend upon the existence of pertinent information, such as knowing that distributors are displeased with a competitor's new policy of quantity discounts and as a result may be willing to place increased orders for your product.

Analyze the Problem or Opportunity

Once a problem or opportunity has been recognized, it must be analyzed. Until the nature and sources of the problem have been analyzed, no alternative courses of action can be considered. Sometimes the symptoms of the problem are recognized first, and there may be several problems that produce the same set of symptoms. An analogy using the human body may help in understanding this point. A person experiencing a headache (symptom) may be suffering from a sinus infection, stress, the flu, or a host of other illnesses (potential problems). Treating the headache may provide temporary relief, but not dealing with the root problem will ensure its return, perhaps worsening physical conditions.

The same type of phenomenon occurs in business. A firm, experiencing a decline in sales (symptom), may find it to be the result of a decline in total industry sales, lower prices by competitors, low product quality, or a myriad of other potential problems. No alternative courses of action should be considered until the actual problem has been analyzed. Thus, information aids the manager at this stage in the decision-making process by analyzing the problem.

In some cases an entire research project must be devoted to defining the problem or identifying an opportunity because of a lack of prior knowledge of a particular area. This type of study is usually called an exploratory study and will be discussed more fully in Chapter 4.

Identify Alternatives

The third stage in the decision-making process involves identifying viable alternatives. For some problems, developing alternatives is a natural outcome of analyzing the problem, especially if that particular problem or opportunity has occurred before. A manager's past knowledge and experiences are used to develop the alternatives in these situations. However, in other situations a real contribution of research is to inform the decision maker of the options available to him or her. A company considering introduction of a new product may use consumer information to determine the position of current offerings to evaluate different ways its new product could be positioned in the market. Information on the significant product attributes and how consumers position existing products on these attributes would be an evaluation of possible "openings" (options) available at a given time.

Select an Alternative

The final stage in the decision-making process is the choice among the alternative courses of action available to the decision maker. Information provided by research can aid a manager at this stage by estimating the effects of the various alternatives on the decision criteria. For example, a firm considering introduction of a new product may test market two versions of that product. The two versions of the product are two alternatives to be considered, and the sales and profits resulting from test marketing these two versions become the information needed to choose one alternative over another. Another example is the pretest of television commercials using different themes, characters, and scripts to provide information on consumer reactions to alternative commercials. This information also aids the decision maker in selecting the best advertising approaches to use.

Information collected through research must be directly related to the decision to be made in order to accomplish its purpose of risk reduction. Thus, the focus of research should be the decision-making processes in general and, specifically, the decision to be made in a given situation, rather than the data or the techniques used to collect the data. There is always the danger of a person involved in business research viewing himself or herself as a research technician rather than as someone who provides information to help managers make decisions to solve problems and take advantage of opportunities. In fact, it is safe to say that the best researchers think like decision makers in search of information to make decisions rather than as researchers in search of answers to research questions.

STRATEGIC VERSUS TACTICAL INFORMATION NEEDS

Managers are called upon to make two broad categories of decisions, strategic and tactical. The strategic decisions are those that have long-run implications and effects. These decisions are critical to a firm's success and may not be altered if successful. Tactical decisions are short run in scope and effect and are usually altered on a regular basis. An example of these two types of decisions will help clarify the distinction and also clarify what many researchers and managers have failed to understand.

A company analyzing a market for possible entry would be considering a strategic move—entering a new market. This requires information on such things as competitor strengths and weaknesses, market shares held by competitors, market growth potential, production, financial and marketing requirements for success in the industry, strategic tendencies of competitors and the like. This is strategic information. Once the decision to enter the market has been made, information on current prices charged by specific competitors, current package designs and sizes, and other criteria is needed to make the tactical decisions for the short run—a year or less. This is tactical information.

Thus, strategic decisions require strategic information, and tactical decisions require tactical information. Failure to recognize the distinction between decision types and information types will result in information that deals with the right areas—prices for example—but with the wrong time frame. For tactical decisions, a manager needs to know competitive prices and their emphasis by both competitors and consumers. For strategic decisions, the manager is more interested in competitors' abilities and tendencies to use pricing as a retaliatory weapon.

The researcher and the manager must be certain the time frame for the decision is specified in advance to ensure that the right type of information is collected. This should be a joint effort by both information user and provider.

THE NATURE OF BUSINES RESEARCH

It is obvious at this point that the key to understanding when business research can be of greatest value to organizations is to understand the decisions facing managers. These areas and the related forms of business research include the following:

Concept/product testing. A concept or product test consists of evaluating consumer response to a new product or concept. This is often a part of the test market in the development of a new product. It is also used to determine how a product or service can best be positioned in a particular sector of the marketplace. For example, product testing would answer what the consumer's perception of new products or services to be offered might be. It can also examine how users perceive a product's value as well as its attributes and benefits or how perceived values and attributes relate to actual need and demand.

Tracking study. A tracking study is an ongoing periodic survey of prerecruited consumers who record their use of various products or services. Specific preferences are measured and compared to evaluate changes in perceptions, preferences, and actual usage over time.

Absenteeism. An absenteeism study is conducted by or for a human resources department and assesses the direct and indirect costs of employee absences in the production of the firm's products and services. Once these costs are determined, the firm can look for ways to reduce absenteeism.

Product or brand service usage. Product or brand usage studies serve to determine current demand for the various brands of a product or service. This type of approach may also determine which brand name has primary awareness in consumers' minds or which they prefer as well as how often and why it is used.

Advertising penetration. Advertising penetration analyses evaluate the message that is actually being communicated to the target audience. This type of study serves to determine if the intended message is understood, how persuasive it is, or how well it motivates. These studies may also evaluate the effectiveness of individual media for a particular target market.

Image evaluation. Image studies provide feedback relative to the image a company, product, or service has in the eyes of the consumers. Image studies may reveal attribute perceptions of a particular brand or determine its strengths and weaknesses.

Public opinion surveys. Public opinion surveys determine the key issues in the minds of the public or specific customers (or investors), relative to specific issues, individuals, or business sectors. They reveal whether opinion is positive or negative, determine the degree of importance of specific issues, or evaluate awareness levels of key issues.

Copy testing. Copy testing allows for an evaluation of consumer response to ad copy being considered. It determines how well the intended message is actually being communicated. Copy tests ensure the wording used is consistent with the language of the target audience. Copy testing is used most effectively in the conceptual stages of copy development to allow for consumer feedback on concepts portrayed by various preliminary ad copy.

Performance evaluation. Many larger companies have a formal employee evaluation system. Research is regularly conducted to make sure the system is fair, objective, measures desired performance, and meets all EEOC requirements.

Test marketing and product placements. Product placements are a bit more extensive than product tests. Product tests take place in a controlled setting, such as a shopping

Jstone/Shutterstock.com

mall, where consumers are recruited to test a product. In a product placement study, the product to be test marketed is placed in the home of the consumer for a specific period of time. After this period a personal or telephone interview is used to record the specific responses of the user concerning the product. This type of study will determine how consumers respond to a product that often has no name or packaging appeals associated with it.

Roman Rybaleov/Shutterstock.com

Taste tests. Taste tests are conducted in a controlled environment where consumers are recruited to taste a product and give their evaluations. Taste tests serve to determine the acceptance of a product without brand or packaging appeals relative to attributes of flavor, texture, aroma, and visual appeal. Taste tests may be conducted with variations of a single product or with samples of competitors' products tasted for comparison testing.

Risk management. Risk management studies assess the potential property, liability, and environmental hazards the firm faces and the best method to reduce or mitigate potential lossless.

Market segmentation. Market segmentation studies determine how a market is segmented by product usage, demand, or customer profiles. These studies usually develop demographic, psychographic, product preference, and lifestyle profiles of key market segments.

Media measurement. These studies determine what share of the market the medium being tested actually has and how a target market is identified demographically and psychographically. Media studies also evaluate preferences in programming as well as promotional appeals that are most effective in reaching and expanding a particular target audience.

Financial analysis. Research in finance helps the firm decide the best method for obtaining money for a new product or service. For example, a firm might study the pros and cons of debt financing as opposed to equity financing.

Market feasibility. A market feasibility study analyzes the market demand for a new product, brand, or service. This type of study usually evaluates potential market size, determines what kind of demand might be expected, what market dynamics are interacting, and what market segments might be most receptive to the introduction of a new product or brand. Feasibility studies may also determine market feedback relative to similar product or services, attributes sought, as well as pricing and packaging perspectives.

Location studies. For local customer-intensive businesses, the location must be determined. Location studies serve to evaluate the size of the potential market surrounding a proposed location and whether local demand will support the facility.

Market share and market size studies. Market share and market size studies determine what products are being purchased at what volume and the actual size of sales being realized by each competitor. These studies can also identify and determine the strength of new firms that have recently entered the market in a strong growth mode.

Competitive analysis. A competitive analysis is often part of a market share and market size study. It consists of an evaluation of the strengths and weaknesses of competitors. It may also include

Lissandra Melo/Shutterstock.com

pertinent data relative to locations, sales approaches, and the extent of their product lines and manufacturing capabilities.

Positioning studies. Positioning studies evaluate how leading companies or brands are viewed in the minds of consumers concerning key product or image attributes. This type of study will evaluate perceived strengths and weaknesses of each, as well as determine key attributes consumers associate with their idea of an "ideal" supplier of a particular product or service.

Customer satisfaction studies. Customer satisfaction studies evaluate the level of satisfaction existing customers have with the products or services of a company or organization. The basic philosophy is that it is cheaper to keep an existing customer than to try to attract a new one. Therefore, continuous analysis of existing customers provides input on how to change what is being done to increase satisfaction or lessen dissatisfaction.

Business Research for Small Organizations

While it is true that larger corporations would account for the largest share of expenditures for the aforementioned applications of research, small businesses and entrepreneurial ventures are certainly interested in obtaining research results that can help them make better decisions in these areas. Such firms would typically seek answers to the following types of questions as well.

Customer Research

- Which customer groups represent the best target markets for my product or service?
- How large is the existing and potential market? What is its rate of growth?
- What unfulfilled needs exist for my product? How are customers currently fulfilling those needs?
- Under what circumstances would customers use the product? What benefits are customers seeking to gain in these circumstances?
- Where would customers expect to buy the product? What decision process do they go through when buying the product?
- Who makes the purchase decision for this type of product? How are they influenced by others in the household (or company) when making this decision?
- What is the value customers place on having their needs fulfilled by this type of product?

Competitor Analysis

- Who are my competitors (i.e., alternatives to addressing the needs of potential customers)?
- How brand loyal are customers to my competitors?
- How do potential buyers perceive competitors' offerings?
- What are my competitors' competitive advantages and how are they exploiting them through their marketing programs?

Operational Environment

- By what means (channels, methods) is this type of production made available to customers? Is there an opportunity to innovate here?
- How are customers made aware of this type of product? What opportunities exist to increase efficiency and effectiveness in promotion?
- What technological developments are likely to occur in this market and how will they affect our competitive position?
- What cultural/social environmental trends could impact our business? How?

- What will be the impact of the regulatory environment on our business now and in the foreseeable future?
- What economic and demographic trends are occurring which could affect the nature of the market opportunity? How?

These examples of issues of interest to small businesses are typical of the kinds of questions that business research can seek to answer. How research arrives at the answers to these questions can vary from project to project.

The Nature of Conventional and Unconventional Research

It is important to reiterate that a study of business research should begin with this understanding—business research is not focused on the use of surveys or experiments or observations (i.e., techniques). Business research is about finding solutions to management problems and aiding in better decision making. Therefore, the goal of using business research is not to propagate convention in the use of research methods, but rather to find solutions. When it is obvious that the best method of finding a solution to a problem is to conduct a survey (or conduct an experiment, or use observational methods), then it is important to use such techniques scientifically, so that we have faith that the findings contain as much "truth" as we can afford. Sometimes the method we use to search for the truth in order to reduce uncertainty and make better decisions follows convention. Sometimes it is unique and unconventional. We do not "score points" for conventionality; we succeed by finding efficient and effective means of gathering information which aids decision making. The following example will help to illustrate this point:

wrangler/Shutterstock.com

A producer of frozen dinner entrees set an objective that the company's food products should not just be good heat-and-serve meals, but should aim higher and be considered excellent cuisine in general. At an advanced stage of product development they wanted to see how close they were getting to their objective, and decided upon a somewhat unconventional method of testing product quality. They rented the ballroom of a local hotel noted for its excellent catering service and under the guise of a professional organization invited local business professionals to attend a meeting where a well-known speaker would make a presentation on a topic of interest to the business community. Unbeknownst to the attendees, the company had the hotel kitchen heat and serve the food company's frozen entrees instead of the hotel's usual catered meal. At each table of eight in the audience the company had a member of its staff playing the role of just another invited guest. During the meal the employee would engage others at the table in a discussion of the quality of the food (e.g., "I see you got the lasagna while I got chicken Kiev. How is the lasagna here?"). After the meal and speech the other guests at each table were debriefed about the ruse.

By taking this approach the firm was able to obtain insights into how close they were to having a product that could compare favorably to cuisine prepared by chefs and with high expectations by diners. Although not the only research conducted by the firm for this line of products, this rather unconventional method gave them good insights at this stage of the process that might have exceeded what traditional taste tests could have achieved. Once again, our overriding objective is to improve decision making, not pursue convention.

We would be remiss, however, if we did not follow up that admonition with this caveat—we are not suggesting an "anything goes" approach to research. We must always ensure that we pursue research that is both related to the management problem and its related decisional issues, *and* must make certain our methods are scientific and represent the most efficient means of seeking answers to our questions. Figure 1.2 helps to show the possible combinations of these variables.

Better decision making by using research results only comes from research which falls in cell #1. However, you can imaginatively apply scientific methodology that goes against

		Is Research Relevant to a Real Management Problem?	
		YES	**NO**
Does the Research Follow Scientific Methods?	YES	1. Results are relevant and believable.	2. Results are believable, but not relevant.
	NO	3. Results are relevant, but not believable.	4. Results are neither relevant nor believable.

FIGURE 1.2 Outcomes of Research

"convention" and still end up in cell #1. The point here is that when we set out to do our research we do not set out to write a questionnaire, or conduct in-depth interviews, or run an experiment, we set out to solve a problem, to evaluate an opportunity, or to test hypotheses so that we can reduce uncertainty and improve our decision making. So, we need to understand that it is possible to be both scientific *and* unconventional, and we must be open to using whatever method represents the most efficient and effective means of generating relevant and believable results, and not be bound by our past proclivities to use certain "comfortable" methods.

STEPS IN A BUSINESS RESEARCH PROJECT

1. Define the Management Problem

2. State Research Objectives

3. Determine the Research Methodology

4. Collect Data

5. Analyze and Interpret the Findings

6. Present the Results

Silver, Stevens, Kernek, Wrenn & Loudon

FIGURE 1.3 Basic Steps in a Business Research Project

Ensuring that data collected in a research project not only is related to management's information needs, but also fits management's time frame, requires an approach to research that is centered on the management problem—the decision to be made. Such an approach is shown in Figure 1.3.

A venerable work adage states, "Plan your work; work your plan," and this is the approach that should be used in carrying out a research project. A research project does not begin with a questionnaire or a focus group interview or any other research technique, but with a carefully thought-out plan for the research that includes: (1) a statement of the management problem or opportunity, (2) a set of research objectives, and (3) a statement of the research methodology to be used in the project.

Define the Management Problem

The starting point in a research project should be an attempt by both the user and the provider of information to clearly define the problem. Mutual understanding and agreement are vitally necessary at this point in the research process. Failure by either party to understand or clearly define the major issue requiring information will surely lead to disappointment and wasted effort. Studies have shown that the proper utilization of the findings from business research by managers is directly affected by the quality of interactions that take place between managers and researchers, plus the level of researcher involvement in the research decision-making process.[5] Many information users, especially the uninitiated, have been "burned," never to be "burned" again, by someone who has collected some data, then collected the money and left them with a lot of "useful" information.[6]

A health care administrator recently related such a story. He had heard a great deal about marketing and the need for having information on consumers, although he was unclear about both. He was approached by a marketing research firm that offered to supply a lot of "useful marketing information" for a reasonable fee. Several months after he had received the final report and the marketing research firm had received his check, he realized that he had no idea of how to use the information or if it was what he really needed.

This type of problem can be avoided, or at least minimized, through user-provider interaction, analysis, and discussion of the key management

dizain/Shutterstock.com

issues involved in a given situation. The information provider's task is to convert the manager's statement of symptoms to likely problems and decision issues and then finally to information needs. Two key questions that must always be dealt with at this stage are: (1) what information does the decision maker believe is needed to make a specific decision and (2) how will the information be used to make the decision? Asking these questions will cause the information user to begin thinking in terms of the information needed to make the decision rather than the decision itself. Also, the user can move to a level of thinking specifically about how the information will be used.

An example of this interaction process will help clarify this point. An executive vice president for a franchise of a national motel-restaurant chain was evaluating his information needs with one of the authors about a major remodeling of one of the chain's restaurants. The author posed the question about how the information was going to be used in the decision-making process. The chain's vice president then realized that corporate policy would not permit deviating from the established interior designs currently used even if information were available that an alternative design would be more acceptable to consumers. He then concluded that he did not need the information! The information could have been easily obtained through a survey, but the bottom line would have been management's inability to act on it. The manager realized that he needed to work on a policy change at the corporate level and if information was needed, it would be to evaluate that particular policy.

A problem exists when there is a difference between the ideal state and the actual state. An opportunity exists when the environment favorably values something the organization can do. Ask the client to describe "the bottom line" of what he or she sees as the problem or opportunity that requires research in order to make decisions. This is a starting point, but more work is needed to determine the focus of the research.

Research Project Tip

One type of question that can aid in the process of identifying the real problem in its proper scope is the "why" question. The researcher uses the why question to help separate what is known (i.e., facts) from what is merely assumed (i.e., hypotheses). The following example of a manufacturer of capital equipment will help illustrate the use of the why question.

The Compton Company was a capital equipment manufacturer with a market share larger than its next two competitors combined. All companies in this business sold through independent distributors who typically carried the lines of several manufacturers. Compton had for several years been suffering a loss of market share. In an effort to regain share they fired their ad agency. The new agency conducted a study of end-use customers and discovered that the fired ad agency had done an outstanding job of creating awareness and interest in the Compton line. The study also revealed that these end-users were buying competitor's equipment from the distributors. The switch from interest in Compton to the competition was not a failure of the advertising, but rather the result of distributors' motivation to sell the products of manufacturers' running sales contests, offering cash bonuses, and supplying technical sales assistance.[7]

If a business researcher had been called in to help address Compton's problem the resulting conversation might have been as follows:

Manager: We need you to help us find a new advertising agency. Researcher: Why do you believe you need a new ad agency? Manager: Because our market share is slipping.

Researcher: Why do you believe that is the fault of your ad agency?

Manager: Because we think they have not created a high enough level of awareness and interest in our product among target market members.

Researcher: OK, but why do you believe that? What evidence do you have that ties your declining market share to a problem with advertising?

At this point it will become obvious that the company does not have any evidence that supports the contention that poor advertising is the source of the decline in market share. This realization should open the door for the researcher to suggest that the issue be defined as a decline in market share, and that some research could be done to identify the source of the problem. Asking "why" questions allows all parties involved to separate facts from hypotheses and give direction to research that can help solve real problems in their proper scope. Once the problem has been determined, the researcher can enter into discussions with the decision maker regarding the appropriate purpose for the research.

Research Project Tip	You will need to ask "why" questions similar to the Compton Company example to distinguish between facts and hypotheses. Sometimes the client believes a hypothesis so strongly that it has become a "fact" in the client's mind. Asking "why" questions helps focus researchers and decision makers on the real problem (i.e., the problem in its proper scope).

Specify Research Purpose[8]

It is important to establish an understanding between the decision maker and the researcher as to the role the research will play in providing information for use in making decisions. This suggests that one of the first things researchers should do is identify the decision alternatives facing the decision maker.

Identify Decision Alternatives

As has been repeatedly stressed in this chapter, effective research is research that results in better decision making. Hence, as a first step in determining the role of research in solving the management problem, the researcher should ask "what if" questions to help identify the decisions under consideration. For example, continuing the Compton Company dialog between researcher and decision maker:

Researcher: *What if* the research revealed that potential customers believed our products failed to offer features comparable to our competitors, and so bought competitor's products?

Manager: Well, I do not think that is happening, but if it were then we would change our product to offer those features.

A review of such "what if" questions will identify those areas in which decisions might be made to solve the management problem. If the answer to the question is that knowing such information would not make a difference in the decisions made, then the researcher knows not to include that issue in the research since it would not positively influence decision making. It is obvious that it is necessary for the researcher to think like a decision maker in order to know what questions to ask. Putting yourself in the position of a decision maker, thinking what decisions you might be faced with, and then asking "what if" questions to determine if the actual decision maker sees things as you do is an effective means of beginning the process of determining the research purpose.

Research Project Tip	Asking "what if" questions aids the researcher in determining the purpose of the research. Write down all the topics where the answers to "what if" questions reveal decisions that are to be made based on such findings. Research will attempt to provide information that makes a difference in decision making.

Determine Decisional Criteria

Once the decision alternatives facing the decision maker seeking to solve the management problem have been specified, the researcher must determine what criteria the manager will use to choose among the alternatives. Different managers facing a choice among alternatives might desire different information, or information in different forms, to feel comfortable in distinguishing which alternative is best. The decisional criteria are those pieces of information that can be used to identify which alternatives are truly capable of solving the problem. For example, in the Compton Company case the dialog to help identify one of the decisional criteria might have looked like the following:

Researcher: So, one area we might want to consider making a decision in would be redesigning the product with the latest features. What information would you need to have in order to make those types of decisions?

Manager: I would want to know the features desired by our target market customers, and how those features are expected to deliver specific benefits to those customers. I would also like to see how our customers compare our products to our competitors' products.

You may have to ask a series of probing questions intended to get the client to reveal what information in what form he or she will need in order to make the decisions faced. Sometimes these criteria have not been explicitly identified before such questioning. By thinking like a business decision maker you can determine if the client might be interested in the same information you might use if you were in the client's position.

Research Project Tip

A similar dialog would help to identify other decisional criteria. Through this process of specifying decisional alternatives and the criteria used to choose among the alternatives, the researcher is also helping the decision maker to clarify in his or her own mind how to arrive at a decision to solve the real management problem.

Indicate Timing and Significance of Decisions

Other areas of concern to the researcher trying to arrive at a statement of research purpose are the amount of time available to the decision maker within which to make the decision, and how important the decision is to the firm. The same management problem could result in very different research purposes if decision makers see the timing and significance of the research differently. Researchers are responsible for ensuring that the research purpose not only fits the decisional criteria needs, but is also consistent with the timing and significance accorded the research and the associated decision making process.

Statement of research purpose. Once the decision alternatives, criteria, and timing and significance of the decisions have been considered, it is useful for the researcher to construct a one (or two) sentence declaration of the research purpose. For the Compton Company case such a sentence might be as follows:

Research Purpose: To determine the cause(s) of the decline in our market share and identify possible actions that could be taken to recover the lost share.

The researcher would need to obtain agreement with the decision maker as to the appropriateness of such a statement, as well as agreement with the research questions.

State Research Objectives

Research objectives consist of questions and hypotheses. The research questions represent a decomposition of the problem into a series of statements that constitute the end results sought by the research project. The questions should be stated in such a way that their accomplishment will provide the information necessary to solve the problem as stated. The objectives serve to guide the research results by providing direction, scope of a given project, and serve as the basis for developing the methodology to be used in the project.

In the area of research questions, both the user and provider should interact to maximize the research results that the user and provider are anticipating. The provider of the information usually assumes the role of interpreting needs and developing a list of questions that serve as a basis of negotiation for final research objectives. It is helpful to use the form of questions so that the researcher can think in terms of finding ways to provide answers to those questions. The following illustration will help make this clear.

In the Compton Company case the research questions might be framed as follows:

- Where has market share declined (e.g., products, geographic areas, channel type)?
- What is the level of awareness and interest in our products among target market members?
- What competitive actions have attracted our customers?
- What are the perceptions of our dealers and distributors for our policies and practices (i.e., what is the status of our relationships with dealers)?
- How do customers rate the quality, features, and price of our products versus competitors?

Other questions could be stated. Note that in each case research must be done (sometimes internal to the company, sometimes external) to discover information that can answer the research questions.

Research Project Tip	Be sure your research questions are in the form of questions, and require research of some type (internal or external to the organization) to get answers to the questions. Plan on spending a fair amount of time developing these questions (and hypotheses) since all the remaining steps of the research process will be seeking to get answers to these questions (and testing your hypotheses).

Research Project Tip	Since the research process from this point on will focus on achieving the research objectives (i.e., answering the research questions and testing the hypotheses), the researcher needs to step back and objectively look at these objectives and ask the question: *Do I really believe that getting answers to these questions (and testing these hypotheses) will provide the information needed to make the necessary decisions to solve management's problem?* Sometimes all the research questions look good individually, but collectively they just do not provide the information necessary to make the decisions. In this case more research questions are needed.

Hypotheses are speculations regarding specific findings of the research. They are helpful to researchers when their presence results in actions taken by the researcher that might not have occurred in the absence of the hypothesis. If the presence of an hypothesis in no way affects the research or the analysis of the data, the hypothesis is superfluous and does not need to be stated. If, on the other hand, the hypothesis influences the research in any one of the following ways, it should be included:

1. ***Choice of respondents.*** If the researcher believes that an important part of the research is to determine if a speculated difference in attitudes, behaviors, and preferences exists between two groups of respondents, the hypothesis is useful to the research. For example:

Hypothesis: Customers on the west coast favor this product feature more than customers on the east coast.

Research Project Tip

Hypotheses can be very helpful in identifying issues for the research to investigate, but are superfluous if they do not work, as the three examples illustrate. Include them when their presence results in the research being somehow different than it would be if they were not there.

Such a hypothesis affects the research by causing the researcher to include customers from both coasts in the sample. Without the need to test such a hypothesis, the sample may not include enough customers on the east and west coasts to allow for comparisons. Of course, as with all research questions and hypotheses, there should be some decision-making relevance in pursuit of an answer to the question or testing the hypothesis.

2. *Questions asked.* A second area where hypotheses work for researchers is in influencing the questions asked of respondents. For example:

Hypothesis: Customer interest in our product declines when they see what it costs.

Research Project Assignment

Prepare a short (no more than three single-spaced pages) Statement of Management Problem, Research Purpose (include decision alternatives, criteria, timing, and importance), Research Objectives, and Hypotheses based on your dialogs with the client. Get the client's reactions, revise as necessary, and submit to your instructor.

To test this hypothesis the researcher must find some way to ask questions that determine the role of price in affecting customer interest in the product. So, hypotheses that aid the researcher by suggesting variables to be included in the data collection instrument are useful.

3. *Analysis of data.* Another use of hypotheses that argues for their inclusion is when the hypothesis identifies analytical tasks that must be performed to test the hypothesis, as shown below:

Hypothesis: Sales declines for this product are not uniform across the country.

Here, a test of the hypothesis requires the researcher to examine the sales data on a regional, district, state, or some other appropriate geographical breakout. Absent such a hypothesis, the data might not be examined in this manner.

Definition of Terms: Management Problems/Opportunity, Research Purposes, Research Questions, Hypotheses

Management Problem/Opportunity

Idle curiosity is an insufficient reason to undertake research. To justify research, management must need research information in order to reduce the risk of making decisions intended to either solve a problem or investigate an opportunity. A problem exists whenever the ideal state differs from the actual state (e.g., sales are down and management doesn't know why). An opportunity is a chance to improve performance if the correct decisions can be made (e.g., what do we need to know about the market that can help us determine whether we should introduce this new product line or not?).

(continued)

Research Purpose

Decision Alternative

What actions might we take to solve the problem or exploit the opportunity if the research reveals those actions are warranted (e.g., change our target market, promote convenience as our competitive advantage)?

Decisional Criteria

The information we need to know from the marketplace that helps us choose among the decision alternatives (e.g., if we discovered the opportunities to grow our current target market we'll better know if we should change our target market; if we know the prospective customers' attraction to convenience as a selling point we'll know if that should be our Unique Selling Proposition).

Research Purpose

A declarative statement that indicates how the research will contribute to solving the problem or evaluating the opportunity (e.g., "To determine the cause(s) of our sales decline and the possible actions to reverse the decline.").

Research Questions

The specific questions that must be answered by the research in order to provide all the decisional criteria information needed. In other words, what exactly does the research need to discover that will help us know what we should do to ultimately solve our problem or exploit our opportunity? For example, our decision alternatives include changing our target market, our criterion is the extent of the opportunity to grow our current target market, and our questions might include:

- What are our current target market's needs? Have they changed? Why?
- Does our current target market believe our product fully satisfies their needs? Why or why not?
- How well do our competitors satisfy the needs of the target market?
- What is the expected growth rate of the current target market (i.e., people who share this need)? Other market segments?

We'll need numerous questions answered before we are fully ready to choose among our decision alternatives.

Research Hypothesis

Possible findings from the research that could make a difference in what we decide to do (e.g., Hypothesis: Our product appeals more to the older market segment than the younger.).

This possible finding (we don't know whether it is true or not until we do the research) could affect our target market selection. To determine whether it is true or not requires that we ask both young and old consumers in our research about the attractiveness of our product.

Develop Research Design

Once we have established the research questions and hypotheses we must plan a research design by which we will get answers to our research questions and test our hypotheses. While it is important that the researcher be precise and comprehensive in the development of research questions and hypotheses in order that the research design directly address those research needs, the researcher must also be flexible in order to make changes to both the research questions/hypotheses and the design in the course of conducting the research. This flexibility is important because unanticipated discoveries during the research may require re-formulation of the questions and hypotheses and the research design followed to address them.

The research design will involve the use of one or more of three broad categories of research approaches: exploratory, descriptive, and causal. Exploratory research is usually called for if the management problem is vague or can be only broadly defined. Research at this stage may involve a variety of techniques (literature review, focus groups, in-depth interviews, psychoanalytic studies, and case studies) and is characterized by the flexibility allowed to researchers in the exploration of relevant issues. Descriptive research is conducted when there is a need to measure the frequency with which a sampled population behaves, thinks, or is likely to act or to determine the extent to which two variables co-vary. Research must be highly structured in descriptive research so that any variation in the variables under investigation can be attributed to differences in the respondents rather than to variations in the questioning. Causal research is also highly structured, and includes exercise of control over variables in order to test cause-and-effect relationships between variables. While exploratory research is used to generate hypotheses, both descriptive and causal research are used to test hypotheses.

Select Data-Collection Methodology

A research design provides the overall plan indicating how the researcher will obtain answers to the research questions and test hypotheses. The researcher must also identify the specific methodology that will be used to collect the data. These decisions include determining the extent to which the questions can be answered using **secondary data**—data that have already been collected for purposes other than the research under investigation—or must be answered by the use of **primary data**—which are collected explicitly for the research study at hand. If primary data must be collected, decisions must be made with regard to the use of communication and observation approaches to generating the data, the degree of structure and disguise of the research, and how to administer the research—observation by either electronic, mechanical, or human methods; communication in person, through the mail, over the phone; or via computer.

Secondary data data that have already been collected for purposes other than the current research project.

Primary data data that is collected explicitly for the research study at hand.

Determine Measurement and Data-Analysis Methods

The next research decision area concerns the methods used to measure and analyze the data. The major criterion used in making this decision is the nature of the data to be analyzed. The purpose of the analysis is to obtain meaning from the raw data that have been collected.

For many researchers the area of data analysis can be the most troublesome. While some data-analysis techniques do require an understanding of statistics, it is not true that all research results must be managed by statistical experts to be interpretable or useful. However, use of the *proper* data-analysis approach will mean the difference between capitalizing on all the careful work done to generate the data versus not being able to discover the answers to research objectives, or worse, drawing erroneous conclusions.

It is important to identify how the information will be measured before a data-collection instrument is developed because it is necessary to know how one plans to use the data in getting answers to research objectives before the question that generates the data can be asked. For example, if one needs to examine the differences in attitudes of people aged 13 to 16, 17 to 20, 21 to 24, and 25 to 28, one cannot ask about the respondent's age by using categories less than 18 years, 18 to 25, or 25 and older.

The researcher is therefore trying to determine the answer to this difficult question: "How will we measure what we need to measure?" For example, if attitudes are to be measured, which technique will be used? The method of equal-appearing intervals? The semantic differential? The Likert technique? In many cases no validated measuring techniques are available, so the researcher must rely on what has been used in past studies and on his or her own judgment to decide upon the appropriate technique.

It is extremely important that the researcher develop operational definitions of the concepts to be measured and that these be stated explicitly. Even seemingly simple concepts, such as awareness, can be defined in several ways, each having different meaning and relative importance. To know that 60 percent of the respondents said they had heard of Kleenex is not the same as 60 percent saying that Kleenex is what comes to mind when they think of facial tissues. Yet both of these approaches could be considered as measuring awareness.

Design Data-Collection Forms

The specific instruments (forms) that will be used to measure the variables of interest must now be designed. This would involve the design of the observation form or questionnaire. In either case, these forms should coincide with the decisions made with respect to what should be measured and how.

Constructing a data-collection form is part art and part science. We are attempting to construct an instrument that is capable of generating the measures and allowing for the data-analysis procedures determined in the previous step. However, we are also focusing on the decision that we are faced with making that was both the beginning point and the end point of our research. Thus the data collection instrument must accomplish more than merely generating measures; it must provide the insights needed that lead to better decision making. As we'll see in Chapter 6, there is a great deal more to achieving such a goal than merely converting our needed measures (data) into questions capable of producing those measures. For example, in addition to expressing the study objectives in question form (i.e., obtaining measures), a questionnaire must contextualize the information collected, create harmony and rapport with the respondent, and generate data that might not have been specified in the study objectives, but that is needed to direct decision making. These goals require a blend of both art and science to be successfully achieved. We won't ultimately be successful, however, if we ask the wrong people the right questions. Hence the importance of our next step in the process.

Define Sampling Methods

The next step in the research is to define the population or universe of the study. The research universe includes all of the people, stores, or places that possess some characteristic management is interested in measuring. The universe must be defined for each research project, and this defined universe becomes the group from which a sample is drawn. The list of all universe elements is sometimes referred to as the sampling frame.

It is extremely important that the sampling frame include all members of the population. Failure to meet this requirement can result in bias. If, for example, the researcher is trying to estimate the potential market for a new memory impaired nursing home and intends to use currently diagnosed Alzheimer patients as the population listing or sampling frame, at least two problems would be encountered. First, not everyone who is memory

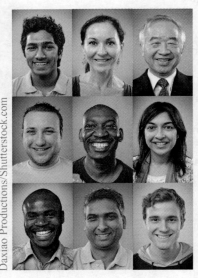

Daxiao Productions/Shutterstock.com

impaired has Alzheimer as there are other forms of dementia. Additionally, there is a percentage of the population with the disease who have not been diagnosed. Thus, the difference between the sampling frame (Alzheimer patients) and area residents could be substantial and would bias the results.

It is imperative that the population be carefully identified and a sampling technique used that minimizes the chance of bias introduced through the sampling frame not containing all elements of the population. Sampling methods also include determination of techniques and sample size. Two separate decisions are called for in this step. The first is how specific sample elements will be drawn from the population. There are two broad categories of sampling techniques: probability and nonprobability. The approach selected depends on the nature of the problem and the nature of the population under study. For probability designs the objective is to draw a sample that is both representative and useful. For nonprobability designs the objective is to select a useful sample even though it may not be representative of the population it comes from. These distinctions will be clarified later, but it is important to note that the sample design influences the applicability of various types of statistical analysis—some analysis types are directly dependent upon an assumption about how sample elements are drawn.

Sampling issues are pertinent even when we are dealing with decision makers who say "I cannot afford the time or money to do a big survey. I just want to get a feel for the market opportunity and then I will take my chances." For example, if in the Compton Company case the decision makers held such an opinion about what competitor policies were with dealers, the researcher is still faced with the need to define the population of interest (all dealers, dealers of a certain volume of business or location), develop a sampling frame (list) of the dealers, and determine how many and who to talk with in order to get answers to the research questions.

Sample size represents the other side of the decision to be made. Determining how many sample elements are needed to accomplish the research objectives requires both analysis and judgment. The techniques for determining sample size are discussed in Chapter 9, including a whole series of other nonstatistical questions, such as costs, response rate, homogeneity of sample elements, which must be considered to determine sample size. In some studies the cost may dictate a lower sample size than would be required given requirements about sampling reliability.

Collect, Analyze and Interpret the Data, and Present the Results

Once the previous steps have been completed and the planning stage of the research project has been carried out, the plan is now ready for execution. The execution stages involve collecting the data from the population sampled in the ways specified, and analyzing the data using the analysis techniques already identified in the research plan. If the research plan or proposal has been well thought out and de-bugged early through revisions of objectives and research designs, then the implementation steps will flow much better.

Once the data are collected and analyzed, the researcher must interpret the results of the findings in terms of the management problem for which the data were collected. This means determining what the results imply about the solution to the management problem and recommending a course of action to management. If the purpose of the research project was to determine the feasibility of introducing a new product and the results of the research project show that the product will produce an acceptable level of profits, then the research should recommend introduction of the product unless there are known internal or external barriers to entry that cannot be overcome. This means the researcher must move beyond the role of the scientist in objectively collecting and analyzing data. Now a researcher must assume the role of a management consultant in a science that states: Given these facts and this interpretation, I recommend this action. This does not, of course, mean that the action recommended will be followed by management. Since the researcher is usually in a staff capacity, only recommendations for action can be offered. Management can accept or reject the recommendations; this is management's prerogative. However, to be effective in getting results implemented, the researcher must assume this role of recommending action. The researcher should be involved in the problem definitions and objectives to be able to recommend courses of action based on interpretation of results.

To some this approach may seem to be overstepping the researcher's responsibilities to make recommendations. Yet most managers appreciate this approach since it at least represents a starting point in deciding what action should be taken given certain research results. Remember, information has not really served its basic purpose until it is used in decision making.

BUSINESS INFORMATION SYSTEMS

Some organizations have moved beyond the stage of thinking of information needs in terms of projects and have focused attention on creating information systems that provide a continuous flow of information to users. While such a focus may shift priorities in terms of the amount spent on information for a database and that spent for specific projects, it should be pointed out that even if information is collected on a regular basis as a part of the information system, the principles of good business research set forth in this book are still applicable to these information systems. The fact that information is collected on a regular basis does not negate the need for relating it to the decisions to be made and for using correct sampling techniques. The basic principles outlined are applicable to all information flows; some directly and others indirectly, but nonetheless applicable. Therefore, an understanding of these principles will help ensure better quality of information regardless of the nature of the system or procedures used to provide the information.

SUMMARY

This chapter focused on the purpose, use, and overall approaches to gathering information for making management decisions. An understanding of the decision-making process and how information can aid management is the basis for planning and implementing research projects. Research projects, in turn, should be carried out in such a way that this focus of providing problem-solving information is central to the research process.

KEY TERMS

Applied business research (p. 4)
Basic business research (p. 4)
Business research (p. 4)
Opportunity (p. 5)

Primary data (p. 19)
Problem (p. 5)
Secondary data (p. 19)

DISCUSSION QUESTIONS

1. "The best business researchers think like decision makers." Discuss the validity of this statement, using examples from the text, class discussion, and other readings to make your point.

2. The Compton Co. made a serious error in problem formulation. Describe what happened and what lessons we can learn from their experience.

3. Describe what should have been the statement of management problem, research purpose, and research questions for Compton had they done research instead of making a decision without collecting information.

4. Which is more important to get right if research that contributes to better decision making is to occur: the management problem, the research purpose, or the research objectives? Defend your answer.

5. Why is it necessary for business research to be both managerially relevant and scientifically believable to result in better management decision making? Use examples from the text and class to help illustrate your answer.

6. Define the following terms and describe the process used by the researcher in determining what they would be for a research project: management problem or opportunity, decisional alternatives, decisional criteria, research questions, research hypotheses. Use specific examples to illustrate your points.

ENDNOTES

1. For a discussion of studies conducted on the value of being market oriented see Bruce Wrenn, "The Marketing Orientation Construct: Measurement and Scaling Issues," *Journal of Marketing Theory and Practice*, 5(3, 1997), pp. 31–54.

2. "The Perils of Typecasting," American Demographics, (February 1997), p. 60; Karen Benezra, "Fritos Around the World," *Brandweek,* (March 27, 1995), p. 32; "Chinese Cheetos," *The New York Times*, (November 27, 1994), p. 31; "Cheetos Make Debut in China but Lose Cheese in Translation," *USA Today,* (September 2, 1994), p. B-1.

3. See John Yokum, "Invest for Success: It's Research That Makes Winning Programs," *Marketing News,* (June 6, 1994), p. 22.

4. See William D. Perreault, Jr., "The Shifting Paradigm in Marketing Research," *Journal of the Academy of Marketing Science*, 20(4, 1992), pp. 369–381.

5. See N. B. Zabriskie and A. B. Hurellmantel, "Marketing Research as a Strategic Tool," *Long-Range Planning,* 27(1994), pp. 107–118.

6. Christine Moorman, Gerald Yaltman, and Rohit Desponde, "Relationships Between Providers and Users of Marketing Research: The Dynamics of Trust Within and Between Organizations," *Journal of Marketing Research,* 24(3, 1992), pp. 314–328.

7. Adapted from Irving D. Canton, "Do You Know Who Your Customer Is?" *Journal of Marketing*, (April 1976), p. 83.

8. Discussion of Research Purpose and Research Objective is adapted from David Aaker, V. Kumar, and George Day, *Marketing Research* (New York: John Wiley and Sons, 1998).

Ethics in Business Research

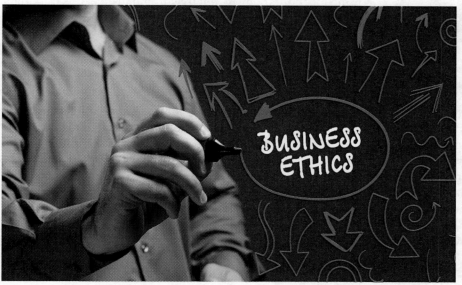

Photon photo/Shutterstock.com

Chapter Outline

Learning Objectives

Upon completing this chapter, you should understand:

- Differences in approaches to ethics.
- What it means to do research in an ethical manner.
- What is meant by term "informed consent" and why it is critical to ethical research.
- How codes of ethics aid in making ethical decisions in research.

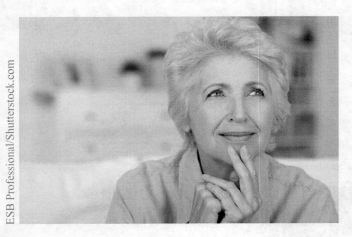

ESB Professional/Shutterstock.com

The word **"ethics"** comes from the Greek *ethos,* which is translated as "character" in English. Yet, *ethos* means more than character. It also refers to the fundamental set of values one uses to make decisions. Thus, we can define ethics, for our purposes, as the set of values and standards we use to make decisions about right and wrong. In terms of business research, these values should include that no harm comes from our research to subjects, clients, society, or the environment.

People use several approaches in governing their ethical decision making. These include: **moral philosophy**, the rights principle, utilitarianism, relativism, and justice. It is important to note that these approaches are not mutually exclusive. That is, most people use some combination of these to make their decisions.

MORAL PHILOSOPHY

Ethics the set of values and standards we use to make decisions about right and wrong.

Moral philosophy (also known as virtue ethics) this school of thought posits that ethical decisions are based on one's moral virtue.

Rights principle this principle holds that a decision is ethical when it is the same decision most people would make based on universal morals (i.e., morals held by all people such as respect for life). This leads to the concept that an ethical decision is correct if it can be applied to all similar situations.

Utilitarianism (also known as teleology) the greatest good for the greatest number of people.

Also known as virtue ethics, this school of thought posits that ethical decisions are based on one's moral virtue. As described by Aristotle, a decision in a certain situation is the one a mature person with good character would make. The virtues that constitute good moral character are timeless and can be taught. Moreover, these virtues transcend and are a higher order than community standards or consensus.

Aristotle believed that a person learned character from the people he or she associated with. If one associates with others of good moral character, then that person will develop the proper virtues. Many adherents of virtue ethics today believe that such institutions as places of worship and schools should be used to foster the proper virtues.

The Rights Principle

Underlying the **rights principle** are the rights of individuals and the intentions of behavior with respect to those rights. Originally expressed by Immanuel Kant (1724–1804) this principle holds that a decision is ethical when it is the same decision most people would make based on universal morals (i.e., morals held by all people such as respect for life). This leads to the concept that an ethical decision is correct if it can be applied to all similar situations. For example, if it is wrong to lie, it is wrong to lie at all times including "white lies" one may tell to spare someone's feelings. This is known as Kant's "moral imperative." The concept goes beyond legal requirements and insists that people volunteer the truth in situations where they are not obligated to reveal information. As an example, when buying a used car, the salesperson is not obligated to reveal information not requested by the buyer. Under the moral imperative, the salesperson is obligated to reveal the information whether asked or not. The rights principle is often compared to the Golden Rule. Therefore, decision makers need to ask, is this decision the same decision that I would expect most moral people to agree with?

Marzolino/Shutterstock.com

Utilitarianism

Another approach to ethics is called **utilitarianism** (also known as *teleology*), which means the greatest good for the greatest number of people. Teleology comes from the Greek word *telos* which means "end." Thus, individuals who espouse utilitarianism seek a decision that benefits everyone in the best way. This is commonly referred to as the "greatest good for the greatest number." Often this process includes a cost/benefit analysis. That doesn't mean this approach will yield the best ethical result. For example, an automobile defect may injure only a few people. Instead of recalling the defective model, however, the automobile company pays the damages to the few injured. The injured get compensation while the automobile manufacturer saves money. It may appear that everyone in this situation wins, but there is still a risk that other consumers will be harmed by the defects, even if these consumers are notified of the defects. This is an example of how utilitarianism suggests that resources be implemented in the most efficient form. Even though there is still a risk of harm to consumers, individuals who use this approach feel they have made the best ethical decision.

The Justice Principle

The **justice principle** refers to the fairness of processes and rewards when dealing with others. There are three categories: 1) distributive justice, 2) procedural justice, and 3) interactive justice. **Distributive justice** deals with the equitable determination of rewards. For example, if it is announced that promotion to sales manager will go to the year's top salesperson, then the top salesperson should get the position. To give the sales manager job to someone who came in second or third violates the equitable determination of rewards.

Procedural justice involves the "rules of the game" and if they are followed. In the above example, if the one salesperson falsely manipulates sales figures and comes out as number one for the year, the rules have been violated. Once procedural justice has been breached, distributive justice is also brought into doubt.

Interactive justice involves the communication used in the relationship. Again, using the example above, if the announced rules for the promotion are that the position goes to the top salesperson; but if management fails to stipulate that it is the most profit on sales and not the most revenue, the lack of communication will violate the concept of interactive justice. Such a violation will undermine employees' beliefs in distributive and procedural justice as well.

Relativism

Relativists make ethical decisions based on the people around them or the specific context in which they find themselves. Often, they simply follow a group's consensus rather than applying any ethical standards of their own. As consensus or context changes, the relativist changes his or her ethical decisions. Everyone has heard the old saying, "When in Rome, do as the Romans do." This sums up the relativist position—ethics change as context changes.

There is a strong tendency for business researchers and other business practitioners to become relativists in international situations. Despite the temptation, core standards still need to be followed in foreign cultures. It is also important to understand the law both in the host country and in the United States. Researchers and other business professionals may be prosecuted for violation of U.S. law (e.g., bribery) while in a foreign country.

ETHICS IN BUSINESS RESEARCH

It is critically important that business research be conducted in an ethical manner because managers often rely on such research to make decisions. Data and information improperly collected or interpreted has the potential to mislead managers in their decision process. Thus, ethical business research requires business researchers to use honesty in all research techniques. To know more about the identified problem, researchers need respondents or study subjects. In order to ensure their rights and encourage their participation,

Justice principle refers to the fairness of processes and rewards when dealing with others.

Distributive justice deals with the equitable determination of rewards.

Procedural justice involves the "rules of the game" and if they are followed.

Interactive justice (also known as interactional justice) involves the communication used in the relationship. Communication should be clear, understood by all, and the dignity of the individual respected.

Relativism ethical decisions based on the people around the decision maker or the specific context in which the decision maker finds him- or herself.

respondents need to be treated with respect. Subjects also need to know that they are free to make a choice about whether or not to participate in a research project. Respondents have the right to be informed about the research being conducted, how their information is going to be used, and a right to privacy. The safety of respondents is extremely important because of legal requirements, and because respondents quit participating if their safety is at risk. In conducting the study, the researcher needs to practice the concepts of justice discussed above.

A helpful tool to guide business research is to have a code of standards. Companies that develop such standards have employees who are better equipped to distinguish between ethical and unethical scenarios. A code of standards may aide researchers from the beginning of the research process, including development of the research question. For example, a proposal to study smokers' reaction to tobacco advertising raises ethical questions even if the research is never conducted. The idea of research on tobacco advertising presupposes that increased tobacco consumption or persuading consumers to change cigarette brands is preferable to encouraging people to quit using tobacco.

Code of Standards

Organizations that conduct business research often develop a code of standards to guide investigators, employees, and any subcontractors involved in the research process. Several research and professional trade groups have written codes of ethics to guide their members. A list of the groups and their web addresses are displayed in Table 2.1.

These organizations offer templates for a research firm or other organization to develop its own code of standards tailored to the firm's particular situation. There are several steps involved in the process of developing a code that applies not only to research but to the entire organization. These steps are outlined in Table 2.2 (see next page).

The term *code of standards* is used in lieu of "code of ethics" to illustrate that the firm should go beyond traditional ethical issues. A code of standards is more inclusive. As well as ethics, a code of standards addresses:

- Client confidentiality
- Duty of care to the environment and community
- Conflicts of interest
- Fair pricing policies
- Equitable treatment of employees
- Quality management/assurance
- Non-discriminatory policies
- Corporate citizenship

TABLE 2.1 Websites of Research Groups

American Marketing Association	www.marketingpower.com
Council of American Survey Research	www.casro.org
Business Research Organization	www.marketingresearch.org
Association of Internet Researchers	www.aoir.org
American Accounting Association	www.aaahq.org
Academy of Management	www.amanet.org

TABLE 2.2 Steps in the Development of a Code of Standards

Get everyone involved	Employees will feel more ownership if they help craft the document. Other shareholders such as customers and vendors can also add valuable insight.
Decide whether to do the job in-house or outsource to a consultant	If the firm lacks the knowledge and expertise necessary to write a code of standards, a consultant may be helpful. The consultant's role, however, is just that—to consult. The firm still needs to take ownership of the document.
Make sure the standards apply to everyone in the organization	A code of standards is ineffective if anyone in the organization is held to a different criterion. This is especially true if senior executives are allowed to engage in behavior for which other employees would be sanctioned.
Avoid legalese	Keep the firm's code of standards in simple language, easily understood by those who will implement it.
Publicize	Publicize the code of standards on the firm's Web page, in brochures and in sales presentations. Publication aides in implementation, provides good publicity, and builds pride among employees.
Provide training	Employees, subcontractors, and others should not be held to standards of behavior of which they are not aware. Hold regular training on the code of standards and make sure all new hires understand the conduct expected.
Implement and follow-up	Make sure all supervisory personnel are implementing the new plan. At the same time, gather feedback from employees and other stakeholders and make necessary adjustments. It is a good idea to have a regular time frame (e.g., annually) to revise the standards to keep up with changing conditions and technology.
Enforcement	Have procedures in place to sanction those who violate the standards. Apply the concepts of procedural and distributive justice to the enforcement process.
Ombudsman	Provide employees, clients, and other stakeholders with a senior executive to whom violations can be reported outside of the chain of command. Employees need to be assured that they can report a supervisor's unethical behavior without fear of retaliation.

Other Organizational Factors in Business Research

Institutional context is also an important ethical concern. This is especially true when there is a perceived power difference between the institution conducting the research and the research subjects. Academic research provides an illustration of this power difference. A professor may require students to participate as research subjects in a study regarding sex and advertising. Some students may view such a study as hostile environment sexual harassment. Yet, the power and authority of the professor may cause reluctant students to keep silent.

Organizations that either commission or conduct business research have a responsibility to conduct and report such research in an unbiased manner. An organization that conducts research on its own products may influence the design, execution, and reported results of a study. For example, Merck and Company, Inc. had to withdraw its pain reliever Vioxx because of potentially dangerous side effects. The U.S. Food and Drug Administration accused the company of presenting false results, and that Merck employees knew all along of the potentially serious problems.[1]

Other problems may arise when advertising agencies have subsidiary business research firms. Pressure to bias the research process or results may be put on researchers if the client has a large account with the agency. Additionally, because the firm is a subsidiary, executives at the agency may assign it research for which it is not qualified and which should be outsourced.

One particularly troubling aspect of business research is known as *advocacy research,* where a firm conducts a study in order to defend a legal action. Advocacy research design is determined by the court and may not adhere to common business research guidelines. Further, researchers may find themselves in an ethical dilemma when they are commissioned to conduct a study aimed not at finding the truth but at supporting the sponsoring organization's specific claim.

In order to avoid many of the ethical problems associated with sponsored research, firms may take the following steps:

1. Price the research adequately so that pressure for bias is reduced.
2. State to clients that bias in interpretation of data will not be condoned.
3. Treat respondents with dignity and respect.
4. When selling research services, avoid unnecessary promotion or pressure on salespeople.
5. Conduct research in accordance with accepted codes of ethics such as the American Marketing Association, the American Accounting Association, The Academy of Management, or the Council of American Survey Research.[2]

International Organization for Standardization

International Organization for Standardization a voluntary organization representing 163 countries, ISO develops common standards of measurement and quality to facilitate world trade.

The **International Organization for Standardization (ISO)** has developed ISO 2052, which applies ISO quality management standards to market, opinion, and social research. The standards were developed to standardize business research worldwide, including ethical standards such as consistency and transparency, so that consumers and research clients can be confident of study results. The standards apply to the manner in which business research studies are planned, conducted, supervised, and reported. According to the Council of American Survey Research, the key elements of the standards are: [3]

- Documented quality management system that can be audited
- Staff training and development
- Control of subcontractors
- Transparency to clients including client review of key steps and reporting
    - Proposal/quotation content
    - Validation and verification of major process steps

ISO also developed standards, definitions, and guidelines for researchers using panels in market, opinion, and social research (ISO 26362). Each of these standards should benefit both research clients and study participants. Clients are assured that the research process has been conducted in ways recognized by the research industry and that research firms are accountable for the quality of their results. Study participants know that ethical standards relating to research have been consistently applied.

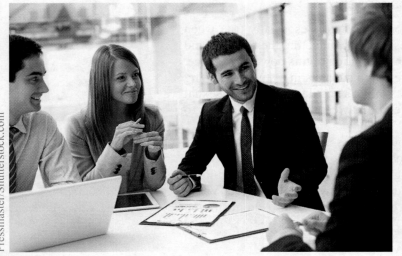

Institutional Review Board (IRB)

Governments at all levels have developed rules and regulations for research involving human subjects.

These laws have led to the creation of the **Institutional Review Boards (IRB)**, which are required for any institution that conducts research for the Federal government and specifically the Department of Health and Human Services. Beyond the Federal government, states have also insisted on IRBs at state-funded universities and state agencies that conduct research. Most private universities have also put boards in place.

The purpose of an IRB is to approve, monitor, and review any research that involves humans. At universities this normally applies to education and the social sciences. Increasingly, however, it also applies to marketing and management studies.

The process requires researchers who wish to study human behavior to submit an outline of the study to the review board, including the name of the investigator, title of the project, time period of the study, any outside funding, how the study will be conducted, how **privacy** and **confidentiality** will be assured, and a copy of the informed consent form the researcher will use.

An advantage of the human subjects form is that it requires the researcher to develop a sound and valid research methodology. A well-designed study is less likely to encounter unexpected ethical problems than one that is not well thought out. Planned research studies also require proper interpretation and application of research findings. This is important because often the results of a study will find its way to the popular press. Most of the people who read about the study will not be trained in interpretation of the information. Additionally, the limitations of the results and conclusions of the study will not likely be revealed because of the space required and the lack of reader interest. Therefore, it is imperative that the researcher to design the study well, interpret the data accurately, and disclose any limitations or lack or generalizability about the results. Figure 2.1 is a sample of an IRB request form.

Institutional Review Board (IRB) the purpose of an IRB is to approve, monitor, and review any research that involves humans.

Privacy researchers must identify themselves when conducting a study, avoid any unwanted intrusion, and set interviews at mutually convenient times. Researchers must also follow all state and Federal privacy laws.

Confidentiality data collected in the research process is not to be shared in any way that it can be identified with any particular individual.

REQUEST FOR APPROVAL OF HUMAN SUBJECTS RESEARCH

This application should be submitted to the Chair of the Human Subjects Research Review Committee.

1. Principal Investigator's Name:_____
   Department & Campus Address:_____
   Campus Phone No.:_____ Home No.:_____

2. If you are a student, provide the following:
   Home Address of Student:_____
   Name of Faculty Sponsor: _____
   Phone Ext:_____
   Is this your thesis research? Yes___ No___

3. Title of Project:_____
   _____

4. Total Project Period: From:_____ To:_____

5. Is a proposal for external support being submitted? Yes__ No__
   If "Yes," you must submit one complete copy of that proposal as soon as it is available and complete the following:
   a. Is notification of Hum. Subj. Approval Required? Yes__ No__
   b. Is this a renewal application? Yes___ No___
   c. Funding agency's name:_____

6. Has this proposal already been approved and you are seeking annual renewal?
   Yes___No___

7. In making this application, I certify that I have read and understand the guidelines and procedures developed by the University for the protection of human subjects, and I fully intend to comply with the letter and spirit of the University's policy. I further acknowledge my responsibility to report any significant changes

FIGURE 2.1 Institutional Research Board (*Continued*)

in the protocol, and to obtain written approval for these changes, in accordance with the procedures, prior to making these changes. I understand that I cannot initiate any contact with human subjects before I have received approval and/or complied with all contingencies made in connection with that approval.
Signature of Principal Investigator and Date

_____   _____

8. Approval by Faculty Sponsor (required for all students): I affirm the accuracy of this application, and I accept the responsibility for the conduct of this research and supervision of human subjects as required by law.
Signature of Faculty Sponsor and Date

_____   _____

9. I have included copies of all pertinent attachments including, but not limited to: questionnaire/survey instrument, informed consent, letters of approval from cooperating institutions, copy of external support proposal if applicable, etc.

   Yes____ No____ (If no, explain on an attached sheet)
   For the following items, attach your answers, appropriately numbered on a separate sheet of paper.

10. Identify the sources of the potential subjects, derived materials, or data. Describe the characteristics of the subject population, such as their anticipated number, age, sex, ethnic background, and state of health. Identify the criteria for inclusion or exclusion. Explain the rationale for the use of special classes of subject, such as fetuses, pregnant women, children, institutionalized mentally disabled, prisoners, or others, especially those whose ability to give voluntary informed consent may be in question.

11. Provide a description of the procedures to be used in the study including major hypotheses and description of the research design.

12. Describe the recruitment and consent procedures to be followed, including the circumstances under which consent will be solicited and obtained, who will seek it, the nature of information to be provided to prospective subjects, and the methods of documenting consent. (Include applicable consent form(s) for review purposes). If written consent is not to be obtained, specifically point this out and explain why not.

   (Note: Informed consent must normally be obtained in a written form which requires the subject's signature or that of the subject's legally authorized representative. A waiver of this requirement may be granted by the HSRRC if adequate justification for the requirement is provided by the investigator in # 12. However, if the procedures pose no more than minimal risk to the subjects, informed consent may be documented via a written cover letter which does not require the subject's signature. In all cases, a copy of the written informed consent must be given to the subject. Consult the document "Research Involving Human Subjects at _____ University" for more information on informed consent requirements and specific examples of possible informed consent documents.)

13. Include a discussion of confidentiality safeguards, where relevant.

14. Describe the anticipated benefits to subjects, and the importance of the knowledge that may reasonably be expected to result.

15. Describe the risks involved with these procedures (physical, psychological, and/or social) and the precautions you have taken to minimize these risks. Do the benefits described above outweigh the described risks?

NOTE: While every effort is made to ensure the accuracy of these pages, errors may occur on occasion.

FIGURE 2.1 (Continued)

COMMON ETHICAL RESEARCH ISSUES

There are various issues that are common to almost every study. It is imperative that the researcher understand and address each of these issues before, during, and after a study as appropriate. An understanding of these common concerns helps avoid ethical problems and misunderstandings of participants, and aids in completing Institutional Review Board requests.

Beneficence

One purpose of Institutional Review Boards is to ensure that the **principle of beneficence** is followed. In research terms, beneficence refers to the benefits of a study as opposed to its risks. In short, the IRB asks the researcher to answer the question, "Does this study benefit more people than are the risks associated with it?" Additionally, investigators need to show that while their research may be of benefit to one group, it does not harm or disadvantage another group. For example, in the case of the Tuskegee Syphilis Study, hundreds of African American men who had syphilis were studied to determine the outcomes of the disease. The study lasted 40 years, but there was an effective treatment within the first 10 years of the study. Even though the researchers learned a great deal about the effects of syphilis, it was unethical for the study to continue after a treatment became available. The broader population had the advantage of understanding the disease, but the study participants were a disadvantaged group because of the research.

Principle of beneficence beneficence refers to the benefits of a study as opposed to its risks.

Informed Consent

Autonomy refers to people's freedom to make their own decisions and to choose the activities they wish to engage in and which activities to avoid. Therefore, potential participants need to understand that they have complete freedom to participate or refuse to participate in a research study. In order to ensure autonomy, participants must give their **informed consent** to participate in a study.

Autonomy people's freedom to make their own decisions and to choose the activities they wish to engage in and which activities to avoid.

Informed consent the researcher fully discloses the purposes and procedures involved in the research and obtains an affirmative acceptance from the subject before the research begins.

Informed consent is at the heart of business research ethics and involves communication between the research participants and the researcher. The ethical researcher fully discloses the purposes and procedures involved in each study. Subsequent to this disclosure, the researcher may ask the potential subject to consent to participation in the project. If the research involves children (e.g., effects of TV advertising on children), a parent or legal guardian needs to agree to a child's participation.

In order for a person to make an informed consent concerning participation in a study, the researcher should identify the sponsor, estimate the time needed to complete the interview or survey, and remind the subject that participation is completely voluntary. Mail surveys, on the other hand, do not normally require signed or verbal consent. If the participant completes and returns the survey, consent is implied. Figure 2.2 is a sample informed consent form.

Mangostar/Shutterstock.com

INTRODUCTION

The following information is provided for you to decide whether you wish to participate in the present study. You may refuse to sign this form and not participate in this study. You should be aware that even if you agree to participate, you are free to withdraw at any time. If you do withdraw from this study, it will not affect your relationship with the researcher or the research sponsor in any way.

PURPOSE OF THE STUDY

(Insert description of the purpose of the study).

PROCEDURES

(Insert description of the procedures that will be followed in the study. Address the participants, i.e. "you will be asked to . . ." Include the time commitment involved. If you plan to use video or audiotapes, state that here. Also state what will be done with the tapes, i.e., used by the researchers only and stored in a locked cabinet).

RISKS

(Insert a description of all burdens, inconveniences, pain, discomforts and risks associated with participation in the study. If no risks are anticipated, this should be stated explicitly).

BENEFITS

(Insert a description of the potential benefits, if any, to the research subject. Clarify if these are direct benefits (e.g., to the subject), or indirect benefits, (e.g., to society). If there are no anticipated benefits, this should be stated explicitly).

PAYMENT TO PARTICIPANTS

(Insert a statement regarding whether or not participants will be paid and if so, how much and on what schedule. Include the following statement if participants are being paid:

Investigators may ask for your social security number in order to comply with federal and state tax and accounting regulations).

PARTICIPANT CONFIDENTIALITY

(Include a general statement about confidentiality and the length of time the researcher intends to keep the information).

If researchers are sharing respondents' information in any way, respondents should be informed and given a choice on whether they agree to the use of their private information. Researchers must not share respondents' information in other research studies, or with other researchers. The research should clearly explain how the information is going to be used and researchers must follow those guidelines to keep the respondents information private.

REFUSAL TO SIGN CONSENT AND AUTHORIZATION

You are not required to sign this Consent and Authorization form and you may refuse to do so without affecting your rights in any way.

CANCELLING THIS CONSENT AND AUTHORIZATION

You have the right to cancel your permission to use and disclose further information collected about you, in writing, at any time, by sending your written request to: (Name and address of researcher or research firm).

If you cancel permission to use your information, the researchers will stop collecting additional information about you. However, the research team may use and disclose information that was gathered before they received your cancellation, as described above.

PARTICIPANT CERTIFICATION:

I have read this Consent and Authorization form. I have had the opportunity to ask, and I have received answers to, any questions I had regarding the study. I understand

FIGURE 2.2 Example of Adult Informed Consent Statement (*Continued*)

that if I have any additional questions about my rights as a research participant, I may call (name and address or researcher or research firm).

I agree to take part in this study as a research participant. By my signature I affirm that I am at least 18 years old and that I have received a copy of this Consent and Authorization form. (Form is modified if a parent or legal guardian needs to consent for the research subject).

_____   _____
Type/Print Participant's Name   Date

_____
Participant's Signature
(Researcher contact information goes here)

FIGURE 2.2 *(Continued)*

Privacy and Confidentiality Rights

Privacy follows the concept of informed consent and requires business researchers to protect the privacy of respondents and the confidentiality of their information. Privacy, in terms of research, is concerned with participation in the research process. Even if a subject signs an informed consent form, he or she has the right to not answer specific questions, not to admit a researcher into his or her home and to refuse to answer the telephone. In addition to informed consent, problems in these areas can be addressed by scheduling times for interviews, respecting the subject's time, and reminding them of their right to refuse to answer questions.

Privacy requires that the person conducting the research identify him- or herself when conducting the study, avoiding any unwanted intrusion and setting interview times that are mutually convenient. Additionally, researchers must comply with all applicable privacy laws whether at the state or Federal level. If the research is being conducted in an international context, the privacy laws of the country where the research takes place should be obeyed. Research organizations with subsidiaries or subcontractors are responsible for such entities following privacy laws. After the conclusion of a study, firms may want to destroy any unneeded information such as survey responses, audio or videotapes.

Privacy on the Web

A recent development in business research ethics involves privacy concerns when conducting online business research. Hiding one's status as a researcher is of particular concern, especially for netnographers and other qualitative researchers. As Robert Kozinets explains, netnographers are "professional lurkers."[4] Specifically, is online information public or private? Moreover, how does one obtain proper informed consent for online research? Finally, is it ethical to deliberately hide the researcher's identity online?

For example, in terms of online information, is there a difference in information posted on Facebook and information discussed in a limited chat room? An additional concern involves the age of the online subject. Facebook requires a person to be thirteen to have a Facebook page, yet this is below the normal age of eighteen required for informed consent. Researchers also need to consider if the participants in the online community consider themselves study subjects or simply people who are voluntarily sharing information with the public. One question a researcher can ask to determine the answer to these questions is, "If the content of a subject's communication were to become known beyond the confines of the venue being studied, would harm likely result?"

Whether a netnographer should act as a member of or remain outside the community under study is another ethical issue. Participation in the online community as a member will affect the results of the research. For business research, influencing the study results is counterproductive. Thus, business researchers should honestly disclose that their interest in the online group is that of researcher, despite that such disclosure may make it more difficult to gain trust and participant influence.

Honest disclosure leads to the key ethical concept of informed consent. Netnographers and other online researchers may find obtaining informed consent difficult. Some online conversations involve thousands of people, many of whom are transient through the community. Nonetheless, the business researcher should disclose his or her actions and let subjects know they can opt out by not participating.

Additionally, people who participate in chat rooms and other online forums often use pseudonyms. The researcher needs to ask if he or she is under the same obligation to protect the privacy of a pseudonym as would be the case for a real person. There are no easy answers to these questions and the researcher's judgment is critical for addressing these matters.

Survey research on the Internet also presents privacy concerns. When conducting survey research via email, study participants should have a reasonable expectation that they may be contacted for survey purposes. This happens when there is a preexisting relationship between the potential subjects and the firm supplying the email addresses or the research firm itself. This also presupposes that the participants have not opted out of email communication. Finally, the firm conducting the research is required to disclose the same information as a survey that is conducted face-to-face.

Active agent technology is software designed to track people's behavior on the Internet including sites visited, online transactions, and advertising click-through and purchase information. The software is also capable of obtaining information from emails and other documents. Active agents are not cookies. Cookies gather much less data and are less intrusive. Moreover, computer users can easily disable cookies.

Downloading of active agent software to someone's computer without permission is clearly unethical. The concept and procedures associated with informed consent must be followed. In addition to consent, research firms need to disclose the types and amount of data sought. As the study continues, participants should be reminded periodically of the presence of the active agent software. Further, active agent software should not disable anti-spam, anti-virus programs or otherwise disable or disrupt participants' computers.

In summary, the issues for online research are varied and complex. Various organizations, including The Association of Internet Researchers (aoir.org/documents/ethics-guide) and the Council of American Survey Research Organizations (www.casro.org) have published ethics codes for online research.

Confidentiality

Confidentiality concerns what is done with the data collected. Since study subjects often provide researchers with personal information, it is imperative that this information not be shared in such a way that it can be identified with any particular individual. Any disclosure of personal information requires informed consent by the study subject.

Moreover, business research studies should clearly explain how information obtained will be used and privacy protected. As noted in the informed consent form discussed above, the length of time research data will be held by the research, the disposition of that data (locked in a safe and password protected), and with whom the data will be shared all need to be disclosed to the participant. It should be noted, the smaller the research group, the more easily it can be identified with a particular subject. This could be especially true in certain qualitative studies where only a few subjects provide in-depth interviews. In these cases, it is imperative that extra caution be taken to avoid disclosure of the identity of participants.

Participant data is protected when research firms properly train and supervise employees who interact with the subjects or have access to the subjects' data. A further step is to have front-line researchers remove as much of the participants' information as possible (e.g., telephone numbers and addresses).

There are instances where a subject's data may be disclosed. For example, a research firm may disclose specific participant information so that its client may compare the data with that of its customers. In such cases, the research firm should obtain, in writing, a commitment from the client firm to use the information only for comparison or model building purposes. In no case should such information be used to embarrass or harass the participant or to use the information as a lead generation for salespeople.

The concept of confidentiality of participant information applies to legal proceedings as well. Information subject to subpoena should be opposed by the research firm until the release of such information is ordered by the court.

Avoiding Deception

Deception occurs when study subjects are lead to believe something the researcher knows is not true. Examples of deception involve misleading promises of privacy or confidentiality, improper or false disclosure of sponsors, and a lack of informed consent. Researchers, for example, may guarantee privacy and at the same time track survey responses with numbered questionnaires or invisible ink. In another situation, researchers may not inform study subjects that they are being observed with two-way mirrors or hidden cameras. These instances of deception violate the important tenant of informed consent.

Deception occurs when study subjects are lead to believe something the researcher knows is not true.

The disclosure of a researcher sponsor is an area of ethical concern for business researchers. Often a firm may conduct business research to determine the viability of a new product or to gather information on entering a new market. In these instances, the company may want to remain anonymous so as not to inform the competition of its activities. In this instance, the researcher will want to safeguard the identity of the sponsor while at the same time informing the subject of the general nature of the study. The confidentiality of the sponsor is perfectly acceptable as long as it does not in any way harm participants or interfere with their informed consent.

Institutional review boards in academic settings and ethics committees in industry may approve deception in the research process if the goals of the research cannot otherwise be achieved or the expected benefits of the research are sufficient to justify the deception. If deception is used, it should be disclosed to the participants during the debrief.

Paying people to participate in research is a common practice. Many mail survey researchers will include a token payment of a one dollar bill, for example, while some medical studies pay considerably more. Research participation has been declining for the past few years for mail, telephone, and interview research.[5] Therefore, paying research

kuzmafoto/Shutterstock.com

subjects may increase mail survey response and aid in recruitment for sensitive research studies, yet this practice may create more problems than it solves.

One problem is that paying participants may violate the tenet of informed consent. Depending on the situation, compensation may cause participants to feel coerced to participate in a study. The researchers who choose participants must decide on an amount that provides incentive but does not coerce participants—particularly subjects who are members of disadvantaged populations.

Another problem associated with paying participants is that it may cause study subjects to tell the researcher what the subject thinks the researcher wants to hear. For example, a month's supply of free laundry detergent in order to study consumer attitudes toward the product may cause the participants to feel obligated to give the detergent a favorable review.[6]

A clearly deceptive method of increasing response rates is to mislead participants about the length of the questionnaire. For example, a business research firm may call homes in a particular neighborhood to determine attitudes toward a new product. In order to gain participants, the phone solicitor tells the subject that the survey will take less than five minutes. At the end of the survey, the researcher tells the participant that a supervisor just handed him or her a few more questions and would the participant mind just a few more minutes. The researcher is relying on the subject's initial commitment to the process and goodwill to continue although the researcher knew all along that the survey would take more than five minutes.

Researchers may also tell potential research subjects that many others, including the subject's friends and family, have completed the survey, implying that refusal to participate will result in becoming a social outcast. Even if the statement of others' participation is true, the method contains an element of deception.

Debrief

Participants should be debriefed after the study is completed. The **debrief** includes information about the results and conclusions of the research. Any questions participants may have are answered. Researchers may also take this opportunity to express gratitude to study participants. The debrief also allows the researcher to lay the groundwork for any future study participation.

Debrief debrief informs the study subjects of the results and conclusions on the research.

If deception has been used (e.g., intentionally misleading the participants as to who the sponsoring organization is), this is the time to explain what deception was used and why. As previously noted, there are times deception may be justified. However, after the study is completed, there should not be any mistaken ideas about the research.

Natural Environments

In addition to not harming study subjects in any way, researchers should take care not to harm the environment as well. Research must avoid harming the planet's resources. The community the research is conducted in needs to be out of harm's way as well. This may require consent on the part of the community as well as individual participants.

Business researchers need to protect the world we live in by making business decisions in the world's best interest. Consumers are judging businesses based on the ways they are preserving or damaging the planet. For consumers to accept business research data, the research needs to be conducted in a way that isn't harmful to the environment. Businesses can make these decisions based on the 3Rs: reuse, recycle, and reduce.[7]

Dangers of Unethical Business Research

To better understand the dangers of unethical business research, it helps to understand the problems that business researchers are faced with. These problems may cause distortions of data that lead to loss of credibility. Communication problems with employers may lead to data distortion. Unethical research by another employee may risk the credibility of other employees. Pressures from clients lead to time constraints, incomplete research, unobtainable data, and information being held from respondents, which all can lead to distortion of data. When distorted data is given to research users, poor decisions are made. All these problems hurt the credibility of the research firm and researcher.

Communication Problems with Clients

Business researchers can have communication problems with their clients. The client may take the information that the researcher has provided and translate it in a different manner. The business researcher may have conducted the research ethically, but the client is translating the information unethically. It is extremely important that the business researcher explain the data and present it without any distortions. The research user should clearly understand that it is unethical to distort the data that has been given to them. When clients distort the data that has been presented to them, the research firm may lose credibility.

Another Employee Makes an Unethical Decision

It is important for all business researchers to work together ethically and hold each other accountable for unethical actions. It becomes difficult when a supervisor or other senior employee is making unethical decisions. For example, a vice president deliberately distorted research findings. The business research director decided to ignore it because the vice president is above his position, and therefore knows what he or she is doing. Business researchers need to be careful with situations such as these because they can be held responsible for the unethical action. The firm's Code of Standards and the position of ombudsman may help alleviate this type of situation.

Time Constraints

Due to time constraints, a researcher may not finish conducting a survey or interview. A business researcher may be tempted to invent an outcome or data that never was discovered. The business researchers may not falsify the outcome, but do the research in a way they know will show the desired results. Researchers may be running out of time and omit information that doesn't support what the client wants. This is no different than changing the information and it makes a business researcher's work dishonest.

Incomplete Research

Another pressure clients may force on business researchers involves stopping the research when a trend is noticed. A business researcher plans to conduct a set number of interviews, but discovers a trend in the findings. The employer wants the interviewing to stop because of time constraints, and the trend has been the same in the respondents that have already been interviewed. The researcher has saved time, but this can greatly affect the findings; and, once again, the credibility of the researcher and research firm. There may be a current trend, but maybe another trend might have been discovered. It can't be concluded that there even is a trend at all until the research is completed.

Client Wants Unobtainable Data

Business researchers need to have good business judgment. A client may want to conduct research that a business researcher knows won't yield the results that the client expects. Should the business researcher take the job? The most ethical action is to inform the client, in a professional manner, that the research will not yield the desired results. While the researcher may cite previous studies in support of his or her contention, one should keep in mind that proof from a previous client's research can't be shared without that client's permission.

There are those who would argue that the client wants the information and therefore the researcher should do it. The suggestion is that another firm will do the research for the client anyway. However, to take the job and not inform the client of your professional opinion, the researcher is putting the firm at risk of losing credibility. The researcher has wasted time and resources and the results will not satisfy the client. The result will be negative publicity and a reputation for poor research.

Making Poor Business Decisions from Faulty Data

When faulty data is used, clients may introduce a new product or service that should've been avoided. When clients make poor decisions from faulty data they imperil the financial health of their firms. Clients may also miss out on an opportunity when faulty data is presented and used to make decisions. The client isn't the only one that loses from a poor decision. Consumers and society at large are also harmed. For the research firm, negative word of mouth will destroy the organization's credibility.

ETHICAL DECISION MAKING

An old Chinese proverb is, "To starve to death is a small thing, but to lose one's integrity is a great one." To keep our integrity, we need to make good ethical decisions. Unfortunately, most ethical situations do not present themselves as simple right or wrong problems, but instead are most often complex and ambiguous. Ethical situations may also be ill-defined and difficult to recognize. As business becomes more globalized, technology advances, and workers gain more knowledge, ethical problems take on increasing complexity. These factors put ethical decision makers at "ethical risk."[8] That is, managers and others who make the wrong ethical decisions put their organizations, employees, and the public at risk of physical, social, or environmental harm.

Ethical decision making will remain difficult, but there are guidelines researchers can employ to assist in making the right choices. Table 2.3 illustrates these guidelines.

In addition to these factors, ethical decision makers should reflect on their own moral philosophy. A person's values guide actions, and the better one understands his or her values, the easier ethical decisions will be.

TABLE 2.3 Factors to Consider When Assessing an Ethical Decision

Follow the rules that are mutually understood and agreed upon. Everyone needs to operate under the same rules of the game.
Be able to discuss and defend your choices. An ethical decision maker needs to be open about how a decision was reached. Openness indicates a confidence in one's attempt to make the right decision.
Be able to discuss and defend your choices. An ethical decision maker needs to be open about how a decision was reached. Openness indicates a confidence in one's attempt to make the right decision.
Employ the Golden Rule. That is, would you want to be on the receiving end of your actions? Additionally, consider what society would look like if everyone acted as you did.

Adapted from L. G. Bolman and T. E. Deal, (2008). *Reframing Organizations: Artistry, Choice, and Leadership, 4th edition Jossey-Bass: San Francisco, CA.*

SUMMARY

Ethics involves the study of how individuals govern their decisions of right or wrong behavior. In business research, right behavior is to protect study subjects, research clients, the community at large, and the environment. Ethical problems, however, are often not clear and easy to understand. Thus, it is incumbent upon business researchers to understand the different schools of ethical thought and to apply a set of ethical standards to their studies. While there are standards common to all ethical business research, individual firms need to develop a more detailed code of standards that applies additional contextual criteria.

Additionally, as ethical decision makers, business researchers need to understand their own values. This requires a certain amount of reflection *before* one is presented with an ethical dilemma. There are factors to consider when making an ethical decision and a number of resources to assist in making the best choice.

KEY TERMS

Autonomy (p. 31)
Confidentiality (p. 29)
Debrief (p. 36)
Deception (p. 35)
Distributive justice (p. 25)
Ethics (p. 24)
Informed consent (p. 31)
Institutional Review Board (IRB) (p. 29)
Interactive justice (also known as interactional justice) (p. 25)

International Organization for Standardization (p. 28)
Justice principle (p. 25)
Moral philosophy (also known as virtue ethics) (p. 24)
Principle of beneficence (p. 31)
Privacy (p. 29)
Procedural justice (p. 25)
Relativism (p. 25)
Rights principle (p. 24)
Utilitarianism (also known as teleology) (p. 24)

DISCUSSION QUESTIONS

1. Characterize the differences between *utilitarianism* and *the rights principle*. Discuss if it is ever morally acceptable to lie. Explain your answer.
2. Do you agree with Aristotle that virtue can be taught? Explain your answer.
3. What is the purpose of an Institutional Review Board? How do such boards help business researchers?
4. Why is informed consent so central to research ethics?
5. What organizational pressures might business researchers face? What are some ways for investigators to deal with these situations?
6. What is the value of a Code of Standards? What are the steps in developing one?
7. What are some guidelines in making good ethical decisions?

ENDNOTES

1. Alsmadi, S. (2010). "Business research and Social Responsibility: Ethical Obligation Toward the Society." *Journal of Accounting, Business & Management 17(1)*, 42–47.
2. Constantineseu, M. (2011). "The Relationship Between Quality of Life and Marketing Ethics." *Romanian Journal of Marketing 6(3)*, 41–44.
3. www.casro.org/iso_faq.cfm Accessed 04/11/2012
4. Kozinets, Robert V. (2002) "The Field Behind the Screen: Using Netnography for Business Research in Online Communities," *Journal of Business research*, February 2002, volume 39, issue 1, p. 68.
5. Head, E. (2009). The ethics and implications of paying participants in qualitative research. *International Journal of Social Research Methodology,* 12 (4), October, pp. 335–344.
6. Alsmadi, S. (2010). *Ibid.*
7. Thiel, Chase E., Zhanna Bagdasarov, Lauren Harkrider, James F. Johnson, Michael D. Mumford (2012). "Leader Ethical Decision-Making in Organizations: Strategies for Sensemaking." *Journal of Business Ethics, 107,* 49–64.
8. Bolman, L. G., & Deal, T. E. (2008). *Reframing Organizations: Artistry, Choice, and Leadership, 4/e.* Jossey-Bass: San Francisco, CA.

APPENDIX

Resources for Ethics

American Counseling Association	www.counseling.org
American Marketing Association	www.marketingpower.com
American Psychological Association	www.apa.org
Aspen Institute	www.aspeninstitute.org
Association of Internet Researchers	www.aoir.org
Council of American Survey Research Organizations	www.casro.org
Ethics Resource Center	www.ethics.org
Global Ethics	www.globethics.net
Josephson Institute	www.josephsoninstitute.org
Business Research Organization	www.marketingresearch.org
Online Ethics Center	www.onlineethics.org
Public Relations Society of America	www.prsa.org
Resources for Research Ethics Education	www.research-ethics.net

Secondary Data and Research Designs

mrmohock/Shuttertock.com

Secondary Data

CHAPTER **3**

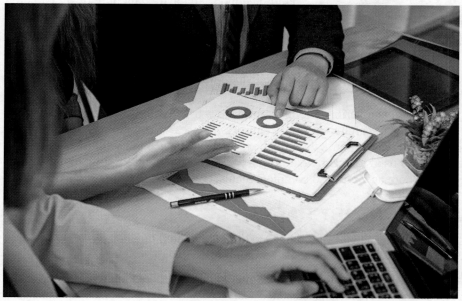

Amnaj Khetsamtip/Shutterstock.com

Chapter Outline

Uses of Secondary Data
Advantages of Secondary Data
Disadvantages of Secondary Data
Secondary Data Sources
Summary
Key Terms
Discussion Questions
Endnotes

Learning Objectives

Upon completing this chapter, you should understand:

- The difference in secondary and primary data.
- The advantages and disadvantages of secondary data.
- What is meant by a search strategy.
- How secondary data can help in the collection of primary data.
- The different sources of secondary data.

Research design, as discussed in Chapter 4, is the road map for the researcher, indicating the route the researcher will take in collecting the information to ultimately solve the management problem or evaluate an opportunity under consideration. The types of data collected in executing this research design will be either (1) *primary data* or (2) *secondary data*. Primary data are those data that are collected for the first time by the researcher for the specific research project at hand. Secondary data are data previously gathered for some other purpose. There is some confusion about the terms "primary" and "secondary." These terms have nothing to do with the relative importance of the information. Whether the data are primary or secondary is determined by whether they originated with the specific study in consideration or not.

The first tenet of data gathering among researchers is to exhaust all sources of secondary data before engaging in a search for primary data. Many research questions can be answered more quickly and with less expense through the proper use of secondary information. However, caution must be used to ensure that primary sources of secondary data are used since they are generally more accurate and complete than secondary sources of secondary data.

Research design the road map for the researcher, indicating the route the researcher will take in collecting the information to ultimately solve the management problem or evaluate an opportunity under consideration.

Primary data data that is collected explicitly for the research study at hand.

Secondary data data that have already been collected for purposes other than the current research project.

USES OF SECONDARY DATA

There are several important uses of secondary data even though the research design might require the use of primary data. The most common uses are:

1. In some cases the information and insights gained from secondary data are sufficient to answer the research question.
2. Secondary data can provide the background necessary to understand the problem situation and provide an overview of the market dynamics.
3. Secondary data often can provide exploratory information that can aid in the planning and design of the instruments used to gather primary data.
4. Secondary data can serve as a check and standard for evaluating primary data.
5. Secondary data can give insight into sample selection.
6. Secondary data can suggest research hypotheses or ideas that can be studied in the primary data phase of the research process.

The extensive use of secondary data reduces the possibility of reinventing the wheel by gathering primary data that someone else has already collected.

ADVANTAGES OF SECONDARY DATA

Secondary data are data gathered for some purpose other than the research project at hand. Consequently, researchers must understand and appreciate the relative advantages and disadvantages of this secondary information. To properly use and evaluate secondary information, its value must be assessed.

Secondary data possess the following advantages:

1. *Low cost.* The relatively low cost of secondary data is one of its most attractive characteristics. The cost of this data is relatively low when it is obtained from published sources. There is no design cost and only the cost of the time required to obtain the data is incurred. Even when the secondary information is provided by a commercial firm, it is normally less expensive than primary data because it is available on a multiclient basis to a large number of users rather than being custom designed on a proprietary basis for a single client.

2. **Speed.** A secondary data search can be accomplished in a much shorter time frame than can primary data collection that requires design and execution of a primary data-collection instrument.
3. **Availability.** Some information is available only in the form of secondary data. For example, census information is available only in secondary form. Some types of personal and financial data cannot be obtained on a primary basis.
4. **Flexibility.** Secondary data is flexible and provides great variety.

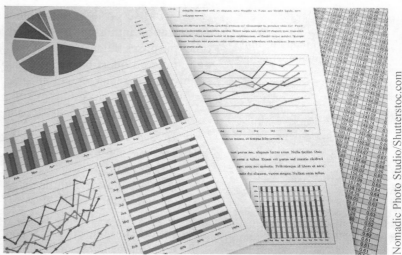

DISADVANTAGES OF SECONDARY DATA

Since secondary data, both internal and external, were generated for some purpose other than to answer the research question at hand, care must be taken in their application. The limitations of secondary data must be considered. Secondary data have the following potential limitations or disadvantages:

1. **A poor fit.** The secondary data collected for some other research objective or purpose may not be relevant to the research question at hand. In most cases, the secondary data will not adequately fit the problem. In other cases, secondary data collected from various sources will not be in the right intervals, units of measurement or categories for proper cross-comparison. The secondary data may not have been collected from the correct or most representative sample frame.
2. **Accuracy.** The question of accuracy takes several things into consideration. First of all, there is the question of whether the secondary data came from a primary or secondary source. Secondary sources of secondary data should be avoided. The next consideration is the organization or agency that originally collected the data. What is the quality of their methodology and data-gathering design? What is their reputation for credibility?
3. **Age.** A major problem with published and secondary data is the timeliness of the information. Old information is not necessarily bad information; however, in many dynamic markets, up-to-date information is an absolute necessity.
4. **Quality.** Information quality is sometimes unknown. The reputation and capability of the collecting agency is important to assessing the quality of the information provided. To verify the overall quality of secondary information, it may be necessary to know how the data were collected, what the sampling plan was, what data collection method was used, what field procedures were utilized, what training was provided, what degree of nonresponse was experienced, and what other sources of error might exist.

SECONDARY DATA SOURCES

The first problem that confronts a researcher in initiating a secondary data search is the massive amount, wide variety, and many locations of secondary data. Some method of logically summarizing the sources of secondary data is helpful. Most textbooks on the subject divide secondary data sources into two groups: (1) internal data sources and (2) external data sources.

Internal secondary data sources are closest at hand since they are found within the organization initiating the research process. These internal data have been collected for other purposes but are available to be consolidated, compared, and analyzed to answer the new research question being posed. This is particularly true of organizations that have sophisticated management information systems that routinely gather and consolidate useful marketing, accounting, and production information.

Specific internal records or sources of internal secondary data are:

1. Invoice records
2. Income statements (various cost information)
3. Sales results
4. Advertising expenditures
5. Accounts receivable logs
6. Inventory records
7. Production reports and schedules
8. Complaint letters and other customer correspondence
9. Salesperson's reports (observations)
10. Management reports
11. Service records
12. Accounts payable logs
13. Budgets
14. Distributor reports and feedback
15. Cash register receipts
16. Warranty cards

vinnstock/Shutterstock.com

Even though most research projects require more than just internal data, this is a very cost-efficient place to begin the data search. Quite often a review of all internal secondary data sources will inexpensively give direction for the next phase of data collection. The internal search will give clues to what external data sources are required to gather the information needed to answer the research question.

External secondary data originate outside the confines of the organization. There is an overwhelming number of external sources of data available to the researcher. Good external secondary data may be found through libraries, Web searches, associations, and general guides to secondary data. Most trade associations accumulate and distribute information pertinent to their industry. Quite often this includes sales and other information gathered from their members. The *Directory of Directories* and the *Encyclopedia of Associations* are excellent sources for finding associations and organizations that may provide secondary information for a particular industry.

Datamining is a term commonly used to describe the process by which companies extract consumer behavioral patterns from analysis of huge databases containing internally and externally generated data. These databases contain information gleaned from customer Web site visits, warranty cards, calls to toll free numbers, retail purchases, credit card usage, car registration information, home mortgage information, and thousands of other databases, including the U.S. Census. The use of neural network and parallel processing technology allows marketers to search through these databases to find behavioral patterns that can help identify the best prospects for:

■ Upgrading customers to more profitable products
■ Cross-selling different products or services offered by the company

- Special offers or offers combining several companies (e.g., travel packages)
- Continued long-term relationship building
- "Weblining"—similar to the practice of "redlining" where vigorous customer service is reserved for only a firm's best customers and withheld from the marginal customers, all based on the customer records in the database[1]

The use of the Internet as a key channel of distribution has allowed many companies to develop even more sophisticated databases for business purposes.[2] For example, customers clicking on NextCard, Inc.'s ad for a credit card on the Quicken.com financial Web site can have their credit history checked and a card issued (or application rejected) in thirty-five seconds.

Secondary Data Sources on the World Wide Web

The Web has become the first, and too often the only, source to be used by the business researcher in search of pertinent secondary data. It is reasonable to assume the reader of this text has had experience surfing the Web, and therefore is familiar with Web browsers (e.g., Google Chrome, Safari, or Microsoft Internet Explorer), search engines or portals (e.g., Bing, , Google, , and Yahoo!), indexes of business and other periodical literature (e.g., EBSCOHOST), Web search strategies (e.g., use of parentheses, and, or, not, +, −, quotation marks, and asterisk), and use of newsgroups (i.e., Internet sites where people can post queries or respond to other people's queries or post comments. Hundreds of thousands of news-groups exist, each devoted to a specific topic). The savvy researcher can harness these and other resources and methods of using the Internet to discover relevant secondary data available over the World Wide Web. Our objective in this section is not to inundate the reader with a long list of websites, but rather to focus on those megasites—sites with the most comprehensive information databases including links to other sites—that can be "bookmarked" and regularly used in secondary research. Perhaps the best way to conceptualize the types of secondary information on the web is the following pyramid:

At the top of the pyramid are the search engines that provide access to all that is on the web. Underneath that are two types of searches—those that seek information about markets (either business to business markets, or business to consumer markets) or research (either companies that offer research services, or the process of research itself). We will provide some suggestions for websites of primary interest for each of these categories.

General Search Engines

A. ***www.Google.com or www.Yahoo.com.*** While virtually everyone reading this book will have had experience using Google or Yahoo as their portal to the web, it bears mentioning that a well-designed search (using appropriate Boolean logic, field searches, proximity operators, truncation, nesting, and limiting) will generate thousands, perhaps millions, of hits where the object of the search appears on the web. Readers unfamiliar with the use of sophisticated search strategies can save considerable time and frustration by learning how to do targeted search before using these engines.

B. ***www.Teoma.com.*** Bought by Ask Jeeves in 2001, this search engine quickly finds "communities" (groups of websites related to the search topic) without generating unproductive links, as is sometimes the case with Google.

C. ***Multi-Search Engines.*** These search multiple search engines for information. The most popular are ***Dogpile.com***, ***Metrocrawler.com,*** and ***Search.com***.

Markets

A. Business to Business Markets

1. Government Sources. ***www.ntis.gov*** Links to 100 federal agencies issuing statistical data. B2B researchers will probably be most interested in information contained in the Economic Census (see ***www.census.gov/programs-surveys/economic-census.html***). Insert the previous year in the URL (e.g., insert /ec14/ if you are doing a search in 2014). Of particular interest will be data contained in the North American Industry Classification System (NAICS) at ***www.census.gove/eos/www/naics***

2. Commercial Sources. ***www.ama.org*** The website of the American Marketing Association has hyperlinks to other websites that identify over 40,000 research reports, including many on B2B markets.

B. Business to Consumer Markets

1. Government Sources. See ***www.ntis.gov*** for government information about the consumer market of interest.

2. Commercial Sources. In addition to search ***www.ama.org*** for reports on the consumer market of interest, commonly used websites for determining the size of a market would include the Survey of Buying Power at ***www.salesandmarketing.com*** and a similar database called *DemographicsUSA* at ***www.city-data.com.com***, which offers calculation of a Buying Power Index (BPI) like the Survey of Buying Power, but at a more specific level (e.g., a BPI for high tech products). Also of use to the marketer of consumer goods is the geodemographic information available at ***www.claritas.com***, whose PRIZM system is perhaps the best known of the geodemographic consumer market segmentation sources.

Marketing

A. Companies. To see a directory of marketing service firms that can be used for a wide variety of marketing services (e.g., advertising, new product or brand development, and research) go to ***www.ama.org*** and see their marketing services directory.

B. Process. By "process" we mean the marketing process itself. That is, when you are seeking information about some aspect of marketing (e.g., sales promotion customer satisfaction research, etc.) that has been published in a business periodical or is otherwise available to the public. Primary sources of information for business-related material are OCLC, Proquent, dialog, Lexis Nexis, and Ebsco, which cover hundreds of sources.

Your Local Library

One source of secondary data that should never be underestimated is a local public or college library, particularly if it is a federal depository. A well-equipped library will not only contain many of the sources mentioned below but will also have a variety of helpful indexes, directories, abstracts, and personnel who can assist in locating specific information. Any thorough search for secondary data should include a comprehensive library search. Not only is the public library an important source of information, but various institutions maintain excellent libraries in their various areas of specialization. Research foundations, financial institutions, energy companies, engineering firms, utilities, universities, and manufacturing establishments often maintain good libraries. The reference librarian can help you find your way through the maze of data sources.

Syndicated Data Sources

Specific syndicated sources are available to provide marketing information. Several specific syndicated services are mentioned below:

Nielsen Retail Index—This service measures consumer activity at the point of sale. It is based on national samples of supermarkets, drug stores, mass merchandisers, and beverage outlets. The store audits track volume at the retail level such as sales to consumers, retail inventories, out-of-stock conditions, prices, dealer support, and number of days' supply.

Roper Reports and the Harris Survey—These surveys deal with public opinion on social, political, and economic subjects. Both involve large national samples and are conducted approximately every month.

National Purchase Diary Panel (NPD)—This diary panel of over 13,000 families provides monthly purchase information about approximately fifty product categories.

Nielsen Television Index—Perhaps the most well-known service, the Nielsen Television Index measures television show ratings and shares among a panel of 1,200 television viewers who are matched according to U.S. national statistics.

Arbitron Radio Market Reports—These reports, based on a representative sample in each market, provide information concerning radio listening habits.

Simmons MRB Media/Marketing Service—Based on extensive data collection from a national sample of about 20,000 individuals, this service reports information concerning media exposure as well as purchase behavior in several hundred product categories. Simmons offers a software package (Choices) which allows the user to create almost unlimited comparisons and cross-tabulations of the extensive database.

Starch Readership Reports—These reports provide measures of exposure to print ads in a wide variety of magazines and newspapers using a large number of personal interviews.

BehaviorScan—This service, provided by Information Resources, Inc. (IRI), uses supermarket scanners to measure the consumption behavior of a panel of consumers.

Consumer Data Sources

Guide to Consumer Markets—Published annually by Conference Board, this source provides data on the behavior of consumers, under the headings of: population, employment, income, expenditures, production and distribution, and prices.

Historical Statistics of the United States from Colonial Times to 1970—This volume was prepared as a supplement to the *Statistical Abstract*. This source provides data on social, economic, and political aspects of life in the United States. It contains consistent definitions and thus eliminates incompatibilities of data in the Statistical Abstracts caused by dynamic changes over time.

Consumer Market and Magazine Report—Published annually by Daniel Starch, this source describes the household population of the United States with respect to a number of demographic variables and consumption statistics. The profiles are based on a large probability sample and they give good consumer behavioral and socio-economic characteristics.

County and City Data Book—Bureau of the Census (Government Printing Office)—Published every five years, this publication gives statistics on population, income, education, employment, housing, retail, and wholesale sales for various cities, SMSAs, and counties.

Sales Management Survey of Buying Power—Published annually by *Sales and Marketing Management* magazine, this source provides information such as population, income, retail sales, and other categories, again broken down by state, county and SMSA, for the United States and Canada.

***Rand McNally Commercial Atlas and Marketing Guide* (Chicago: Rand McNally Company)**—Published annually, this source contains marketing data and maps for some 100,000 cities and towns in the United States. It includes such things as population, auto registrations, basic trading areas, manufacturing, transportation, population, and related data.

Marketing Information Guide—Published monthly by the Department of Commerce, this source lists recently published studies and statistics that serve as a useful source of current information to marketing researchers.

***Census of the Population* (Government Printing Office)**—Taken every ten years, this source reports the population by geographic region, with detailed breakdowns according to demographic characteristics, such as sex, marital status, age, education, race, income, and others.

Editor and Publisher Market Guide—Published annually by Editor and Publisher Co., it contains information on 265 metro areas including population, number of households, industries, retail sales, and climate.

Company Data Sources

Fortune Directory—Published annually by *Fortune* magazine, this source presents information on sales, assets, profits, invested capital, and employees for the 500 largest U.S. industrial corporations.

Middle Market Directory—Published annually by Dun & Bradstreet, this source lists companies with assets in the range of $500,000 to $999,999. The directory offers information on some 30,000 companies' officers, products, sales, and number of employees.

Million Dollar Directory—Published annually by Dun & Bradstreet, this source offers the same information as the Middle Market Directory, only for companies with sales over $9 million or 180 employees.

Thomas Register of American Manufacturers—Published annually by the Thomas Publishing Company, this source gives specific manufacturers of individual products, as well as a company's address, branch offices, and subsidiaries.

Moody's Manuals—This source list includes manuals entitled *Banks and Finance, Municipals and Governments, Public Utilities, Transportation*. These manuals contain balance sheet and income statements for various companies and government units.

Standard and Poor's Register of Corporations, Directors, and Executives—Published annually by Standard and Poor, this source provides officers, sales, products, and number of employees for some 75,000 U.S. and Canadian corporations.

Almanac of Business and Industrial Financial Ratios—Published annually by Prentice-Hall, this source lists a number of businesses, sales, and certain operating ratios for several industries. The computations are from tax returns, supplied by the IRS, and the data allow comparison of a company's financial ratios with competitors of similar size.

Wall Street Journal Index—Published monthly, this source lists corporate news, alphabetically, by firm name, as it has occurred in *The Wall Street Journal*.

Moody's Manual of Investments—This source documents historical and operational data on selected firms and five years of their balance sheets, income accounts, and dividend records.

Directory of Intercorporate Ownership—Published by Simon & Schuster, Volume 1 contains parent companies, with divisions, subsidiaries, overseas subsidiaries, and American companies owned by foreign firms. Volume 2 provides an alphabetical listing of all the entries in Volume 1.

Sheldon's Retail Directory of the United States and Canada—Published annually by Phelon, Sheldon & Marsar, Inc., this source supplies the largest chain, department, and specialty stores, by state and city, and by Canadian province and city. This source also includes merchandise managers and buyers.

State Manufacturing Directories—Published for each state, these sources give company addresses, products, officers, and other information, by geographic location.

Fortune Double 500 Directory—Published annually in the May-August issues of *Fortune* magazine, this source offers information on assets, sales, and profits of 1,000 of the largest U.S. firms, 50 largest banks, life insurance companies, and retailing, transportation, utility, and financial companies. In addition, this source ranks foreign firms and banks.

Directory of Corporate Affiliations—Published annually by National Register Publishing Company, Inc., this source lists approximately 3,000 parent companies and their 16,000 divisions, subsidiaries, and affiliates.

Moody's Industrial Manual—Published annually, this source provides information on selected companies' products and description, history, mergers and acquisition record, principal plants and properties, principal offices, as well as seven years of financial statements and statistical records.

Reference Book of Corporate Management—Published annually by Dun & Bradstreet, this source gives a list of 2,400 companies and their 30,000 officers and directors.

Hoover's Handbook of American Business—Published by Hoover's Business Press, this two-volume work provides profiles of 750 large companies in the U.S.

Mergent's Manuals—Published annually, this source provides income statements and balance sheets for companies and government units.

Market Data Sources

Bureau of the Census Catalog (**Government Printing Office**)—Published quarterly, this source is a comprehensive guide to Census Bureau publications. Publications include agriculture, foreign trade, governments, population, and the economic census.

Directory of Federal Statistics for Local Areas: A Guide to Sources (**Government Printing Office**)—This source looks at topics such as population, finance, income, education, and education in a local perspective.

Measuring Markets: A Guide to the Use of Federal and State Statistical Data **(Government Printing Office)**—This publication lists federal and state publications covering population, income, employment, taxes, and sales. It is a useful starting point for the business researcher who is interested in locating secondary data.

Business Conditions Digest. **Bureau of Economic Analysis, Department of Commerce (Government Printing Office)**—Published monthly, this source gives indications of business activity in table and chart form.

Economic Indicators. **Council of Economic Advisors, Department of Commerce (Government Printing Office)**—Published monthly, this source gives current, key indicators of general business conditions, such as GNP, personal consumption expenditures, etc.

Federal Reserve Bulletin **(Washington, DC: Federal Reserve System Board of Governors)**—Published monthly, this publication offers financial data on interest rates, credit, savings, banking activity; an index of industrial production; and finance and international trade statistics.

Monthly Labor Review—Bureau of Labor Statistics (Government Printing Office). Published monthly, this source presents information on employment, earnings, and wholesale and retail prices.

Predicasts **(Cleveland, OH: Predicasts, Inc.)**—This abstract gives forecasts and market data, condensed to one line, from business and financial publications, trade journals and newspapers. It includes information on products, industries and the economy, and it presents a consensus forecast for each data series.

Statistical Abstract of the United States— Bureau of the Census (Government Printing Office). Published annually, this source serves as a good initial reference for other secondary data sources. It includes data tables covering social, economic, industrial, political and demographic subjects.

Survey of Current Business—**Bureau of Economic Analysis, Department of Commerce (Government Printing Office).** Published monthly, this source presents indicators of general business, personal consumption expenditures, industry statistics, domestic trade, earnings and employment by industry, real estate activity, etc.

Market Guide **(New York: *Editor and Publisher Magazine*)**—Published annually, this source presents data on population, principal industries, transportation facilities, households, banks, and retail outlets for some 1,500 U.S. and Canadian newspaper markets.

Census of Business **(Government Printing Office)**—Published every five years, this source supplies statistics on the retail, wholesale, and service trades. The census of service trade compiles information on receipts, legal form of organization, employment, and number of units by geographic area.

Census of Manufacturer **(Government Printing Office)**—Published every five years, this source presents manufacturers by type of industry. It contains detailed industry and geographic statistics, such as the number of establishments, quantity of output, value added in manufacture, employment, wages, inventories, sales by customer class, and fuel, water, and energy consumption.

Business Cycle Developments. **Bureau of the Census, (Government Printing Office)**—Published monthly, this source provides some 70 business activity indicators that give keys to general economic conditions.

County Business Patterns—Departments of Commerce and Health, Education and Welfare. Published annually, this source gives statistics on the number of businesses by type and their employment and payroll broken down by county.

Commodity Yearbook—Published annually by the Commodity Research Bureau, this source supplies data on prices, production, exports, and stocks for 100 commodities.

Handbook of Economic Statistics—Economics Statistics Bureau. Published annually, this source, presents current and historical statistics of U.S. industry, commerce, agriculture, and labor.

Economic Almanac—Published every two years by the National Industrial Conference Board, this source gives data on population, prices, communications, transportation, electric and gas consumption, construction, mining and manufacturing output, in the U.S., Canada, and other selected world areas.

Directories of Federal Statistics for Local Areas, and for States: Guides to Sources—Bureau of the Census. These two directories list sources of federal statistics for local areas, and for states, respectively. Data includes such topics as population, health, education, income, and finance.

American Statistics Index: A Comprehensive Guide and Index to the Statistical Publications of the U.S. Government—Published monthly by the Congressional Information Service, this source indexes statistical publications of federal agencies, and it is a useful starting point for obtaining market data.

Business Statistics—Department of Commerce. Published biennially, this source is a supplement to "The Survey of Current Business." It provides information from some 2,500 statistical series, starting in 1939.

Standard and Poor's Trade and Securities Statistics—Published monthly by Standard and Poor Corporation, this source contains statistics on banking, production, labor, commodity prices, income, trade, and securities.

Market Analysis—A Handbook of Current Data Sources. Written by Nathalie Frank and published by Scarecrow Press of Metuchen, NJ, this book offers sources of secondary information broken down on the basis of indexes, abstracts, directories, and other references.

Business Periodicals Index—This source lists articles by subject heading from 150 or more business periodicals. It also suggests alternative key words that can be used to determine a standard of relevance in environmental analysis.

F and S Index—This detailed index on business-related subjects offers information about companies, industries, and products from numerous business-oriented newspapers, trade journals, financial publications, and special reports.

Reader's Guide to Periodical Literature—This index presents articles from magazines of a general nature, such as *U.S. News and World Report, Time, Newsweek, Saturday Review*, etc. It also suggests alternative key words that provide initial insight into the nature of the environment.

Statistics of Income—Internal Revenue Service, published annually, this source gives balance sheet and income statement statistics, prepared from federal income tax returns of corporations, and broken down by major industry, asset size, and other criteria.

Public Affairs Information Services Bulletin (PAIS)—Similar to, but different from, the Business Periodicals Index, this source includes more foreign publications, and it includes many books, government publications, and many non-periodical publications.

Census of Retail Trade (**Government Printing Office**)—Taken every five years in the years ending in 2 and 7, this source provides information on 100 retail classifications. Statistics are compiled on number of establishments, total sales, sales by product line, size of firms, employment and payroll for states, SMSAs, counties and cities of 2,500 or more.

Census of Selected Service Industries (**Government Printing Office**)—Taken every five years, in years ending in 2 and 7, this source compiles statistics on 150 or more service classifications. Information on the number of establishments, receipts, payrolls, and other information is provided for various service organizations.

Census of Wholesale Trade (**Government Printing Office**)—Taken every five years, in years ending in 2 and 7, this source provides statistics of 150 whole-sale classifications. Information includes numbers of establishments, sales, personnel, payroll, and other criteria.

Census of Transportation (**Government Printing Office**)—Taken every five years, in years ending in 2 and 7, this source presents three specific surveys: Truck Inventory and Use Survey, National Travel Survey, and Commodity Transportation Survey.

U.S. Industrial Outlook (**Government Printing Office**)—Published annually, this source provides a detailed analysis of approximately 200 manufacturing and nonmanufacturing industries. It contains information on recent developments, current trends, and a ten-year outlook for the industries. This source is useful in forecasting the specific marketing factors of a market analysis.

Merchandising—Published annually in the March issue of this magazine is the "Statistical and Marketing Report," which presents charts and tables of sales, shipments, product saturation and replacement, trade in, and import/export figures for home electronics, major appliances, and housewares. Also appearing annually in the May issue is the Statistical and Marketing Forecast. This gives manufacturers' sales projections for the coming year and is useful in forecasting certain market factors.

Standard and Poor's Industry Survey—Published annually, this source offers current surveys of industries and a monthly Trends and Projections section, useful in forecasting market factors.

Monthly Labor Review—Published monthly by the U.S. Bureau of Labor Statistics, this source compiles trends and information on employment, wages, weekly working hours, collective agreements, and industrial accidents.

Ayer Directory of Publications—Published annually by Ayer Press, this source is a comprehensive listing of newspapers, magazines, and trade publications of the United States, by states, Canada, Bermuda, Republics of Panama and the Philippines, and the Bahamas.

Cost Data Sources

Moody's Investors Services, Inc.—Published by Standard and Poor Corporation (NY), this is a financial reporting source that includes many large firms.

Standard Corporation Records—Published by Standard and Poor Corporation (NY), this is a publication of financial reporting data of the larger firms.

Encyclopedia of Associations—Published by Gale Research Co. May acquaint a researcher with various associations for cost data pertaining to desired industry.

Business Publication Rates and Data—Published by Standard Rate & Data Service, Inc. This index lists various trade publication sources.

Economic Census (**Government Printing Office**)—A comprehensive and periodic canvass of U.S. industrial and business activities, taken by the Census Bureau every five years. In addition to providing the framework for forecasting and planning, these censuses provide weights and benchmarks for indexes of industrial production, productivity, and price. Management uses these in economic or sales forecasting, and analyzing sales performance, allocating advertising budgets, locating plants, warehouses and stores, and so on.

Gale Directory of Databases—Published by Gale Research Co. twice a year, this directory lists more than 12,000 databases, 3,000 database producers and 2,000 online services and vendors.

General Advice

There is no question that the number and complexity of information sources may discourage the novice secondary source researcher from pursuing this line of research. Our advice to the uninitiated researcher is to take the problem to the business reference librarian at the nearest university library. He/she can save considerable wasted time and effort by directing the researcher to those sources most likely to provide the solution to information problems. We also recommend the following short list of sources for those researchers who want to pursue their searches alone, but who need a few broad-based sources to get started.

Directories in Print—*Gale Research Co.* Indexes over 10,000 published directories.

Encyclopedia of Business Information Sources—Also by Gale Research, this encyclopedia is updated frequently.

Business Information, How to Find It, How to Use It—Michael R. Gavin, author. The second edition was published in 1992 by Oryx Press. More recent editions may be available.

Directory of On-Line Databases—Euadra Associates, Santa Monica, CA. Updated periodically.

Encyclopedia of Associations—Gale Research lists over 20,000 trade associations by subject area, including addresses and phone numbers. Many trade associations are very helpful in meeting information needs.

Research Project Tip   Virtually all research projects will benefit from conducting a literature review of secondary data sources. While this will undoubtedly include the use of the web, you should also visit a university or public library. It is not enough to merely print out those articles available as a full-text print option on EBSCOHOST, for example. Other very important articles and secondary data sources are available only by visiting your library. Conducting a literature review only from in front of your computer screen is not sufficient. This is not a time to take shortcuts. Key information may be available only with the expenditure of time and hard work.

SUMMARY

Whenever research requirements are defined, secondary data should be exploited first to give background, direction, and control over the total research process. Beginning with a secondary data search will ensure that the maximum benefit is derived from the collection of primary data. All pertinent secondary data should be gathered before moving to the primary gathering stage because it is generally quicker and cheaper to collect secondary data.

Good secondary data can be found both internally and externally. Library facilities, as well as the web, should be used as a starting point in gathering secondary data, while the federal government is the largest single source of secondary information.

Although secondary information may answer the research question, generally it pro-vides only the springboard for a collection of specific custom-designed information.

KEY TERMS

External secondary data (p. 46)
Internal secondary data (p. 46)
Primary data (p. 44)

Research design (p. 44)
Secondary data (p. 44)

DISCUSSION QUESTIONS

1. Why is a search of secondary data almost always a good way to begin a research project? Provide an example from your research project to illustrate your points.
2. What precautions need to be observed when using secondary data to get answers to research questions? Provide an example from your research project to illustrate your points.

3. Describe in depth a search strategy you would use to get an answer to this question: How have conceptions of what constitutes good customer service changed over time for American consumers, and what has been the trend in customer complaints about airline travel in the past decade?

ENDNOTES

1. See Marcia Stepanek, "Weblining," *Business Week E-Biz Supplement,* (April 3, 2000), pp. EB26–EB34.

2. See Heather Green, "The Information Gold Mine," *Business Week E-Biz Supplement,* (July 26, 1999), pp. EB17–EB30.

Research Designs: Exploratory and Qualitative Research

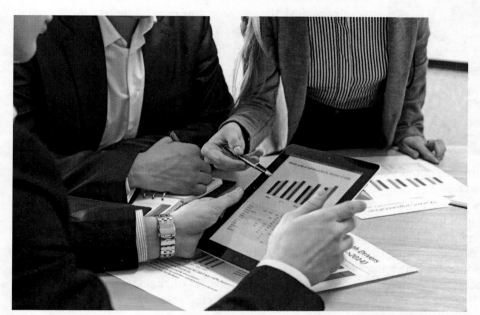

Alex Brylov/Shutterstock.com

Chapter Outline

Types of Research Designs

Exploratory Research

Tools Used to Conduct
    Exploratory Research

Summary

Key Terms

Discussion Questions

Endnotes

Learning Objectives

Upon completing this chapter, you should understand:

- Differences in exploratory, descriptive, and causal research.
- How exploratory and qualitative research differs from quantitative research.
- When exploratory and qualitative research should be used.
- How exploratory and qualitative research can improve the development of the quantitative research process.
- Different types of exploratory/qualitative methodologies.

As described in our outline of the research process, the next step after stating the management problem, research purpose, and research hypotheses and questions, is to formulate a research design. The starting point for the research design is, in fact, the research questions and hypotheses we have so carefully developed. In essence, the **research design** answers the question: How are we going to get answers to these research questions and test these hypotheses? The research design is a plan of action indicating the specific steps that are necessary to provide answers to those questions, test the hypotheses, and thereby achieve the research purpose that helps choose among the decision alternatives to solve the management problem or capitalize on the market opportunity (see Figure 4.1).

TYPES OF RESEARCH DESIGNS

A research design is like a roadmap—you can see where you currently are, where you want to be at the completion of your journey, and can determine the best (most efficient and effective) route to take to get to your destination. We may have to take unforeseen detours along the way, but by keeping our ultimate objective constantly in mind and using our map we can arrive at our destination. Our research purpose and objectives suggest which route (design) might be best to get us where we want to go, but there is more than one way to "get there from here." Choice of research design is not like solving a problem in algebra where there is only one correct answer and an infinite number of wrong ones. Choice of research design is more like selecting a cheesecake recipe—some are better than others but there is no one which is universally accepted as best. Successfully completing a research project consists of making those choices that will fulfill the research purpose and obtain answers to the research questions in an efficient and effective manner.

Choice of design type is not determined by the nature of the strategic decision faced by the manager such that we would use research design A whenever we need to evaluate the extent of a new product opportunity, or design B when deciding on which of two advertising programs to run. Rather, choice of research design is influenced by a number of

Research design the road map for the researcher, indicating the route the researcher will take in collecting the information to ultimately solve the management problem or evaluate an opportunity under consideration.

FIGURE 4.1 The Relationship between Research Design and the Solution to Management's Problem

variables such as the decision-maker's attitude toward risk, the types of decisions being faced, the size of the research budget, the decision-making time frame, the nature of the research objectives, and other subtle and not-so-subtle factors. Much of the choice, however, will depend upon the fundamental objective implied by the research question:

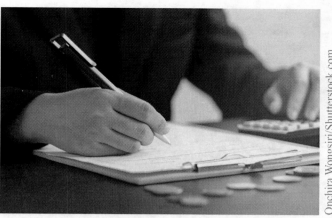

Onchira Wongsiri/Shutterstock.com

- To conduct a general *exploration* of the issue, gain some broad insights into the phenomenon, and achieve a better feel for the subject under investigation (e.g., What do customers mean by good value?).

- To describe a population, event, or phenomenon in a precise manner where we can attach numbers to represent the extent to which something occurs or determine the degree two or more variables ovary (e.g., determine the relationship between age and consumption rate).

- To attribute *cause* and effect relationships among two or more variables so that we can better understand and predict the outcome of one variable (e.g., sales) when changing another (e.g., advertising).

These three broadly different objectives give us the names of our three categories of research designs: exploratory, descriptive, and causal. Before we discuss each of these design types a cautionary note is in order. Some might think that the research design decision suggests a choice among the design types. Although there are research situations in which all the research questions might be answered by doing only one of these types (e.g., a causal research experiment to determine which of three prices results in the greatest profits), it is more often the case that the research design might involve more than one of these types performed in some sequence. For example, in the case of the Compton Company described in Chapter 1, if research had been conducted, the research objectives might first have required **exploratory research** to more precisely define the problem, followed by descriptive research which could have determined the frequency that distributors recommended a competing brand, or the extent to which purchase intent covered by previous experience with the Compton brand. Some research questions might have been completely answered using just one of the research design types, while others required a sequence of two or all three types. The overall research design is intended to indicate exactly how the different design types will be utilized to get answers to the research questions or test the hypothesis.

A further cautionary note is needed to warn the reader that while it may appear that any sequence would be exploratory, then descriptive, then causal, that is not always the case. For example, some companies may do an annual survey of consumers to determine the frequency with which certain behaviors are performed (e.g., washing dishes by hand) followed by exploratory research that probes to gain an in-depth understanding of the circumstances surrounding that behavior (i.e., descriptive then exploratory rather than exploratory then descriptive). It is not hard to imagine a research design that might sequence as exploratory, then descriptive, then exploratory again; or causal, then descriptive. It is important to remember that, because a research design is a plan of action to obtain answers to the research questions, it is those questions that suggest which design types are necessary and any sequence that is needed. An example later in this chapter will be used to illustrate this point. With these cautions in mind we will discuss exploratory research in this chapter and address descriptive and casual methods in Chapter 5.

Exploratory research research that is undertaken when a problem is not well understood and there is no prior research available. Exploratory research is often used to better develop an understanding of the problem to aid in future research projects.

EXPLORATORY RESEARCH

Exploratory research is in some ways akin to detective work—there is a search for clues to reveal what happened or is currently taking place, a variety of sources might be used to provide insights and information, and the detective follows where his or her nose leads in the search for ideas, insights, and clarification. Researchers doing exploratory research must adopt a very flexible attitude toward collecting information in this type of research and be constantly asking themselves what lies beneath the surface of what they are learning and seeing. An insatiable curiosity is a valuable trait for exploratory researchers.

Such curiosity will serve the exploratory researcher well when, for example, he or she sees the need to ask a follow-up question of a respondent who has mentioned some unanticipated answer to that researcher's query. The follow-up question is not listed on the researcher's interview guide, but the curious interviewer instinctively knows that the conversation should begin to deviate from the guide because the unexpected response may be revealing much more important issues surrounding the topic for investigation than were originally anticipated by the researcher. A willingness to follow one's instincts and detour into new territory is not only acceptable in exploratory research, it is commendable! Inspired insight, new ideas, clarifications, and revelatory observations are all the desired outcomes from exploratory research, and decision makers should not judge the quality of the idea or insight based on its source.

Although we do not want to give the impression that any approach is acceptable for doing exploratory research, or that all methods are of equal value in providing desired information, it is true that exploratory research is characterized by a *flexibility* of method that is less evident with descriptive and causal designs.

Exploratory research is needed whenever the decision maker has an objective of:

1. More precisely defining an ambiguous problem or opportunity (e.g., Why have sales started to decline?).
2. Increasing the decision maker's understanding of an issue (e.g., What do consumers mean by saying they want a "dry beer"?).
3. Developing hypotheses that could explain the occurrence of certain phenomena (e.g., Different ethnic groups seek different levels of spice in our canned beans.).
4. Generating ideas (e.g., What can be done to improve our relationships with independent distributors?).
5. Providing insights (e.g., What government regulations are likely to be passed during the next year that will affect us?).
6. Establishing priorities for future research or determining the practicality of conducting some research (e.g., Should we try to survey all our salespeople on this issue or just talk with the leading salesperson in each region?).
7. Identifying the variables and levels of variables for descriptive or causal research (e.g., We will focus our attention on determining the level of consumer interest in these three product concepts because exploratory research shows no interest in the other two.).

Research Project Tip   Your choice of a research design goes beyond simply saying which type(s) of approaches you will use (exploratory, descriptive, or causal). You must indicate the specific way you will get answers to each research question.

TOOLS USED TO CONDUCT EXPLORATORY RESEARCH

As previously noted, our research design is a plan of action indicating the specific steps that are necessary to provide answers to the questions we have developed and, in some cases, to test hypotheses. It is possible, however, that we do not know enough about a question to formulate a hypothesis, or we are more interested in describing a particular event or discovering the meaning of an event for the research subjects than we are in frequency of event occurrence or differences between groups. The research method we use in these situations is known as **qualitative research** and is outlined below.

Explanation of the Qualitative Research Process

Qualitative research is beneficial for studying ill-structured problems, which are defined as "non-routine problems that have no clear solution."[1] Traditional survey research methods are inadequate for this type problem because, by definition, the problem cannot be verbalized. Effective qualitative methods may help by eliciting images, nonverbal cues, and unconscious thoughts that lead to a statement of the problem.

Qualitative research refers to a variety of methods and, as such, a variety of definitions. There are differences between qualitative and quantitative research that address not only research questions to be investigated but the role of the researcher and assumptions about the world in which we live. Additionally, qualitative research is often a multi-method process with the particular method employed depending, at least to some extent, on the results of the ongoing study.

Qualitative research is often conducted in a natural setting. An underlying assumption is that humans create their own reality and that observation and description of this reality is the only way to understand human behavior. Often a qualitative researcher will immerse herself in the situation. For example, in order to understand the consumption behavior of homeless people, the researcher may join a homeless community and live as they do for the duration of the study. Thus, qualitative research is phenomenological in that it is concerned with the meanings people attach to events, the dominant culture, advertising, and business.

Qualitative methods include ethnography, extended case studies, immersion techniques, **in-depth interviews**, focus groups, projective techniques, and grounded theory. Data is collected in a variety of ways including field notes, videos, voice recordings, historical artifacts, company reports and advertisements, and storytelling. Thus, qualitative research can be defined as a set of methods that are investigative in methodology, naturalistic in approach, and are dependent on description, observation, and categorization.[2]

As previously noted, market researchers employ qualitative methods when not enough is known about a problem to develop a workable hypothesis, or when the researcher is interested in discovering the root cause or deeper meaning of an event, such as a purchase decision. Thus, researchers can use qualitative research to explore questions people are unwilling or unable to answer. For example, a study subject may be unwilling to admit his decision to buy a gift for his girlfriend was to reflect on his financial success rather than attempting to please her. A more acceptable answer would be that the gift was practical or the right color. Various qualitative methods (such as projective techniques discussed below) can develop the true reason for the purchase.

People often make decisions for reasons they do not understand or cannot articulate. Depth interviews, projective techniques, ethnography, and other qualitative research methods can help the researcher tap the subject's subconscious and help him or her articulate the decision process. These methods are also valuable in discovering which sensory feelings are important in areas such as purchase decisions.

Qualitative methods differ from quantitative research methods, and there is tension between those who favor one method over the other. We will examine these differences and the controversy surrounding them next.

Qualitative versus Quantitative

Many academic and practitioner business researchers are skeptical of the value of qualitative research. Increased sophistication of statistical software results in less measurement error than was true in the past. Additionally, managers and business researchers find value in the ability of quantitative studies to generalize from a sample to the population. Qualitative research, however, is catching the attention of both industry and researchers. There are three primary issues that arise in the qualitative versus quantitative argument.

First, there is a difference between a numbers approach and word approach to research. Words, actions, and records are emphasized in qualitative research while numerical assignments to words, actions, and records signify qualitative methods.

Next, the qualitative researcher attempts to understand study subjects in the context of their environment In fact, many qualitative researchers do not consider themselves objective observers (as do quantitative investigators) but as actors who are part of the research process. That is, they are observers and participants.

Finally, qualitative research is designed to discover patterns and trends that take place in a particular context. This differs from quantitative research that takes a relatively small sample and attempts to generalize findings across contexts.[3]

Table 4.1 (below) outlines the differences in qualitative and quantitative research in terms of various research processes.

Qualitative research has been criticized as "soft science" or just plain journalism. Qualitative researchers who immerse themselves in the study context are accused of bias, value-laden results, or even a political agenda. At best, critics of qualitative research believe that it is valuable only as an exploratory method and is unsuited for descriptive or causal research designs. Yet, each approach has limitations. Quantitative methods tend to force people into groups that are artificial, while qualitative research often fails to provide results that can be generalized beyond the current study. Despite these criticisms, businesses have embraced qualitative research as part of an overall, effective business research program.

Another criticism of qualitative research is that, because of the methods used, there is no way to statistically determine the validity of a study. To answer this criticism, there are several steps the qualitative researcher can take. First, and most important, researchers should be very careful and precise in designing the study, from deciding on the management question to the interpretation and reporting of results.

Another method of increasing the validity of a qualitative study is to view the management question from different perspectives. This method is known as triangulation. In this approach, the same questions are addressed from a different perspective. For example, an ethnographic study may observe children's television viewing habits. To look at the question from a different perspective, depth interviews may be conducted with the children's parents.

TABLE 4.1 Qualitative vs. Quantitative Methods

	Qualitative	Quantitative
Objective or Purpose	Gain understanding of underlying motives; explore ill-structured problems.	Test hypotheses; generalize from sample results to the population of interest.
Sample or Data Collection	Small sample; unstructured, flexible, data collection involving observation, interviews, and field notes.	Large sample; numerical values assigned to subjects' responses; primary survey data or secondary data.
Data Analysis	Continuous as data is collected; analysis affects next step in the research; non-statistical analysis.	Analysis takes place after all data collected; statistical methods used
Planned Outcome	Develop an initial understanding description; begin theory development.	Provide a specific recommendation

A third approach is to combine qualitative and quantitative methods into one study. This often happens when one method alone is not sufficient to measure all aspects of a phenomenon. Refer to the example of children's TV viewing habits; a survey might be given to the parents while the children are observed in their homes.

Designing the Qualitative Study

Qualitative methods require the researcher to be able to tolerate ambiguity and vagueness. Both require flexibility and patience on the part of the researcher. Ambiguity refers to a situation that can be understood in more than one way, while vagueness means the situation lacks precision. Qualitative researchers need to approach a project with a willingness to change qualitative methods as the situation begins to take a specific direction or the meaning becomes clearer. With qualitative methods, data unfolds as the study progresses. In this sense, qualitative research is in some ways akin to detective work—there is a search for clues to reveal what happened or is currently taking place, and the detective follows where his or her nose leads in the search for ideas, insights, and clarifications. The keys to success in qualitative research are flexibility and an insatiable curiosity.

In contrast to quantitative methods that use random sampling to recruit study participants, qualitative researchers rely on purposive sampling where the research participants and the setting (school, business, consumption experience) are carefully selected depending on the study question. A qualitative sample needs to be information rich.[4] For example, if we are conducting a study to determine the consumption pattern of problem gamblers, we would look for participants who display this characteristic, rather than recreational gamblers who stay within their budgets. In other cases we may want to select participants who are experts on the subject under study, or we may want the most heterogeneous sample we can assemble. The qualitative researcher needs to be aware, however, that as the study progresses, newer participants may be very different from those originally chosen. Again, as previously noted, the qualitative researcher needs to be flexible and go where the study leads. Below is a list of factors to consider when designing a qualitative study.

Roman Globa/Shutterstock.com

1. The management question should not be narrowly drawn, but should be exploratory and descriptive. Qualitative studies evolve as data is collected and analyzed. The analysis of collected data often determines the next set of questions or subjects to be interviewed.

2. Spend time determining the initial sample of participants. Study subjects reside in the context of the phenomenon being investigated. For example, if we are studying the breakfast eating habits of elementary school children, we would want to select families where both parents worked outside the home and families where one parent stayed home. This gives us variability in our sample. In contrast, quantitative methods use random sampling, which is designed to achieve the same variability with a large sample size.

3. An important characteristic of qualitative research is that personal meaning is tied to the context within which a behavior takes place. Therefore, it is best to collect data from participants where they live, work, or play.

4. The data we collect in qualitative research is often people's language and behavior. In order to be accurate, researchers might use field notes, audio, or videotapes, and collection of relevant documents. It is important that the data collection process be organized and complete because the decision about which data is relevant may change as the study progresses.

5. Data is constantly analyzed and interpreted during a qualitative study. This allows for important aspects of the study to emerge as it processes. Again, this process

differs from quantitative research in several ways. First, data is analyzed at the end of a quantitative study. Secondly, quantitative research is designed upfront and the design does not change as the study progresses. Finally, and not critically, the quantitative researcher decides what is important in a study, while the qualitative researcher takes a participant perspective. That is, the data collected and analyzed is based on what is important to the study participants.

6. Qualitative findings are best reported in a narrative such as a case study. The length of the report may range from a few pages to an entire book. The longer the report, the more excerpts from interviews and observations can be included. While quantitative reports suggest to readers that generalizing the results depends on the sample, qualitative reports provide enough information for readers to make this determination on their own.

Qualitative Research Methods

Literature Review

Literature review an investigation of previous research related to the research issues under study.

More often than not the proper place to begin a research study is to investigate previous work related to the research issues under study. Exploratory research seeks to generate ideas, insights, and hypotheses, and reading what others have done and discovered about the topic in which you are interested can save valuable time and resources in the search for those ideas. For example, if your research objective consists of developing an instrument to measure customers' satisfaction with your product or service, a search of previously published studies measuring customer satisfaction could generate many ideas and insights useful in developing your own instrument. This can be done by using one or more of numerous books on the subject currently available, or by doing a search of a library database where key words such as "customer satisfaction" or "customer service" are used to reveal articles published on the subject during a specific time period (e.g., the previous three years) or searching the Web for information. Chapter 3 discussed sources and uses of secondary data in more depth.

In-Depth Interviews

One of the best ways to obtain desired insights, hypotheses, and clarifications is to talk with someone whose experience, expertise, or position gives them unique perspective on the subject of interest. While in some cases such key informants are obvious, such as talking with secretaries about changes in your word-processing software, sometimes valuable insights come from not-so-obvious sources, such as talking with shoeshine people about executive footwear or golf caddies about golf equipment. The key to achieving your research objective of gaining insight and ideas through exploratory personal interviews is to be flexible and think about what you are hearing. Your objective in conducting the interview is not to get your seven questions asked and answered in the course of the conversation. The questions are the means to the objective of gaining insights; they are not the objective itself. My objective is to gain *insight* and I might be able to achieve that objective far better by asking questions related to what I am hearing than doggedly pursuing my original questions.

Researchers should never confuse the exploratory in-depth interview with one conducted in descriptive research. Descriptive-research interviewing requires a consistency in the questions asked and the way the questions are asked which is not conducive to achieving exploratory objectives. With descriptive, we need to eliminate the variance of results due to differences in interviewing circumstances so that we can attribute the results to variances in respondent attitudes and behaviors; hence the need for consistent interviewing behavior. With exploratory, we are not trying to precisely measure some variable, we are trying to gain penetrating insights into some important issue. Hence, each of our exploratory interviews might take a different tack as we seek to probe and query each key informant to gain full benefit of their unique experiences.

For example, if we are researching the use of digital music player devices by college students, the exploratory in-depth interviews may probe issues about what features are desired, when and how they are used, which devices are currently popular, and why, etc. The order these topics are addressed in the interviews and how the question is asked to elicit discussion of these topics is immaterial and can vary from interview to interview. We are looking for insights, not numbers here, and we must let the interview flow naturally to cover these topics and perhaps digress into areas we hadn't anticipated if those areas promise even greater insights. We might find that after 20 or so of these interviews we start hearing the same responses, so we stop conducting interviews. Or, we are continuing to generate more and more ideas from these interviews that we explore in subsequent interviews, and end up conducting 40 interviews instead of the 25 we had originally planned. Again, flexibility in both conducting the interviews and knowing when to stop is the key to getting the most from our exploratory research.

Researching this same topic in descriptive research interviews would not afford such flexibility. Here we want to know how many students prefer one product feature over another, would pay $50 more for twice as much storage capacity, or intend to buy in the next six months, etc. Every interviewer in the descriptive research must ask each question in the same way and in the same order for each interview in this research design. This is necessary so that the data generated reflects the market characteristics instead of the peculiarities of the interviewer-interviewer interaction. In other words, in descriptive research interviews we want the results of the interview to be the same no matter who did the interviewing. In exploratory, each interview can be a unique experience that results in original insights and ideas.

In the same sense, descriptive-research interviewing may require a probability sample of respondents so that we can compute sampling errors and be able to make statements such as, "We are 95 percent confident that somewhere between 77 percent to 81 percent of dealers prefer brand A over brand B." Never, however, should exploratory research use a probability sample since our entire objective in talking with people is to select those who are in a position to shed an unusual amount of light on the topic of interest. They are chosen precisely because they are in the best position to shed some light on the subject. Another way of thinking about this is to answer the question "How many people do you need to talk with to get a good idea?" The answer, of course, is one person—the *right* person. In exploratory research we are not measuring behavior, we are seeking inspiration, clarification, and perspective, etc., so we must seek out those people who can do that for us. Chapter 8 discusses in more detail interviewing approaches that would be used in descriptive research.

Focus group a small number of people (usually eight to twelve), convened to address topics introduced by a group moderator.

Focus Groups

One of the most popular techniques for conducting exploratory research is the **focus group**, a small number of people (usually eight to twelve), convened to address topics introduced by a group moderator. The moderator works from a topic outline developed with input from moderator, researcher, and decision maker. Focus groups have proven to be of particular value in:

- Allowing managers to see how their consumers act, think, and respond to the company's efforts.
- Generating hypotheses that can be tested by descriptive or causal research.
- Giving respondent impressions of new products.
- Suggesting the current temperament of a market.
- Making abstract data real—such as seeing how a "strongly agree" response on a survey appears in the faces and demeanor of real people.

Focus groups are popular because they not only are an efficient, effective means of achieving these goals but also because decision makers can attend them, observing the responses of the participants live. This observation can be a double-edged sword, for while it does make the abstract real, it can deceive the novice into believing that the entire market is represented by the consumers in the focus group. Conducting more focus groups to see a larger number of respondents does not convert the exploratory findings into descriptive data. Focus groups are one of several means of achieving the objectives of exploratory research and should not be overused or believed to be generating results that were never the intent of this technique.

Why Conduct Focus Groups?

The standard reasons for conducting focus groups include:

- *Idea Generation.* Participants or knowledgeable experts may provide a good source of new products or other ideas in the fertile environment of a group setting.

- *Reveal Consumers' Needs, Perceptions, Attitudes.* Probing participants on why they think or act the way they do may reveal less obvious, but no less important, reasons for their behavior.

- *Help in Structuring Questionnaires.* Hearing the way participants think and talk about a product, activity, or consumption experience not only generates hypotheses that might be tested in a descriptive research design, but also informs the researcher about how to word questions in ways directly relevant to the consumer's experience.

Some less frequently mentioned reasons for conducting focus groups include:

- *Post quantitative Research.* Focus groups are most often mentioned as research done prior to a survey, but they might be of equal value in helping researchers to flesh out quantitative research. Discovering that a certain percentage of participants behave in a particular fashion may make it desirable to probe a group of those participants in some depth to discover why and how they came to act in that manner.

- *Making the Abstract Real.* One of the most memorable qualities of focus groups is their ability to make real what was heretofore only considered in a very

abstract manner. For example, it is one thing for a product manager of a brand of dog food to know that many dog owners really love their dogs. It is quite another for that product manager to see dog owners in a focus group take obvious delight in recounting their Ginger's latest adventure with a raccoon, or grow misty-eyed in remembering Jason, now dead ten years, or hear the soft lilt in their voice as they describe the relationship they have with Kate and Bailey, their golden retrievers. Attendance at a focus group can infuse lifeless data with new meaning and make its implications more memorable and meaningful. One checklist for management using focus groups to obtain a more three-dimensional understanding of their actual customers includes the following advice: [5]

1. Do not expect the people in the focus group to look like idealized customers. Fitness seekers may not look like aerobic instructors—they are just *trying* to.
2. It can be shocking to find that your customers may not like you very much. Listening to what they have to say about your company's products and personnel and your ideas can be ego-bruising. You cannot argue with them—be prepared to listen to the good and bad news.
3. Your customers are unlikely to think or care as much about your product as you do. It may be what you worry about for ten hours a day, but not them.

4. Do not expect focus group participants to be just like you are—or to be totally different either.

5. People are not always consistent in what they say. That does not mean they are liars or hypocrites—just human.

6. Your moderator is a good resource to put the study in a context with other research he or she has done. Are the responses more or less positive than he or she has seen in other focus groups?

7. If your screening process was effective, you are looking at real customers—whether you like what you see or not.

8. Be honest about what you expected to see. We all have preconceptions, just ask whether yours are based on research or prejudice.

■ *Reinforcing Beliefs.* Judith Langer recounted an experience by The Gillette Company which illustrated the ability of focus groups to convey a message much more powerfully to employees than repeat admonitions by management:

> A focus group with women showed that consumers are more demanding and "educated" about quality than in the past. This comment was typical:
>
> "I think as consumers we're becoming more aware of what goes into a product. For myself, I have become more aware of the ingredients—food or clothing or whatever. I feel that I'm not the same shopper I was perhaps six years ago. That was just fad buying. Now I look at something."
>
> Business, business research, and research and development people observe the group; the videotape of the session has since been shown to others in the company. Hans Locater, Gillette's research director, says that the focus group made what top management has been saying more tangible and believable

■ *Early Barometer.* Focus groups may provide an early warning system of shifts in the market. Probing consumers on lifestyle changes, consumption patterns, opinions of new competitive entries, and the like may reveal threats and opportunities entering the market long before they might be revealed in a large-scale survey. Keeping an open mind and maintaining an active curiosity allow for researchers to see the far-reaching significance of seemingly innocuous observations made by focus group participants.

Focus Group Composition

Conventional industry wisdom suggests that focus groups should consist of eight to twelve people selected to be homogeneous along some characteristic important to the researcher (e.g., do a lot of baking, own foreign luxury cars, manage their own retirement account with more than $100,000 invested). Usually recruitment of focus group participants strives to find people who fit the desired profile but who do not know each other—thus reducing the inhibitions of group members to describe their actual feelings or behaviors. Typically, group sessions last from one and a half to two hours. Going against such conventional wisdom may be necessary in some cases. For example, one of the authors conducted research for a food company that wanted a few direct questions asked prior to presenting participants with prepared versions of their food products, as well as their competitor's. While not a taste test per se, the client wanted to hear the subjects' reactions to the products and a discussion of the circumstances under which the products would be used in their homes. For this study a series of one-hour group sessions was run with five people per group. The more structured discussion and the desire to query each participant made the shorter time and smaller group more conducive to achieving the study's objectives.

Selection and Recruitment of Group Participants

The research objectives and research design will indicate the types of people to be recruited for a focus group. If a facility especially designed for focus group use is contracted the management of the facility typically will conduct recruitment of focus group members. If a business research firm is being hired to conduct the groups, they usually hire the facility; identify, recruit, and select the participants; moderate the groups; and make an oral and written report of the findings. Sometimes the client organization will provide a list of possible participants taken from a master list of customers, members, users, and others. It is usually necessary to provide *at least* four names for every respondent needed (i.e., approximately fifty names per focus group).

Prospective participants are screened when contacted to ensure their eligibility for the group, but without revealing the factors used to assess their eligibility. For example, if the researcher is interested in talking with people who have traveled to Europe in the past year, he or she would also ask about other trips or activities to camouflage the central issue under investigation. This deception is helpful in discouraging respondents from answering in ways strictly intended to increase or diminish chances for an invitation, and to discourage selected participants from preparing "right" answers for their participation in the group sessions. It is advisable to provide a general idea of the topic for discussion (e.g., personal travel) to encourage participation. Actual participants are usually rewarded with an honorarium (say $25 to $50 per person) for their time. The size of the honorarium depends upon the type of participant (e.g., physicians expect more than homemakers). The focus group facility's management usually covers the cost of recruiting, hosting, and compensating the groups in their fee. The following are six rules for recruiting focus group members.

1. Specifically define the characteristics of people who will be included in the groups.
2. If an industrial focus group is being conducted, develop screening questions that probe into all aspects of the respondents' job functions. Do not depend on titles or other ambiguous definitions of responsibilities.
3. If an industrial focus group is being conducted, provide the research company with the names of specific companies and employees, when possible. If specific categories of companies are needed, a list of qualified companies is critical.
4. Ask multiple questions about a single variable to validate the accuracy of answers. Therefore, if personal computer users are to be recruited, do not simply ask for the brand and model of personal computer they use. In addition, ask them to describe the machine and its function; this will ensure that they are referring to the appropriate equipment.
5. Do not accept respondents who have participated in a focus group during the previous year.
6. Have each participant arrive fifteen minutes early to complete a prediscussion questionnaire. This will provide additional background information on each respondent, reconfirm their suitability for the discussion, and help the company collect useful factual information.

Moderator Role and Responsibilities

The moderator plays a key role in obtaining maximum value from conducting focus groups. The moderator helps design the study guide, assists the researcher who is seeking the information, and leads the discussion in a skillful way to address the study's objectives while stimulating and probing group participants to contribute to the discussion. The following are ten traits of a good focus group moderator.

1. Be experienced in focus group research.
2. Provide sufficient help in conceptualizing the focus group research design, rather than simply executing the groups exactly as specified.
3. Prepare a detailed moderator guide well in advance of the focus group.
4. Engage in advance preparation to improve overall knowledge of the area being discussed.

5. Provide some added value to the project beyond simply doing an effective job of conducting the session.
6. Maintain control of the group without leading or influencing the participants.
7. Be open to modern techniques such as visual stimulation, conceptual mapping, attitude scaling, or role-playing, which can be used to delve deeper into the minds of participants.
8. Take personal responsibility for the amount of time allowed for the recruitment, screening, and selection of participants.
9. Share in the feeling of urgency to complete the focus group while desiring to achieve an excellent total research project.
10. Demonstrate the enthusiasm and exhibit the energy necessary to keep the group interested even when the hour is running late.

Trends in Focus Groups

Several new variations in the traditional focus group approach are being successfully used by some companies. One is two-way focus groups, which involves conducting a focus group, then having a specific group of respondents interested in the comments of the first focus group view the video of the focus group during their own focus group session. This approach could be expanded to a three-way focus group setting. One of the authors of this text worked with a company that supplied food products to fine restaurants that used a three-way focus group approach. In this instance the first group consisted of patrons of expensive restaurants talking about their experiences at such restaurants. The video of these consumers was then viewed in a focus group of chefs and restaurant managers who commented on what they were seeing and were asked what they might do to address the needs of these consumers. The video of the chef's focus group was then observed by the food brokers used by the food service company who talked about what they could do differently to better serve the needs of the chefs. Managers from the sponsoring food service company attended all three focus groups (multiple groups of each level of focus groups were conducted).

Matej Kastelic/Shutterstock.com

Quads is another variation of focus groups that has been used. In these groups usually four respondents (hence the name quads) discuss a limited set of topics, perhaps engage in a taste test, and might complete a short evaluation of products. Quads take less time to complete than the usual focus group (less than one hour as opposed to one and one half to two hours), allowing for more of them to be conducted in an evening than traditional focus groups. The attraction of quads is the ability to get 100 percent participation of respondents (in a ten-person focus group, participation by each person is more limited) on a short, specific set of issues, allowing observers to more easily focus on the differences in responses and generate hypotheses regarding those observations. Conducting more groups allows for more fine tuning of discussion questions and methodology and changes to be made from one group session to the next. Both two-way and quad variations of focus group approaches (and many more variations practiced by research firms) illustrate the flexibility inherent in conducting good exploratory communication research.

Internet focus groups are rapidly gaining in popularity. Internet focus groups are, like all focus groups, an exploratory research technique that capitalizes on the efficiency afforded by the Internet to engage people in diverse geographic locations together in a discussion of a topic of interest to the researcher and participants. Such groups can be conducted within a company with employees, or externally with customers or members of a target market. If confidentiality is a concern with employees, they can use a hyperlink embedded in e-mail to go to a secure Web site where they can participate anonymously.

Internet focus groups with consumers have an obvious advantage in cost savings over traditional focus groups (approximately one-fifth to one-half the cost) as well as allowing for greater diversity among participants. Participants may in some situations be able to enter their input and reactions to other participants anytime during the extended focus group time frame—twenty-four hours a day. Use of IRC (Internet Relay Chat) or Web chat sites make it easy for participants to contribute to a discussion set up at that specific site for a specific purpose. It is then possible to immediately generate transcripts of twenty to thirty pages of verbatim responses for analysis. Advantages include speed of recruitment, savings in travel costs and time away from the office, ability of respondents to participate from the comfort of their own home, and anonymity of responses. Disadvantages include a loss of observable information (e.g., facial expressions, body language, sense of excitement, confusion, and the like), which veteran focus group moderators use in analyzing traditional group sessions. Also, it is not possible to ensure that the person engaging in the focus group session is really the person you wanted. It is not possible to effectively screen people for certain desirable and easily verifiable characteristics (e.g., age, gender, or racial background), and be certain the person on the Internet actually fits the desired profile. Also, unless the topic is about the use of the Internet itself, the people who are available for Internet focus groups may or may not be representative of the complete target market.

Some research companies operate Internet focus groups by recruiting and building a database of respondents from screening people visiting their Web site or through other recruitment methods. These people are then profiled through a series of questions, which allows the research firm to select respondents with the characteristics desired by the client organization. Potential respondents are e-mailed, asking them to go to a particular Web site at a particular time (using a hyperlink embedded in the e-mail). The moderator types in questions and responds, probes, and clarifies during the session by typing in queries. Several companies do these types of focus groups.

Iakov Filimonov/Shutterstock.com

Immersion Groups

Some researchers are turning away from the traditional format of focus groups with a moderator and eight to ten people, and have instead begun interacting directly with fewer participants in what has begun being called "Immersion Groups".[6] At Yahoo, for example, researchers meet directly with four or five consumers in work sessions to design new services. A new online community for auto buffs who desire more opportunities to chat with other members was designed using immersion research. The advocates of these immersion groups believe that some consumers are not honest about their feelings and behaviors in front of other consumers around the focus group table. Hands-on work sessions with consumers break down such inhibitions.

Ethnography

Ethnography the researcher experiences life events along with the study participants—asking questions, observing, and recording their own feelings as they share the experience.

Companies are increasingly adapting the ethnographic research methodologies of cultural anthropologists to study consumers. Typically, **ethnography** involves a researcher experiencing life events along with their participants—asking questions, observing, and recording their own feelings as they share the experience. Volkswagen engineers couldn't understand why Americans treat their cars as homes on wheels until they spent three and one-half grueling hours on a Greyhound bus traveling between Seattle and Portland. That experience and spending 18 months traveling across the U.S. by car, talking with fellow travelers at rest stops and fast food outlets, going to malls, visiting the Rock and Roll Hall of Fame, tailgating at a NASCAR race, attending drag races, and observing other travelers on similar long car trips helped drive home the differences in the American and European car cultures. "If you lose your car here you're done," was the revelation of one of the researchers.[7] Additionally, they took subways, drove rental cars, and took red-eye flights. They shadowed mothers who spent the day taking kids to soccer practice, picking up the dry cleaning, and shopping for groceries. Their conclusion: "In Germany it's all about driving, but here it's about everything but driving." Designs for all VW products sold in the U.S. market are expected to be affected by the ethnographic research results.

Procter & Gamble likewise conducts ongoing ethnographic studies to keep abreast of consumption practices. The company routinely sends scores of researchers armed with video cameras into consumer households around the world to tape daily routines and procedures of consumers in all their boring glory. Typically the ethnographer-filmmakers arrive at the home of the participant when the alarm clock goes off, and stay until bedtime, usual for a four-day stretch. Sometimes the camera is left on without an attendant in a room while family members go about their daily tasks. Taping a mother feeding a child in the consumer's own home can reveal many actions that would go unreported in a focus group session on that subject. Observing multitasking behaviors occurring during such sessions could inspire packaging and product designs that could provide a competitive advantage when they reach the market.[8] Each year more companies pursue such ethnographic studies to supplement other exploratory research methods.

Netnography

In recent years, e-commerce has become an important component of retail sales. Moreover, consumers join discussion boards, chat rooms, and other online forums to trade information about products, services, and businesses. Thus, methods to conduct research on the World Wide Web have been developed. One such method is **netnography**, which is ethnography that studies the consumer behavior of online communities. The research methodology is the same as traditional ethnography in that the researcher should begin with specific research questions and learn as much as possible about the online groups to be studied. Data collection can consist of copies of computer-mediated communications of the online community or transcriptions of what the researcher observes in monitoring online forums.

Netnography ethnography that studies the consumer behavior of online communities.

For example, while many may believe that the coffee market has been adequately addressed by Starbucks, a study of coffee drinkers using netnography indicates that there is an online community of coffee drinkers with an almost religious fervor about coffee that has yet to be exploited. These consumers possess discriminating tastes and snob appeal. They also are not interested in the in-person social aspects of coffee consumption at a place like Starbucks but are more interested in products they can use at home.[9]

Grounded Theory

Grounded theory is based on the concept that people act in response to environmental clues, objects, and other people based on the meanings people assign to them. That is, grounded theory researchers believe that personal conduct is programmed by social norms. In order to understand behavior in a particular situation, then, the researcher enters into the subject's context.

Grounded theory based on the concept that people act in response to environmental clues. The theory evolves during the research process.

A variety of research methods might be used in grounded research including depth interviews, ethnography, and immersion groups. A researcher might choose to use only one method or more than one method in the same study. The method to use after the initial method is chosen is driven by the research.

The key concept of grounded theory is that the theory evolves during the research process. That is, unlike quantitative methods where the researcher tests an existing theory, grounded theory research is designed to *develop* a theory. Another important element of grounded theory is that there is a constant interplay between the data collected and its analysis. Thus, as data is collected the theory evolves along with the method. Additionally, there is no pre-determined sample with grounded theory. Researchers continue to collect data until they learn nothing new from additional data. This is known as theoretical sampling.

Grounded theory is used when researchers want to study an area of interest without preconceptions. Thus, the method is more difficult for study subjects with long, empirically based literature. Grounded theory researchers attempt to avoid even any unconscious predispositions concerning the area of study.

Analysis of Selected Cases

Analysis of selected cases case analysis involves the study of a specific situation similar to the current research problem. It is particularly valuable for complex research problems.

Another means of achieving the objectives of exploratory research is to conduct in-depth **analysis of selected cases** of the subject under investigation. This approach is of particular value when a complex set of variables might be at work in generating observed results, and intensive study is needed to unravel the complexities. For example, an in-depth study of a firm's top salespeople and a comparison with the worst salespeople might reveal characteristics common to stellar performers. Here again, the exploratory investigator is best served by an active curiosity and willingness to deviate from the initial plan when findings suggest new courses of inquiry might prove more productive. It is easy to see how the exploratory research objectives of generating insights and hypotheses would be well served by use of this technique.

Projective Techniques

Projective techniques a form of research that is effective in discovering the hidden (latent) motives and attitudes of the research subjects. It is also useful when dealing with sensitive subjects.

Researchers might be exploring a topic where respondents are either unwilling or unable to directly answer questions about why they think or act as they do. Highly sensitive topics involving their private lives are obviously in this category, but more mundane behaviors may also hide deep psychological motivations. For example, in a case investigating why some women persisted in preferring a messy, expensive spray to kill roaches instead of using a more efficient trap that the women acknowledged to have more benefits than their sprays, researchers discovered that the women transferred hostilities for the men who had left them to the roaches and wanted to see the roaches squirm and die. The method used to uncover these hidden motives is one of the so-called **projective techniques**, named because respondents project their deep psychological motivations through a variety of communication and observable methods. These methods typically include:

1. *Word association.* Respondents are given a series of words and respond by saying the first word that comes to mind. The response, the frequency of the response, and time it takes to make the response are keys to understanding the underlying motives toward the subject. If no response is given, it is interpreted to mean that emotional involvement is so high as to block the response.

2. *Sentence completion.* Similar to word association, sentence completion requires the respondent to enter words or phrases to complete a given sentence such as: People who use the Discover credit card are _____. Responses are then analyzed for content.

3. *Storytelling.* Here respondents are given a cartoon, photograph, drawing, or are asked to draw a scene related to the subject under investigation and tell what is happening in the scene. In theory, the respondent will reveal inner thoughts by using the visual aid as a stimulus to elicit these deep motivations. Therefore, if the picture is of two people sitting and looking at a computer screen in an office, the story that is told about the people will reveal how the respondent feels about using computers in a work environment.

4. *Third-person technique/role-playing.* This technique is a reflection of what Oscar Wilde meant when he said "A man is least himself when he talks in his own person; when he is given a mask he will tell the truth." Respondents are told to explain why a third person (a coworker or a neighbor) might act in a certain way. For example, a stimulus might appear as: We are trying to better understand what features people might consider when buying a garden tractor. Please think about people you know and tell us what features would be important to them for such a product. Role-playing requires the respondent to play the role of another party in a staged scenario, such as asking a retailer to play the role of a customer coming into a retail establishment.

5. *Collages.* This technique involves asking the respondent to cut pictures out of magazines and arrange them on poster board to depict some issue of interest to the researcher. For example, respondents might be asked to choose pictures that tell a story of how they decided to start exercising daily, or to find pictures that convey their image of the Compaq computer brand.

art4all/Shutterstock.com

6. *Music association.* Here the researcher plays a variety of music selections and asks the respondent to associate the music with one of the brands being evaluated. The objective is to determine a brand's emotional content for the respondent (e.g., associating one brand of vodka with hard rock music and another brand with cool jazz).
7. *Anthropomorphizing.* In this approach the respondent is asked to describe what the product or service being researched would look like if it were a person—age, gender, attractiveness, how would he or she be dressed, what would his or her occupation be, what kind of car would he or she drive, or health status and the like. A variation of this is asking what famous person the product or service would be.

As can be seen from the description of these techniques, one must be skilled not only in structuring these approaches, but also must be an experienced professional in interpreting the results. Also, their use is often bimodal—either an organization (such as an advertising agency or marketing consulting firm) uses them extensively or not at all. These techniques have been shown to provide intriguing new insights into behavior, but are best left to experts to operate and interpret.

The Value of Exploratory Research

All of these exploratory techniques, when properly applied, can be successfully used to achieve the research objectives of generating ideas, hypotheses, and clarifying concepts. Quite often in a multistage research project, one might start with exploratory research, then use the results to help structure a descriptive research questionnaire or a causal research experiment. While that is frequently the case, exploratory results do not have value only as preliminary work before the real research takes place. Depending on the research purpose or attitude of the decision maker toward risk, exploratory research may be the only research that is done. For example, if in-depth interviews with twenty selected purchasing agents generate only ridicule of a new product idea, it is not necessary to conduct a structured survey of 500 to kill the idea. However, if you want to ultimately produce an ad that says your paintbrush is preferred two to one over a major competitor's by professional painters, exploratory research will not be sufficient to support your claims. If a decision maker is a high risk taker, exploratory research may be all that is desired before a decision can be reached. If the stakes increase, however, that same decision maker may want to follow up the exploratory research with more structured and quantifiable descriptive or causal research.

The point we are trying to make here is that well-conducted exploratory research can be extremely valuable in achieving the objectives endemic to that type of research, apart from its contributing to later phases of the research study. The fact that it does not generate precise quantifiable data is not a weakness of the approach. When properly conducted and interpreted it can serve as a powerful aid to decision making, depending upon the decisions being faced and the decision-making style of the manager.

To know whether exploratory research is alone sufficient or should be followed by descriptive or causal research, the researcher should examine the research questions, the decisional criteria, the time available to do the research, and the research budget. An example might help to illustrate the interplay of these factors in determining whether exploratory research should be followed by quantitative research.

In the case of the Compton Company described in Chapter 1, the managers decided, incorrectly as it turned out, to get a new advertising agency instead of doing research to discover the cause of their declining market share. If they learned a lesson from this experience and next time decide to do research before making a decision, their preferred decision-making style might be to rely on exploratory approaches rather than a full-scale quantitative study.

So, a research question such as: "Are our dealer policies competitive?" might with some decision makers involve doing exploratory research to first clarify concepts, formulate the issue more precisely, and gain valuable insights into dealer relations, then descriptive research to discover the frequency with which dealers rate your company's policies as fair, motivating, and understandable compared to your competitors. The Compton Company managers, however, may merely want you to have in-depth conversations with a few key dealers (i.e., the decision criteria of Compton's decision makers), report the results of your conversations, and then they are ready to make their decision. Whether the research would be staged as exploratory followed by descriptive, or exploratory only would therefore depend upon how the decision makers (with the help of the researchers, see Chapter 1) defined the decision alternatives and criteria that would be used to choose among the alternatives, the time available for the research, and the research budget.

In some cases the research question itself suggests descriptive research will be needed to follow up exploratory findings. If, in collaboration with the decision maker, the researcher writes the research question as: "What percentage of dealers rate our company as having the best customer service?", then it will be necessary to follow the exploratory research with descriptive research. Here the exploratory clarifies terms such as "best" and "customer service" and identifies what areas of customer service are most important to dealers, and the descriptive determines the percentage of dealers rating the company's and its competitors' customer service along those important dimensions. It is descriptive, not exploratory, that provides quantification of responses.

Research Project Tip | If your research questions require some exploratory research to gain insights, ideas, and generate hypotheses, either to answer the questions entirely or before you can go on to descriptive or causal research, you should indicate in detail how that exploratory research is to be conducted. For example, indicate not only that a literature search is to be conducted to help answer research question #3, but also describe what literature is to be reviewed. Wherever possible include a photocopy of a page or two of the document being reviewed. For in-depth interviews, profile the specific types of people you plan to interview and list the topics you plan to cover in the interview. Link each research objective with the exploratory techniques you plan to use to answer the question, along with a detailed discussion of exactly what the use of that technique will involve.

SUMMARY

Research designs are like roadmaps that help us determine the most efficient and effective methods to conduct our business studies. The three basic research designs are exploratory, descriptive, and causal.

In this chapter, we focused on exploratory research design with an emphasis on qualitative methods. It was noted that exploratory research helps us gain broad insights to an issue or an ambiguous problem. Exploratory research might also help us develop hypotheses we will use in descriptive and causal research designs.

Qualitative research methods are one set of tools we can use to conduct exploratory research. Qualitative research is often a multi-method process that is flexible in design and depends on the researcher's observation and interpretation of behavior and or non-numerical data. Methods include case analysis, ethnography, netnography, immersion groups, depth interviews, grounded theory, and projective techniques.

Qualitative methods are still rejected by many who consider them to be soft science that fails to reflect objective reality. Despite these reservations, many companies are incorporating qualitative methods into their market research activities.

KEY TERMS

Analysis of selected cases (p. 72)
Ethnography (p. 70)
Exploratory research (p. 59)
Focus group (p. 65)
Grounded theory (p. 71)
In-depth interview (p. 61)

Literature review (p. 64)
Netnography (p. 71)
Projective techniques (p. 72)
Qualitative research (p. 61)
Research design (p. 58)

DISCUSSION QUESTIONS

1. What are the objectives of exploratory research?
2. How does exploratory research differ from descriptive and causal research?
3. Define qualitative research.
4. What are the main issues in the debate between qualitative and quantitative researchers?
5. If you were asked to study the breakfast cereal consumption habits of children 8–10, which qualitative method would you use? Why?

ENDNOTES

1. Zaltman, G. (1997). Rethinking market research: Putting people back in. *Journal of Marketing Research, 34(4)*, p. 458.
2. Denzin, N. & Lincoln, Y. S. (1994) Introduction: Entering the Field of Qualitative Research, in N. K. Dentin & Y. S. Lincoln (Eds), *Handbook of Qualitative Research:* 1–17. Thousand Oaks, CA: Sage.
3. Mayut, Pamela (1994). Introduction: Entering the Field of Qualitative Research, in N. K. Dentin & Y. S. Lincoln (Eds), *Handbook of Qualitative Research*: 1–17. Thousand Oaks, CA: Sage.
4. Ibid.
5. Catterall, M. & Maclaran P. (2006). Focus Groups in Marketing Research in R. W. Belk (Ed) *Handbook of Qualitative Research in Marketing*, 255–267. Northhampton, MA: Edward Elgar.
6. See David Kiley, "Shoot the Focus Group," *Business Week* (November 14, 2005), pp. 120–121.
7. Gina Chon, "VW's American Road Trip", *Wall Street Journal,* January 4, 2006, p. B1ff.
8. Emily Nelson "P&G Checks Out Real Life", *Wall Street Journal,* May 17, 2001, p. B1ff.
9. Kozinets, Robert V. (2002) "The Field Behind the Screen: Using Ethnography for Marketing Research in Online Communities," *Journal of Marketing Research*, February 2002, volume 39, issue 1, pp. 61–72.

Research Designs: Descriptive and Causal Research

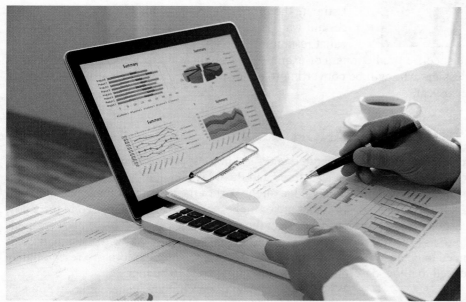

Doidam 10/Shutterstock.com

Chapter Outline

Descriptive Research

Causal Research

Experimentation

Exploratory, Descriptive, or Causal Observation

Dangers of Defining Design by Technique

Summary

Key Terms

Discussion Questions

Endnotes

Learning Objectives

Upon completing this chapter, you should understand:

- How exploratory or qualitative, descriptive, and causal research differ.
- The factors influencing the choice of research design.
- How descriptive designs differ from experimental designs.
- The differences between a quasi experimental, preexperimental, and true experimental design.
- What is meant by the terms: treatments, experimental units, and experimental designs.
- The differences in the application of experiments to test marketing.

Ollyy/Shutterstock.com

As the name implies, **descriptive research** seeks to *describe* something. More specifically, descriptive research is conducted when seeking to accomplish the following objectives:

1. Describe the characteristics of relevant groups. For example, 20 percent of our customers who generate 80 percent of our business. Having a description of our heavy users can define a target for our future management efforts intended to find more prospects similar to our best customers.
2. Determine the extent to which two or more variables covary. For example, does consumption rate vary by age of consumer?
3. Estimate the proportion of a population who act or think a certain way. For example, how often do childless couples eat at restaurants in a typical month?

4. Make specific predictions. For example, we might want to forecast the number of wholesalers who will be converting to a new inventory tracking software system in the next year.

Descriptive research research that *describes* something. It is much more structured than exploratory research and assumes more prior knowledge of the research problem.

DESCRIPTIVE RESEARCH

Descriptive research is highly structured and rigid in its approach to data collection, compared to exploratory research's unstructured and flexible approach. As such, descriptive research presupposes much prior knowledge on the part of the researcher regarding *who* will be targeted as a respondent, *what* issues are of highest priority to be addressed in the study, *how* the questions are to be phrased to reflect the vocabulary and experience of the respondents, *when* to ask the questions, *where* to find the respondents, and *why* these particular questions need to be answered in order to make decisions. Thus, exploratory research may often be needed to allow descriptive research requirements to be met.

pixfly/Shutterstock.com

While exploratory research may generate a hypothesis (e.g., Hispanics offer a more attractive market for our product than do Asians), it is descriptive research (or causal) that provides for a test of the hypothesis. Exploratory research may be needed to answer the who, what, when, where, why, and how of doing descriptive research (e.g., who should be the respondents of the survey), while descriptive research answers these same questions about the market (e.g., who are the high consumers of our product). Whereas exploratory research *suggests,* descriptive *quantifies.*

Finding answers to these who, what, when, where, why, and how questions in descriptive research demands disciplined thinking on the part of the researcher.[1] This is illustrated by the following example:

Suppose a chain of food convenience stores was planning to open a new outlet and wanted to determine how people begin patronizing such a store. Imagine some of the questions that would need to be answered before data collection for this descriptive study could begin.

■ Who is to be considered a "patron"? Anyone who enters the store? Even those who participate in only the grand-opening prize giveaway? Someone who purchases anything from the store?

■ Should patrons be defined on the basis of the family unit or as individuals?

■ What characteristics should be measured: age, gender, where they live, or how they learned about the store? Should we measure them before, during, or after shopping? Should they be studied during the first weeks of operation, or after sales have stabilized? Should they be measured outside or inside the store, or at home?

Should we measure them by using a questionnaire or by observing their behavior? If using a questionnaire, will it be administered by telephone, mail, or personal interview?[2]

Research Project Tip

While a detailed description of what you plan to do in conducting the descriptive phase of the research might need to wait until you have done the exploratory research (i.e., get specifics of the who, what, and the like for the descriptive research), you should be able to describe in general terms the rationale for doing descriptive research. Provide a preliminary description in your research design of which research question and hypotheses will require descriptive research, a rationale for why descriptive is needed, and your initial ideas for answers to the who, what, and other questions, understanding that these may change after reviewing the exploratory findings.

These questions reveal the need for the researcher to arrive at answers by thinking like a decision maker. That is, the researcher must think how the research findings will be used to make the decisions facing the decision maker. If you are trying to attract more single, elderly patrons to food convenience stores, for example, you know the who question would need to include a representative sample of that group. Your exploratory research might have been needed to identify the importance of that type of patron (helping supply the answer to the who question), but the descriptive research can not be conducted until that and other questions, such as those listed above, have been answered. All answers should be supported by an underlying rationale related to the decisions being faced.

→ Labor & Delivery
→ 401 - 429
→ Maternity Waiting
→ Nursery
→ Obstetric Center
→ Post Partum
→ Sleep Disorders Ctr.

← Outpatient Care Ctr.
← 430 - 443

Descriptive research is more than an efficient means of collecting quantifiable facts. Facts can be a plentiful and useless commodity unless coupled with the "glue of explanation and understanding, the framework of theory, the tie-rod of conjecture."[3] We should determine how the information collected in a descriptive research study will be analyzed and used to test hypotheses, indicate the characteristics of a population, and other things before we ever design the data-collection instrument. For example, exploratory research conducted by a hospital may have generated the hypothesis that women of child-bearing age with higher incomes and education demand a variety of birthing options, education classes, and father participation and presence in the delivery room, including during a cesarean section. Secondary data may reveal that the hospital is located in an area of high concentration of women of above-average income and education, and that pregnancy rates are average for the area. Descriptive research may seek to test the hypotheses that these women:

- Do demand and expect their hospital to provide an obstetrics program with those characteristics.
- Are not presently satisfied with the options available from other hospitals.
- Are looking for and would be attracted to a hospital that did offer an obstetrics program that satisfied their wants and needs.

Here, the exploratory research generated, but could not test, the hypotheses, and the descriptive research generated facts in a form that provided the means of testing the hypotheses. It is important to note that researchers would have determined how the hypotheses would be tested *before* they designed questions in the questionnaire to generate the desired facts. That is, they would have set up dummy tables or chosen the multivariate statistical techniques to be used to test the hypotheses, then determined how data would be collected to allow for the use of these procedures for hypotheses testing. For example, sample dummy tables can be seen in Figure 5.1.

Sibling Education Classes	Household Income Per Year			
	≤$25,000	$25,001–$40,000	$40,001–$55,000	>$55,000
High				
Medium				
Low				

Father in Delivery Room	Household Income Per Year			
	≤$25,000	$25,001–$40,000	$40,001–$55,000	>$55,000
High				
Medium				
Low				

Nurse Midwife	Household Income Per Year			
	≤$25,000	$25,001–$40,000	$40,001–$55,000	>$55,000
High				
Medium				
Low				

Physician Referral Service	Household Income Per Year			
	≤$25,000	$25,001–$40,000	$40,001–$55,000	>$55,000
High				
Medium				
Low				

FIGURE 5.1 Sample Tables for Hypothesis Testing

By setting up this table before we even design the questionnaire or determine the number and type of respondents to survey, we have in effect helped specify the parameters for those parts of the research design. One hypothesis is that we should see the percentages on the top row of these tables get larger as we move to higher incomes (e.g., higher-income expectant mothers put more emphasis on such services in choosing a hospital than do lower-income expectant mothers). Other dummy tables would be developed to show how other hypotheses would be tested. This table was developed because researchers were intent on testing the hypotheses arising out of the exploratory research, and will be used, once completed, to influence decisions about service design, promotion, and other aspects of the marketing program. Design of such a table also permits researchers to develop a data-collection instrument such as a questionnaire that can provide the data in a form that permits the hypotheses to be tested. While sounding somewhat convoluted, it is true that we determine how the data will be analyzed before we develop the questions that provided the data. Remember, "No problem is definitely formulated until the researcher can specify how [he or she] will make [his or her] analysis and how the results will contribute to a practical solution."[4] The basic types of descriptive research studies used to provide such data are cross-sectional and longitudinal studies.

Cross-Sectional Designs

Cross-sectional analysis research that involves a sampling of a population of interest at one point in time. Also revered to as a *sample survey*.

The best known and most frequently used descriptive design, **cross-sectional analysis**, involves a sampling of a population of interest at one point in time. This technique is sometimes referred to as a *sample survey,* because it often involves a probability sampling plan intended to choose respondents who will be representative of a certain population. As with all descriptive research, sample surveys are characterized by a high degree of structure—in both the data-collection instrument and in the data-collection process itself. The only way we can be sure we are measuring frequency or variation in the phenomenon under investigation is to build a high degree of structure into the instrument and process. That structure was not only *not* needed in exploratory research, it would have been a deterrent to achieving our objectives of insight, ideas, hypotheses, clarification, and others. Chapter 7 will discuss how to conduct sample surveys via questionnaires or observation in order to achieve the goals of a descriptive research study.

Cross-sectional surveys do not always have to involve selection of a one-time sample of respondents from the population. Several firms such as The Home Testing Institute, Market Facts, and National Family Opinion (NFO) operate omnibus panels that consist of hundreds of thousands of U.S. households that have been selected to proportionately represent the U.S. population along key dimensions such as age, income, sex, ethnic composition, and geographic dispersion. Members of such households are recruited to serve on the panel and agree to participate in answering questionnaires or trying products when requested to do so by the company maintaining the panel. Using such a panel allows an organization to select certain demographic characteristics for respondents (e.g., single males under thirty-five years of age) and send a questionnaire to them, knowing that the cost of finding and getting a response from a targeted number of this group (e.g., 1,000 completed questionnaires) is much less than trying to complete such a project in the general population where response rates may be as low as one or two percent.

These panels are particularly cost-effective when research is being conducted on a topic where the incidence rate in the population is very low (e.g., vegetarians, people with three-car garages, or people with weight training machines in their homes). In such cases it is possible to buy a few screening questions on the monthly questionnaire sent to, say, 50, 000 panel members to identify those members who fit the desired profile, then send only those qualified panelists a longer questionnaire to obtain the detailed information being sought. Firms maintaining such omnibus panels turn over membership frequently to avoid participating households becoming "professional respondents," which would reduce the respondents' representativeness for the general population.

Some organizations recruit and maintain their own panels. For example, Parker Pen maintains a panel of people who use writing pens frequently. Such corporate panels are useful when a company wants to assess targeted consumers' attitudes on a scheduled basis, try out potential new products in an in-home setting before making a go/no-go decision, or seek information on awareness and knowledge of competitive promotions. These panels are used more than once over time, similar to the longitudinal panels discussed below, but since the subject of the research changes constantly it is best to think of these panels as company-run omnibus cross-sectional survey research panels.

Ambient Ideas/Shutterstock. comcom

Longitudinal Studies

Whereas cross-sectional studies are like taking snapshots of a target population at a point in time, **longitudinal studies** are similar to filming videotapes of the respondents. The primary objective of longitudinal research is to monitor behavior over time and thereby identify behavioral (or attitudinal) changes. Sometimes referred to as *true panels,* these longitudinal panels report the same information (e.g., grocery store purchases, or purchases and use of a particular product or service) at specific points in time. This information can be combined with other pertinent information to determine, for example, if brand switching occurred after exposure to a trial sample, coupon, or advertisement.

One of the best-known panels for consumer goods is Information Resource's BehaviorScan, which continuously tracks tens of thousands of households in a number of different markets. A specially coded card that tracks optically scanned purchases by household members at selected grocery stores. BehaviorScan can be used for test-marketing purposes by splitting the panel into two or more matched groups based on household

Longitudinal study research that monitors behavior over time and identifies behavioral or attitudinal changes.

TABLE 5.1 Two Cross-Sectional Sample Surveys

Number of Consumers Buying	Period 1	Period 2
Brand A	100	100
Brand B	150	150
Brand C	250	250
Total	500	500

TABLE 5.2 Longitudinal Panel

Brand Purchased in Period 1	Brand Purchased in Period 2			
	Brand A	Brand B	Brand C	Total
Brand A	50	20	30	100
Brand B	20	80	50	150
Brand C	30	50	170	250
Total	100	150	250	

demographics, and then sending different promotional appeals to the groups via direct mail, newspaper ads, or even TV. Changes in purchasing patterns can be measured after the promotional appeal is made. A.C. Nielsen Company offers a similar service, where households use hand-held scanners in their homes to track purchases.

The ability to use longitudinal panels for tracking changes in purchase behavior and brand loyalty has advantages over the use of cross-sectional surveys. For example, consider Table 5.1 and information taken from two cross-sectional sample surveys.

It appears that no brand switching occurred between the two surveys taken in time periods 1 and 2. A longitudinal analysis, however, might reveal a very different story, as shown in Table 5.2.

Table 5.2 shows that in fact there was considerable brand-switching behavior, and that brand C enjoyed the greatest brand loyalty, brand A the least. Longitudinal panels also have an advantage over sample surveys in that panel members record purchases immediately and therefore generate accurate purchase data, whereas cross-sectional surveyors often must rely on respondents' memories for reporting purchases. However, cross-sectional studies may often be more representative of the target population due to the difficulties of recruiting and maintaining a representative sample in a panel design.

CAUSAL RESEARCH

While descriptive research is effective in identifying covariation between variables (e.g., blue packages outsell red ones, consumption rate varies by education level) it cannot truly indicate causality (e.g., color causes sales, education causes consumption). When we are in need of determining if two or more variables are causally related we must turn to causal-research procedures. While there might be a tendency to see many research objectives from a causal perspective ("We really want to know what causes consumers to act that way"), there is a difference between causality in the vernacular and how it is defined by scientists. Quite often decision makers do not need to test for a causal relationship in order to make good decisions. I might need to know only that blue packages outsell red ones or that consumption of my product increases with educational level in order to make appropriate management decisions. Testing for causality is a risky, expensive, time-consuming proposition and may not in the end permit better decisions than those made by simply acknowledging the covariation that descriptive research identified.

However, in some cases a test of our hypothesis requires **causal research** (e.g., greater sales will result from having four shelf offerings of our product in stores under 60,000 square feet than having two facings in stores over 80,000 square feet). Remember that we stated that descriptive research is characterized by its more structured approach as compared to exploratory? Causal research is also highly structured, but is characterized also by the use of *control* procedures used during the experimental designs associated with tests of causal relationships.

Our interest in causal research is to determine the degree to which one variable is causally related to another (e.g., Does ad "A" cause people to remember its message better than ad "B"? Does a 10 percent decrease in price cause an increase in profit compared to no price change?). Obviously, in all such cases we are concerned with truly determining the impact of our independent variable (ads A and B, or price in the examples above) on our dependent variable (ad recall or profit in the examples), and not some extraneous variable that "leaks" into our test (e.g., a competitor's actions, an environmental event). Therefore, when we conduct a causal experiment we do three things:

Causal research research that determines if one variable (the *independent variable*) causes a change in another variable (the *dependent variable*).

1. *Manipulate:* We manipulate the causal or independent variable such as ad message or price.
2. *Measure:* We measure the effect or dependent variable such as ad recall or profit.
3. *Control:* We control other variables which could have an impact on our dependent variable, such as making sure that our product with price P1 in store S1 is found on the same shelf level as that product with price P2 in store S2.

In addition to manipulation, measurement, and control, we should also think of causal research as requiring three types of evidence: concomitant variation, time order of occurrence, and elimination of other possible causal factors.

Concomitant Variation. Cause and effect must vary together in some predictable manner. They may vary in a positive (i.e., the cause and effect both increase or decrease together) or inverse relationship (i.e., one increases while the other decreases).

Statistical tests indicate the degree of the concomitant variation, such as chi-square tests, correlation, regression, or analysis of variance. Concomitant variation, when we are dealing with the actions of people as with marketing research, is a matter of degree and is not absolute or perfect in the correlation of movement between cause and effect. Scientists infer cause and effect relationships if the presence of the cause makes the occurrence of the effect more likely from a statistically significant standpoint. However, no matter how strong that relationship, mere concomitant variation alone is insufficient to infer a causal relationship. We must see the next two pieces of evidence present.

Time Order of Occurrence. To demonstrate that X causes Y, we must be able to consistently see that X occurs first before we see Y, and not vice versa.

Elimination of Other Possible Causal Factors. Conducting experiments under actual market conditions ("in the field") makes it difficult to control for other possible factors that could influence the effect variable. For example, if we are trying to determine how the amount of shelf space influences the sales for a particular brand of cereal, we realize that other variables such as price, advertising, sales promotion and environmental events (e.g., good or bad publicity about the product), not to mention the activities of our competition, could also influence sales. So when we say we must design an experiment that involves manipulation, measurement, and control, what we are saying is that we must find ways of holding all other possible causal factors constant while manipulating the causal factor(s) under investigation. Otherwise, when we measure our effect variable we will not know if the observed change was due to our manipulated variable, shelf space, or some other variable, such as competitor pricing.

When we cannot exercise physical control (i.e., physically putting the products on the same level of store shelf), we can in effect still have control over the experiment by measuring the nonphysically controlled variable. For example, we cannot control our competitor's pricing in our test markets, but if we can measure the competitor's price, we can use our statistical analysis procedure to control for differences in competitive pricing by making all else equal and just measuring the effect of our price change on our sales. How this is done is beyond the scope of this discussion, but researchers should be aware that control can be exerted through both physical means as well as via measurement. The key in both cases is to anticipate what variables, other than the ones being manipulated, could have an effect on the dependent variable and then exercise control in some form over those variables. Manipulation, like control, may also occur in two ways: physical manipulation (e.g., altering the price) or naturally occurring manipulation. For example, if you are seeking to determine if store size has an effect on sales of a particular product, store size is the causal variable, and would be manipulated. Obviously you can't physically manipulate store size but you can find stores of different sizes naturally occurring the market and randomly assign product placement in 10,000 or 20,000-square-foot-sized stores. Why can't you merely check existing sales data to determine store size effect on sales? Because you haven't also met the conditions we've discussed here, and therefore can't know for sure if a cause-effect relationship exists.

As previously mentioned, causal research is often conducted through the use of controlled experiments to allow for testing of cause and effect. We will now discuss experimentation in business research.

EXPERIMENTATION

What Is Experimentation?

goory/Shutterstock.com

Experimental design the researcher not only measures variables, as in other research designs, but also attempts to control some or all of the conditions under which the data are collected.

Experimental designs differ from other research designs in the degree of control exerted by the researcher over the conditions under which data are collected. When observational or survey descriptive designs are employed, the researcher measures the variables of interest but does not attempt to manipulate or control the variables. However, in experimental (causal) designs, researchers are exercising control over the variables of interest.

For example, a retailer trying to isolate the influence of price changes on the sales volume of a product must identify the nonprice variables such as location of the product in the store, time period of the day or week, and promotion, and control these variables because they also influence sales volume. Simply altering price and measuring sales is not an adequate design because of the impact of nonprice variables on sales.

Essentially, the key differences in experimentation and other designs are:

1. In an experiment, one or more of the independent variables are deliberately manipulated while others are controlled.
2. Combinations of conditions (particular values of the independent variables, such as different prices) are assigned to sample elements (such as different stores) on a random basis. This reduces the likelihood of preexisting conditions affecting the results.

The Terminology of Experimentation

There are several terms that are used to describe the concepts involved in an experiment. Knowledge of these terms is essential to understanding experimental designs.

Experimental Treatments

The term "treatment" is used to describe a specific manner of manipulating an independent variable. For example, if an experiment was designed to measure the influence of three different levels of advertising on sales, then each level of advertising would be a different treatment. If the effects of the three levels of advertising were combined with two levels of price, then there would be six experimental treatments as shown in the following:

Price level one with:
Advertising level one
Advertising level two
Advertising level three

Price level two with:
Advertising level one
Advertising level two
Advertising level three

Since price level one with advertising level one represents a specified combination of independent variables, it is referred to as an experimental treatment. Each combination of price and advertising level creates another experimental treatment. Therefore, this example consists of six different treatments.

Experimental Units

Experimental units are the geographic areas, stores, or people whose responses are measured in determining the effect of the different treatments. If the price and advertising levels described earlier are used in different geographical areas, then the areas represent experimental units. Each group of experimental units is a sample of all possible units and is used for comparing the impact of the treatments. Continuing the example, each of the six treatments may be assigned to 40 different geographic locations for a total of 240 units. If we took a measure of sales before and after each treatment in each location, we would have a total of 480 (i.e., 240 $\times$ 2) observations.

Experimental Designs

The experimental design is the specific process used to arrange independent variables into treatments and then assign treatments to units. There are many possible designs, and great care should be exercised in choosing or modifying the design. Choosing the best design is the most important aspect of experimentation. Several designs will be discussed in a later section, but it should be noted that researchers unfamiliar with experimentation should seek advice in setting up an experiment.

Control Group

In many experiments the use of a **control group** is a necessary element of the design. A control group is randomly selected just like other groups of units in the experiment. However, the control group does not receive a treatment and thus serves as a benchmark for comparing the effects of treatments. If an experiment were used to determine the impact of two new levels of price on sales, prices held at the previous level in some areas would enable these areas to serve as controls in analyzing the results.

Control group a randomly selected group of units in the experiment that does not receive a treatment and thus serves as a benchmark for comparing the effects of treatments.

Validity and Experimentation

While there are a number of different types of validity, the two major varieties are considered here: **internal validity** and **external validity**. Internal validity has to do with whether the independent variables that were manipulated caused the changes in the dependent variable, or whether other factors involved also influenced the dependent variable. There are many threats to internal validity. Some of the major ones are:

1. *History.* During the time that an experiment is taking place, some events may occur that affect the relationship being studied. For example, economic conditions may change, new products may be introduced, or other factors may change that alter the results.
2. *Maturation.* Changes may also take place within the subject that are a function of the passage of time and are not specific to any particular event. These are of special concern when the study covers a long period of time, but may also be a factor in tests that are as short as an hour or two. For example, a subject can become hungry, bored, or tired in a short time and this can affect response results.
3. *Testing.* When pretreatment and posttreatment measures are used, the process of taking a test can affect the scores of a second measurement. The experience of participation in the first measurement can have a learning effect that influences the results on the second measurement.
4. *Instrumentation.* This threat to internal validity comes from changes in measuring instruments or observers. Using different questions or different observers or interviewers is a validity threat.
5. *Selection.* One of the more important threats to internal validity is the differential selection of subjects to be included in experimental and control groups. The concern is over initial differences that exist between subjects. If subjects are randomly assigned to experimental and control groups, this problem can be overcome.
6. *Statistical regression.* This potential loss of validity is of special concern when subjects have been selected on the basis of their extreme scores. For example, if the most productive and least productive salespeople are included in an experiment, there is a tendency for the average of the high scores to decline and the low scores to increase.
7. *Mortality.* Mortality occurs when the composition of the study groups changes during the experiment. Subjects dropping out of an experiment, for example, cause the makeup of the group to change.

While internal validity concerns whether experimental or nonexperimental factors caused the observed differences, external validity is concerned with whether the results are generalizable to other subjects, stores, or areas. The major threats to external validity are:

1. *Subject selection.* The process by which test subjects are selected for an experiment may be a threat to external validity. The population from which subjects are selected may not be the same as the target market. For example, if college students were used as subjects, generalizing to other types of consumers may not be appropriate.
2. *Other factors.* The experimental settings themselves may have an effect on a subject's response. Artificial settings, for example, can give results that are not representative of actual market situations. If the subjects know they are participating in a price experiment, they may be more sensitive to price than normal.

Andrey Arkusha/Shutterstock.com

Field versus Laboratory Experiments

There are two types of settings in which experiments are conducted—field and laboratory. **Field experiments** result in an experimental setting which is more realistic in terms of modeling actual conditions and is therefore higher on external validity. Field experiments are carried out in a natural setting with a minimum of artificial elements in the experiment. The downside of field experiments is that they usually cost more, have lower internal validity due to lack of control over variables that influence the dependent variable, and also may alert competition to changes a company is contemplating in its business strategy.

Laboratory experiments are experiments conducted under artificial conditions, such as testing television ads in a movie theater rather than in buyers' homes. Such experiments usually are lower in cost, have higher internal validity due to more control of the experimental environment, and provide greater secrecy of potential marketing actions. It is also possible to use more elaborate measurement techniques in a laboratory setting than in field experiments.

Disadvantages of laboratory experiments include loss of realism and lower external validity. These are due to the artificial conditions used in the experiment. For example, an experiment where people are given play money and asked to shop in a laboratory setting may reveal a great deal about some aspects of consumer behavior, but there would be great difficulty in trying to generalize the findings to the purchase environment encountered in the marketplace.

The type of information to be generated from the experiment and its intended use dictate which type of experimental setting is more appropriate in a given situation. It is even possible to use both—a laboratory experiment followed by a field experiment—to validate the findings of the laboratory study under actual market conditions.

Experimental Design Symbols

Certain symbols have been developed to help describe experimental designs. These symbols have been used because they help in understanding the designs. These symbols include:

- X = exposure of a group of subjects to an experimental treatment or a level of an independent variable (e.g., to a particular ad or product price). If different levels are used, then such as $X_1, X_2, X_3, \ldots, X_n$ are used.
- O = observation or measurement of the dependent variable in which the researcher is interested.
- R = random assignment of people to groups or groups to treatments.

Other notations are also helpful. The left-to-right notation indicates the time sequence of occurrence of events. Thus the notation

RO_1XO_{2s}

would mean that subjects were randomly assigned to this group (R); a before measure (O_1) was taken; the subjects were then exposed to the treatment (X); and then an after measure (O_2) was taken.

All the notations on a single line refer to a single group of respondents, and notations that appear together vertically identify events that occurred at the same point in time. Thus,

$O_1 \ X_1 \ O_2$

X_1O_3

refers to two groups of subjects, one of which received a pretest measure and a posttest measure (O_1 and O_2), whereas the other received only a posttest measure (O_3). Both groups were exposed to the same treatment (X_1) and the treatment and posttest measures occurred at the same time for both groups.

Field experiments experiments that are carried out in a natural setting with a minimum of artificial elements in the experiment.

Laboratory experiments experiments conducted under artificial conditions, such as testing television ads in a movie theater rather than in buyers' homes.

Ethics and Experimentation

Over the past few years, there has been increasing concern for protecting the rights of subjects used in research projects. This is a potential problem in all studies involving human subjects. The researcher should give careful consideration to the potential negative effects on those participating in an experiment to avoid violating the subjects' rights and deflect potential lawsuits. Luckily, most business research experiments are not likely to involve negative effects, but the possibility of such effects should be carefully evaluated.[5]

Experimental Research Designs

There are many possible experimental designs, and they vary widely in terms of both complexity and effectiveness. The most widely accepted classifications of designs are: (1) pre-experiments, (2) true experiments, and (3) quasi experiments. While complete coverage of experimental designs is beyond the scope of this book, a brief explanation and examples of these follows:

Preexperimental Designs

Preexperimental designs are designs that are weak in terms of their ability to control the various threats to internal validity. This is especially true with the one-shot case study.

One-Shot Case Study. This design may be noted as:

$$X_1 O_1$$

An example of such a study would be to conduct a sales training program without a measure of the salespeople's knowledge before participation in the training program. Results would reveal only how much they know after the program but not how effective the program was in increasing knowledge.

One-Group Pretest-Posttest. This design can be represented as:

$$O_1 X_1 O_2$$

It is an improvement on the one-shot case study because of the addition of the pretest measurement, but it is still a weak design in that it fails to control for history, maturation, and other internal validity problems.

Static-Group Comparison. This design provides for two study groups, one of which receives the experimental treatment while the other serves as a control. The design is:

$$X_1 O_1$$

$$O_2$$

The addition of a control group makes this design better than the previous two designs. However, there is no way to ensure that the two groups were not different before the introduction of the treatment.

True Experimental Designs

The major deficiency of the previous designs is that they fail to provide groups that are comparable. The way to achieve comparability is through the random assignment of subjects to groups and treatments to groups. This deficit is overcome in the following true experimental designs.

Pretest-Posttest Control Group. This design is represented as:

$$RO_1 X_1 O_2$$

$$RO_3 O_4$$

In this design, most internal validity problems are minimized. However, there are still some difficulties. For example, history may occur in one group and not the other. Also, if communication exists between the groups, the effect of the treatment can be altered.

Posttest-Only Control Group. Pretest measurements are not used in this design. Pretest measurements are well-established in experimental research design but are not really necessary when random assignment to groups is possible. The design is represented as:

$$RX_1O_1$$

$$R\ O_2$$

The simplicity of this design makes it more attractive than the pretest-posttest control group design. Internal validity threats from history, maturation, selection, and statistical regression are adequately controlled by random assignment. This design also eliminates some external validity problems as well. How does this design accomplish such notable achievements? We can think of the O_1 observation as a combination of the treatment effect (such as a change in price, or the advertising campaign we ran, or a change in package design), plus the effect of all the extraneous variables (i.e., history, maturation, testing effect, instrumentation, selection, statistical regression, and mortality). However, since O_2 will theoretically be subject to all the same extraneous variables, the only difference between what we observe between O_1 and O_2 (that is, a measure of sales at two stores) will be the fact that O_1 (such as, sales at store #1) was measured after the treatment X_1 (that is, where prices were lowered), and O_2 (such as, sales at store #2) did not receive the treatment. Therefore, all the other extraneous variable effects wash or cancel out between the two observations, so any difference in the observations must be due to the treatment. These results are dependent, however, on the random assignment of multiple units (stores in this example) to either the test or control conditions. Sample sizes for each of the test and control conditions must be large enough to approach a normal distribution of stores so that we can assume that the only difference that we see between O_1 and O_2 is the result of the treatment, and not due to some extraneous variable differences between the test and control stores.

Quasi Experiments

Under actual field conditions, one often cannot control enough of the variables to use a true experiment design. Under such conditions, quasi experiments can be used. In a quasi experiment, comparable experimental and control groups cannot be established through random assignment. Often the researcher cannot even determine when or to whom to expose the experimental variable. Usually, however, it is possible to determine when and whom to measure. The loss of control over treatment manipulation (the when of the experimental variable exposure) and the test unit assignment (the who of the experimental variable exposure) greatly increases the chance of obtaining confounded results. Therefore, we have to build into our design the ability to account for the possible effects of variables outside our control in the field, so that we can more safely conclude whether the treatment was, in fact, the thing that caused the results we observed.

A quasi experiment is not as effective as a true experiment design, but is usually superior to available nonexperimental approaches. Only two quasi-experimental designs will be discussed here.

Nonequivalent Control Group. This is one of the most widely used quasi-experimental designs. It differs from true experimental design because the groups are not randomly assigned. This design can be represented as follows:

$$O_1X_1O_2$$

$$O_3\ O_4$$

Pretest results are one indicator of the degree of comparability between test and control groups. If the pretest results are significantly different, there is reason to doubt the groups' comparability. Obviously, the more alike the O_1 and O_3 measures are, the more useful the control group is in indicating the difference the treatment has made (that is, comparing the difference in the O_2 to O_1 with the difference between O_4 to O_3). Close similarity allows for control over the extraneous variables of history, maturation, testing, instrumentation, selection, and mortality. However, statistical regression can be a problem if either the test or control group has been selected on the basis of extreme scores. In such a case, the O_2 or O_4 measures could be more the result of simply regressing back from the extreme to the average score, rather than the result of anything that intervened between the first and second observation of either group.

Separate Sample Pretest-Posttest. This design is most applicable in those situations where we cannot control when and to whom to introduce the treatment but can control when and whom to measure. The design is:

$$R\ O_1$$

$$R\ X_1 O_2$$

This design is more appropriate when the population is large and there is no way to restrict who receives the treatment. For example, suppose a company launches an internal marketing campaign to change its employees' attitudes toward customers. Two random samples of employees might be selected, one of which is interviewed regarding attitudes prior to the campaign. After the campaign the other group is interviewed.

Limitations of Causal Research

It is natural for managers to be attracted to the results that can be gained from doing experimentation. After all, are we not often looking to know what really causes the effects we see, such as satisfied customers, rising (or falling) sales, and motivated salespersons? However attractive causal research may be, managers should recognize the following limitations:[6]

1. Field experiments can involve many variables outside the control of the experimenters, resulting in unanticipated differences in conditions surrounding treatment groups.
2. It may be difficult or expensive to gain the cooperation of retailers and wholesalers when setting up the experiment.
3. Researchers or other personnel may lack knowledge of experimental procedures, reducing the chance of results which demonstrate causality.
4. Experiments are notoriously expensive and time consuming.
5. The experimenter must be careful not to introduce bias into the experiment by saying or doing something that may consciously or unconsciously affect the behavior of the test participants.

Ex Post Facto Research

Ex post facto (after the fact) studies are those that try to discover a causal relationship without manipulation of the independent variable or control over respondent exposure to treatment conditions. These studies are characterized by an observance of an outcome followed by attempts to find the causal factor that caused the observed outcome. Consider this example:

A research manager for a regional bank was concerned with assessing customer images of their various branch locations. A mail survey asked whether customers were satisfied with the services provided by the branch location that they used. Each respondent rated his or her branch location on a number of attributes such as friendliness of bank personnel, convenience of location, parking facilities, and so forth. After receiving the questionnaires, the manager divided the sample into two groups: those who expressed satisfaction with the branch location and those who expressed dissatisfaction. An analysis of these two groups revealed that compared with customers who expressed satisfaction, dissatisfied customers rated their branch location as unsatisfactory with respect to friendliness of service. The researcher concluded that friendliness of services is the primary factor leading to customer satisfaction, and, consequently, it plays an important part in the decision about which bank to use.[7]

In this example, there is an attempt to identify a cause-effect relationship ex post facto, without manipulation of variables, assignment of respondents to treatments, or control of extraneous variables. The observed association between friendliness of service, customer satisfaction, and choice of bank may in fact be spurious and the correlation possibly in fact due to another variable not included in the analysis.

For example, the people who rated their branch lower on the friendliness and satisfaction scales may be from an area populated by high-income households who may have higher expectations of all aspects of service and who are more difficult to please in general. In such a case, the same level of service and friendliness of personnel among the branches is perceived differently by respondents, as is their level of overall satisfaction. It is obvious that any causal inference drawn from ex post facto research, while indicating a *possible* causal relationship, must be supplemented with true experimental or quasi-experimental studies before we can draw cause-effect conclusions. However, in some cases, merely demonstrating covariation between variables of interest is sufficient for management purposes. We merely must be careful not to assume we know more than we can legitimately claim we do.

Test Marketing

Test marketing is the name given to a set of experimental or quasi-experimental (field) studies that are intended to determine the rate of market acceptance for (usually) a new product. A company typically would use test marketing to determine such information as:

- The sales volume and market share expectations of the new product
- Some estimate of the repurchase cycle and likelihood of repurchase
- A profile of trier-adopters
- An understanding of competitor reactions to the new product
- Some feel for the effect of the new product sales on existing product sales
- Performance of new product package design in generating trial and satisfaction

Test marketing a set of experimental or quasi-experimental (field) studies that are intended to determine the rate of market acceptance for (usually) a new product.

With the cost and likelihood of new product failure, it is easy to see the incentive of managers conducting test markets to avoid large-scale introduction of products destined to fail. On the other hand, test marketing itself may cost millions of dollars, delay the cash flow of a successful new product, and alert competitors to your plans, so the costs might be high in either case. However, when the stakes are high and the costs of failure are very significant, test marketing may be the best of the unattractive options available.

There are several points to ponder when making the decision whether or not to test market a product.[8]

1. It is necessary to weigh the cost and risk of product failure against the profit and profitability of success. The higher the probability of success and lower the costs of failure, the less attractive is test marketing.
2. The difference in the scale of investment involved in the test versus national launch route has an important bearing on deciding whether to test. The greater the investment called for in manufacturing, the more valuable a test market becomes in indicating the payout of such an investment before it is made.
3. Another factor to be considered is the likelihood and speed with which the competition will be able to copy the new product and preempt part of your national market or overseas markets, should the test market prove successful.
4. Investments in plant and machinery are only part of the costs involved in a new product launch. The investment in marketing expenses and effort may be extensive, as well as the fact that sometimes the new product will only be given space at the retail level previously occupied by your existing products. Stock returns and buybacks for unsuccessful products likewise increase the costs of failure, not to mention the psychological impact of failing on a national scale. The higher these associated costs, the greater the potential value of test marketing in helping decision makers arrive at the best decision regarding large-scale product launch.

A.C. Nielsen data indicate that 75 percent of products that undergo test marketing succeed, while 80 percent of products not test marketed fail.[9] Careful readers, however, may identify this implied causal relationship between test marketing and success as ex post facto research—we observe the relationship and identify the implied causal factor instead of conducting a controlled test to determine causality. In this case, it could be that the type of firms doing test marketing (large, big-budget firms with considerable marketing expertise), or not doing test marketing (small, low-budget firms without high-priced marketing talent), may explain more of the success rate than does test marketing itself.

Three Types of Test Markets

Standard Test Markets. In a standard test markets the firm uses its own regular distribution channels and sales force to stock the product in selected test areas. Test site selection is an important consideration. Some criteria for selecting test sites are:[10]

1. There should be a balance in the size of a test area between being large enough to generate meaningful results but not so large as to be prohibitively expensive (a good rule of thumb is that test areas should comprise at least two percent of the potential market).
2. They should provide representative media that would be used in a national launch, but be self-contained so that media in test areas will not bleed over into other test areas or control sites.
3. They should be similar along demographic dimensions with the full-scale market area (i.e., region or entire United States).
4. The trading area should be self-contained to avoid transshipments between test and control areas or two test areas.
5. Competition should be representative in test areas.
6. Test areas should provide for testing under different conditions that will be encountered on a national scale (such as both hard and soft water sites for water soluble products).

Additional considerations include what measures will be used to indicate performance (such as trial rates, repeat purchase rates, percentage of households using, and sales) and length of the test (that is, depends upon the repurchase cycle, competitive response, and consumer response, but a minimum of ten months for new consumer brands). Standard test markets are subject to the problems associated with after-only experimental designs and are time consuming and expensive.

Controlled Store Test Markets. Controlled store test markets are run by research firms such as Audits & Surveys Worldwide, or A.C. Nielsen, who, for a fee, handle warehousing, distribution, product pricing, shelving, and stocking. Typically, these organizations pay a fee to distributors to guarantee shelf space. Sales and other performance measures are also gathered by the research firm.

Advantages of controlled test markets are that competitors cannot know test results because they are available only to the research firm conducting the test (and are not available through syndicated sales tracking services, which would track standard test market data), they are faster to run since it is not necessary to move the product through a distribution channel, and they are less costly to operate than standard test markets. Disadvantages include use of channels that might not be representative of the firm's channel system; the number of test sites is usually fixed and limited, making projections difficult; firms will not get a read on the willingness of the trade to support the product under normal conditions; it can be difficult to mimic nationally planned promotional programs; and the care of the research firms to avoid stock-outs, optional shelf positioning, correct use of point-of-purchase materials, and so on may not duplicate conditions existing with the normal launch of a product. Nevertheless, controlled store test markets are often used as a check before going to standard test markets. If the results are promising, a standard test market follows. If not, the product is killed or revised.

Simulated Test Markets. A simulated test market is not conducted in the field, but rather in a laboratory setting. Firms providing such services (such as, Burke; M/A/R/C; NPO

Research; Yankelovich Clancy Shulman; Custom Research, Inc.) follow a procedure that usually includes the following:

1. Respondents are recruited and screened to fit the desired demographic and usage patterns of the target market.
2. Respondents are shown ads for the tested products as well as competitive products, or are shown product concepts or prototypes.
3. Respondents are asked to record their attitudes toward the product on structured questionnaires and are either asked to indicate their purchase interest or are given a chance to buy the product or competitive products in a simulated shopping environment. For example, an aisle might be set up similar to an aisle in a drugstore with your tested cough syrup along with competitive cough syrups. Respondents can purchase any of the brands they desire.
4. Those who choose the tested product take it home and use it as they would under normal conditions, and are contacted after an appropriate time period and asked a series of attitudinal, repurchase intent, and usage-related questions.
5. Data from these steps are processed by a computer programmed to calculate estimated sales volume, market share, and other performance data based on assumptions of a marketing mix incorporated into the program.

Simulated test markets do *not* assume that the attitudes and behaviors evidenced in the simulation will be exactly duplicated in the market, but rather depend upon observed relationships that have been discovered historically between laboratory and eventual market findings. While costing in the low six-figures, simulated test markets are cheap compared to a full-blown standard test market, they are confidential, and permit easy modifications in a marketing mix to calibrate the most successful plan for introduction. The disadvantage is that they operate under a series of assumptions about what will really happen, while standard test markets *are* the real thing. Reported accuracy of simulated test markets is within 29 percent of forecast 90 percent of the time.[11]

EXPLORATORY, DESCRIPTIVE, OR CAUSAL OBSERVATION

The previous discussion of research designs followed the generally accepted practice of discussing the techniques for carrying out the research without distinguishing between the data-collection methods of communication or observation. We will discuss those two methods at greater length in Chapter 7, but the reader should be alerted to the fact, at this point, that observation can be legitimately conducted as a part of exploratory, descriptive, or causal research. The use of observation for collecting causal data is perhaps most obvious (such as sales data collected in a test market represents observation). Less obvious is the use of observation in exploratory or descriptive research. This situation is at least partly explained by the lack of categories used to classify observation techniques such as exist for communication methods (like focus groups, or cross-sectional sample surveys).

The difficulty in classifying observational techniques does not diminish the value of these techniques; however, it just makes their discussion a little more difficult. It is perhaps best to think of observational research, whatever the technique, as being appropriately used when it is consistent with the overall objectives of the research design under which it is being applied. Therefore, observational research in exploratory designs is being used to gain insights, ideas, and clarification, while descriptive observational research is determining frequency of occurrence, the extent to which two observational behaviors covary, and causal observation is conducted in a controlled setting to determine if a causal relationship exists between carefully defined variables. Such desirable consistency is the rule whether observation is the sole data-collection method, or combined with communication. For example, in a focus group intended to gain insight into consumer attitudes about a brand, the body language of consumers observed by the researchers provides additional insights into their feelings. Likewise, in descriptive research, coupling survey information with diary of purchases (i.e., observed data) can provide opportunity to see if attitudes and behavior covary. However observation is done, it is the objective of research that will determine how it is applied—flexibility inherent in exploratory observation, structure inherent in descriptive observation, and control inherent in causal observation.

In another example, observation data collected by optical scanners in supermarkets could be used to generate ideas or hypotheses in the exploratory phase of a research project (maybe large packages are outselling smaller packages because they seem to offer better value), test hypotheses via covariation in the descriptive phase (package size purchases covary with number of people in the household), or test hypotheses via experimental design in the causal phase (varying coupon amounts has a greater effect on sales of the 16 oz. package size of Brand A than the 8 oz. size). In this example it is important to note that the only reason the data could be used in the descriptive and causal research designs is that it was originally collected by using a methodology that generated quantifiably precise data. In other words, we cannot use information that was originally generated using exploratory research methodology in making descriptive or causal research calculations (for example, focus groups cannot generate descriptive data if we do a hundred of them instead of three because the methodology is not intended to generate quantifiable information—it was intended to provide insights, ideas, and the like.)

DANGERS OF DEFINING DESIGN BY TECHNIQUE

Just as it is not appropriate to define a research design by data-collection method (for example, exploratory research is not always done via communication; causal, not always by observation), it is also inappropriate to think research tools are the province of only one design. While some techniques are associated with only one design, such as experiments with causal and projective techniques for exploratory, other techniques might be used successfully under all three designs. Therefore, it is dangerous to define a design by a technique. Rather, designs are defined by the objectives and resulting methodology pursued which is consistent with the methodology. An example will help make this point. Table 5.3 shows the difference in using a survey when doing exploratory, descriptive, or causal research.

TABLE 5.3 Differences in Using a Survey by Research Design Type

	Exploratory Research	Descriptive Research	Causal Research
Objectives	Gain insights, ideas	Quantify	Test variables for causal relationships
Hypotheses Are	Generated	Tested via covariation	Tested via experimentation
Sampling Method	Nonprobability	Probability	Random assignment to treatments
Survey Questions	Can change over course of research	Fixed	Fixed
Structure of Data Collection	Loosely structured	Highly structured	Controlled
Example of Survey Question	"Why did you first start using Tide?"	"Which of the following reasons best explains why you first started using Tide?"	"Do you recall seeing any TV commercials in the past 24 hours for a laundry detergent?" (Unaided recall measures after testing a new TV commercial.)

While acknowledging that surveys can be and are used for exploratory research, we should emphasize that the preferred methods for achieving the objectives of exploratory research remain the five techniques (literature review, in-depth interviews, and the like) discussed earlier in this chapter. They are more capable of generating the depth of insight desired as an outcome from exploratory research.

Describe the design to be used in conducting the research for your project. Be as specific as possible in detailing exactly how you will get answers to your research questions and test your hypotheses. For example, don't just say you will do exploratory research; rather say you will do a literature search of census data for research question #4, which will provide information needed to do descriptive research in the form of a mailed sample survey to get answers to research questions #6 and #7, and so on.

Research Project Tip

SUMMARY

Good strategy and good management decisions do not just happen. They are grounded in accurate, timely, and useful business intelligence. Such information is obtained only through the careful translation of management problems into a research purpose, a research purpose into a set of research objectives, and those research objectives into a research design. Such a design is a road map that helps us arrive at our planned destination of having the information we need for decision making. The research design might involve one or more of the three categories of research: exploratory, descriptive, or causal. Our research objectives suggest that one or combinations of these types will be needed to obtain the desired information.

Whenever researchers must find answers to research questions dealing with cause and effect inferences, they must consider the need for experimentation. Experimental designs differ from exploratory or descriptive designs in the degree of control exerted by the researcher over relevant variables. Experiments involve manipulation, control, and measurement of variables in order to allow for causal inference. In some cases such experiments must be conducted in the field, rather than in a controlled laboratory setting, and are referred to as quasi-experiments. Several experimental designs were discussed, along with test marketing, one of the most commonly conducted causal experimental approaches used by marketers.

KEY TERMS

Causal research (p. 83)
Control group (p. 85)
Cross-sectional analysis (p. 80)
Descriptive research (p. 78)
Experimental design (p. 84)
External validity (p. 86)

Field experiments (p. 87)
Internal validity (p. 86)
Laboratory experiments (p. 87)
Longitudinal study (p. 81)
Test marketing (p. 91)

DISCUSSION QUESTIONS

1. Explain why the three key words ("flexible" for exploratory, "rigid" for descriptive, "control" for causal) were chosen to indicate the approaches used for each of the three types of research designs. Use examples to illustrate your points.

2. How do you know which one, or combination, of the three research designs to use to achieve your research purpose in any given situation? How do you know which technique (focus groups, sample survey, for example) to use for the research design? Use examples to help illustrate your points.

3. What do we mean by stating that descriptive research requires a clear specification of the who, what, where, why, and how of the research before we can design the descriptive study? Why is this required?

4. If you had been asked by the Compton Co. to design research to help them solve their problem, what research would you have suggested? Describe and defend your choice.

5. There have been a number of complaints in your city that minorities have received discriminatory treatment from local retailers of major appliances with respect to

trade-ins, prices, sales assistance, and credit terms. How would you investigate this issue (that is, describe and defend a research design and data collection method).

6. You are the business research manager at Proctor and Gamble. A brand manager comes to you and says she wants you to design a causal research study that will allow her to determine the motivations people have for buying Tide detergent. How would you respond? Be comprehensive in your response.

ENDNOTES

1. Donald R. Cooper and Pamela S. Schindler, *Business Research Methods*, 10th Edition, 2008, McGraw-Hill Irwin, New York, NY, p. 151.

2. Adapted from Gilbert A. Churchill, *Basic Marketing Research,* Second Edition (Fort Worth, TX: Dryden Press, 1992), pp. 130–131.

3. Robert Ferber, Donald F. Blankertz, and Stanley Hollander, *Marketing Research* (New York: The Ronald Press, 1964), p. 153.

4. Ibid., p. 171.

5. For a discussion of the ethics of marketing research see N. Craig Smith and John A. Quelch, "Ethical Issues in Researching and Targeting Consumers," in N. Craig Smith and John A. Quelch (Eds.), *Ethics in Marketing* (Homewood, IL: Irwin, 1993), pp. 145–195.

6. Thomas C. Kinnear and James R. Taylor, *Marketing Research* (New York: McGraw-Hill, 1991), p. 285.

7. William R. Dillon, Thomas J. Madden, and Heil H. Firtle, *Marketing Research in a Marketing Environment,* Third Edition (Burr Ridge, IL: Irwin, 1994), p. 180.

8. These points were taken from N. D. Cadbury, "When, Where, and How to Test Market," *Harvard Business Review,* (May–June 1985), pp. 97–98.

9. "Test Marketing: What's in Store?" *Sales and Marketing Management,* 128 (March 15, 1982), pp. 57–58.

10. Donald S. Tull and Del L. Hawkins, *Marketing Research,* Sixth Edition (New York: Macmillan, 1993), pp. 252–258.

11. Material provided by the Burke Institute on their BASES simulated test-marketing program.

Measurement, Data Collection, and Sampling

Alumin/Shutterstock.com

Measurement

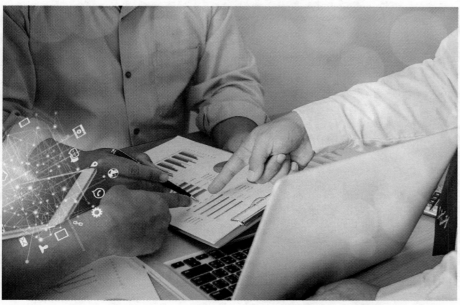

KeemMiDo/Shutterstock.com

Learning Objectives

Upon completing this chapter, you should understand:

- What is meant by the measurement process.
- The differences in nominal, ordinal, interval, and ratio levels of measurements.
- The concepts of validity and reliability of measurement.
- What is meant by a measurement scale.
- How scales are used in business research.

INTRODUCTION

In Chapter 1 we described business research as producing the information managers need to make management decisions. In that chapter we also listed numerous examples of how the results of business research can inform management decisions such as in concept and product testing, market segmentation, competitive analysis, customer satisfaction studies, and the like. These, and many other examples of business research studies, illustrate the need for *measurement*: "rules for assigning numbers to objects in such a way as to represent quantities of attributes."[1] Several things we should note about this definition:

Gearstd/Shutterstock.com

1. Not all of what researchers do involves measurement. Researchers are interested in generating *information,* which leads to *knowledge,* which leads to better *decisions.* Sometimes that information is in the form of insights from exploratory research studies such as focus groups, in-depth interviews, projective research, and similar methods. For these techniques we are generating information, but we are not assigning numbers to objects, so we are not measuring. As we have said before, information does not have to have numbers attached to it to have value; we are dangerously oversimplifying our analysis when we favor information with numbers over that without, simply because it has the appearance of being hard evidence.

2. The "rules for assigning numbers" will be discussed in greater depth in this chapter, but we should note here that those rules exist so that we can be more scientific in our measures, and can place more confidence in the numbers that those rules help generate (see Figure 1.2). We want to make decisions that are grounded in information that we believe correctly represent reality. This means the assignment of numbers should map the empirical nature isomorphically (i.e., on a "one-to-one" basis).

   For example, if we assign the number "5 pounds" to represent the weight of an object, we want to make sure that the weight is 5 pounds and not 8 pounds or 3 pounds. Using a carefully calibrated scale is how we ensure in this example that we have correctly measured the item's weight—assigned numbers to the object to accurately represent the quantity of its attribute of weight. The mundane nature of this example disappears when we find ourselves confronted with the need to measure variables of interest to marketers such as intentions, attitudes, and perceptions. How can we be sure that the number "4" correctly captures the intensity with which a respondent holds an intention, for example? We will devote further discussion to the ways of ensuring good measures in our research in this chapter.

3. The definition states that we attach numbers to the attributes of an object and not to the object itself. For example, we cannot measure the quantity of what you are now holding in your hand or viewing on your screen. There is no scale for measuring the amount of "bookness" in a book. We can, however, measure the attributes of a print book—its weight, dimensions in inches, number of pages, and so forth. We can even measure qualities less obvious such as its stature as great literature or its educational value; but, as described in point number 2, the rules for assigning numbers to those attributes will involve different measuring devices than those used to measure its physical properties. This caveat also holds true for the measurement of variables of interest to marketers.

bestv/Shutterstock.com

We measure a consumer's attitudes, income, brand loyalty, and other things, instead of measuring the consumer. In some cases, such as attitudes, we go a step further and measure the subcomponents of the variable. Attitudes, for example, are said to consist of cognitive, affective, and conative components that we would want to measure to ensure we have captured the essence of how strong a person's attitude was toward an object. For example, if we are to claim we have measured a parent's attitude toward a new product concept for a child's fruit drink, we need to measure beliefs and knowledge (the cognitive component of attitudes), how positive or negative he or she feels about the concept (the affective component), and the parent's predisposition to behave toward the product (the conative component).

4. Scientists in the physical sciences such as physics, chemistry, and biology have something of an advantage over behavioral scientists because the things physical scientists are interested in measuring have a physical reality, and the devices used to measure these things can be physically calibrated. Accurate measures are generated by carefully calibrating the measuring devices (such as micrometers and weight scales). Behavioral scientists, such as business researchers, cannot see or feel those things of interest to them (perceptions, intentions, brand loyalty, attitudes), and so must find ways of determining if the process they use to attach numbers is trustworthy in order to know if the numbers resulting from that process are trustworthy. In other words, while a chemist can trust that the weight of a chemical is what a carefully calibrated scale says it is, the business researcher can trust that he or she has obtained a good measure of intent to purchase only by having faith in the measurement process used to attach numbers to that intention. There is no way of comparing the numbers on the intention scale to a standardized measure for intentions the way a chemist can check the measures of weight against a standardized scale for weight. We trust the numbers because we trust the process used to attach those numbers.

THE PROCESS OF MEASUREMENT

Information gained from conducting business research contributes to better decision making by reducing risk, which can happen only if researchers are able to collect information that accurately represents the phenomenon under study. When it is appropriate to measure that phenomenon, that is, attach numbers to reflect the amount of an attribute inherent in that object of interest, we must try to ensure that the process we use to take those measures is a good process. We have nothing to compare those numbers with to determine if they are good numbers, so we make sure the process is trustworthy so that

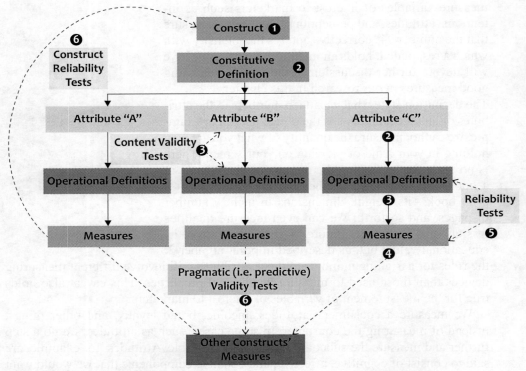

FIGURE 6.1 Measurement Hierarchy

Note: Circled numbers represent the stage of the process outlined in Figure 6.2 that the activity occurs.

we can believe the numbers resulting from the process are trustworthy and can indeed reduce the risk of decision making. The following process can help generate good measures (see Figures 6.1 and 6.2).

Step 1: Determine the Construct(s) of Interest

Constructs are abstract constructions (hence, the name) that are of interest to researchers. Some examples of constructs of interest to business researchers are customer satisfaction, heavy users, channel conflict, brand loyalty, and marketing orientation. These constructs are typical of the type of constructions of interest to marketers—they have no tangible reality apart from our defining them (unlike, for example, a botanist's plant), we define and study them because we need to understand them in order to make decisions based on that understanding (for example, changing our policies on return of purchases in order to increase customer satisfaction). Because they have no tangible reality they are generally not directly observable. We cannot see customer satisfaction, but we can indirectly observe it by asking customers a series of questions that we believe reveal how satisfied customers are with our firm in specific areas. As an example of measuring a construct we will use "marketing orientation"—a core construct of the marketing discipline.

Step 2: Specify the Construct's Domain

We must take care that we are accurately capturing what should be included in the definition of that construct. We previously mentioned that the tricomponent model indicates that an attitude contains in its domain cognitive, affective, and conative components. Social scientists have studied the construct "attitude" over many years and have generally agreed that its domain includes these three components. We specify a construct's domain by providing a constitutive definition for the construct. A constitutive definition defines a construct by using other constructs to identify conceptual boundaries, showing how it is discernable from other similar but different constructs. A construct's constitutive definition is what has been generally accepted in the marketing literature as a definition. Consider the constitutive definitions for the following related, but different, constructs:

Marketing orientation is the attention to identifying and satisfying customer needs, integration of effort by all areas of the organization to satisfying those needs, and focusing on the means by which an organization can achieve its goals most efficiently while satisfying those needs. *Market orientation* is the systematic gathering of information on customers and competitors, both present and potential, the systematic analysis of the information for the purpose of developing marketing knowledge, and the systematic use of such knowledge to guide strategy recognition, understanding, creation, selection, implementation, and modification.[2]

The definition of *market* orientation is distinguished from *marketing* orientation by what it adds (a focus on potential customers as well as present customers and on competitors as well as customers), and subtracts (an interfunctional coordination).

Step 3: Establish Operational Definitions

The constitutive definition makes it possible to better define the construct's domain by use of an **operational definition**. An operational definition indicates what observable attributes of the construct will be measured and the process that will be used to attach numbers to those attributes so as to represent the quantity of the attributes. Often, a construct's attributes are identified in the constitutive definition.

We need to establish operational definitions of our constructs to move them from the world of abstract concepts into the empirical world where we can measure them. Marketing orientation remains an abstract concept until we say exactly what its attributes are and how, specifically, we intend to measure those attributes.

One example of operationalizing the marketing orientation construct[3] in a hospital setting involved identifying five attributes of the construct (customer philosophy, marketing information systems, integrated marketing effort, strategic orientation, and operational efficiency), and then generating a set of nine statements for each attribute which fell along a strength of marketing orientation continuum anchored by the end points of "primitive" to "world class." These statements were assigned a score on the nine-point scale by a panel of expert judges. The following are two examples of statements whose average score by the judges fell at different points on the scale. Respondents (hospital administrators) would choose which statements most accurately reflected the marketing practices at their hospital.

These examples were two of forty-five item statements (nine statements for each of five attributes), which represent the operationalization of the marketing orientation construct.

Another operationalization[4] of marketing orientation involved identifying four attributes of the construct (intelligence generation, intelligence dissemination, response design, and response implementation), and then generating thirty-two item statements, each

Step 1:
Determine the Construct(s) of Interest

Step 2:
Specify the Construct's Domain

Step 3:
Establish Operational Definitions

Step 4:
Collect Data to Test Measures

Step 5:
Purify the Measures

Step 6:
Conduct Validity Tests

Step 7:
Analyze Research Findings

FIGURE 6.2 Developing Good Measures: The Measurement Process

Operational definition indicates what observable attributes of the construct will be measured and the process that will be used to attach numbers to those attributes so as to represent the quantity of the attributes.

"Marketing here is more than a staff function—it is heavily involved in line decision making." (8.35)

Example Statements (Integrated Marketing Effort Attribute)

"The feeling in my organization is that marketing activity is often contrary to the values of this hospital." (1.25)

FIGURE 6.3 Strength of Marketing Orientation

of which would be scored on a five-point scale ranging from strongly disagree to strongly agree. Some examples of these operationalizations of the intelligence dissemination attribute (respondents were executives at manufacturing firms) are:

We have interdepartmental meetings at least once a quarter to discuss market trends or strategies.

1	2	3	4	5
Strongly	Disagree	Neither agree or disagree	Agree	Strongly agree

Data on customer satisfaction are disseminated at all levels in this business unit on a regular basis.

1	2	3	4	5
Strongly	Disagree	Neither agree or disagree	Agree	Strongly agree

---

Note that these two operational approaches differ in the identification of the construct attributes, the item statements used to operationalize the attributes, and the method used to attach numbers to the item statements (also part of the operationalization process). Both examples, however, share in common the operationalization process of describing a specific set of operations that must be carried out in order to empirically measure the construct's attributes (i.e., move it from mere abstract conceptualization to the real world where it can be measured by establishing a process for attaching numbers to represent the quantity of the attribute—in these cases the degree to which a firm exhibits marketing-oriented behavior). Researchers might not choose the same means of operationalizing the constructs of interest. How can we tell if our chosen approach represents good measurement methods if it is different from the methods used by other researchers, who can demonstrate that their methods have resulted, in fact, in good measures? The answer to this question lies in the next steps of the measurement process.

Step 4: Collect Data to Test Measures

In this step we use our operationalized measures to collect data from our target population (i.e., the measures in Figure 6.1). We need this data to help us determine if we are on the right track with our operationalized measures. That is, have we done a good job in developing the operational definitions and measuring processes so that they accurately represent our constructs of interest? As was mentioned before, since we have no standardized measures that can be calibrated to give us accurate data, such as a chemist using a carefully calibrated weight scale, we must use data to help us determine if the methods used to collect that data were good. If the process of measurement is good the results of the process will also be assumed to be good. "Collecting data" in the previous two examples would consist of using the questionnaires to collect responses from the target populations (hospital administrators in the first example, executives at manufacturing firms in the second).

Step 5: Purify the Measures

In Step 5 we use the data collected in Step 4 to determine which items in our original list of operationalized items are reliable. Some items we thought would be good ways to operationalize our abstract constructs may not be as good as we thought. We can determine which item statements are keepers and which are to be rejected for our final item list by conducting reliability tests. We will discuss **reliability** in greater detail later in this chapter, but for now we are using some statistical procedures to help identify which item statements work together as a set, capturing the various aspects of the construct's attributes we were seeking to measure in our operationalizations.

Reliability a reliable measure is one that consistently generates the same result over repeated measures.

For example, the two statements that were used to illustrate the attributes for marketing orientation in the two studies described in Step 2 were keepers—they passed the statistical tests intended to use the collected data to determine which item statements were appropriate pieces of the whole attribute we sought to measure. Other item statements might have failed those tests (the statements did not contribute to describing the attribute as we thought they would), and are eliminated from the final version of our measuring device (questionnaires in these two cases).

Step 6: Conduct Validity Tests

Once we have purified the scale by eliminating item statements that fail to pass our reliability test, we are ready to conduct another test to determine how much faith we will place in the results of our research. Here we are testing for **validity**—did we actually measure what we were trying to measure? Validity will also be discussed in greater depth later in this chapter. Here, we should merely make note of the need to determine how successful we were in establishing measures that did correctly reflect the quantities of those attributes of our constructs of interest. Did we, in fact, accurately measure the degree to which an organization was marketing oriented?

Validity the extent to which differences found among respondents using a measuring tool reflect *true* differences among respondents.

Step 7: Analyze Research Findings

If we have successfully developed measures that are reliable (Step 5) and valid (Step 6) we are now ready to analyze our data to achieve the objectives of our research study: answer research questions, test hypotheses, check for cause and effect relationships, describe the extent to which a population behaves in a specific manner, and the like. A report can then be written that states the results of the research.

Commentary on the Measurement Process

Note that in this seven-step process data are actually analyzed two different ways. In Steps 5 and 6 data are being analyzed not to determine what are the findings of the research itself (i.e., not to obtain answers to the research questions), but rather to determine if the process used to collect the data generated results which can be trusted—did the process generate reliable, valid information? Both of these measures of data trustworthiness are matters of degree instead of binary yes or no conclusions. We determine the degree of reliability and validity rather than determining whether the data are or are not reliable or valid. Once we have established degree of reliability and validity we are in a better position to know how secure we can be in our research conclusions when we analyze the same data in Step 7 to achieve the purpose of doing the research study itself.

We should also point out that some measurement processes[5] suggest collecting data twice—once to determine which item statements are reliable (after Step 4), then again after unreliable item statements have been eliminated (between Steps 4 and 5), performing reliability and validity tests on the second set of data, followed by analysis of the data for research findings (Step 7).

marvent/Shutterstock.com

Now a reality check: Do all or most business research studies actually follow a measurement process similar to the seven step process outlined here? Well, yes and no. Marketing scholars doing research on topics of interest to the discipline of management (such as "Does being marketing oriented increase a firm's profit?"), would have to do something like this process or they might not get their research results published! However, applied business-research studies, such as described in this text, are less vigilant in conducting such measurement processes. It should be obvious that all researchers are concerned whether or not they have measures that can be trusted before drawing conclusions and making decisions based on research findings. Therefore, attention to issues of construct domain, proper operational definitions, appropriate data-collection methods, and reliability and validity checks are efforts intended to generate data that accurately represent the object of the research and can lead to better decisions.

WHAT IS TO BE MEASURED?

There are many different types of measures used in business research. However, most measures fall into one of the following three categories:[6]

1. States of being—age, sex, income, education, and the like.
2. Behavior—purchase patterns, brand loyalty, and the like.
3. States of mind—attitudes, preferences, personality, and the like.

Table 6.1 shows examples of the types of measures frequently used in consumer and industrial business research. The criterion for selecting what to measure is based on our knowledge or expectation that what we want to measure will provide insight into or help solve the management decision problem for which data are being collected. Thus, the relevant measures for any study are based on the research objectives, which indicate the types of information needed.

The research objectives indicate the concepts (constructs) that must be measured. For example, customer satisfaction, store loyalty, and sales performance are all concepts that relate to management problems. However, most concepts can be measured in

TABLE 6.1 Types of Measures

	Type of Buyer	
Measurement Type	**Ultimate Consumers**	**Industrial Customers**
States of Being	Age Sex Income Education Marital status	Size or volume Number of employees Number of plants Type of organization
Behavioral	Brands purchased Coupon redemption Stores shopped Loyalty Activities	Decision makers Growth markets Public vs. private Distribution pattern
States of Mind	Attitudes Opinions Personality traits Preferences	Management attitudes Management style Organizational culture

more than one way. Store loyalty, for example, could be measured by: (1) the number of times a store is visited, (2) the proportion of purchases made at a store, or (3) shopping at a particular store first. These alternate measurement approaches are our operational definitions. We develop operational definitions for two types of variables: discrete and continuous.

Discrete variables are those that can be identified, separated into entities, and counted. The number of children in a family is an example of a discrete variable. Although the average may be 3.5, a given family would have 1, 2, 3, or 4 or more children, but not 3.5.

Continuous variables may take on any value. As a simple rule, if a third value can fall between the two other values, the variable is continuous. It can take on an infinite number of values within some specified range. Temperature, distance, and time are continuous variables, and each can be measured to finer and finer degrees of accuracy. Frequently, continuous variables are rounded and converted to discrete variables expressed in convenient units such as degrees, miles, or minutes.

WHO IS TO BE MEASURED?

The question of the object of the measurement process may appear to have obvious answers: people, stores, or geographic areas. However, more thoughtful answers would reveal a multiplicity of possible objects to be measured.

For example, the level of influence on decision making of a husband and wife depends in part upon the product or service being purchased. The resulting decision might be wife dominated, husband dominated, joint, or autonomic (either solitary or unilateral). Moreover, such decision-making influence can change over time, as evidenced in recent trends toward female heads of households making financial decisions.[7] Husband-wife decision making also varies from culture to culture.[8] In another study of children's influence on decision making in the family, it was discovered that about 17 percent of the nine-to-twelve-year-old children survey considered themselves the main decision maker with regard to a decision to go to a restaurant, and 40 percent thought themselves the primary decision maker in choice of restaurant.[9] Thus, collecting data from the "decision maker" does not always represent an obvious choice of respondent.

The buying-center concept used in understanding organizational buying patterns provides a useful framework for other consumer and industrial purchasers.[10] A buying center consists of everyone involved in a buying action.

Buying-center participants play different roles. These roles must be identified and understood to select the type of respondents to be measured in a research project. These roles are:

- Users—those who actually use the product
- Gatekeepers—those who control the flow of information or access to decision makers
- Influencers—those who influence the choice of product or supplier by providing information
- Deciders—those who actually make the choice of product or supplier
- Buyers—those who actually complete the exchange process for a family or organization

The major point of this discussion is to emphasize the need to judiciously select the respondents, stores, areas—the "who" to be measured. If we ask questions of the wrong people, we will still get answers, but they will not be meaningful and could even be misleading.

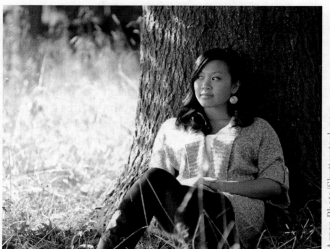

Aspen Photo/Shutterstock.com

HOW TO MEASURE WHAT NEEDS TO BE MEASURED

Measurement involves a system of logical decision rules incorporated into a scale. Four scales widely used in business research are nominal, ordinal, interval, and ratio scales. These are listed in order of the least sophisticated to the most sophisticated in terms of the amount of information each provides. The scale classification of a measure determines the appropriate statistical procedure to use in analyzing the data generated through the measurement process.

The Nominal Scale

Nominal scale the lowest level of measurement. It measures difference in kind (male, female, member, nonmember, and the like).

The **nominal scale** is the lowest level of measurement. It measures difference in kind (male, female, member, nonmember, and the like). Many people consider a nominal scale a qualitative classification rather than a measurement. It produces categorical data rather than the metric data derived from more advanced scales. While numbers may be used as labels (e.g., 0 for males, 1 for females), they can be replaced by words, figures, letters, or other symbols to identify and distinguish each category. Nominal scales are said to recognize differences in kind, but not differences in degree. As a result, nominal scales tend to oversimplify reality. All items assigned to the same class are assumed to be identical.

Summaries of data from a nominal scale measurement are usually reported as a count of observations in each class or a relative frequency distribution. A mode, or most frequently observed case, is the only central tendency measure permitted. Since the nominal scale does not acknowledge differences in degree, there are no useful measures of dispersion (such as range, standard deviation, and variance). This scale calls for nonparametric statistical techniques such as chi-square analysis.

The Ordinal Scale

Ordinal scale goes a step further than the nominal scale to introduce a direction of difference.

The **ordinal scale** goes a step further than the nominal scale to introduce a direction of difference. If measurement can be ordered so that one item has more than, or less than, some property when compared with another item, measurement is said to be on an ordinal scale. Ordinal scales are frequently used in ranking items such as best, or second best. Such a ranking reveals position, but not degree. For example, if favorite vacation destinations are rank ordered, it may be determined that Florida ranks first, the Rocky Mountains second, and New England third, but it is not clear if all three are relatively close in desirability, or if Florida is much more desirable and the Rockies and New England are distant second and third choices.

The most appropriate statistic describing the central tendency on an ordinal scale is the median. Dispersion can be quantified using the range, interquartile range, and percentiles.

The Interval Scale

Interval scale a scale with two features: (1) a unit of measurement, and (2) an arbitrary origin. The arbitrary origin of the interval scale means there is no natural origin or zero point from which the scale derives.

Measurement is achieved on an **interval scale** with two features: (1) a unit of measurement, and (2) an arbitrary origin. Temperature, for example, is measured by interval scales. Each scale has a unit of measurement, a degree of temperature. An interval scale indicates a difference, a direction of difference, and a magnitude of difference, with the amount expressed in constant scale units. The difference between 20 and 30 degrees represents the same difference and direction as the difference between 100 and 110 degrees.

The arbitrary origin of the interval scale means there is no natural origin or zero point from which the scale derives. For example, though both Fahrenheit and Celsius scales are used to measure temperature, each has its own zero point.

The arithmetic mean is the most common measure of central tendency or average. Dispersion about the mean is measured by the standard deviation. Many researchers will assume their measures are interval level measures to permit the use of more powerful statistical procedures. Great care must be used here to avoid the use of inappropriate statistical procedures.

TABLE 6.2 Scales of Measurement

Measure	Results	Sample Questions	Measure of Central
Nominal	Classification of variables	Which brand do you own? A ___ B ___ C ___	Mode
Ordinal	Order of variables	Rank your preference for stores. First ___ Second ___ Third ___	Median
Interval	Differences in variables	The salespeople were friendly. Strongly Agree ___ Agree ___ Neutral ___ Disagree ___ Strongly Disagree ___	Mean
Ratio	Absolute magnitude of differences in variables	What was your sales volume by store last year? Store A $___ Store B $___ Store C $___	Geometric mean

Source: Adapted from Robert F. Hartley, George E. Prough, and Alan B. Flaschner, *Essentials of Marketing Research,* 1983, p. 145. Tulsa, OK: PennWell Books, Inc.

The Ratio Scale

The most advanced level of measurement is made with a **ratio scale**. This scale has a natural origin. Zero means a complete absence of the property being measured. Properties measured on a ratio scale include weight, height, distance, speed, and sales. Measurement on a ratio scale is less frequent in business research than in the physical sciences. All the common descriptive and analytical statistical techniques used with interval scales can be used with ratio scales. In addition, computation of absolute magnitudes are possible with a ratio scale, but not with an interval scale. Therefore, while it cannot be said that 100°F is twice as hot as 50°F (it is not when converted to Celsius), it can be said that $2 million in sales is twice as much as $1 million in sales.

Table 6.2 is a summary of these measurement levels along with sample types of variables and questions used in their measurement.

Ratio scale this scale has a natural origin. Zero means a complete absence of the property being measured. Properties measured on a ratio scale include weight, height, distance, speed, and sales.

ASSESSING RELIABILITY AND VALIDITY OF OUR MEASURES

In a perfect world our measures would exactly represent the construct under study, with no bias or error introduced into the measurement process. Since we live in an imperfect world we must expect that the numbers we collect in our research to represent our constructs will contain a certain amount of error. In other words, if M represents our measures (i.e., numbers) and T represents the true, accurate quantity of our construct we are trying to measure, we could represent the relationship as

$$M = T + E$$

where E represents errors introduced into the measure. Here we see that any numbers that are collected in the measurement process to represent the attributes of the construct of interest contain the true quantity of the attribute plus a certain amount of error. How does this error enter into our measures? There are several explanations why we might see a difference between the measured value and the true value:[11]

1. Short-term characteristics of the respondent such as mood, health, fatigue, and stress.
2. Situational factors such as distractions or other variations in the environment where the measures are taken.
3. Data-collection factors introducing variations in how questions are administered (such as different tone of voice for different interviewers) and variations introduced by the interviewing method itself (that is, Internet, phone, mail, personal contact).
4. Measuring instrument factors such as the degree of ambiguity and difficulty of the questions and the ability of the respondent to provide answers.
5. Data analysis factors introduced during the coding and tabulation process.

Reliability

A reliable measure is one that consistently generates the same result over repeated measures. For example, if a scale shows that a standardized one pound weight actually weighs one pound when placed on the scale today, tomorrow, and next Tuesday, then it appears to be a reliable scale. If it reads a different weight, then it is unreliable, the degree of unreliability indicated by how frequently and by how much it reads an inaccurate weight. A reliable scale will also indicate that a different weight placed on the scale consistently shows a different measure than the one pound weight (that is, a scale is not reliable if it says a one-pound weight weighs one pound consistently, but says every other weight is also one pound because it is stuck on that measure). We can determine whether our measures of psychological constructs are reliable using one of several types of tests.

Test-Retest Reliability. The objective with test-retest reliability assessment is to measure the same subjects at two different points in time under approximately the same conditions and compare results. If there was actually no change in the object of measurement (such as someone's preferences or attitudes), a reliable measuring device (such as a questionnaire) would generate the same results. Obvious problems are that it may not be possible to get the same respondents to respond to the test, the measurement process itself may alter the second responses, and conditions may be difficult to duplicate.

Alternative Form. The deficiencies of test-retest reliability measures can be overcome to some degree by using an alternative form of the measuring device. If you have at least two equivalent measuring forms (such as questionnaires), researchers can administer one form and then two weeks later administer the alternative form. Correlating the results provides a measure of the reliability of the forms.

Internal Consistency. Measuring reliability using an internal consistency approach usually involves the use of different samples of respondents to determine reliability of measures. A typical way to assess internal consistency would be to use a split-half technique, which involves giving the measuring instrument (such as a questionnaire) to all the respondents, then randomly dividing them into halves and comparing the two halves. High correlation represents good reliability. Another type of split-half comparison involves randomly splitting the item statements intended to measure the same construct into halves and comparing the results of the two halves of the statements for the entire sample. Again, high correlation of results (the way the respondents answered the item statements) suggests good reliability. Another way of testing for internal consistency is to use a statistical test such as Cronbach's alpha for intervally scaled data or KR-20 for nominally scaled data. These measures will indicate how well each individual item statement correlates with other items in the instrument. A low correlation means the item statement should be removed from the instrument. Cronbach's alpha is a common test done in Step 5: Purify the Measures of Our Measurement Process (see Figure 6.2). Also note that in Figure 6.1, reliability tests are using measures (data such as answers to questionnaires) to test whether our operational definitions (questionnaire questions) are reliable (e.g., internally consistent).

Validity

Validity is the extent to which differences found among respondents using a measuring tool reflect *true* differences among respondents. The difficulty in assessing validity is that the true value is usually unknown. If the true value were known, absolute validity could be measured. In the absence of knowledge of the true value, the concern must be with relative validity, that is, how well the variable is measured using one measuring technique versus competing techniques. Validity is assessed by examining three different types of validity: content, predictive, and construct.

The **content validity** of a measuring instrument is the extent to which it provides adequate coverage of the topic under study. To evaluate the content validity of an instrument, it must first be decided what elements constitute adequate coverage of the problem in terms of variables to be measured. Then the measuring instrument must be analyzed to assure all variables are being measured adequately. Thus, if peoples' attitudes toward purchasing different automobiles are being measured, questions should be included regarding attitudes toward cars' reliability, safety, performance, warranty coverage, cost of ownership, and the like, since those attributes constitute attitudes toward automobile purchase.

Content validity rests on the ability to adequately cover the most important attributes of the concept being measured. It is testing to determine how well we have specified the domain of our construct (see Figure 6.1). It is one of the most common forms of validity addressed in practical business research. A common method of testing for content validity is to ask experts to judge whether the item statements are what they purport to be. For example, if you are trying to develop item statements intended to measure customer satisfaction with the content of a Web site, you could get several experts on customer satisfaction for Web sites to judge the adequacy of your item statements, or use item statements previously found to have passed content validity tests.

Predictive or pragmatic validity reflects the success of measures used for estimating purposes. The researcher may want to predict some outcome or estimate the existence of some current behavior or condition. The measure has predictive validity if it works (see Figure 6.1). For example, the ACT test required by many colleges has proved most college students has proved useful in predicting success in college courses. Thus, it is said to have predictive validity. Correlation of the independent (ACT test score) and dependent (college GPA) variables is often used to test for predictive validity.

Construct validity involves the desire to measure or infer the presence of abstract characteristics for which no empirical validation seems possible. Attitude scales, aptitude tests, and personality tests generally concern concepts that fall in this category. In this situation, construct validity is assessed on how well the measurement tool measures constructs that have theoretically defined models as an underpinning. For example, a new personality test must measure personality traits as defined in personality theory in order to have construct validity. Construct validity is usually determined by testing to see if measures converge (convergent validity) when they are supposed to measure the same thing, but by different means or by different respondents, and discriminate (discriminant validity) when they are measuring different things. Construct validity is obviously important—if we are not really measuring what we thought we were measuring (we thought we were measuring brand loyalty but we were actually measuring store loyalty), we cannot have confidence that our decisions based on the research will achieve their goals. When two independent methods of measuring the same construct converge as expected (such as two different measures of the degree of a consumer's

Content validity is the extent to which it provides adequate coverage of the topic under study.

Predictive or pragmatic validity the success of measures used for estimating purposes.

Construct validity involves the desire to measure or infer the presence of abstract characteristics for which no empirical validation seems possible.

brand loyalty), then we have some degree of convergent validity (see Figure 6.1). When two measures diverge as expected (such as brand loyalty and eagerness to try a new brand), then we have some degree of discriminant validity. How each of these tests of construct validity is determined varies for different research studies.

Commentary on Reliability and Validity

As stated previously, researchers conducting research in order to make management decisions rarely conduct the kinds of formal tests of reliability and validity described here. However, it should be obvious to the reader that good research is good, at least to some degree, because it generates data we have faith in as a picture of reality—i.e., it uses a data collection instrument which could consistently generate similar results when used repeatedly (it is reliable), and it measures what it is intended to measure (it is valid). An illustration will help make the point about the wisdom of being concerned about these issues when doing research, even nonacademic practical research. Let's say our construct of interest is an accurate rifle. If we were living on the frontier, an accurate rifle would not only be an abstract concept of intellectual interest, it could be a life or death matter! That is practical in the extreme! We want to do reliability and validity tests on the rifle before we make decisions based on its use, so we clamp it in a vise to make it steady (and remove the variability of the skill of the shooter) and sight it at the center of a target a reasonable distance away. We do this at an indoor shooting range where conditions are held constant (so we can avoid the problems previously mentioned about environmental variables that can affect our measures). The rifle is then fired numerous times using a mechanical triggering device. Figure 6.4 displays several different possible results of our test.

   A. Neither Reliable nor Valid
   B. Reliable, but not Valid
   C. Reliable and Valid

As shown in (a), the rifle is very inconsistent (unreliable) in its shot pattern, and does not hit the center of the target very often (it is not valid as an accurate rifle). In (b), there is much better consistency (it is reliable), but it still fails to be what it is supposed to be—an accurate rifle. That is, the construct "accurate rifle" means it hits what it is aimed at, and the rifle in both (a) and (b) does not do that. Reliability is obviously less important than validity here. You would take little comfort in knowing your rifle could consistently hit six inches above and a foot to the left of a charging mountain lion. In (c) we see that the rifle can consistently (reliably) hit what it is aimed at (it is a valid accurate rifle), which increases our faith in it as a tool of practical value.

In the same way, we will have more faith in our ability to make good decisions if we believe the data we analyze to make those decisions were generated using valid and reliable data collection instruments. As mentioned at the beginning of the chapter, since we do not have a standard, calibrated set of results to compare our results to in order to

FIGURE 6.4 Possible Results of Firing a Rifle to Test for Reliability and Validity of an "Accurate Rifle"

know if the results are good, we must determine if the results were collected using good measuring devices. If the devices (questionnaires, observation methods, and the like) are good, then we believe the results from use of those devices are good—that is, reliable and valid representations of the reality we sought to measure. For example, we want to be sure that our efforts to measure consumer preference and intention to purchase product designs A or B have accurately represented consumers' actual desires and likely behavior, so that we can have faith in our decision to introduce design A instead of B because the research supports that decision.

Research Project Tip

Indicate how you will check to ensure that the results of your research are reliable and valid. This may not necessarily involve statistical tests, but should involve actions that check to ensure that you are in fact measuring what you say you are measuring and that the results are replicable. At a minimum you should indicate how you will test for content validity. Also, take special care in establishing your operational definitions. A careful and thorough literature search of research previously conducted on your topic is one of the best ways to improve the reliability and validity of your data collection instrument. You are able to better define the domain of your construct and perhaps even find questionnaires that have been tested for validity and reliability in the literature.

If we do not know whether we can trust the results of the research, why do research at all? The alternative to good research is to make your decision and hope for the best. By doing business research we are saying that we want to reduce the uncertainty of the decision-making process. But we can only reduce the uncertainty by a reliable and valid representation of the real state of our constructs of interest. So, even if formal methods of testing for validity and reliability are not used, the wise researcher devotes thought to the construction of research instruments and using research methods that have proven over time to generate valid and reliable results. Interested readers should refer to some of the major works on the subject.[12]

MEASURING PSYCHOLOGICAL VARIABLES

Measurement of most variables depends upon self-report, that is, by the respondents volunteering the information when asked, instead of through observation. While a state of mind is obviously not directly observable (you cannot see a motive for purchasing an item), many behaviors are also not observable. Consequently, business researchers must ask people to respond to questions intended to measure (attach numbers to) an attribute of a construct in ways that reveal the quantity of the attribute. Researchers have developed scales that are believed to capture the quantity or intensity of the construct's attribute.

Many of the states of mind mentioned are typically measured using scales developed for that purpose. We will describe several scales used for measuring various states of mind after discussing attitude measurement, a common object of measurement for business researchers.

Attitude Measurement

Attitudes are one of the most frequently measured constructs business researchers. Why are attitudes of such universal interest? Because management decision makers are interested in them. Why are management decision makers interested in attitudes? Because they believe there is a close connection between the way a person thinks (their attitude) and what they are likely to do (their behavior). Why, then, don't we just study behavior, since marketers are actually ultimately interested in understanding and influencing people's behavior, not just their attitudes? There are several good reasons why marketers do focus on attitudes instead of exclusively on behavior:

1. Marketers may not have access to observation of or reporting of a person's behavior. The behavior may occur over a long period of time or in private settings only, and therefore observation is either not possible or prohibitively expensive. Also, sometimes the behavior itself is of a nature that people will not voluntarily report it, but will answer attitude questions related to the behavior.

2. Sometimes the behavior cannot be reported because it has not yet occurred. Marketers seeking to determine the best combination of attributes for a new product must ask attitudinal questions about the desirability of those features since the product itself has yet to be produced and, hence, there is no behavior that can be recorded concerning the product.

3. Attitudes, under certain circumstances, are reasonably good predictors of behavior. Consequently, by measuring someone's attitudes we can obtain a good indication of their likely behavior in the future. The connection between attitudes and behavior has, however, been the subject of extended debate among business researchers.[13] Attitudes can help us understand *why* certain behaviors occur.

If attitudes are such good surrogates for behavior, why do we hear of the marketing blunders like New Coke, (see Figure 6.5) where making decisions on the basis of attitudes got marketers in some very hot water? The answer is that the research focused on only a limited set of attitudes toward the new formula versus the old (taste), and failed to measure other attitudes (how people felt about the idea of altering a formula for a product they had used for many years). Consider also the problems of using attitudes to predict behavior (see Figures 6.6 and 6.7).

When the Coca-Cola Company unveiled its formula for New Coke, executives were certain that it was the right move to make. They described as "overwhelming" the results of taste tests with 190,000 consumers, most of whom preferred the new recipe over old Coke.

The record is now clear that the introduction of New Coke ranks right up there with the debut of the Edsel as one of the greatest marketing debacles of all time. What went wrong? After all, if a marketer cannot rely on the findings from 190,000 consumer taste tests, then what good is research in aiding management decisions?

Analysts now agree that the problem was Coke failed to measure the psychological impact of tampering with a venerable ninety-nine-year-old soft drink brand. "When you have a product with a strong heritage that people could always count on being there, the mind becomes more important than physiological responses," said the research director for a rival cola.

FIGURE 6.5 Coca-Cola's "New" Coke Fiasco

Source: Adapted from Ronald Alsop, "Coke's Flip-Flop Underscores Risks of Consumer Taste Tests," *The Wall Street Journal,* July 18, 1985, p. 27.

Food companies have usually conducted their market research by asking people about their eating habits and preferences. Then they develop new products based on the results. The problem is that people do not always tell the truth. To counter this problem, NPD distributed the usual questionnaires to members of 1,000 households asking them questions about their attitudes on nutrition and food. In addition, the company asked each household to record in a diary every snack or meal consumed during a two-week period in each of the two years the survey spans.

NPD found that its subjects divide roughly into five groups: meat and potato eaters; families with kids, whose cupboards are stocked with soda pop and sweetened cereal; dieters; natural-food eaters; and sophisticates, those moneyed urban types. The study focused mainly on the last three groups because food companies are mostly interested in them. It was found that, as expected, each group frequently consumed the following:

Naturalists—Fresh fruit, rice, natural cereal, bran bread, wheat germ, yogurt, granola bars

Sophisticates—Wine, mixed drinks, beer, butter, rye and pumpernickel bread, bagels

Dieters—Skim milk, diet margarine, salads, fresh fruit, sugar substitutes

More surprisingly, however, each group was also found to frequently consume:

Naturalists—French toast with syrup, chocolate chips, homemade cake, pretzels, peanut butter and jelly sandwiches

Sophisticates—Prepackaged cake, cream cheese, olives (probably in drinks), doughnuts, frozen dinners

Dieters—Coffee, zucchini, squash

FIGURE 6.6 Do Attitudes Predict Behavior? Part I

Source: Adapted from Betsy Morris, "Study to Detect True Eating Habits Finds Junk-Food Fans in the Health-Food Ranks," *The Wall Street Journal,* February 3, 1984, p. 19.

Early lifestyle travel studies conducted by a Chicago ad agency showed a positive trend in the attitude that "meal preparation should take as little time as possible." It would be safe to predict, therefore, that during the same period consumer use of frozen vegetables would also increase.

Wrong, according to the agency's senior vice president and director of research services. "There was actually a precipitous decline in the use of frozen vegetables," he said, "when an extraneous factor entered the picture. During the years of the study, the real price of frozen vegetables increased sharply, especially when compared with the cost of other ways to simplify meal preparation. Remember that frozen vegetables represent only one of a number of acceptable ways to shorten meal preparation time. The link between the desire to make meal preparation easier and the use of frozen vegetables is neither necessary nor direct."

The ease of meal preparation/frozen vegetable case illustrates the point that broad attitude trends do not always predict specific trends in consumer behavior.

FIGURE 6.7 Do Attitudes Predict Behavior? Part II

Source: Adapted from "Broad Attitude Trends Don't Always Predict Specific Consumer Behavior," *Marketing News,* May 16, 1980, p. 8.

In Figure 6.6 we see that peoples' attitudes toward their diet resulted in their being classified in specific groups. Separate measures of their behavior indicate not all of what they eat would be predicted from their attitudes. Why this inconsistency? Just as in the

New Coke example, we see that people hold a multiplicity of attitudes toward an object, and not all attitudes will be consistent with a specific behavior (solid lines indicate consistency, dotted lines inconsistency):

Here, we see that attitude A1 is consistent with behavior B1, but not with behavior B2, while attitude A2 is consistent with behavior B2, but not B1. In other words, because people have a *multiplicity of attitudes,* focusing on any one attitude (A1) may not permit successful prediction of a single behavior (B2).

In Figure 6.7, we see that people were increasingly in agreement with the attitude that meal preparation should take as little time as possible. This fact failed to lead to an increase in sales of frozen vegetables. Why this inconsistency? In this case a *multiplicity of behaviors* are possible, only some of which are consistent with the attitude concerning meal preparation time.

Lesson

Attitudes and behavior are complex phenomena. When we try to simplify what is inherently complex for our own convenience we often draw erroneous conclusions. We are seekers after truth, not simplicity. If truth is complex, let's try to understand its complexity. If it is simple, let's just be thankful for its simplicity. What these examples do tell us is that we must strive very hard to make sure we have correctly sampled the domain of the attitudes we are seeking to measure (that is, have good content validity). For example, if we are trying to measure peoples' attitudes toward eating healthfully, we would want to have a number of item statements that would be divided among the three components of attitudes. Example attitude questions about eating healthfully might be:

		Strongly Agree	Strongly Disagree
Affective	I like the taste of healthy foods.		_____
Cognitive	I believe eating healthfully will increase my life span.		_____
Conative	I try to buy healthy foods whenever possible.		_____

We would also want to correctly sample from the domain of the behavior of interest to us. We will now discuss the use of scales to measure attitudes and other psychological variables of interest to marketers.

Itemized Rating Scales

Itemized rating scales are just that—the points on the scale are itemized, with a description of the scale point provided. Several choices confront the researcher using an itemized rating scale:

Itemized rating scales the points on the scale are itemized, with a description of the scale point provided.

1. The number of item statements and scale points. Research has indicated that scale reliability improves, up to a point, with increases in the number of item statements and scale points.[14] So, for example, a questionnaire that asks for attitudes toward healthy eating is more reliable if it uses twelve attitude item statements (an example of an item statement is a declarative statement with itemized responses such as "I like the taste of most healthy foods" with responses like strongly agree, agree, neither agree nor disagree, disagree, strongly disagree), rather than three item statements—but thirty item statements is probably less reliable than twelve. Why? Because of the fatigue factor—respondents grow weary of answering too many questions, and their responses are made more to get finished rather than as a true representation of their state of mind. The same is true for response points on the scale; five is better than three, but more than ten points does not improve reliability. Typically, the number of scale points varies between five to seven (see examples).
2. Odd or even number of points. Is a scale with an even number of points preferable to an odd number, or is the odd number preferable? There is no hard evidence that supports either choice. The odd number provides a midpoint on the scale, while the even number forces respondents to lean toward one end of the scale or the other. This remains a matter of researcher preference.
3. Use of "don't know" and "no opinion." The general tendency for interviewers is to discourage respondents from choosing a "don't know" or "no opinion" option when responding to a scaled item statement. Many respondents then select the midpoint of an odd-number scale as the default option. Obviously, researchers analyzing the data are then unable to determine how many people marked "3" on the five-point scale because that expressed the intensity with which they held an attitude, and how many marked "3" because they did not know how they felt, and chose the midpoint because it was the safest option available. These kinds of compromises to the validity of the instrument argue persuasively for a scale that provides for both a "don't know" and a "no opinion" option for respondents, and for instructions to interviewers to accept these responses from respondents.

It is generally conceded that itemized rating scales generate intervally scaled data, although there is an ongoing debate in the social sciences as to whether that position is defensible or not (some researchers believe itemized rating scales generate only ordinal data).

Examples of Itemized Rating Scales

Likert Scales

ATTITUDES

Strongly Agree	Agree	Neither Agree or Disagree	Disagree	Strongly Disagree
5	4	3	2	1

PERFORMANCE OR QUALITY

Excellent	Very Good	Good	Fair	Poor
5	4	3	2	1

SATISFACTION

Completely Satisfied		Very Satisfied		Fairly Well Satisfied		Somewhat Dissatisfied		Very Dissatisfied
10	9	8	7	6	5	4	3	2	1

IMPORTANCE

Of Critical Importance	Very Important	Somewhat Important	Of Little Importance	Not at all Important
5	4	3	2	1

EXPERIENCE

Far Exceeded My Expectations	Exceeded My Expectations	Met My Expectations	Did Not Meet My Expectations	Far Below My Expectations
5	4	3	2	1

INTENTION

Extremely Unlikely	Very Unlikely	Somewhat Unlikely	About 50-50 Chance	Somewhat Unlikely	Very Unlikely	Extremely Unlikely
7	6	5	4	3	2	1

BEHAVIOR

Always	Frequently	Occasionally	Infrequently	Not at All
5	4	3	2	1

More Than Once a Week	About Once a Week	Two or Three a Week	About Once a Month	Less Than Once a Month	Almost Never	Never
7	6	5	4	3	2	1

Likert scale determine the strength of someone's attitude, positive or negative, toward an object by summing their scores for each of the item statements.

Strictly speaking, a **Likert scale** is a five-point itemized rating scale with specific descriptors for the scale points. We list it separately here because it is one of the most frequently used scales for measuring attitudes. Developed by Rensis Likert,[15] it has undergone many variations over the years. It consists of five points of agreement for measuring intensity of an attitude.

Strongly Agree	Agree	Neither Agree nor Disagree	Disagree	Strongly Disagree

Variations have been made to turn it into a seven-point scale,

Strongly Agree	Agree	Somewhat Agree	Neither Agree nor Disagree	Somewhat Disagree	Disagree	Strongly Disagree

or a bipolar scale,

Strongly Agree ___ ___ ___ ___ ___ ___ ___ **Strongly Disagree**

which is not technically an itemized rating scale since the points of the scale are not itemized with a description.

The Likert scale is sometimes referred to as a summated ratings scale, because we can determine the strength of someone's attitude, positive or negative, toward an object by summing their scores for each of the item statements. Consider, for example, how persons A and B answered the following questions:

	Strongly Agree	Agree	Neither Agree Nor Disagree	Disagree	Strongly Disagree
	5	4	3	2	1
The hotel was helpful	A		B		
The hotel is		A	B		
The hotel has	A				B

The summated rating score for person A is $5 + 4 + 5 = 14$, and for person B it is $3 + 3 + 2 = 8$. Person A has an overall more positive attitude toward the hotel than person B. Note that we would not then state that person A's attitude is 75 percent more positive ($14 = 8 = 1.75$) than person B's. Such a statement requires ratio-scaled data, and attitudes can never be measured on a ratio scale (there is no absolute zero point for attitudes). At best, a Likert scale generates interval data.

Rank-Order Scales

In a **rank-order scale** the respondent puts objects in an order of some variable under study (such as order of liking, preference, intention to buy, or quality, generating ordinal data. An example of such a scale is shown below:

Rank-order scale the respondent puts objects in an order of some variable under study (such as an order of liking, preference, intention to buy, or quality) generating ordinal data.

Rank-order the following sporting events in terms of most desirable to least desirable for you to attend (1 = most desirable, 2 = second most desirable, and so on):

___ Super Bowl
___ World Series
___ NBA Championship Game
___ NHL All-Star Game
___ NCAA Basketball Championship
___ Masters Golf Tournament

The advantages of a rank-order scale are that it is easy for the respondent to understand and respond to, and it is a realistic representation of choice behavior (some objects would be purchased before others according to the rank order). The disadvantages are that the rank order appears without the researcher knowing his or her location on a like-dislike continuum. That is, all the items may be toward the highly liked end of the scale, or spread out along the scale so that number one is liked while the bottom numbered item is disliked, or all located at the disliked end of the scale (put another way, even the item ranked number one is only the least disliked of the entire group of disliked items rank-ordered). Another disadvantage is that data analysis is limited to those procedures permissible for ordinal-ranked data. Also, the respondents' actual first choice may not have been included on the list, but researchers would not know this. Finally, we do not know how far apart the items are on the list in terms of desirability (1 and 2 may be highly desirable and close together, 3, 4, and 5 are much less desirable and far down the list), and we do not know why the items were ranked in that order.

Comparative Rating Scales

Comparative rating scale also known as a *constant-sum scale*, this scale requires respondents to divide a fixed number of points, usually a 100, among items according to their importance to the respondent.

The **comparative rating scale** (also called a constant-sum scale) requires respondents to divide a fixed number of points, usually 100, among items according to their importance to the respondent. The result provides researchers with some understanding of the magnitude of the difference between the items' importance to the respondent. An example is:

> Please allocate 100 points among the items below such that the allocation represents the importance of each item to your choice of a hotel. The higher the number of points, the greater its importance. If an item has no importance you would assign no points to it. Please check when finished to ensure that your point total is 100.
>
> Hotel belongs to a national chain ____
> I receive frequent guest points for my stay ____
> Location is convenient ____
> Is good value for the money ____
> Listed as a top quality hotel in guide book____
> Total   100 points

The task of allocating points becomes more difficult with a large number of items. Ten items are generally considered the maximum limit for the comparative rating scale.

Semantic Differential Scales

Semantic differential scale a seven-point scale using pairs of adjectives or phrases that are opposite in meaning.

The **semantic differential scale** is a seven-point scale using pairs of adjectives or phrases that are opposite in meaning. Each pair of adjectives measures a different dimension of the concept. The respondent chooses one of the seven scale positions that most closely reflects his or her feelings. A large number of dimensions would be needed to completely measure a concept.

Two forms of a semantic differential scaled statement are:

Clean	1	2	3	4	5	6	7	Dirty
The store was clean	1	2	3	4	5	6	7	The store was dirty.

Again, the numbers assigned to the positions on the scale indicate order, so at least an ordinal level of measurement has been achieved, although many researchers assume interval level data are obtained through this method. Semantic differential scales can also be graphed to show comparisons by group or objects by plotting medians or means.

FIGURE 6.8 Profiles of Two Restaurants Using a Semantic Differential Scale

Stapel Scales

The **Stapel scale** is used as a substitute for the semantic differential when it is difficult to construct pairs of bipolar adjectives. The following example illustrates a Stapel scale for measuring airline performance on seating comfort.

Stapel scale used as a substitute for the semantic differential when it is difficult to construct pairs of bipolar adjectives.

	Delta	United	American	Northwest
Comfortable Seating	+3	+3	+3	+3
	+2	+2	+2	+2
	+1	+1	+1	+1
	−1	−1	−1	−1
	−2	−2	−2	−2
	−3	−3	−3	−3

Respondents would be instructed to circle positive numbers for when the adjective increasingly accurately describes the airline seating in economy class, and negative numbers when the adjective is increasingly less accurate in describing the airline. Stapel scales generate results similar to the semantic differential, but are easier to construct and administer, particularly over the phone.

Commentary on Scales

Some types of scales are designed to collect measures of a specific type of construct, while others can be used for more than one type of construct. For example, Likert, semantic differential, and Stapel scales were all originally designed as attitude-rating scales. They are also generally thought of as interval scales (generating intervally scaled data).

A comparative rating scale, in contrast, is an interval scale (or quasiinterval—scientists are not in agreement about this) that could be used to measure several constructs. See the following examples.

Motives. Allocate 100 points among this list of items with respect to their importance in selecting a university for an undergraduate degree:

Parents attended the university _____
National reputation for quality _____
Student-teacher ratio _____
Cost of tuition _____
Close to home _____
Total 100 points _____

Preferences. Allocate 100 points among this list of items with respect to your preference for places to vacation:

Disneyworld _____
Mountains _____
Beach _____
Golf Resort _____
Total 100 points _____

A rank-order scale is similar in versatility to the comparative rating scale (could measure motives, preferences), but is an ordinal scale.

Example: Rank-order your preferences for places to vacation (first choice = 1, second choice = 2, etc.):

Disneyworld   ____

Mountains   ____

Beach   ____

Golf Resort   ____

See Table 6.3 for further clarification.

TABLE 6.3 Types of Scales and Their Properties

	Types of Data	Used to Measure	Typical Number
Itemized Ratings	Interval	Many Different Constructs (see examples in this chapter)	Varies
Likert	Interval	Attitudes	Five
Rank-orders	Ordinal	Several constructs	Varies
Comparative Rating	Interval or quasi	Several constructs	Varies
Semantic Differential	Interval	Attitudes	Seven
Stapel	Interval	Attitudes	Six

SUMMARY

The researcher must be sure that the measurement process is carefully analyzed to ensure good measurement tools are used in research. All the questions of what, who, and how to measure must be dealt with to yield valid and reliable measures of management concepts. Failure to exercise care throughout measurement procedures can result in misleading information and ineffective decisions. The process of developing measures to be used in research projects should constitute a substantial part of the researcher's time and effort in the planning stages of each project. Using the proper scale for responding to questions measuring psychological variables is an important step in obtaining good measures. Care should be taken that attitude measures do not lead to improper and erroneous predictions of behavior.

KEY TERMS

Comparative rating scale (p. 120)
Construct (p. 102)
Construct validity (p. 111)
Content validity (p. 111)
Interval scale (p. 108)
Itemized rating scales (p. 117)
Likert scale (p. 118)
Nominal scale (p. 108)
Operational definition (p. 103)

Ordinal scale (p. 108)
Predictive or pragmatic validity (p. 111)
Rank-order scale (p. 119)
Ratio scale (p. 109)
Reliability (p. 105)
Semantic differential scale (p. 120)
Stapel scale (p. 121)
Validity (p. 105)

DISCUSSION QUESTIONS

1. Do we test for construct and pragmatic (predictive) validity before or after we use the questionnaire to collect data from respondents? Explain.

2. Discuss how a thorough literature search can help improve the validity of the measures we will obtain in the descriptive research phase of a research project.

3. Describe how we could use Figures 6.1 and 6.2 to develop a questionnaire that could be used to measure attitudes and behavior toward a healthy diet. Provide examples of questions that could be generated from this process. Discuss how we would test the questionnaire for reliability and validity.

ENDNOTES

1. Jim C. Nunnally, *Psychometric Theory,* Second Edition (New York: McGraw-Hill, 1978), p. 3.

2. Shelby D. Hunt and Robert N. Morgan, "The Comparative Advantage Theory of Competition," *Journal of Marketing,* 59(April 1995), pp. 1–15.

3. Bruce Wrenn, "What Really Counts When Hospitals Adopt a Marketing Orientation: The Contribution of the Components of Marketing Orientation to Hospital Performance," *Journal of NonProfit and Public Sector Marketing,* 7(1/2, 1996), pp. 111–133.

4. Bernard J. Jaworski and Ajay K. Kohl, "Marketing Orientation: Antecedents and Consequences," *Journal of Marketing,* 57(July 1993), pp. 53–70.

5. Gilbert Churchill, "A Paradigm for Developing Better Measures of Marketing Constructs," *Journal of Marketing Research,* 16(February 1979), pp. 64–73.

6. Robert D. Buzzell, Donald F. Cox, and Rex V. Brown, *Marketing Research and Information Systems: Text and Cases* (New York: McGraw-Hill, 1969), p. 133.

7. Raymond, Joan. 2000. "For Richer and for Poorer," *American Demographics,* (July), pp. 58–64.

8. Ford, John B., Michael S. LaTour, and Tony L. Henthorne. 1995. "Perceptions of Marital Roles in Purchase Decision Processes: A Cross-Cultural Study," *Journal of the Academy of Marketing Science,* Vol. 23, No. 2, pp. 120–131.

9. Labrecque, J. and L. Ricard. 2001. "Children's Influence on Family Decision-Making: A Restaurant Study," *Journal of Business Research* (November), pp. 173–176.

10. Michael D. Hutt and Thomas W. Spegh, *Industrial Marketing Management* (Hinsdale, IL: The Dryden Press, 1985), pp. 65–69.

11. Thomas C. Kinnear and James R. Taylor, *Marketing Research* (New York: McGraw-Hill, 1996), p. 231.

12. For an in-depth discussion of the measure process see Jim C. Nunnally, *Psychometric Theory*, Second Edition (New York: McGraw-Hill, 1978); Claire Selltiz, Lawrence S. Wrightsman, and Stuart W. Cook, *Research Methods in Social Relations*, Third Edition (New York: Holt, Rinehart and Winston, 1976); Fred N. Kerlinger, *Foundations of Behavioral Research*, Third Edition (New York: Holt, Rinehart and Winston, 1986).

13. For a discussion of some of the associations between attitudes and behavior see Richard Lutz, "The Role of Attitude Theory in Marketing," in Harold Kassarjian and Thomas Robertson (Eds.), *Perspectives in Consumer Behavior*, Fourth Edition (Upper Saddle River, NJ: Prentice-Hall, 1991), pp. 317–339; John Mowen and Michael Minor, *Consumer Behavior* (Upper Saddle River, NJ: Prentice-Hall, 1998), p. 263.

14. Gilbert A. Churchill, Jr. and J. Paul Peter, "Research Design Effects on the Reliability of Rating Scales: A Meta-Analysis," *Journal of Marketing Research,* 21 (November 1984), pp. 360–375.

15. Rensis Likert, "A Technique for the Measurement of Attitudes," *Archives of Psychology,* (140, 1932).

Primary Data Collection

Maksim Kabakau/Shutterstock.com

Learning Objectives

Upon completing this chapter, you should understand:

- What is meant by the term primary data.
- The different types of "primary data" that can be collected in a research project.
- Basic methods of collecting primary data.
- The advantages and disadvantages of the different methods of data collection.

The search for answers to our research questions, or the tests of our hypotheses to determine whether or not they are supported by the information we collect, may require us to go beyond the examination of existing data. When we find ourselves in such a situation we are in need of **primary data**—data not available in a secondary form that must be collected to address the specific needs of our research. Research studies can be at any point on a continuum, which at one end answers all research questions with secondary data and at the other end where no existing secondary data can be used to answer the research questions (Figure 7.1). Chapter 3 provided guidance on how and where to look for secondary sources of information. In this chapter we examine the search for primary data.

FIGURE 7.1. Continuum of Answers to Research Questions

Primary data data not available in a secondary form that must be collected to address the specific needs of our research.

It is important not to lose sight of how we arrived at the point of acknowledging our need for primary data. We are seeking to make decisions to solve a management problem (or assess a market opportunity), and we want those decisions to be *informed* decisions, rather than be based on hunches or guesswork. Consequently, we have identified a purpose for the research and a specific set of research questions to keep ourselves on track as we seek information to inform our decision making. Thus, the primary data we seek is in a form needed to answer a question, test a hypothesis, or in some way contribute to better decision making. We would know, for example, that we needed to measure consumer preferences because they were one of the criteria decision makers want to consider when choosing among decision alternatives (such as, do consumers prefer product design A or design B). In other words, we do not automatically include any particular type of primary data in our research—there must be a reason for its inclusion, which ultimately can be traced to its contribution to making better decisions.

SOURCES OF PRIMARY DATA

Primary data originate from various sources. Some of the major sources are:

1. *The organization itself.* We generally think of the organization as a source of internal secondary information; however, the organization can also be a valuable beginning source of primary data for answering research questions (such as a survey of the sales force).
2. *The environment.* The market environment includes customers and potential customers, as well as competitors. Customers are very important sources of information

related to their demands and intentions. An emerging factor relative to the market environment is competition. Competition is increasing in importance, and the next decade will be one of severe marketing warfare among competitors. Customers, and even potential customers, can be surveyed and information can be gathered from them much more easily than from competitors. It is difficult to obtain information directly from competitors. Competitive intelligence and analysis is an important type of primary data.

3. *The distribution channel.* Wholesalers, retailers, manufacturers, and various suppliers and users can be vital sources of information for an organization. In fact, the role of wholesalers and retailers has increased greatly in importance in recent years in many product categories.

TYPES OF PRIMARY DATA

Primary data come in a variety of forms. Some of the more common types of primary data are:

Demographic and Socioeconomic Data

Information such as age, education, occupation, marital status, sex, income, ethnic identification, and social status are of interest to managers because when combined with other types of primary data (such as consumption rates, attitudes), these descriptions help managers profile target market members or other groups of interest. Consequently, through media plans, channels of distribution, and other ways, marketing plans can reflect the type of people who are our targets. In other words, this information is quite often of interest to us because the means by which we get our message and product to our target market is most often described in terms of **demographic and socioeconomic data** (such as magazine subscription lists, typical retail customers, TV viewers, and the like). The equivalent of demographics for industrial marketers (such as sales volume, number of employees, location, North American Industrial Classification System [NAICS] code) is likewise used in combination with other information for targeting purposes.

Another reason for collecting this information is to test hypotheses that are related to groupings of people by demographic or socioeconomic category (young people will prefer concept A and middle-aged people will prefer concept B; consumption rate is directly correlated with income; people with college degrees do this behavior more frequently than those with no college education).

Attitudes

Attitudes refer to a person's feelings, convictions, or beliefs for an object, idea, or individual. Attitudes are a common object of measurement for business researchers because it is believed that they are precursors of behavior. While marketing managers are ultimately responsible for influencing behavior, not just attitudes, we are not always able to observe and measure behaviors. For example, for a potential new product we may have to measure attitudes toward the product concept instead of behavior toward a product that does not yet exist. Also, attitudes help us to understand why people behave as they do, and managers always want to know *why* behavior occurs, in addition to the frequency with which it occurs. Chapter 6 discussed some of the more common means of measuring attitudes.

Please check the highest educational level you have achieved:

Less than high school	☐
High school graduate	☐
Some college	☐
College graduate	☐
Some graduate school	☐
Post-graduate degree	☐

Demographic and socioeconomic data information such as age, education, occupation, marital status, sex, income, ethnic identification, and social status.

Attitudes refer to a person's feelings, convictions, or beliefs for an object, idea, or individual.

I like the taste of healthy foods.

Strongly agree	☐
Agree	☐
Neither agree or disagree	☐
Disagree	☐
Strongly disagree	☐

Psychographics and Lifestyle Data

Psychographics and lifestyle data is concerned with people's personality traits, what interests them, how they live, and their values. It is sometimes referred to as a person's AIOs—activities, interests, and opinions. While empirical evidence linking someone's personality with their purchase and consumption behavior is weak, managers find that combining psychographics and lifestyle information with demographics provides a three-dimensional perspective of a target market, permitting a much better focus to a marketing program.

If I have an hour of free time,
I would rather (check one):

Read a book	☐
Watch TV	☐
Pursue my hobby	☐
Take a walk	☐

Psychographics and lifestyle data this type of data is concerned with people's personality traits, what interests them, how they live, and their values.

Intentions

Intentions refer to the anticipated future behaviors of an individual. This is a subject of interest to managers who factor the planned behavior of their consumers heavily into business plans. Intentions may be specific to the research project under investigation, or may be the kinds of purchase intentions routinely measured by such organizations as the Survey Research Center at the University of Michigan. While there will always be some disparity between what consumers say they will do, and what they actually do, managers feel that obtaining some measure of planned future behavior is useful in distinguishing the potential of several alternative offerings.

Read the product concept below and indicate the likelihood of whether you will buy such a product:

Definitely will purchase						Definitely will not purchase
7	6	5	4	3	2	1

Intentions refer to the anticipated future behaviors of an individual.

Awareness and Knowledge

Which brands of riding lawn mowers have you ever heard of? [Interviewer: Do not read list. Check all brands mentioned.]

☐ John Deere   ☐ Case
☐ Simplicity   ☐ Lawn Boy
☐ Craftsman   ☐ Other
☐ White

Referring to what subjects do or do not know about an object of investigation, **awareness and knowledge** is of interest to managers who wish to distinguish the image, experience, and feelings of consumers who are familiar with a product from those who are not. If I am interested in determining my brand's image, for example, I want to first determine which consumers are aware of and knowledgeable about my brand. Other areas for determining awareness (unaided or aided) and extent of knowledge are advertisement recall, retail store familiarity, manufacturers, country of product origin, and so on.

Awareness and knowledge referring to what subjects do or do not know about an object of investigation.

Motivations

Motives consist of inner states that direct our behavior toward a goal. Other terms used to describe motives are urges, drives, or impulses. Our concern with motives centers around an interest in why people act as they do. When we ask respondents to indicate how important each of several product attributes is in influencing their choice, we are attempting to identify what motives are influencing their behavior. Other ways of assessing motives include projective techniques (see Chapter 4), open-ended questions asking why people acted as they did, and a variety of other exploratory, descriptive, or even causal techniques intended to probe the needs that channel a person's actions.

Motivations inner states that direct our behavior toward a goal.

Degimages/Shutterstock.com

How important is each of the following in influencing your choice of a laundry detergent for the first time?

	Very Important	Somewhat Important	Important	Not Very Important	Not at All Important
Advertisement	☐	☐	☐	☐	☐
Consumer	☐	☐	☐	☐	☐
Magazine test	☐	☐	☐	☐	☐
Coupon	☐	☐	☐	☐	☐
Friend or relative	☐	☐	☐	☐	☐
Sale	☐	☐	☐	☐	☐
Sample	☐	☐	☐	☐	☐

Behaviors

Behaviors are the actual actions taken by respondents. Managers may have an interest in any number of specific behaviors enacted by selected groups of respondents, but typically purchase and consumption behaviors are of significant interest. Obtaining information about a person's behaviors might be accomplished through either self-report (asking someone to indicate how often they consume a particular product), or through observation, either disguised or undisguised, of a subject's behavior as it occurs.

How often do you go out to see a movie?

☐ Less than once a month
☐ Once a month
☐ Two or three times a month
☐ Once a week or more

METHODS OF COLLECTING PRIMARY DATA

The design of any research project is developed to obtain answers to the questions and objectives of the study. This will call for specific types of information and also indicate specific methods of gathering the data. The primary methods of collecting primary data are (1) *communication* and (2) *observation*. **Communication** includes various direct approaches of asking questions of respondents either by personal interview, telephone survey, electronic survey, or mail questionnaire. Observation, on the other hand, involves the process of viewing market situations either in the field or in laboratory settings. In this method of data collection, an observer records activities of the entity being observed, either in a structured (descriptive or causal research) or unstructured (exploratory) fashion. Sometimes the actions of interest are recorded by mechanical devices instead of using an observer.

Behaviors actual actions taken by respondents.

Communication includes various direct approaches of asking questions of respondents either by personal interview, telephone survey, electronic survey, or mail questionnaire.

Choosing Between Observation and Communication Methods

How does a researcher know when to use communication or **observation methods** to collect primary data? Each approach has inherent advantages and disadvantages that can affect the decision of when to appropriately use it for collecting information.

Observation methods involves the process of physically or mechanically recording some specific aspect of a consumer's activity or behavior.

Advantages and Disadvantages of the Communication Method

Communication methods have the advantages of versatility, speed, and cost. *Versatility* is the ability to cover a wide spectrum of types of primary data. Examining our list of primary data types reveals that communication is the preferred (and sometimes only) method of collecting information on attitudes, intentions, awareness and knowledge, motives, demographics and socioeconomic factors, and behaviors (such as self-report of past behaviors). Obtaining accurate and truthful answers to questions on these topics is always a concern, but certainly communication methods are a versatile means of addressing the need for information in such areas.

Communication also provides the benefits of speed and cost. These two benefits are interrelated and refer to the degree of control the researcher has over data collection. It is much faster and less expensive to develop questions that ask people to recount their experiences (behaviors) than it is to set up an observational research process and wait for the behavior to occur in order to record it. A telephone interviewer, for example, might conduct four extensive interviews in the same hour the observational researcher is still waiting to observe the first relevant behavior.

Disadvantages of the communication method involve the lack of cooperation on the part of the research subject. Some subjects may either be unable or unwilling to answer questions. Perhaps worse than being unable to answer questions is when they do not recall the facts in questions yet invent an answer so as to not disappoint the interviewer! Another disadvantage, then, is the bias in responses that may be introduced in the process of asking questions. We will discuss this at greater length in Chapter 10.

Advantages and Disadvantages of the Observation Method

Observation has several advantages over the communication method. The disadvantages of the communication method—inability or unwillingness for subject to communicate, interviewer bias—are not present with observation. Also, some types of behavior, such as observing small children at play or solving problems, lend themselves much more readily to observational study than communication. Observational information is thought to have an advantage over communication in objectivity and accuracy. Subjects wishing to portray themselves in the most positive light will respond to questions accordingly, but when unknowingly observed, a record of their behavior may reflect more objectivity and accuracy. Also, descriptive observational research, such as scanner data from a supermarket, generates more accurately and objectively determined data than achieved by communication (like trying to recall purchases and list them on a questionnaire).

Two disadvantages characterize the observation method. First, some information internal to subjects such as attitudes, intentions, and motives, cannot be observed. It is important to remember this when tempted to attribute such things to people based on an observation of their behavior. For example, you might observe someone examining the back of a food carton and believe they are studying the product's nutritional content when they were looking for the name of the producer. Second, the observed behavior must be of short duration and occur frequently enough to permit a cost-effective plan for its measurement.

Often communication can be productively combined with observation to gain the benefits of both, with none of the disadvantages, since the disadvantages of one method are the advantages of the other. The usual sequence would be to observe behavior and then ask questions about why the person behaved as he or she did. For example, if a company were trying to build a better infant highchair they might observe mothers feeding their infants using currently available brands, then ask what they liked or disliked about them, why they performed particular acts in using the highchairs, and the like.

Research Project Tip	When writing up the preliminary results of your research you should describe the methodology you used in detail. It is not enough, for example, to say you conducted a search of the literature and then completed four in-depth interviews with consumers. You should describe the databases you used in your search, the key words used in searching the computer databases (e.g., LEXIS/NEXIS), include a photocopy of the printout of the results of the search (e.g., articles list, abstracts, or first page of published article or report). In-depth interviews should indicate the criteria you used in selecting people to interview, a description of the people interviewed, a copy of interview guides, and so on.

COMMUNICATION METHODS

At the risk of repeating ourselves, we will note that the communication method (and observation too) can be used for information collection using exploratory, descriptive, or causal research designs. As we have already indicated, the most commonly used communication method, the survey, can be used in all three research designs, although it is most commonly thought of as a primary tool of descriptive research. We will discuss a common exploratory research communication method—focus groups—then discuss the descriptive communication survey research method.

Exploratory Communication—Focus Group Interviewing

As discussed in Chapter 4, one of the most popular and widely used exploratory research techniques, **focus group interviewing**, consists of a small group of people (usually eight to twelve) assembled for the purpose of discussing in an unstructured, spontaneous manner topics introduced by a group moderator. The objective of conducting focus groups is *not* to accomplish the goals of a survey at a lower cost. In fact, focus groups, as an exploratory research technique, cannot be substituted for a descriptive research's survey design.

Focus group interviewing consists of a small group of people (usually eight to twelve) assembled for the purpose of discussing in an unstructured, spontaneous manner topics introduced by a group moderator.

Focus groups are a popular technique and when appropriately used, they can effectively and efficiently achieve the following goals of exploratory research:

■ Generate new ideas or hypotheses, which can be tested in later phases of the research study

■ Clarify concepts, actions, or terms used by consumers

■ Prioritize issues for further investigation

■ Provide an opportunity for management to see how their real consumers think, feel, and act

■ Obtain an early read on changing market trends

Focus groups are good at accomplishing such objectives because their relatively unstructured approach permits a free exchange of ideas, feelings, and experiences to emerge around a series of topics introduced by a moderator. The moderator works from a topic outline that covers the major areas of interest to the client firm, but because each group session consists of different individuals with their own feelings, desires, and opinions, no two sessions with the same agenda will be exactly the same in conduct or findings. The term "focus group" is used because the moderator focuses the group's attention on the predetermined subjects, without letting the discussion go too far afield. However, it is considered unstructured in the sense that a good moderator will consider the particular dynamics of each group when introducing these topics and the order in which they are brought up for discussion. Because they are so frequently used in business research, several books have been exclusively devoted to a discussion of how to conduct and analyze focus group sessions.[1] We will confine our discussion here to a few of the more important aspects of using focus groups as a qualitative exploratory research approach.

Sequencing of Focus Groups and Surveys

While the usual sequence of focus groups and surveys is to do focus groups first to generate hypotheses and then a descriptive survey to test the hypotheses, there are some advantages to doing focus groups after descriptive research as well as before. Advantages of conducting focus groups after doing descriptive research are:

1. Managers are not as likely to be unduly influenced by anomalous responses. When you have already determined the frequency with which certain behaviors are performed, you have a perceptual framework to use when listening to people describe their behavior and the motives behind it. When you hear something that deviates

significantly from the norm you do not have to wonder if the person represents a significant number of people in the market, you already know the frequencies with which such behavior is performed. You can concentrate on probing to understand the relevant behavior.

2. The descriptive data allows you to better screen focus group respondents to ensure they represent the people you are most interested in understanding in greater depth.

3. You are better able to delve into the nuance of consumer phenomena understood in statistical terms from the descriptive research. For example, identifying the statistical profile of your heavy users is undoubtedly useful information, but understanding what makes them tick and how vulnerable they are to competitor appeals may be best determined through qualitative (focus group) work.

4. Descriptive data will usually reveal information that cannot easily be explained with existing knowledge of consumers. Sometimes the statistics are merely puzzling, sometimes they are counterintuitive. The possible competing explanations of the data need to be tested through probing qualitative research to determine *why* the results look as they do. Without such probing, the explanation settled upon may or may not be appropriate, but if repeated often enough it will take on an undeserved verity which could be dangerous. Making the effort to check out the various explanations before making a decision could in some instances be the best money spent in the research project.

Reporting the Results of Focus Groups

In writing the findings of focus groups, care must be taken not to imply that results typify the target population. The groups were not formed in an effort to generate inferential statistics, but rather to clarify concepts, generate ideas and insights, and make the abstract real. Therefore, it is the qualitative rather than quantitative conclusions that should be the focus of the written report. Goldman and McDonald make the following suggestions about writing the report on focus group findings:[2]

1. The report should not be a sequential summary or transcript of the sessions, but rather a "logically organized and coherent interpretation of the meaning of these events."

2. The report should begin with an introductory section that reviews the research purpose, research objectives, and a short description of the research methodology. This is followed by a report of findings, the marketing implications, recommendations, and suggestions for future research phases.

3. An Executive Summary at the beginning of the report should cover the major discoveries as well as the relevant marketing implications that can be justifiably concluded based on the qualitative research results.

4. The results section is not necessarily best done by following the sequence of topics covered in the discussions. It might rather be approached by focusing on marketing problems or market segments, and discussing the findings from the groups that might have been addressed in diverse order during the group sessions.

5. The written analysis should progress from the general to the more specific. For example, a report on a new snack product concept might start with a discussion of general observations about snack eating, then go to a discussion of brand image and loyalty, then address the response to the new snack concepts.

6. The marketing implications section should provide guidance for the development of marketing response to the findings without overstating the conclusiveness of the qualitative findings. Everyone, report writers and readers, should remain aware of the limited objectives for conducting the groups, as well as the limitations of this type of research method in general.

Other forms of exploratory communication techniques were discussed in Chapter 4. We will now discuss what is perhaps the most frequently used of all communication research techniques: the descriptive research sample survey.

Descriptive Communication—Survey Research

In the discussion of descriptive research in Chapter 5, we noted that the primary methods of collecting descriptive data were through cross-sectional sample surveys and panels. Panel data may be collected via surveys or through observation (scanner-based data or the like), but our concern in this section is to describe the use of the cross-sectional sample survey method of collecting descriptive data.

Surveys are frequently used to collect all the types of primary data described earlier in this chapter. Surveys generate data that make it possible to test various types of hypotheses that suggest relationships between those variables and between respondent groups. For example, we might use a survey to segment a consumer population and then test hypotheses that some segments are more price sensitive than other segments, or that some segments acquire more information by using the Internet than other segments. A test of a hypothetical relationship between variables might involve determining the degree of influence a set of demographic, attitudinal, or behavioral variables had in explaining a consumer decision (such as membership in a health club). As we will see in our chapters on data analysis, statistical analytical techniques to test such hypotheses require that the data being analyzed be collected through descriptive or causal data collection methods, and most frequently the method for descriptive research is a survey.

SURVEY METHODS

Descriptive research surveys can be conducted in a variety of ways using many combinations of people and electronics and conducted in a variety of locations. Table 7.1 displays a few of the types of survey delivery methods possible from such combinations, including **computer surveys**. We will first discuss the more traditional methods of conducting surveys by telephone, mail, or in person, then discuss some of the newer ways these methods and computer and fax technologies are being used in survey research.

Computer survey computer is utilized in telephone (CATI) interviewing, personal interviews conducted at shopping malls, or at a central location.

Telephone Interviewing

Telephone interviewing is usually employed when the study design requires speedy collection of information from a large, geographically dispersed population that would be too costly to do in person; when eligibility is difficult (necessitating many contacts for a completed interview); when the questionnaire is relatively short; or when face-to-face contact is not necessary.

Telephone interviewing usually employed when the study design requires speedy collection of information from a large, geographically dispersed population that would be too costly to do in person.

TABLE 7.1 Survey Delivery Methods

Location of Interaction	Human/Electronic Involvement			
	Telephone	Mail	Personal	Computer or Fax
Home	WATS or IVR	Self-administered or panels	Door to door	Internet or disk by mail
Work	WATS or IVR	Self-administered or lock box	Executive interview	Internet or fax
Malls	--	--	Mall intercept	Internet or fax
Central Location Research Facility	--	--	On-site	Computer assisted

From the Home

In this case, interviewing is conducted directly from the interviewer's home. The interviewer has all the materials that will be needed to complete an assignment in his or her home and use the specified period (per instructions) on the telephone contacting respondents and conducting interviews.

From Central Location Phone Banks

A research firm may conduct interviewing from its facilities equipped with wide area telephone service (WATS). Central location interviewing has many advantages. It allows for constant monitoring and supervision. If an interviewer has a problem or question, it can be handled on the spot. Mistakes can be corrected; respondents can be called back immediately if the supervisor finds that the interviewer's information is not complete. Interviews can be monitored to ensure correct interviewing procedures and techniques, and that quotas are being filled. Since telephone interviewing is the most commonly used method of data collection, a detailed discussion on the specific procedures of telephone interviewing is located in Chapter 12.

Most business research companies now use some form of computer-assisted telephone interviewing (CATI) system. The survey instrument or questionnaire is programmed into a computer, and the "pages" of the questionnaire appear on the terminal screen in front of the interviewer. The interviewer can input the results either through the keyboard or in some cases by using an electronic light pen that can touch the appropriate response on the screen. The CATI System also provides for automatic skip patterns, immediate data input, and in some cases automatic dialing. This system promotes flexibility and simplification. In addition, increased speed and improved accuracy of the data are accomplished. Various programs of random-digit dialing can be attached to the CATI system. The computer-generated random-digit numbers can eliminate the sampling bias of unlisted numbers.

Predictive dialing is another important feature that makes telephone interviewing more effective. With predictive dialing, the technology does the dialing, recognizes a voice response, and switches to the caller so fast that the interviewer virtually hears the entire "hello." The system predicts how many dials to make to keep the interviewing staff busy without spending over half of their time just making contact. The system automatically redials no-answer and busy numbers at specified intervals. Some predictive dialing systems can be set to identify answering machines automatically and reschedule those calls as well. This results in more efficient calling and higher penetration of the sample list.

Increasingly, research firms are turning to Interactive Voice Response (IVR) systems to conduct surveys by phone. In this approach respondents dial a toll-free number and respond to recorded questions either with a limited set of voice responses indicated (such as "Please answer by saying home, work, or both."), or by using the designated buttons on a touch-tone phone. Respondents might be members of a major panel (such as Market Facts, National Family Opinion, or Home Testing Institute), or just responding to a one-time survey. The use of IVR, or Completely Automated Telephone Surveys (CATS), has been employed to get quality data very quickly and has the advantage of letting respondents call anytime to answer the survey.

The advantage of having an interviewer ask questions of a respondent using a WATS line is, of course, the ability to ask open-ended questions where probing for response is needed and answer respondent questions or provide clarification when necessary. These needs may sometimes be greater than the needs for the speed and cost savings of the IVR approach.

Telephone Communication

As compared to personal or mail interviewing, telephone interviews have the advantage of speed and relative economy. Interviews of this type are also easily validated, and the personal interaction of a qualified interviewer maintains a relatively high degree of control.

TABLE 7.2 Advantages and Disadvantages of Telephone Interviewing

Advantages	Disadvantages
1. Provides ease of making a contact (callback) with a respondent.	1. Exhibits cannot be shown unless a mail/phone or phone/mail/phone methodology is used.
2. Administration and close supervision is provided by professional staff at a central telephone center.	2. Question limitations such as limited scales.
3. Drawing representative samples of persons with telephones is relatively easy.	3. Long interviews are difficult to administer by telephone.
4. Sequential disclosure, and questionnaire flexibility with skip patterns, refer backs, etc., is possible.	
5. Speed in gathering information.	
6. Relatively low cost.	
7. Simplicity at conducting a pretest.	
8. Access to hard-to-reach people.	

The proper sequencing of question response also can be maintained. While not as flexible and productive as a personal interview, a well-designed questionnaire administered by a skilled interviewer can gather relatively comprehensive information. The interviewer also is in a position to probe at appropriate times and follow appropriate skip patterns. Weaknesses of the telephone interview are its inability to be as long or as detailed as personal interviews and its inability to show the respondent any products, pictures, or lists. Specific advantages and disadvantages of telephone interviewing are listed in Table 7.2.

Mail Surveys

Mail surveys are commonly used in either ad hoc (one time) or mail panel research. In ad hoc research projects a sample of respondents is chosen to be representative of the population of interest and a questionnaire is sent by mail. The mail questionnaire may be preceded by and/or followed by a telephone call intended to encourage participation. The combination of telephone and mail is an attempt to reduce the high rate of nonresponse that plagues ad hoc, and to a lesser degree panel, mail surveys.

Mail surveys commonly used in either ad hoc (one time) or mail panel research.

When mail is used in surveying people at work a *lockbox* approach is some-times used to avoid secretaries or assistants completing a survey intended for an executive. Here an accompanying letter tells the respondent the purpose of the survey and that the box is a gift, but the combination will be provided at the time of a phone interview. The respondent opens the box at a scheduled interview time, completes the interview and, in some instances, returns the survey by mail.

Mail surveys are sometimes dropped off at homes or work sites with the intent of having the respondent complete the questionnaire and return it by mail. Such an approach has been shown to increase response rates and has the advantage of allowing the person dropping off the questionnaire to explain the purpose of the interview.

Mail questionnaires allow for wide distribution. Also, the lack of interviewer/respondent interaction can impart the feeling of anonymity that can encourage accurate responses to relatively sensitive questions. In theory, the respondent has time to check records or even confer with someone else to make sure reported information is accurate. Disadvantages include a low response rate that results in nonresponse error. Control of the sample is minimal. Knowing the difference in results between those who participated and those who did not is not possible. Too often participants are those who are either more interested in the subject area or who have more free time to fill out questionnaires. Also, a mail survey

TABLE 7.3 Advantages and Disadvantages of Mail Surveys

Advantages	Disadvantages
1. Cost-effective.	1. Low return rate.
2. Efficiency in reaching large samples.	2. Nonreturn bias; those who return a mail questionnaire may not represent the sample as a whole.
3. Access to hard-to-reach people.	3. No control of who fills out the questionnaire.
4. Self-administered/no interviewer bias.	4. No ability for sequential disclosure of information.
5. Limited use of exhibits is possible.	5. Slow response.
	6. Hard to pretest.
	7. Question limitations.

is slow, less flexible, and does not allow for probing. Control is lost with a mail questionnaire and sequencing is difficult. Further-more, researchers never actually know who completed the questionnaire. Many of these problems can be overcome through the use of mail surveys conducted by consumer panel organizations (see Chapter 4). Table 7.3 lists the advantages and disadvantages of mail surveys.

Personal Interviewing

This face-to-face method is employed when the survey is too long to conduct over the telephone or there might be material to show the respondent. Personal interviews are effective when the interviewer is placing a product in a home or office; the respondent is tasting a product; or the sample necessitates contacting homes in a specific manner, such as every fourth home or going to every home until an interview is conducted, then skipping a specified number of homes before attempting the next contact, as well as other applications.

Personal interviews allow for more in-depth probing on various issues and are the most productive, accurate, comprehensive, controlled, and versatile types of communication. There is ample opportunity for a well-trained interviewer to probe and interpret body language, facial expression, and other nuances during the interaction. Rapport can be developed that would put the interviewee at ease and gain his or her cooperation. The interviewer can explain any misunderstanding the respondent might have and keep the respondent on track and in sequence in responding to the questionnaire. In spite of the advantages of greater depth and productivity, the personal interview does take more time and money to administer. The advantages and disadvantages of **personal interviewing** are listed in Table 7.4.

There are several varieties of personal interviews. The most common are:

Door-to-Door Interviewing

In door-to-door interviewing, the client or field-service director will assign an interviewing location and often the exact address at which to begin. The interviewer then takes a specific direction in order to contact respondents according to the sample pattern that is specified to be followed. The interviewer will ask the questions and record the respondent's answers either during the interview or immediately afterward.

Central Location/Mall Interviewing

The use of a central location or mall area is effective in instances where respondents will taste a product, look at a package design, view a commercial, or listen to a recording or view a videotape and report their impressions. Shopping malls are frequently used because of their high volume of traffic. Other central locations such as a church meeting hall, hotel, or other facility might be used to conduct a large number of personal interviews. When this method of personal interviewing is used, the respondents are generally

Personal interviewing face-to-face method is employed when the survey is too long to conduct over the telephone or there might be material to show the respondent.

TABLE 7.4 Advantages and Disadvantages of Personal Interviewing

Advantages	Disadvantages
1. Exhibits such as ads, packages, pictures can be shown.	1. High cost.
2. Flexibility and versatility.	2. Interviewer bias.
3. Speed can be accomplished with multiple interviews being completed in multiple locations.	3. Administration/execution problems.
4. Sampling can be done in a very representative way.	
5. Observation of the respondent allows for viewing behavior as well as asking questions.	

TABLE 7.5 Strengths and Weaknesses of Methods of Data Collection

	Interviewing			Questionnaire		
	Personal	Telephone	Self-Administered	Mail Back	Internet	Fax
Response Rate	Moderate to High	Moderate to High	High	Low to High	Low to High	Low to High
Timing	Slow	Fast	Moderate	Slow	Fast	Fast
Cost/Coverage	High	Moderate	Low	Low	Low	Low
Interviewer Impact (bias)	High	Moderate	Low	Low	Low	Low
Ability to handle complex questions	High	Low	Moderate	Moderate	High	Moderate
Control	High	High	Low	Low	Low	Low
Length	Long	Short	Long	Long	Moderate to Long	Short
Sample Control	High	High	Moderate	Low	Moderate	Moderate

recruited in advance. Shopping malls may be used as locations for prearranged interviews or involve "intercepts" where shoppers are recruited in the mall for the interviews.

Executive and Professional Interviewing

Interviewing of executives at their places of business is the business-to-business marketing research equivalent to consumer door-to-door interviewing. Locating people of interest to the researcher by title or name can be expensive and time-consuming if an accurate list is not available from a list vendor. Once identified, respondents must be contacted, an appointment scheduled for the interview, and then the survey can be administered in person at the workplace. Highly trained interviewers who are appropriately dressed and knowledgeable about the topic are much more likely to be successful in obtaining response, so this type of interviewing can be costly. As is shown in Table 7.5, each of these data collection methods have strengths and weaknesses. These strengths and weaknesses must be considered when selecting a specific method.

Computer or Fax Survey

It is not uncommon for the computer to be used in telephone (CATI) interviewing, personal interviews conducted at shopping malls, or at a central location. See Table 7.6 for a summary of the various ways the computer might be used in survey research.

TABLE 7.6 Methods of Computerized Data Collection Available to Marketing Researchers

Survey Methods	Characteristics
Computer-assisted personal interviewing	A method in which the researcher reads questions to the respondent off a computer screen, and keys the respondent's answers directly into the computer.
Computer-assisted self-interviewing	A member of the research team intercepts and directs willing respondents to nearby computers. Each respondent reads questions and keys his or her answers directly into a computer.
Computer-assisted telephone interviewing	Interviewers telephone potential respondents, ask questions of respondents from a computer screen, and key answers directly into a computer.
Fully automated telephone interviewing	An automated voice asks questions over the telephone, and respondents use their touch-tone telephones to enter their replies.
Electronic mail survey	Researchers send e-mail or web-based surveys to potential respondents who use electronic mail. Respondents key in their answers and send an e-mail reply or submit the complete web survey.

Source: Adapted from V. Kumar, David A. Aaker, George S. Day, *Essentials of Marketing Research* (New York: John Wiley and Sons), 1999, p. 258.

Internet Research

Tashatuvango/Shutterstock.com

Earlier in this chapter we discussed the use of the Internet for doing exploratory research in the form of Internet focus groups. We will now discuss the use of the Internet for conducting survey research.[3] (Chapter 10 will discuss a firm that specializes in Internet survey research.) Some of the newer, Internet and facsimile-based approaches will be discussed here. Several reasons have been suggested for explaining the rise in the use of the Internet for conducting surveys.[4] First, the questionnaire can be created, distributed to respondents, and electronically sent to the researcher very quickly. Since data are electronically delivered, statistical analysis software can be programmed to analyze and generate charts and graphs summarizing the data automatically. Second, Internet surveys are less expensive than using interviewers or printing, mailing, and tabulating mail surveys. Third, it is possible to create panels of respondents on the Internet and longitudinally track attitudes, preferences, behaviors, and perceptions over time. A fourth reason is that other methods are not as cost effective as is the Internet for asking just a few questions. Another reason is the ability to reach large numbers of people globally very quickly and at low cost. Finally, Internet surveys can be made to look aesthetically pleasing and can, via Netscape or Internet Explorer or similar browsers, add audio and video to the questionnaire.

Internet surveys can either be email or Web-based approaches. Email surveys are simple to compose and send, but are limited to simple text (flat text format), allow for limited visual presentations (no photo- or video-based stimuli) and interactive capabilities, and cannot permit complex skip patterns.

Web surveys, in comparison, are in HTML format and offer much more flexibility to the researcher, providing opportunity for presentation of complex audio and visual stimuli such as animation, photos, and video clips; interaction with respondent; skip patterns; use of color; pop-up instructions to provide help with questions; and drop-down boxes to allow respondents to choose from long lists of possible answers (such as "In which state do you currently reside?"). Based on answers to a set of screening questions, Web-based Internet surveys can direct respondents to customized survey questions specifically designed with those respondent characteristics in mind. These types of HTML format surveys can also be downloaded to the respondent's computer for completion and then either mailed or electronically sent to the researcher. Of course differences in monitor screen size, computer clock speed, use of full or partial screen for viewing questionnaire, use of broadband versus telephone transmission lines, and other variables will result in different presentations of the questionnaire for different viewers. Also, computer navigation skills still vary widely across the population and must be taken into account when designing a Web-based survey. Designing Internet surveys adds another set of challenges to the researcher using questionnaires to collect data, and those researchers interested in using this medium should consult one of the recent publications addressing this topic (see, for example, Don Dillman, *Mail and Internet Surveys*, New York: John Wiley and Sons, 2000, pp. 361–401).

Some of the movement toward the use of the Internet for survey research is due to the increasing number of people with access to and amount of time devoted to being on the Web. Set-up time can be as fast or faster than CATI, with faster survey execution (often the targeted number of completed surveys can be reached in a few days). Also, the ability of the respondent to choose the time for completing the survey gives it an advantage over personal or telephone interviewing.

Not everything about the use of the Internet for survey research is positive, however. At present one of the issues of greatest concern is the degree to which respondents to Internet surveys are representative of a target population. If the survey is meant to be projectable to a population with a high percentage of access to and usage of the Internet (such as university faculty, businesses, groups of professionals, purchasers of computer equipment), then this issue is of less concern. But when the survey is meant to be projectable to the mass market (that is, U.S. population in general or a large portion of it cutting across ages, occupations, and income levels), then conducting research by using the Internet exclusively is problematic. Descriptive research requires the use of probability sampling methods; not only is a large percentage of the U.S. population not reachable at home via the Internet (and is therefore in violation of the "known and equal probability" random sample selection requirement), it is also true that e-mail address directories do not provide all addresses with a known probability of being sampled. "In sum, e-mail and Web surveying of the general public is currently inadequate as a means of accessing random samples of defined populations of households and/or individuals."[5]

In comparison, the sampling frame for telephone interviews is well defined and its coverage biases are documented. With phone interviewing it is much easier to verify that the respondent is the person you targeted than it is with Internet surveys. Voluntary response at a Web site is particularly troublesome as a means of sampling a specified population with particular parameters (for example, geographic, demographic, and experience characteristics). Based on these problems, many researchers restrict Internet surveys to nonprobability-sampling-based exploratory research. However, there are researchers who claim it is just as valid to use the Internet for probability-sampling-based descriptive research as it is to use mall interviews or mail surveys. As previously mentioned, these claims for projectability are more valid when almost the entire target population has Internet access.

Another computer-based survey method is to put the questionnaire on a computer disk and send it by mail to the home or work location of the respondent. The computer disk contains the skip patterns for the questionnaire in its software. For example, if the question is, "Do you have a pet?" and the answer is no, the next question asked is different than if the answer was yes. Some of the same advantages and disadvantages regarding the use of graphics and other visuals, and ease of tabulating and statistically analyzing e-mail surveys, are also true for computer disk by mail surveys.

A Code of Conduct providing guidelines for conducting research over the Internet has been developed by the Marketing Research Society and can be found at www.mrs.org.uk/standards/internet.ht. These standards, published in January 2004, including the following sections:

1. Definition of Internet research
2. Cooperation is voluntary

3. Respondents must not be inconvenienced
4. Respondents must give their informed consent
5. Researcher's identity must be disclosed
6. Respondent's anonymity must be safeguarded
7. Safeguarding data
8. Client-supplied data
9. Research with children and young people
10. Privacy policy statements

Fax Surveys

Fax surveys have also seen increased usage in the past decade. Distributing and receiving results via facsimile machines is much faster than mail. However, despite improved technology the quality of print reproduction by fax is not as good as is available in mail surveys. The much greater incidence of fax machines in businesses compared to homes is a reason why this form of survey delivery is best utilized in business-to-business research. Advantages include quick dissemination and response and preparation of only one paper copy of cover letter and questionnaire. Disadvantages include lower quality reproduction of print, lack of color capability, reduced length of survey, no incentives for response can be included, return transmission cost may discourage response, and it must be possible to receive multiple replies simultaneously or a constant busy signal will discourage some respondents from replying.

OBSERVATION METHODS

Observation involves the process of physically or mechanically recording some specific aspect of a consumer's activity or behavior. Some research designs call for this type of data. Some contend that observation is more objective than communication. However, observation, whether in a field setting or a laboratory, is not very versatile. Observation cannot answer questions concerning attitudes, opinions, motivations, and intentions of consumers. Observation works well when measuring specific behavioral variables but is less effective measuring attitudinal variables. Often a design that starts with unobtrusive observations, followed by communication to obtain information about motives or attitudes behind the observed behavior, is an effective approach. *Direct observation* involves actually watching an individual's behavior. Their purchase behavior is watched or they are viewed while using a specific product. Sometimes this behavior is monitored in a natural setting or real-life situation. Observations can also be made in an artificial setting that is developed by the researcher to simulate a real-life situation. Quite often a contrived store setting is established to simulate consumers' responses to products in an "actual" purchase situation. A major advantage of artificial or simulated observation is the greater degree of control offered researchers to alter specific variables.

An observation might be accomplished with or without the knowledge of the subject. Obviously, the advantage of disguised observation is that the subject has no motivation to alter his or her behavior. *Mechanical observation* is sometimes appropriate to meet the study objectives of the research design. When this is the case various mechanical devices such as cameras and counting instruments are used to make observation. Eye motion, galvanic skin response, perspiration, pupil size, and various counting devices are examples of mechanical methods of measuring and recording activity. Eye tracking equipment can be used to measure where the eye goes in viewing an advertisement, a product package, or promotional display. A specific application of this technology would be to determine the impact of color in advertising and copy on a newspaper page. The tracking equipment records not only where the eye goes on the page, but also how long it focuses on a specific area. People meters are designed to measure both the channel that is being watched as well as which person in the household is doing the watching.

TABLE 7.7 Examples of Data-Collection Methods Used for Generating Exploratory, Descriptive, or Causal Research Information

Data Collection Form	Research Design Types		
	Exploratory	Descriptive	Causal
Secondary			
Communication	Previous industry studies help to define what "customer service" means to consumers.	Annual survey revealing the number of times during the week people wash dishes by hand.	A journal article that reports on testing the hypothesis that public service advertising changes peoples' attitudes toward donating blood.
Observation	A *Wall Street Journal* article reporting that there are a growing number of magazines devoted to Internet usage.	Syndicated data indicating the market shares of various brands of coffee.	A report by a marketing research firm on the use of test marketing by different industries in the past year.
Primary			
Communication	A focus group of distributors that discusses trends in package handling technologies.	A survey of salespeople to determine the frequency with which competitors have given free goods to dealers.	Running two advertisements in matched markets and determining which ad resulted in greater recall and positive attitudes toward the company.
Observation	Watching production line workers using a handheld grinder and gaining insights on product design changes.	Recording license plate numbers in store parking lot and getting R.L. Polk to generate a map showing trade area and distribution of customers.	Doing a test market for a new product and determining if sales reached objectives.

SUMMARY

So far, we have discovered that the pursuit of answers to research objectives necessitates both a research design and data-collection methods that permit the execution of that design. Good research in any particular case could involve collection of information using one or more of the combinations of research design type and data-collection method. Table 7.7 illustrates that all combinations are possible. Which cell(s) a researcher should be in is a function of the research objectives, research budget, time available, and the decision maker's preferred data form for making decisions.

KEY TERMS

Attitudes (p. 127)
Awareness and knowledge (p. 128)
Behaviors (p. 129)
Communication (p. 129)
Computer survey (p. 133)
Demographic and socioeconomic data (p. 127)
Focus group interviewing (p. 131)
Intentions (p. 128)

Mail surveys (p. 135)
Motivations (p. 128)
Observation methods (p. 129)
Personal interviewing (p. 136)
Primary data (p. 126)
Psychographics and lifestyle data (p. 128)
Telephone interviewing (p. 133)

DISCUSSION QUESTIONS

1. What things do you consider when choosing whether to use communication or observation in your research?

2. What differences exist between doing exploratory, descriptive, or causal observation? Use examples to illustrate your points.

3. What is the relationship between the three types of research designs, the two forms of data, and the two methods of data collection?

4. Do you use communication or observation when you are trying to understand someone's motives? Behaviors? Explain.

ENDNOTES

1. Richard A. Krueger, *Focus Groups* (Newbury Park, CA: Sage Publications, 1990); Alfred E. Goldman and Susan Schwartz McDonald, *The Group Depth Interview* (Englewood Cliffs, NJ: Prentice-Hall, 1987).

2. Judith Langer, "Getting to Know the Customer Through Qualitative Research," *Management Review*, (April 1987), pp. 42–46.

3. Ibid.

4. The following sources were referred to in writing this section on Internet research: James Watt, "Using the Internet for Quantitative Survey Research," *Quirk's Marketing Research Review*, (June/July 1997), pp. 18–19, 67–71; "Pro and Con: Internet Interviewing," *Marketing Research*, 11(2, 1999), pp. 33–37; Diane K. Bowers, "FAQs on Online Research," *Marketing Research*, 10(4, Winter 1998/Spring 1999), pp. 45–49; Don Dillman, *Mail and Internet Surveys* (New York: John Wiley and Sons, 2000), pp.352–361.

5. Joe L. Welch, "Research Marketing Problems and Opportunities with Focus Groups." *Industrial Marketing Management*, (14, 1985), p. 248..

Designing the Data-Gathering Instrument

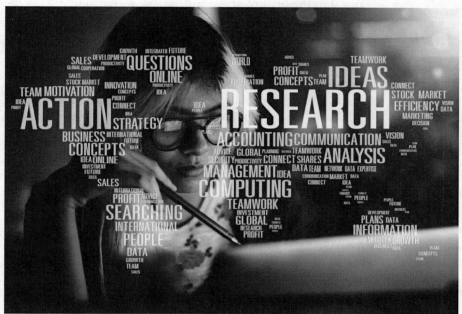

Rawpixel.com/Shutterstock.com

Learning Objectives

Upon completing this chapter, you should understand:

- The goals of a data collection instrument.
- The basic components of a well-designed instrument.
- The different types of questions that can be used in a data-collection instrument.
- The steps involved in designing a questionnaire.
- How pretesting can be used to improve the data-collection process.

imtmphoto/Shutterstock.com

When we use the term "data-gathering instrument," we typically are referring to using a descriptive research design data-collection method. That is because we do not think of collecting data per se in exploratory research (we are generating hypotheses, ideas, insights, clarifying concepts, and prioritizing objectives for the next phase of research). Although we do generate data in causal research, we tend to think in terms of putting together an experimental design rather than designing a data-collection instrument.

The quality of the information gathered is directly proportional to the quality of the instrument designed to collect the data. Consequently, it is extremely important that the most effective data-gathering instrument possible be constructed.

As mentioned in Chapter 5, it is necessary to anticipate the total information needs of the project so the data-gathering instrument can be designed in such a way that it will provide answers to the research questions. The instrument must also gather the data in a form that permits processing it using the analytical techniques selected. As a result of its importance, the data-gathering instrument is the key that holds the research project together and must be done well.

A questionnaire is the main type of data-gathering instrument in descriptive-research designs. A questionnaire is defined in *Webster's New Collegiate Dictionary* as "a set of questions for obtaining statistically useful or personal information from individuals." Obviously, an effective questionnaire is much more than that. Since poor questionnaire design is a primary contributor to nonsampling errors, specifically response errors, the questionnaire should be well designed. The questions should minimize the possibility that respondents will give inaccurate answers. The questions that are asked respondents are the basic essence of a research project. Inquiring by way of specific questions forms the core of survey research. The reliability and validity of survey results are dependent on the way the specific questions are planned, constructed, and executed.

Constructing a questionnaire that generates accurate data that is relevant to solving the management problem is not a simple matter. It is quite possible to construct a questionnaire that flows well from part to part, containing questions easily understood by respondents, addressing the issues identified in the study's research objectives, and lending itself to the appropriate analytical techniques, but totally failing to present an accurate picture of reality conducive to making decisions that lead to a solution of the management problem. How is this possible? As Patricia Labaw notes, a questionnaire is more than just a series of well-worded questions. "It is a totality, a gestalt that is greater than the sum of its individual questions. A questionnaire is organic, with each part vital to every other part, and all parts must be handled simultaneously to create this whole instrument."[1]

A questionnaire must provide data that allows the researcher to determine the information contained in Table 8.1. Without these contextualizing components, it is not possible to extract meaning from the answers respondents give to the questions in a questionnaire.

We need to include questions that reveal respondent consciousness, knowledge, behavior, and environmental situation so that we can know how to interpret, or extract meaning from the answers to those questions that are derived from our research objectives. While our research objectives provide guidance for what questions we will ask respondents, fulfill the research purpose, and permit selection from among our decision alternatives, thereby solving our management problem, those research objectives are not the only source of our questionnaire questions. We will only be able to derive meaning from the answer to those questions by using responses to the four components discussed in Table 8.1 as a filter. For example, we can imagine grouping respondents, based on their answers to some factual questions, into two groups, those knowledgeable about the topic and those not knowledgeable about the topic, and then analyzing the responses by the knowledgeable group in our attempt to make meaningful conclusions from the

TABLE 8.1 Necessary Components of Questionnaires to Allow for Meaningful Analysis

Component	What it means	Evidence of it	Why it is needed	Example
1. Determination of levels of respondent consciousness	Does the respondent see or understand the *implications* of his or her answers to the questions?	Unconscious answers that are inconsistent, not based on objective reality, purely emotional, ignorant, or misleading	If data from answers reflect low level of consciousness, no amount of statistical analysis can help us to predict behavior	Respondent says in answer to one question that they don't believe in abortion "under any circumstances," then say in another answer that abortion is OK to save a mother's life
2. Delineation of the structures or environments affecting behavior	The physical determinants surrounding the respondent's behavior	Such things as age, sex, health, race, locale, mobility, etc., which impinge on respondents ability to behave in certain ways	People, despite their attitudes toward an object, may behave in ways different than their attitude would suggest because of environmental or situational constraints	While a respondent's attitude toward mass transit may be quite favorable, the key determinant of whether he or she will use it is whether it exists in his or her environment
3. Determination of levels of respondent knowledge	Does the respondent really have an understanding of the topic of the questions?	Ability to answer factual questions correctly	Lack of knowledge colors respondent attitudes and behaviors and makes decisions based on such responses very risky	Respondents may answer questions about the positioning of a product relative to its competition without possessing any knowledge of the product, making interpretation of the positioning map impossible
4. Determination of present respondent behavior in specific situations	Respondents reporting what they have already done	Responses to questions asking for the frequency with which specific behaviors are performed	Behavior acts as a measure of experience (or knowledge) with the topic as well as importance of the topic	Someone who smokes reveals more in that behavior than what might be revealed from answering attitudes about smoking (e.g., believing smoking is deleterious to your health)

Source: Adapted from Patricia Labaw, *Advanced Questionnaire Design* (Cambridge, MA: Abt Books, 1980).

data. In fact, answers to well-worded, relevant questions may lack meaning for several reasons:[2]

1. Respondents may not respond truthfully to the question, either to protect their ignorance or true feelings.
2. The questions were understandable, but failed to allow respondents to reveal how they really thought, felt, or behaved because of inadequate response options.
3. Respondents might answer without really being in touch with their own thoughts or emotions (this is a consciousness problem).
4. Respondents provide meaningful answers but they only provide a piece of the total picture. Other questions that could have completed the picture were not asked.
5. Respondents might answer the questions honestly, but the answers were based on incomplete or faulty knowledge. More knowledge might have changed the answers.
6. Researchers might impute meaningfulness to the answers when, in fact, the issues have no importance or salience to the respondents. They answered only because we

asked, and really do not make their decisions by thinking about the issue. It is vitally important to us but not at all important to them.

GOALS OF A QUESTIONNAIRE

Researchers therefore should take great care in designing a data-collection instrument that it is perceived in the gestalt sense—more than just a well-ordered series of questions resulting from our research objectives. A good questionnaire should accomplish the goals below:

Contextualize the Information Collected

This is what we mean by collecting meaningful information, as outlined in Table 8.1. The researcher should include any questions that will aid in the interpretation of those questions that are directly related to the research objectives. In other words, include questions such as those indicated in Table 8.1 and others, which can be used by the decision maker in the decision-making process, even if those additional questions are not directly related to the research objectives. A questionnaire is more than merely a conversion of research objectives into questionnaire questions.

Express the Study Objectives in Question Form

The questionnaire must capture the essence of the study objectives and ask questions that will provide the information needed to answer the various research questions. Quite often, a set of study objectives are adapted to an existing questionnaire that has been effective in the past. Care must be taken that one does not compromise the achievement of the current research study's objectives by trying to force a previous study's questionnaire questions into use in an attempt to economize time and effort. Each project with its unique set of study objectives should have a custom-made questionnaire designed especially for that project. The design of the questionnaire is the wrong place to try to economize during the research process. Judicious selection of questions from previous studies is appropriate in some cases, however.

Measure the Attitude, Behavior, Intentions, Attributes, or Other Characteristics of the Respondent

The questions must be specific and reported in a form that will allow for comparisons to be made and results to be analyzed. The responses to the questions must provide the information that is necessary to answer the research questions and in a format that can be subjected to the appropriate analytical technique (techniques of analysis will be discussed in Chapters 11 and 12).

Create Harmony and Rapport with the Respondent

A well-designed questionnaire targeted at the correct population sample should provide an enjoyable experience for the respondent. The frame of reference of the respondent must be considered in the design, wording, and sequencing of a questionnaire. Occupational jargon, cultural background, educational level, and regional differences can alter the effectiveness of a questionnaire if they are not taken into consideration. Not only should the questionnaire appeal to the respondent, it should be designed so the respondent can easily understand it, be able to answer it, and be made willing to answer it.

Provide Just the Right Amount of Information: No More, No Less

This appears to be a trite statement, but it has much truth to it. There are often honest differences of opinion on just how much information is needed to answer a set of research questions. However, in designing a questionnaire the two basic mistakes are leaving an important question unasked, which makes the survey incomplete, and asking too many irrelevant questions, which makes the survey too long and unwieldy. A researcher must learn to economize in asking questions to avoid respondent burnout, which leads to early terminations and incomplete and inaccurate information. However, care must be taken in the design process to be sure the proper quantity of information is gathered to accomplish the research objectives.

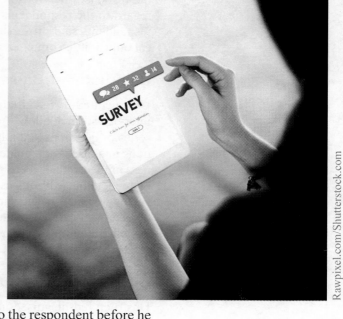

Rawpixel.com/Shutterstock.com

CLASSIFICATION OF QUESTIONS

Questions can be classified in terms of their degree of *structure* and *disguise*. By structure we mean the degree to which the question and the responses are standardized at some point in the data-collection process. When a questionnaire is classified according to disguise, it depends on how evident the purpose of the question or questionnaire is. An undisguised questionnaire is one in which the purpose of the research is obvious to the respondent because of the questions asked. A disguised questionnaire obscures the purpose of the research and tries to indirectly get at a respondent's point of view. Of course the sponsor of the research may or may not be revealed to the respondent before he or she answers the questions, but this is not what is meant by "disguise."

Based on the classification of questions according to structure and disguise, the following general types emerge.

Structured-Undisguised Questions

Structured-undisguised questions are the most commonly used in research today. Every respondent is posed the same questions in the same sequence, with the same opportunity of response. In most cases the purpose of the research is clearly stated in an introductory statement or is obvious from the questions asked. This type of instrument has the advantages of simplicity in administration, tabulation, and analysis; standardized data collection; objectivity; and reliability. The disadvantages include lack of flexibility in changing questions on the fly.

Structured-Disguised Questions

Structured-disguised questions are probably the least-used questions in business research. They maintain the advantages of structuring while attempting to add the advantage of disguise in eliminating possible bias from the respondent's knowledge of the purpose of the survey. The main advantages of this type of questionnaire are ease of administration, coding, and tabulating. An additional advantage is to gain insight on a sensitive issue without alerting the respondent. The problem with this type of research is the difficulties encountered in interpreting the respondent's answer. An example of a structured-disguised question would be:

Which of the following types of people would eat a lot and which would eat a little hot cereal?

	Eat a lot	Eat a little
Professional athletes	_____	_____
Wall Street bankers	_____	_____
Farmers	_____	_____
College teachers	_____	_____

The structure is obvious. The disguise is related to the purpose of the questions, which is to use the responses to determine the image people have of hot cereal. It is easy to tabulate the responses but considerably more difficult to interpret what the responses mean with regard to the respondents' image of the product. (What does it mean that 23 percent of respondents said professional athletes eat a lot of hot cereal, while 18 percent said they eat only a little compared to 31 percent and 22 percent, respectively, for college teachers?)

Unstructured-Undisguised Questions

Unstructured-undisguised questions are appropriate for in-depth interviews and focus group interviews. They allow the interviewer or moderator to begin with a general question or series of questions and allow the discussion to develop following a general series of questions in a discussion guide. Because of the nature of these types of questions, the effectiveness of the depth or focus group interview depends largely upon the skills of the interviewer or moderator. Advantages of this method are that more in-depth and accurate responses can be obtained, particularly for complex and sensitive issues, and greater cooperation and involvement can be obtained from the respondent. The unstructured-undisguised interview is well-suited for exploratory research, gaining background, and generating and clarifying research questions.

Unstructured-Disguised Questions

Unstructured-disguised questions are often used in motivation research to determine the whys of an individual's behavior. Projective methods are often used to get at the subtle issues that are not easily explored by direct questioning. Word association, storytelling, and sentence completion are methods that can be used to try to gain information about a subject without revealing the actual purpose of the research (see Chapter 5).

Descriptive-research questionnaires largely consist of structured-undisguised questions. They are highly structured data-gathering instruments compared to the less structured instruments used in focus groups or in-depth interview guides. In the descriptive-research questionnaire each respondent hears (or sees) the same question and has the same response options. This is obviously true with questions such as:

Would you say you eat away from home more often, less often, or about the same as you did three years ago?

More _____   Less _____   Same _____

Here, both the question and the response categories are highly structured. Open-ended questions are structured but the response is not, at least at the point of gathering the data. An example of an open-ended question:

[If said "less"]

Why do you eat away from home less often than you did three years ago?

_____

_____

The respondent could give any explanation to the interviewer or write in any response if the respondent were completing the questionnaire alone. The responses become structured when the researcher develops categories of the answers based on the type and frequency of the responses (for example, the number of times the researcher sees an answer such as "I work at home now whereas I used to eat lunch out every day at work" or "Our household income has decreased and we cannot afford to eat out as often"). The researcher might establish a number of different categories of responses after considering all the responses and then tabulate the responses for all completed questionnaires by category. Thus, what appears to be an unstructured question is in fact structured as a question before asked, and as an answer after it has been asked (that is, open-ended questions are still structured-undisguised).

Another way of collecting information is when the respondent hears what appears to be the same open-ended question in a phone or personal interview, but the interviewer categorizes the response into predetermined categories at the time the question is asked, such as:

[If "less often" indicated in previous question asked]

Why do you eat away from home less often than you did three years ago? [CHECK ALL THAT APPLY]

___ Economics/less money/lower income

___ Change in household members/circumstance

___ Changed jobs, etc.

___ Other [WRITE IN VERBATIM]

_____

_____

Instructions to the interviewer are in brackets and upper case or capital letters. In this example the interviewer exercises the judgment in categorizing the response (the respondent hears only the questions, the responses are not read). Response categories may have been established based on exploratory research or previous descriptive studies. If a response does not fit any of the given categories, the interviewer is to record the verbatim response, allowing the researcher to later establish new categories to capture the unanticipated responses. The researcher must balance the ease of tabulating and lower expense of having structured responses with the flexibility and richness of the more expensive open-ended responses that must later be structured.

DESIGNING A QUESTIONNAIRE

There is no single generally accepted method for designing a questionnaire. Various research texts have suggested procedures ranging from four to fourteen sequential steps. Questionnaire design, no matter how formalized, still requires a measure of science and a measure of art with a good dose of humility mixed in. In designing a questionnaire, presumption must be set aside. Although for simplicity of format the sequence for developing a questionnaire is given on a step-by-step basis, rarely is a questionnaire constructed in such a routine way. Quite often it is necessary to skip from one step to another and to loop back through a previous series of steps.

The following steps represent a sequential procedure that needs to be considered for the development of an effective survey instrument.

- *Step 1:* Determine the specific information needed to achieve the research objectives.
- *Step 2:* Identify the sources of the required information.
- *Step 3:* Choose the method of administration that suits the information required and the sources of information.
- *Step 4:* Determine the types of questions to be used and form of response.
- *Step 5:* Develop the specific questions to be asked.
- *Step 6:* Determine the sequence of the questions and the length of the questionnaire.
- *Step 7:* Predetermine coding.
- *Step 8:* Pretest the questionnaire.
- *Step 9:* Review and revise the questionnaire.

Remember that a questionnaire is a measurement device, and all the procedures discussed in Chapter 6 on how to develop more scientific measures apply here as well (see Figure 6.2). A brief discussion of each of the questionnaire development steps follows.

Determine the Specific Information Needed

The initial step to be taken in the design of a questionnaire is to determine the specific information needed to achieve the research objectives—answer the research questions and test the hypotheses. Or, another way of thinking of this step is that you are specifying the domain of the constructs of interest and determining the constructs' attributes (Chapter 6). This task can be made much easier if the earlier phases of the research process have been precisely accomplished. Clear study objectives facilitate this important decision. One of the most common and costly errors of research is the omission of an important question on the data-gathering instrument. Once the questionnaire is fielded, it is too late to go back for additional information without significant delay and additional cost.

The researcher must determine all of the information required before the questionnaire is developed. Sometimes the articulation of research objectives into specific questions by setting up dummy tables to be used when analyzing the results will trigger a new idea or research question that should be included in the survey. Every effort needs to be marshaled at this point of the design process to ensure relevant results for the analysis phase of the research process. In some cases it is advisable to conduct exploratory research to ensure that all of the relevant variables are identified. Focus groups, reviews of secondary sources of information, and some selected personal interviews are good ways of making sure that the pertinent variables are identified. Also, contextualizing information such as is listed in Table 8.1 should be determined.

Identify the Sources

Step two involves the important aspect of identifying the sources of the information requirements determined in step one. Sample selection will be discussed in more detail in Chapter 9; however, the characteristics of the sample frame are extremely important in designing the data-gathering instrument. The sophistication, intelligence, frame of reference, location, ethnic background, and other characteristics of the potential respondents are vital to determining the type of questionnaire, the wording of questions, the means of administration, as well as other aspects of the questionnaire. Consider, for example, the difference in the design of a questionnaire if the questions are asked of ten-year-old children or twenty-year-old college students.

Choose the Method of Administration

Step three involves utilizing the results of steps one and two to decide whether the Internet, or a personal interview, telephone survey, or mail questionnaire is most acceptable. Issues such as whether a stimulus is required, the length of the questionnaire, the complexity of the questions, and the nature of the issue being researched must be considered in choosing which type of survey is best. These decisions should be made with respect to the information required and the nature of the sources of the information. Other considerations that affect this decision are the cost and time constraints placed on the research project (see Chapter 7).

Determine the Types of Questions

Step four involves choosing the types of questions to be used in the questionnaire. To accomplish this the researcher must look both backward and forward. The researcher looks back to review the information required and the nature of the respondents. This can dictate various decisions concerning the types of questions selected. The researcher must also look forward to the analysis stage of the research process to ensure that the right form of data is obtained to accommodate the proper analytical techniques.

There are four basic types of questions that might be used in a questionnaire: (a) open-ended, (b) dichotomous, (c) multichotomous, and (d) scales. Most questionnaires have more than one type of question.

Open-Ended Questions

Open-ended questions such as "What did you like about the product?" provide an unlimited range of replies the respondent can make. The major advantages and uses of this type question are that they can be used when the possible replies are unknown, when verbatim responses are desired, and when gaining deep insight into attitudes on sensitive issues is needed. Open-ended questions are also useful to break the ice with the respondent and provide background information for more detailed questions. As discussed earlier, these questions are good for providing respondents with maximum flexibility in answering questions regarding motivations (why they behave as they do), or in explaining attitudes, behaviors, or intentions in greater depth. Their responses can be categorized by the researcher after the questionnaire has been completed, but the extra time for collecting and categorizing responses may add to the expense of the study (thousands of dollars for each open-ended question).

Dichotomous Questions

Dichotomous questions give two choices: either yes or no, or a choice of two opposite alternatives. They are preferred for starting interviews, are easy to tabulate, and can be used as a lead-in for more specific questions to a particular group. A weakness of dichotomous questions is that they can force a choice where none exists or lead to bias (such as the classic "Do you still cheat on your taxes?"___ Yes ___ No). Another weakness is that few questions can be framed in terms of a dichotomy, particularly more complex questions.

Multichotomous Questions

Multichotomous questions provide several alternatives to respondents. In some cases they may be asked to select only one from a list or asked to select as many as are applicable. The advantages of the multichotomous question are: ease of administration, ease of tabulation, and flexibility for factual as well as attitudinal responses. Some disadvantages exist in the length of the list of alternative responses, the fact that response alternatives may not be mutually exclusive, or that reading the list may lead the respondent to a particular response.

Scales

Although a scale can be considered a multichotomous question, it deserves separate consideration. (Scaling was discussed and examples provided in Chapter 6.) The benefit of a scale is that it permits the objective measurement of attitudes and feelings. This allows for the identification of segments who are more favorably inclined toward a product, service, or issue. Scaling is somewhat subject to various frames of reference differences and to the halo effect. Some debate exists concerning whether scales should be balanced or unbalanced. Balanced scales have the same number of responses on the positive side of the scale as on the negative side of the scale. Unbalanced scales have more possible responses on one side of the scale than the other, usually the positive side. Some debate also exists over whether to have a neutral response. Those who feel there should be a neutral option believe so because they think that this is a legitimate response category and for the sake of accuracy the respondent should have that option. People against having a neutral response category argue that most individuals are unlikely to be authentically neutral on an issue. They consider the neutral as an easy way out or a polite negative. Consequently, they feel that it is much better to frame the issue so that the respondent is induced to indicate a preference, however slight.

The "don't know" or "no opinion" response should always be available to respondents. An honest expression of a lack of awareness, experience, or thought given to an issue should be allowed so that these responses are not lumped together with those people who have considered the issue and find their position is the neutral point on the scale.

Earlier we mentioned that the researcher must look ahead to the analysis stage of the research process when determining the types of questions in order to ensure that the right levels of data are obtained to accommodate the planned analytical techniques. By this we mean that the researcher who plans to use specific analytical techniques (such as multiple regression, multidimensional scaling, conjoint analysis, and analysis of variance) to test hypotheses or determine the relationship between variables of interest (such as between sales volume and various attributes of the target market) must have collected data in the form required by the analytical technique. In other words, one cannot just use any data as an input to these techniques. They require raw data in very specific forms before they can be run, just as a production process requires raw material to be in a very specific form to be able to produce a product. It must be determined how to analyze the data even before questions are written that will generate the data. In the interest of simplifying things somewhat, we will confine our questionnaire design suggestions to address analytical procedures no more complicated than cross-tabulation. As will be seen in Chapter 11, that technique is the most widely used and useful approach to getting managerial answers to the research objectives.

Develop the Specific Questions

Step five of the process of constructing a questionnaire is to actually write the specific questions that will be asked (i.e., the operational definitions of our constructs' attributes discussed in Chapter 6). The previous steps regarding the information required and the choices made relative to the types of questionnaire and questions will, to a large extent, control the content of the questions. The wording should be understandable and as explicit as possible. Questions should be worded in ways that avoid leading, pressuring, or embarrassing the respondent. The questions should avoid ambiguous words. Six basic rules for wording questions are:

1. Keep the questions short, simple, and to the point. Reasons for keeping the questions as brief as possible are that longer questions make the response task more difficult, are more subject to error on the part of both interviewers and respondents, cause a loss of focus, and are less likely to be clear. One question should not ask more than one thing at a time.
2. Avoid identifying the sponsor of the survey. In some cases, such as customer satisfaction surveys, the researcher may want to identify the sponsor of the survey. In most cases, however, it is best to not identify the sponsor so more objective responses may be gathered.
3. Keep the questions as neutral as possible. Unless a question can be worded objectively, it should not be asked. Nonobjective questions tend to be leading because they suggest an answer.
4. Do not ask unnecessary questions. Always ask yourself, "Is this question necessary?" Each question should relate or add meaning to a specific research objective. If the question falls in the "nice to know but not necessary" category, leave it out.
5. Avoid asking questions the respondent either cannot answer or will not answer. Since respondents will answer most questions, it is important to determine if a respondent can be expected to know the information desired. On other occasions, respondents will have the information required but may not be willing to divulge it. If a question appears to be sensitive it may be best to leave it out. If it is crucial to the research objective, then it is best to ask the sensitive question later in the survey after a degree of trust has been established with the respondent.
6. Avoid asking leading or overly personal questions. Words or phrases that show bias are emotionally charged and will lead to inaccurate results. When sensitive questions must be asked, they should be asked after a warm-up period or hidden within a series of less personal questions.

Researchers should refer to some of the standard texts on how to word questions.[3]

Determine Question Sequence and Length of the Questionnaire

Step six can be extremely important in the completion rate of the survey. Excessive length may deter some respondents from completing the survey. This step can be equally important to the quality of the results acquired. The sequence of the questions should follow a logical pattern so it flows smoothly and effortlessly from one section to another. Another important consideration is to ensure that questions building on previous questions are placed properly in the questionnaire. Generally, questions will flow from the general to the specific. This warms up the respondents and lets them reflect appropriately before being asked specific questions that require good recall and some degree of detail. Skip patterns for branching questions need to be carefully designed. Quite often, a respondent must be directed to a specific location in the questionnaire based on a previous question such as, "Have you baked brownies in the past three months?" "Yes" respondents go on to answer specific questions about the baking occasion while "No" respondents skip to a different part of the survey. Personal, telephone, and Internet surveys lend themselves more to branching than do mail questionnaires.

Most questionnaires have three basic sections: (a) introduction, (b) body, and (c) classification section.

Introduction

The introduction tells the respondent who the researcher is, why she is requesting the respondent's information, and explains what is expected of the respondent. The introduction should explain the purpose of the questionnaire and enlist the cooperation of the respondent. In the case of a mail survey this may take place in an attached cover letter. On the phone this is accomplished with a positive tone without sounding like a polished sales pitch. Most people want to express their opinion as long as they know it is not a sales gimmick. The introduction should promise to keep the respondent's identity anonymous and his information confidential. Often the introduction will qualify the respondent in a special way to make sure that the interviewer is talking only to the right respondents. Qualification questions may include brand usage, and gender categories, security issues such as whether the respondent or any member of the household works for a competitor of the client, an advertising agency or a business research company.

Body or Content

The body or main content of the questionnaire provides basic information required by the research objectives. This is usually the most substantial portion of the questionnaire. If the respondent has not been qualified in the introduction, the first question of this section should identify the proper respondents and have instructions to end the survey for all others. This section should begin with easy, direct questions. Place questions that are personal or reflect a sensitive issue well toward the end of the body. Once respondents have become interested in the survey, they are more likely to respond to personal or sensitive issues.

Classification Section

The final section is designed to obtain cross-classification information such as sex, income, educational level, occupation, marital status, and age. These demographic data allow for comparisons among different types of respondents. Certain market segments may emerge through the use of this cross-classification data. Many of these questions address the situational or environmental questions described in Table 8.1.

Predetermine Coding

Questionnaires should be precoded so that any difficulties encountered in entering data into computer tabulation and analysis programs can be solved before the data are gathered. Once the questionnaires are completed and returned, the responses can be quickly entered into the database and results generated.

Pretest the Questionnaire

The eighth step is an essential step that should not be ignored. Following the maxim, "the proof is in the pudding," a questionnaire should be pretested before it is administered. A questionnaire may be too long, ambiguous, incomplete, unclear, or biased in some way. Not only will a thorough pretest help overcome these problems, but it will help refine any procedural problems a questionnaire might have. Some of the procedural problems might be improper skip patterns and misunderstanding the interviewer. A pretest will evaluate and fine-tune the questionnaire, estimate the time required for completion of the interview, and allow for setup of coding refinements for tabulations. The pretest should be administered under actual field conditions to get an accurate response. If significant changes result from an original pretest, it is advisable to conduct a second pretest after appropriate revisions have been made. A relatively small number of interviews is sufficient to pretest a normal questionnaire. Once they have been completed, all interviewers who participated should report their findings. They will be able to determine whether the questions work and be able to make suggestions for revision.

Review and Revise the Questionnaire

Based on the pretest and a thorough review of all the previous steps, the questionnaire should be revised. The bottom line for an effective data-gathering instrument is the accuracy of the data collected. Everything that can possibly be done in advance should be done to ensure the accuracy of the instrument.

The steps used to design an effective data-gathering instrument need to be viewed as a dynamic outline and not a sequential step-by-step process. Each step should be applied with a sharp eye on the research objectives and the data needs they require. The finished questionnaire is the result of rearticulating the study objectives into a set of effective questions for extracting the required information from the pertinent set of respondents.

Research Project Tip　　Developing a good questionnaire requires both creativity and highly structured, disciplined thought. You will go through numerous drafts of the questionnaire, so allow plenty of time for this part of the research. Pretest each version of the questionnaire. Refer to the books listed in this chapter's notes for more on questionnaire design. Refer to Appendix B for copies of sample questionnaires.

SUMMARY

Good questionnaire design is both an art and a science. The questionnaire is a gestalt—more than the sum of its parts—and must be designed in such a way that it generates meaningful data. Questions that provide answers to our research questions and test our hypotheses are necessary, but not totally sufficient to the construction of the questionnaire. We must also contextualize the information gained from our research objective-related questions if we are to gather meaningful data that leads to better decision making.

DISCUSSION QUESTIONS

1. Why will good questionnaires collect information beyond that identified in the Research Objectives (research questions and hypotheses)?
2. Discuss when you would typically use structured-undisguised questions and when you would use unstructured-disguised questions.
3. How are dummy tables (discussed in Chapter 5) used to help design the questionnaire?
4. What is meant by saying that a questionnaire is a "gestalt." In what ways does thinking of a questionnaire in this way affect the quality of information obtained from the use of a questionnaire?

ENDNOTES

1. Patricia Labaw, *Advanced Questionnaire Design* (Cambridge, MA: Abt Books, 1980), p. 12.
2. Ibid., p. 61.
3. See Stanley L. Payne, *The Art of Asking Questions* (Princeton, NJ: Princeton University Press, 1951); Seymour Sudman and Norman M. Bradburn, *Asking Questions: A Practical Guide to Questionnaire Design* (San Francisco: Josey-Bass, 1982); Jean M. Converse and Stanley Presser, *Survey Questions: Handcrafting the Standardized Questionnaire* (Beverly Hills, CA: Sage Publications, 1986). Another good source on designing and implementing a mail or Internet questionnaire is Don Dillman, *Mail and Internet Surveys* (New York: John Wiley and Sons, 2000).

Sampling Methods and Sample Size

Study Population

Sample

Target Population

Iamnee/Shutterstock.com

Learning Objectives

Upon completing this chapter, you should understand:

- The difference between a sample and a population or universe.
- Why sampling is preferred over a census.
- What is meant by sampling error, sample bias, and nonsampling error.
- The difference between probability and nonprobability sample designs.
- The steps involved in selecting a sample.
- How sample size is calculated.
- Factors influencing sample size.

ASDF_MEDIA/Shutterstock.com

In the course of most research projects, the time usually comes when estimates must be made about the characteristics or attitudes of a large group. The large group of interest is called the **population or universe**. For example, all of the registered Republicans in Jefferson County or all of the heads of households in Madison, Indiana, would each constitute a universe. Examples of a population are all people in the United States, all households in the United States, or all left-handed Scandinavians in Biloxi, Mississippi. Once the determination of the study universe is decided, several courses of action might be taken. First, the decision might be made to survey all of the entities in the universe. If all of the members of the selected universe are surveyed, this is called a census. With a census, direct, straightforward information concerning the specific universe parameters or characteristics is obtained. A second course of action would be to survey a sample of the universe (population). A sample is the term that refers to the group surveyed any time the survey is not administered to all members of the population or universe. The process of selecting a smaller group of people who basically have the same characteristics and preferences as the total group from which it is drawn is called **sampling**.

Population or universe often this universe is called a target population because of the importance of focusing on exactly who the study objects are and where they are located.

Sampling consists of obtaining information from a portion of a larger group or population.

WHAT IS SAMPLING?

Everyone has some experience with sampling. Anyone who has taken a bite of fruitcake and decided "never again!" or any child who, after a quick taste, has tried to hide her asparagus under the mashed potatoes has experienced sampling.

A famous quote from Cervantes states, "By a small sample we may judge the whole piece." Most of our everyday experiences with sampling are not scientific. However, our satisfaction with the results of our decisions, based on sampling, depends on how representative they are. In business research the goal is to assess target segments efficiently and effectively by designing and executing representative sample plans.

m.jrn/Shutterstock.com

Sampling consists of obtaining information from a portion of a larger group or population. While making estimates from a sample of a larger population has the advantages of lower cost, speed, and efficiency, it is not without risk. However, fortunately for researchers, this risk can be set very low by using probability-sampling methods and appropriate estimating techniques, and by taking a sufficiently large sample. Thanks to the European gamblers of several centuries ago who were eager to establish the odds on various games of chance, some of the best mathematical minds of the day were dedicated to the task. This effort led to the fascinating branch of mathematics known as probability theory. Development in this area laid the foundation for modern scientific sampling.

WHY SAMPLING?

There are many reasons for selecting a sampling technique over a census. In most cases the study objects of interest consist of a large universe. This fact alone gives rise to many advantages of sampling. The most significant advantages of sampling are:

1. *Cost savings*—Sampling a portion of the universe minimizes the field service costs associated with the survey.

2. *Time economy*—Information can be collected, processed, and analyzed much more quickly when a sample is utilized rather than a census. This saves additional monies and helps ensure that the information is not obsolete by the time it is available to answer the research question.

3. *More in-depth information*—The act of sampling affords the researcher greater opportunity to carry the investigation in more depth to a smaller number of select population members. This might be done via focus group, panel, personal, telephone, mail, or Internet surveys.

4. *Less total error*—A major problem in survey data collection comes about as the result of **nonsampling errors**. Greater overall accuracy can be gained by using a sample administered by a trained, supervised field-service group. In fact, the Bureau of the Census used sampling (as opposed to a census) in the year 2000 to improve the accuracy of their data.

5. *Greater* practicality—A census would not be practical when testing products from an assembly line, when the testing involves the destruction of the product, such as durability or safety tests or when the population is extremely large. The U.S. government has great difficulty accomplishing the U.S. Census every ten years.

6. *Greater security*—This is particularly true if a firm is researching a new product or concept. Sampling would be preferred to keep the product or concept a secret as long as possible.

> **Nonsampling error** is introduced into the research results from any source other than sampling.

SAMPLING ERROR, SAMPLE BIAS, AND NONSAMPLING ERROR

It may be somewhat disconcerting to the novice researcher to discover that even with all the attention to developing a valid and reliable data-collection instrument (Chapter 6), there are still numerous ways error can contaminate the research results. We can divide the sources of error into three categories: sampling error, sample bias, nonsampling error.

Sampling Error

Sampling error occurs when the sample does not perfectly represent the population under study. Sampling error occurs either from flaws in the design or execution of drawing the sample, causing it to not be representative of the population. Sampling error also occurs from chance, the random error that is introduced into any sample that is taken from a population. Design or execution errors can be minimized by careful attention to sample selection procedures. Random error cannot be avoided, but can be calculated and reduced by increasing the size of the sample. Convention restricts the definition of sampling error to that calculable error which occurs when a sample is drawn from a population. We will follow that convention by discussing the calculation of sampling error in this chapter and discussing other errors introduced in the sampling process (such as the selection of a sampling frame) and nonsampling error in Chapter 10.

> **Sampling error** occurs when the sample does not perfectly represent the population under study.

Sample Bias

Sample bias is introduced into a sample when the sample varies in some systematic way from the larger population. An example would be using the Internet to do a survey that is supposed to represent the entire population. Those who do not have Internet access may vary in a number of ways from those who do. The same is true for calling people at home during the day—they are different from people who are not at home; or asking only people who ride mass transit about their opinions of mass transit funding and believing you have measured the general public's opinions. Obviously, unlike sampling error, we cannot reduce sample bias by increasing **sample size**. In fact, increasing sample size merely increases the bias of the results. Controlling sample bias is achieved by careful attention to the sampling process—defining a population of interest, carefully selecting a representative sample from the population, and having success in obtaining responses from the sample group.

> **Sample bias** is introduced into a sample when the sample varies in some systematic way from the larger population.

> **Sample size** the size of the sample will be a function of the accuracy of the sample.

Nonsampling Error

Nonsampling error is introduced into the research results from any source other than sampling. It can occur in the data-gathering process whenever research workers either intentionally (by cheating or leading a respondent) or unintentionally (by belonging to an ethnic group, sex, or age category that elicits a particular response from respondents; misunderstanding a response; being tired and missing a response, and so on) introduce errors. Nonsampling error can also occur in the response process whenever respondents intentionally (by lying or not responding) or unintentionally (due to misunderstanding a question, guessing or answering with a response when "don't know" is more accurate, or becoming distracted or fatigued). Other errors can enter the research at the recording, coding, tabulating, editing, or analysis stages of data management.

SAMPLING DECISION MODEL

Sampling involves several specific decisions. This section briefly discusses the steps of a sampling decision model (see Figure 9.1).

FIGURE 9.1 Sampling Decision Model

Step 1: Define the Population or Universe

Once the researcher has decided to apply sampling techniques rather than a census, he or she must make several important sampling decisions. The first decision is to define the population or universe. Since sampling is designed to gather data from a specific population, it is extremely important that the universe be identified accurately. Often this universe is called a target population because of the importance of focusing on exactly who the study objects are and where they are located. Usually any effort expended to do a first-rate job of identifying the population pays generous dividends later in terms of accurate and representative data.

The definition of the population of interest should be related directly back to the original study objectives. Clues to identifying the target population can be found in the statement of research purpose. The research questions and research hypotheses generated from the research purpose should refine the definition of the target population. The sample must be reduced to the most appropriate common denominator. Do the research questions require selecting as sample elements individuals, households, purchase decision makers, or product users? Defining a population improperly can introduce bias into the study. Professional staff experience and insight are required to properly specify the target population.

The definition of a population consists of four parts: element, sampling unit, extent, and time. A slight change in any one of these parts can have a significant impact on the results of the research. For example, consider the impact on a research study whose purpose is to understand the eating habits of single adults when we make changes in two of the four parts.

Population Definition #1

Element: All unmarried persons 18 years of age or older who are shopping in
Sampling Unit: Supermarkets
Extent: In Los Angeles
Time: During the week of January 18–24.
Findings: "Single adults do not eat meals away from home as frequently as previously thought."

Population Definition #2

Element: All unmarried persons 18 years of age or older who are eating in
Sampling Unit: Restaurants
Extent: In Los Angeles
Time: During the week of January 18–24
Findings: "Single adults eat meals away from home more frequently than previously thought."

Obviously, great care must be given to the definition of the population from which a sample will be drawn. In fact, contrary to popular belief, the first step and steps 2 and 3 of the sampling *process* will have a greater impact on the findings of the research than determination of the sample *size*. Reviewing the management problem, research purpose (including decision alternatives and criteria, time frame and budget), and research objectives (questions and hypotheses) is an important prerequisite to establishing the four parts to the definition of the population.

Step 2: Determine the Sampling Frame

The second step in the sampling decision model is to determine the sampling frame. The **sampling frame** is a listing of the members of the target population that can be used to create and draw the sample. It might be such things as a directory, subscribers list, customer list, or membership roster. In some cases, the sampling frame consists of a process instead of a list (such as random-digit dialing, or asking every tenth person passing the interviewer in a mall to complete a questionnaire). The sampling frame might include everyone in the target population defined in step 1 without duplication.

Sampling frame a listing of the members of the target population that can be used to create and draw the sample.

This ideal situation seldom exists in actual experience, however. Sample lists or frames can be purchased from third-party companies specializing in sample preparation, or they can be put together by combining several sources. Because of the incompleteness of sampling frames, several discrepancies develop. In some cases, the sample frame is made up of the subjects of interest but is smaller than the total population. As a result, certain elements of the population are omitted from the survey. In other cases, the sample frame includes all members of the population but is larger than the population. Duplications or inappropriate units are included in the survey in these situations. A third situation occurs when some elements of the population fall in the sampling frame and some elements of the sampling frame are not of the population. In this case, both omissions and undesired inclusions occur.

For general population surveys, a traditional sample frame has been the telephone directory. In the United States, 95 percent of potential respondents can be reached by telephone. However, the telephone directory is an incomplete sample frame because in some metropolitan areas almost two-thirds of the telephone subscribers have unlisted numbers. Not only does this condition cause a large number of people to be left out of the directory, the omission of elements is not proportional across geographical areas. As a result, random digit designs, where phones are programmed to dial random digits, are often used to overcome the exclusion bias inherent in directory-based sampling designs. There are numerous sources of computer-generated, random-digit sample frames for commercial use.

The goal of developing an appropriate sample frame is to get a listing of elements of the target population that is as inclusive and proportionally representative as possible with a minimum of duplication. Survey Sampling, Inc. (SSI) provides computer software that allows researchers to order very specific sampling frames (for example, females aged 25–30, living in Indiana, with MBAs). SSI can then send this sampling frame to the researcher over the Internet.

Step 3: Select the Sampling Method

The third step in the sampling decision model is to select the sampling method. This decision logically follows the decisions to determine the target population and to define the sampling frame. The initial consideration in the selection of a sample is whether or not to employ a probability-sampling procedure or a nonprobability-sampling procedure.

Probability Sampling

Probability sampling samples where each element has a known chance to be included in the sample.

Probability samples are simply those samples where each element has a known chance to be included in the sample. "Known" in this case simply refers to the theoretical ability to calculate the likelihood of inclusion in the sample, rather than actually knowing with precision the probability of inclusion. With nonprobability samples there is no known way of estimating the probability of any given element being included in the sample. With probability sampling a random or a systematic, chance-based procedure is utilized to select the study elements. The researcher preselects the respondents in a mathematical way so that persons in the universe have an equal or known chance of being selected. From a statistical point of view, probability sampling is preferred because it allows a calculation of the *sampling error*. Probability-sampling procedures tend to be more objective and allow the use of statistical techniques.

Nonprobability sampling sampling techniques that do not involve the selection of sample elements by chance.

Nonprobability sampling introduces certain biases, from an operational perspective, but offers the advantage of being less expensive and quicker to implement. However, the fact that a sample is a nonprobability sample does not mean that the sample must be less *representative* than a probability sample. The problem is, with nonprobability samples we cannot compute the degree to which they are representative, and therefore they cannot be used to generate such desirable statistics as confidence intervals. (We cannot say such things as "We are 95 percent confident that 45 percent ± 2 percent of the respondents say they will definitely buy formulation A.").

The most commonly used probability samples are simple random samples, stratified samples, cluster samples, and systemic samples.

Simple random sample a technique that allows each element of the population an *equal* and *known* chance of being selected as part of the sample.

Simple Random Sample. A **simple random sample** is a technique that allows each element of the population an *equal* and *known* chance of being selected as part of the sample. The implementation is often accomplished by the use of a table of random numbers.

Computer and calculator random numbers can also be generated to assist in selecting random samples. A common analogy for a random sample is the traditional drawing of a sample from a fishbowl containing slips of paper with the names of the elements of the sampling frame.

Stratified Samples. When subgroups of the population are of special interest to the researcher, a stratified sample might serve a better purpose than a simple random sample. A **stratified sample** is characterized by the fact that the total population is (1) divided into mutually exclusive subgroups (strata) (different age or income groups and the like) and that (2) a simple random sample is then chosen from each subgroup. This is a modified type of random sample. The method of creating a stratified sample ensures that all important subgroups are represented in the sample. The stratified random-sampling technique is good for classifying consumers by various demographic factors. Stratified samples can be divided into proportionately stratified samples or into disproportionately stratified samples. A proportionately stratified sample allows for a breakdown where the number of items randomly selected in each subgroup is proportionate to their incidence in the total population. A disproportionately stratified sample is a sample where the allocation of sample elements is not established according to relative proportion. This can result in an equal number of elements per subgroup, or it can result in the greater sampling of the subgroups that have the greater potential for variability. This, however, requires prior knowledge of the characteristics of the population. Just as with a simple random sample, there can be no stratified sample if there is no available sampling frame of elements of the population that breaks down the population into the appropriate subgroups. Also, choosing a variable for stratification (such as age or income) means that you believe people *within* the stratum are similar along some dimensions of interest to the decision maker (such as attitudes or behaviors) that ultimately will influence business decisions, and different *between* strata (such as people in different income categories differ in some behavior of interest to managers).

Stratified sample characterized by the fact that the total population is (1) divided into mutually exclusive subgroups (strata) (different age or income groups and the like) and that (2) a simple random sample is then chosen from each subgroup.

Miilles Studio/Shutterstock.com

Some specific reasons for choosing to stratify a population sample include:

1. A desire to minimize variance and sampling error or to increase precision. If a population is segmented into strata that are internally homogeneous, overall variability might be reduced. The required sample size for a well-designed stratified sample will usually be smaller than for a well-designed unstratified sample.
2. A desire to estimate the parameters of each of the strata and have a readable sample size for each one.
3. A desire to keep the sample element selection process simple.

Cluster Samples. In some cases when stratified sampling is not possible or feasible, cluster sampling can be utilized. The first step in selecting a **cluster sample** is the same as in a stratified sample: The population is divided into mutually exclusive subgroups. However, the next step involves the selection of a random sample of subgroups rather than a random sample from each subgroup. Cluster sampling may not be as statistically efficient as a stratified sample, but it is usually more procedurally efficient in terms of cost and time. Cluster sampling is often associated with area sampling. In area sampling, each cluster is a different geographic area, census tract, or block.

Cluster sample the population is divided into mutually exclusive subgroups, and the next step involves the selection of a random sample of subgroups rather than a random sample from each subgroup.

Systematic Samples. A fourth technique of probability sampling is called systematic sampling. In this method of cluster sampling, every element has a known but not equal chance of being selected. Systematic sampling is an attempt to increase the efficiency of

Systematic sample every element has a known but not equal chance of being selected.

the sample at favorable costs. A **systematic sample** is initiated by randomly selecting a digit, *n,* and then selecting a sample element at every *n*th interval, depending on the size of the population and the sample size requirement. This method is often used when selecting samples from large directories. Some loss of statistical efficiency can occur with systematic samples, particularly if there are hidden periodic sequences that cause some systematic variances to occur at the intervals selected. A systematic sample may be more representative than a simple random sample depending on the clustering of objects within the sample frame. The ideal list will have elements with similar value on the key defining characteristics of the sample close together, and elements diverse in value in different locations of the list.

Nonprobability Samples

Nonprobability samples are defined as any sampling techniques that do not involve the selection of sample elements by chance. The most commonly utilized nonprobability sampling techniques are convenience sampling, judgment sampling, and quota sampling.

Convenience sample any process that quickly and easily selects sample elements.

Convenience Sample. The least expensive and least time-consuming of sampling techniques is generally considered to be **convenience sampling**, which is any process that quickly and easily selects sample elements. The sample element close at hand is chosen and surveyed in the application of this technique. Man-on-the-street interviews are examples of this type of sampling. The greatest problem with convenience sampling is the inability to know if the sample is representative of the target population. Consequently, one cannot generalize from the sample to the target population with a high degree of confidence.

Since the convenience sampling technique follows no predesignated method, the sampling error cannot be calculated, and specific precision and confidence level estimates cannot be made. Even with the drawbacks of convenience sampling, it is frequently used, particularly for exploratory research.

Judgment sample a subjective approach to sampling, the knowledge and experience of a professional researcher can create a very representative sample.

Judgment Sample. The representativeness of a **judgment sample** depends on the skill, insight, and experience of the one choosing the sample. Although a judgment sample is a subjective approach to sampling, the knowledge and experience of a professional researcher can create a very representative sample. This is particularly true in industrial studies where a knowledge of the industry dynamics and decision-making procedures is necessary in identifying the correct respondents. In the area of polling, expert opinion, judgment samples can be very effective. Even though judgment samples are more restrictive and generally more representative than convenience samples, they have the same weakness, not permitting direct generalization of conclusions derived to a target population. In the final analysis, representativeness of a judgment sample depends on the experience, skill, knowledge, and insight of the one choosing the sample. Focus group recruitment is an example of a judgment sampling process.

A particular kind of judgment sample is the "snowball sample," which relies on the researcher's ability to locate an initial group of respondents with the desired characteristics. Additional respondents are identified on a referral basis, relying on the initial set of respondents to identify other potential respondents.

Quota Sample. Quota sampling is the third type of nonprobability sampling. It is similar in some respects to stratified and cluster sampling. In quota sampling, the researcher divides the target population into a number of subgroups. Using his or her best judgment, the researcher then selects quotas for each subgroup. The quota method takes great pains to obtain a representative sample by dividing the population and assigning appropriate quotas based on prior knowledge and understanding of the characteristics of the population. Quite often the subgroups of the population are divided into categories such as age, sex, occupation, or other known characteristics. Usually quotas are assigned based on known proportions for these characteristics, such as provided by the U.S. Census. In this way, a quota sample can be drawn to represent the population based on the defining characteristics selected. An example could be to establish quotas based on age and sex proportions provided by the census and known product-usage patterns. While this would not ensure a representative sample, the researcher would know that the respondents come in the same proportion as the total population among product users and nonusers.

The difference between quota sampling and stratified sampling is that **quota samples** do not use random sampling from the categories, as we do in stratified sampling. Also, in stratified sampling we must select the strata based upon a correlation between the category and the respondent behavior of interest (such as expenditures on furniture vary by age of head of household). In quota sampling researcher judgment is used in establishing the categories and choosing the sample from the categories.

The problems with quota sampling are the same as for other nonprobability-sampling methods. The sampling error cannot be calculated, and projection to the total population is risky. A quota sample might be very representative of the quota-defining characteristics; however, there may be some other characteristic that is supremely important in defining the population that is not used to establish quotas. Consequently, this characteristic may be disproportionately represented in the final sample. It is impractical to impose too many cell categories on a quota sample. Despite some of its drawbacks, quota sampling is often used in business research projects.

Quota sample takes great pains to obtain a representative sample by dividing the population and assigning appropriate quotas based on prior knowledge and understanding of the characteristics of the population.

Probability Versus Nonprobability Sampling

The reader by now realizes that probability-sampling methods are the methods of choice for descriptive research and nonprobability methods for exploratory research. This fits our discussion in Chapter 5, when we said exploratory research is best described as flexible, while descriptive is best described as rigid. It also makes sense when we remember the goal of exploratory research is to generate ideas, insights, and better focus the problem—all of which are best done by using a nonrandom-respondent selection process, and choosing a smaller number of people than we would if our goal were to measure or describe a population in terms of frequencies and covariations, as we do in descriptive research. For example, if we are screening people for inclusion in in-depth interviews or for focus groups, we want to use a nonprobability (nonrandom) method of selection so we can talk to those people whose experience puts them in the best position to provide us with the insights and ideas we are looking for.

In contrast, when we do descriptive research we are ultimately measuring the frequency with which something occurs, or the extent to which two variables covary (for example, consumption rate varies with respondent age), which means we want to be able to report results using statistics ("We are 95 percent confident that the average of our heavy users age is 35.2 ± 3 years."). The only sampling method that allows us to report statistical results in this way is probability sampling, and hence, since we want to describe our population in this way when doing descriptive research, we want to use probability-sampling methods.

We previously mentioned that exploratory research sometimes uses surveys, as does descriptive research. But the results of an exploratory-research survey using nonprobability sampling cannot be reported the same way as descriptive-research results. Whereas the descriptive research/probability survey results of a sample of 200 respondents might be stated as: "We are 95 percent confident that the average age of our heavy users is 35.2 ± 3 years;" our exploratory/nonprobability survey results for a sample of 400 (sample size twice as large) could only be reported as: "Our heavy users are roughly in their mid-thirties."

Our nonprobability sample may be as representative as our probability sample, but because it was chosen using a nonprobability method we are not able to calculate the sampling error, and therefore will never know if it was as representative. But again, such a limitation is of no consequence if we are merely looking for ideas, insights, and generating hypotheses. It is of considerable consequence if we are testing hypotheses, trying to establish frequencies, and covariation.

Step 4: Determine Sample Size

The size of the sample will be a function of the accuracy of the sample. Two criteria are used in measuring accuracy: the margin of error and the level of confidence. The first is determined as the tolerated-error range (also known as sample precision) and the second is the probability that the sample will fall within that tolerated-error range. A margin of error of three percent, for example, means that out of all possible samples of a certain determined size of coin flips, 95 percent will differ from the actual population by no more than three percentage points.

Sample-size determination ultimately is a reflection of the value of the information sought. Scientific journals require that reported results must fall in the 95 to 99 percent confidence levels. When the risk involved in the decision alternatives is high, then 95 to 99 percent confidence levels will be required. However, a sampling of well-known television ratings is at the 66 percent confidence level. Even though the margin of error in these ratings is far greater than most scientific research, many business decisions are based on this result. Even low-budget studies, with low-risk decision alternatives that serve as a glimpse into the market environment, should usually not consider a confidence level of less than 80 to 90 percent. The 95 percent confidence level is suggested for most research. Sample sizes can be selected by using either statistical calculations or nonstatistical methods. Each of these will now be discussed.

Statistical Sampling Concepts

The Statistical Side of Sampling. The sample size for a probability sample depends on the standard error of the mean, the precision desired from the estimate, and the desired degree of confidence associated with the estimate. The standard error of the mean measures sampling errors that arise when estimating a population from a sample instead of including all of the essential information in the population. The size of the standard error is the function of the standard deviation of the population values and the size of the sample.

$$\sigma_{\bar{x}} = \frac{\sigma}{\sqrt{\eta}}$$

$\sigma_{\bar{x}}$ = standard error
σ = standard deviation
η = sample size

The precision is the size of the plus-or-minus interval around the population parameter under consideration, and the degree of confidence is the percentage level of certainty (probability) that the true mean is within the plus-or-minus interval around the mean. Precision and confidence are interrelated and, within a given size sample, increasing one may be done only at the expense of the other. In other words, the degree of confidence or the degree of precision can be increased, but not both.

The main factors that have a direct influence on the size of the sample are:

1. *The desired degree of confidence associated with the estimate.* In other words, how confident does the researcher want to be in the results of the survey? If the researcher wants 100-percent confidence, he or she must take a census. The more confident a researcher wants to be, the larger the sample should be. This confidence is usually expressed in terms of 90, 95, or 99 percent.
2. *The size of the error the researcher is willing to accept.* This width of the interval relates to the precision desired from the estimate. The greater the precision (the smaller the plus-or-minus fluctuation around the sample mean or proportion) the larger the sample requirement.

The basic formula for calculating sample size for variables (age, income, weight, height and the like) is derived from the formula for standard error:

$$\eta = \frac{\sigma^2}{\sigma_{\bar{x}}^2}$$

The unknowns in the formula above are $\sigma_{\bar{x}}$ (standard error), σ (standard deviation), and η (sample size). In order to calculate the sample size, the researcher must:

1. Select the appropriate level of confidence.
2. Determine the width of the plus-or-minus interval that is acceptable and calculate standard error.
3. Estimate the variability (standard deviation) of the population based on a pilot study or the previous experience of the researcher with the population.
4. Calculate sample size (solve for n).

For example, a researcher might choose the 95.5 percent confidence level as appropriate. Using the assumptions of the Central Limit Theorem (that the means of samples drawn will be normally distributed around the population means), the researcher will select a standard normal deviate from the following tables:

Level of Confidence	Z Value
68.3%	1.00
75.0	1.15
80.0	1.28
85.0	1.44
90.0	1.64
95.0	1.96
95.5	2.00
99.0	2.58
99.7	3.00

This allows the researcher to calculate the standard error ($\sigma_{\bar{x}}$). If, for example, the precision width of the interval is selected at 40, the sampling error on either side of the mean must be 20. At the 95.5 percent level of confidence, $Z = 2$ and the confidence interval equals: $\pm Z\sigma_{\bar{x}}$.

Then the standard error is equal to 10.

$$CL = \bar{\chi} \pm Z\sigma_{\bar{x}} \quad CL = \pm Z\sigma_{\bar{x}}$$

$Z = 2$ at 95.5% level
$2_x\sigma_{\bar{x}} = 20$

$\sigma_{\bar{x}} = 10$

CL = Confidence limits
CI = Confidence interval

Having calculated the standard error based on an appropriate level of confidence and desired interval width, we have two unknowns in the sample size formula left, namely sample size (η) and standard deviation (σ). The standard deviation of the sample must now be estimated. This can be done either by taking a small pilot sample and computing the standard deviation, or it can be estimated on the knowledge and experience the researcher has of the population. If you estimate the standard deviation as 200, the sample size can be calculated.

$$\sigma_{\bar{x}} = \frac{\sigma}{\sqrt{\eta}}$$

$$\eta = \frac{\sigma^2}{\sigma_{\bar{x}}^2}$$

$$\eta = \frac{(200)^2}{(10)_{\bar{x}}^2}$$

$$\eta = \frac{40,000}{100}$$

$$\eta = 400$$

The sample size required to give a standard error of 10 at a 95.5 percent level of confidence is computed to be 400. This assumes that assumptions concerning the variability of the population were correct.

Another way of viewing the calculation of sample size required for a given precision of a mean score is to use the following formula:

$$\eta = \frac{Z^2 \sigma^2}{h^2}$$

Z = value from normal distribution table for desired confidence level
σ^2 = standard deviation
h = sample size
h = desired precision ±

$$\eta = \frac{(2)^2 (200)^2}{(20)^2}$$

$$\eta = \frac{(4)(40,000)}{(400)}$$

$$\eta = \frac{160,000}{400}$$

$$\eta = 400$$

Tables in most statistical books are provided to allow us, at several given confidence levels, to select the exact sample, size given an estimated standard deviation and a desired width of interval.

Determining sample size for a question involving proportions (those who eat out/don't eat out, successes/failures, have access to Internet/don't have access) or attributes is very similar to the procedure followed for variables. The researcher must:

1. Select the appropriate level of confidence.
2. Determine the width of the plus-or-minus interval that is acceptable and calculate the standard error of the proportion $\sigma_{\bar{\rho}}$.
3. Estimate the population proportion based on a pilot study or previous experience of the researcher with the population.
4. Calculate the sample size (solve for n).

The basic formula for calculating sample size for proportions or attributes is derived from the formula for standard error of the proportion:

$$\sigma\bar{p}=\sqrt{\frac{pq}{\eta}}$$

$\sigma\bar{p}$ = standard error of proportion
p = percent of successes
q = percent of nonsuccess (1-p)

Assume that management has specified that there be a 95.5 percent confidence level and that the error in estimating the population not be greater than ± 5 percent (p ± 0.05). In other words, the width of the interval is 10 percent. A pilot study has shown that 40 percent of the population eats out over four times a week.

$$CI=\pm Z\,\sigma_{\bar{p}}\quad \sigma_{\bar{p}}=\frac{0.05}{2}$$

$$2\sigma_{\bar{p}}=\frac{\pm CI}{2}\quad \sigma_{\bar{p}}=0.025$$

Substituting in:

$$\sigma_{\bar{p}}=\sqrt{\frac{pq}{\eta}}\quad \eta=\frac{(.40)(.60)}{(.025)^2}$$

$$\eta=\frac{p\cdot q}{\sigma_{\bar{p}}^{-2}}\quad \eta=\frac{.24}{.000625}\quad \eta=384$$

Another way to view calculating the sample size required for a given precision of a proportion score is to use the following formula:

$$\eta=\frac{Z^2(p\cdot q)}{h^2}$$

Z = value from normal distribution table for desired confidence level
p = obtained proportion
$q=1-p$
h = desired precision ±

Using the same information as used in the previous example, the same result is obtained:

$$\eta=\frac{(2)^2(.40\times.60)}{(.05)^2}$$

$$\eta=\frac{(.4)(.24)}{.0025}$$

$$\eta=\frac{.96}{.0025}$$

$$\eta=384$$

The sample size required to give a 95.5 percent level of confidence that the sample proportion is within ± 5 percent of the population proportion is .384.

Tables in statistics books provide a simple method for selecting sample size at several alternative confidence levels, given an estimated value of the proportion (p) and a desired confidence interval.

Since sample size is predicated on a specific attribute, variable, proportion, or parameter, a study with multiple objectives will require different sample sizes for the various objectives. Rarely is a study designed to determine a single variable or proportion. Consequently, to get the desired precision at the desired level of confidence for all variables, the larger sample size must be selected. In some cases, however, one single variable might require a sample size significantly larger than any other variable. In this case, it is wise to concentrate on the most critical variables and choose a sample size large enough to estimate them with the required precision and confidence level desired by the researchers or clients.

Nonstatistical Determination of Sample Size. While the formulas previously listed are used to calculate sample size, frequently in business research studies one of the following nonstatistical approaches is used to establish the sample size for a research study.1 Recall that our determination of sample size is a separate step in the sampling process from determination of sampling method (probability versus nonprobability). Therefore, using one of these nonstatistical approaches to establish the size of the sample does not change the way in which we would report our findings from the sampled respondents; it merely affects the ultimate selection of sample size (and hence, with a probability sample, it affects the sampling error). So, using one of these nonstatistical approaches to setting sample size might change a reported result using a probability sampling method from

> "We are 95 percent confident that the average age of our heavy consumers is 35.2 ± 3 years." (Sample of 200)
> to
> "We are 95 percent confident that the average age of our heavy consumers is 35.7 ± 1.8 years." (Sample of 350)

but using the nonstatistical approach does not alter our ability to report statistical results as shown here.

Use Previous Sample Sizes. Companies that do repeated studies over time to gather similar information to compare data and determine trends might automatically use the same sample size every time the research is conducted. Also, if the same type of study is done (such as concept tests of new product ideas), companies will often use the same sample size. Researchers are cautioned against using the same sample size for all research studies—it is possible to be spending too much or too little money compared to the value of the information.

Use "Typical" Sample Sizes. Common wisdom has led to an accepted sample size based upon the number of subgroups that might be used to analyze the data (see Table 9.1). Another typical sample size determination based on the number of subgroups is that

TABLE 9.1 Typical Sample Sizes for Consumer and Institutional Population Studies

Number of Subgroups	Consumer or Households		Institutions	
	National	Regional or Special	National	Regional or Special
0–4	850–1,500	200–500	50–500	50–200
10–May	1,500–2,500	500–1,000	350–1,000+	150–500
Over 10	2,500+	1,000+	1,000+	500+

Source: Adapted from Seymour Sudman, *Applied Sampling,* Academic Press, New York, 1976.

major subgroups should have 100 or more respondents (for example, males and females = 2 major subgroups), and less important subgroups should have approximately 50 respondents (for example, males under 35 years old, 35–50 years old, 51+ years old, plus females under 35 years old, 35–50 years old, 51+ years old = 6 subgroups). Using this rule of thumb, the analysis of males versus females would mean a minimum sample size of 200 (that is, 2 × 100), while males versus females by age categories would mean a minimum sample size of 300 (that is, 50 × 6).

Population

Sample

Use a "Magic Number." Decision makers unaccustomed to reviewing research findings before making decisions may be skeptical of research findings that reveal unexpected results or that go against conventional wisdom. In such cases, researchers should say something like, "It is possible this research will produce findings that may be unexpected. What size sample would you need in order to see the results as legitimate representations of the market and not a fluke?" Sample sizes should then exceed the number given by the decision makers who will review findings in making their decisions.

Use Resource Simulations. Perhaps the most common method of selecting a sample size is "whatever the budget will allow." An example of determining sample size using this method:

Total amount allocated for research	$30,000
Minus fixed costs (research company fees, data analysis costs, overhead, etc.)	−16,000
Amount available for variable costs	$14,000
Divide by cost of completed interview	÷ $15
Equals number of interviews that can be conducted within the budget (i.e., the sample size)	933

Such an approach to determining sample size has appeal because it is expressed in a language managers understand—dollars and cents. Of course, a sample size determined in this way should be checked against the other research information needs to see if the size is satisfactory and efficient.

Ask an Expert. A final nonstatistical approach is to ask an expert in research for advice on appropriate sample size. The expert will probably use one of the statistical or nonstatistical approaches described here, but at least you will feel better about determining the sample size.

Step 5: Select the Sample

Once the target population has been identified, an appropriate sampling frame determined or compiled, all sampling procedures selected, and a sample size determined, it is time for the final step in the sampling-decision mode. The sampling process should be executed in an efficient and professional way. Whether a sample is a probability sample or a nonprobability sample, the important aspect is to obtain as much representative information and eliminate as much sampling and nonsampling error as possible. Generally speaking, the sample size should be increased whenever the population exhibits high variability or whenever high levels of confidence and precision are required.

WHAT IS A SIGNIFICANT STATISTICALLY SIGNIFICANT DIFFERENCE?

Substantive significance refers to the strength of a relationship or the magnitude of a difference between two values.

Henry Clay once said, "Statistics are no substitute for judgment." Just because two values can be adjudicated as statistically different does not mean that they are substantively different, and the reverse is also true. **Substantive significance** refers to the strength of a relationship or the magnitude of a difference between two values. Does the difference imply real-world practicality? If a very large sample is used, very small differences may be concluded to be statistically different; however, they may not be different in any substantive way. On the other hand, the difference between two values in a research project may not test as being statistically significant at a given level of confidence, but if the difference holds up in the real world it could be substantively significant.

SUMMARY

Chapter 9 presents the important aspects of sampling. The nature of the research project determines the type of sample, the sample size, the sample frame, and the method necessary to correctly draw or select the sample.

In some projects, sampling consideration is a critical decision area because of the impact on costs and the need to draw inferences about the population from which the sample is drawn.

KEY TERMS

Cluster sample (p. 163)
Convenience sample (p. 164)
Judgment sample (p. 164)
Nonprobability sampling (p. 162)
Nonsampling error (p. 159)
Population or universe (p. 158)
Probability sampling (p. 162)
Quota sample (p. 165)
Sample bias (p. 159)

Sample size (p. 159)
Sampling (p. 158)
Sampling error (p. 159)
Sampling frame (p. 161)
Simple random sample (p. 162)
Stratified sample (p. 163)
Substantive significance (p. 172)
Systematic sample (p. 164)

DISCUSSION QUESTIONS

1. Discuss the thought process that a manager of home furniture would go through in deciding whether or not to use a stratified sample for research being done to select target markets and set positioning strategies.
2. Give an example of the definition of the population of the business students at your college.
3. Define sampling frame. What would be the sampling frame if the population of interest were the business

students who eat lunch in the school cafeteria at least once a week on average?
4. What considerations go into a decision whether to use probability or nonprobability sampling? How does selection of a sample size differ between probability and nonprobability sample (for example when do you use statistical calculations for determining sample size vs. nonstatistical methods)?

ENDNOTE

1. This section is based upon a discussion in Seymour Sudman and Edward Blair, *Marketing Research* (New York: McGraw-Hill, 1998), pp. 375–378. This book is an excellent reference for marketing research sampling issues.

Fielding the Data-Gathering Instrument

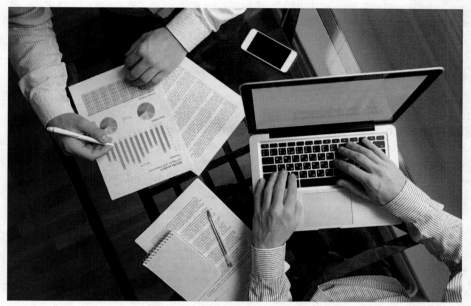

Ditty_about_summer/Shutterstock

Chapter Outline

Learning Objectives

Upon completing this chapter, you should understand:

- The importance of careful planning of the data-collection process.
- The different types of interviews and requirements of each type.
- The importance of identifying qualified respondents and probing.
- The errors of omission and commission of data collection.
- The sources of error in the research process and in data collection.

Roobcio/Shutterstock.com

Once the questionnaire has been completed, it is ready for the field. The field-operation phase of the research process is the occasion that the data-collection instrument is taken to the source of the information. The planning of the field work is closely related to the preparation of the questionnaire and the sample selection. All three of these aspects of data gathering must be well conceived, planned, and executed in order to achieve the objectives of a study. Error can occur in all three phases, and the field collection portion is no exception. The results of any excellently conceived questionnaire drawn from a scientifically selected representative sample can be nullified by errors in the fielding of the questionnaire. Consequently, the data-collection phase of the business research process is extremely important. A poorly executed data-collection effort can nullify the impact of a well-designed sampling scheme and data-collection instrument.

PLANNING

To minimize total error and to gather accurate information as efficiently as possible, the field service of a questionnaire should be well planned. Time, money, and personnel must all be budgeted appropriately. Time for the field portion of a research project is extremely important, since it must fit into the overall time frame of the entire research project. The field service portion should have a realistic completion date with a little leeway built in. This will allow for timely and accurate completion. Since the field work must be done before analysis can occur, good sequencing is necessary.

Budgets

Money must be appropriately budgeted for the field service effort. Cost must be assigned to all the component activities of the field-service phase. Cost estimates must be made for:

■ wages of interviewers, supervisors, and general office support
■ telephone charges
■ postage and shipping
■ production of questionnaire and other forms
■ supplies

Staffing

Personnel are the key to successful field-service operations. Care must be taken to have the best possible personnel to accomplish the research task. There is no substitute for well-trained, experienced interviewers. Consequently, the personnel must not only be selected and scheduled for a project, they must have been trained in the techniques of interviewing. Some of the basic rules of interviewing are discussed later in this chapter. Another important part of preparing the personnel for a specific study is to ensure they are thoroughly briefed on the specific aspects of the questionnaire that will be administered. The personnel must have a clear understanding of the data-gathering instrument and what information is desired.

GUIDELINES FOR INTERVIEWERS

The field-service operation should include the following responsibilities to be carried out by the interviewer:

1. Cover the sample frame in accordance with instructions to ensure representative data. The proper areas and persons must be contacted.

2. Follow study procedures and administer the questionnaire as written. Be familiar with the questionnaire before beginning.

3. Write down open-ended responses verbatim. Record all other responses according to instructions in the proper terms of measurement.

4. Probe, but do not lead. If a person does not understand the question, read it again, verbatim, perhaps more slowly or with more inflection.

5. Establish rapport with the interviewee. Be confident in what you are doing and assume people will talk to you. Most people love to have the opportunity to say what they think. Reflect enthusiasm in what you are doing, but do not lead the respondent.

6. Accomplish a field edit to ensure that the data are being collected in appropriate form.

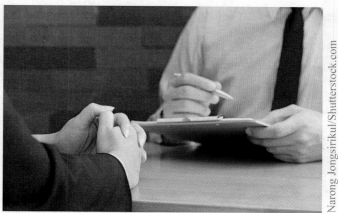
Narong Jongsirikul/Shutterstock.com

TYPES OF INTERVIEWS

Personal Interviews

The requirement of personal interviews creates special problems from the field-service point of view. As discussed in Chapter 7, personal interviews can be done through door-to-door, mall intercept, central location interviewing, or executive interviewing. Interviewers must be located, screened, hired, trained, briefed, and sent out in the proper geographic areas called for in the sampling plan in order to execute a door-to-door survey. A company will often hire outside field-service organizations to conduct this type of interviewing. If a company has subcontracted the entire project to an outside consultant firm, it would be wise to make sure that the research firm has its own in-house field-service personnel or at least has a good network of field services that it subcontracts to. Interviewers must also be well trained in the art of interviewing, but quite often they must also understand technical terms and jargon, particularly in industrial marketing research. This high degree of competence and preparation of interviewers, as well as the time and travel involved, make this door-to-door interviewing quite expensive.

Mall-intercept interviewing is a very popular way to execute personal interviews across a wide geographic area. This method of survey research intercepts shoppers in the public areas of shopping malls and either interviews them on the spot or executes a short screening survey; if respondents qualify, they are invited to a permanent interviewing facility in the mall to participate in a research study. Many different types of studies may be conducted in shopping malls: concept studies, product placement and home use tests, taste tests, clipboard studies (short, simple surveys), simulated controlled-store tests, and focus groups.

Another method of questionnaire administration that involves a personal interview approach is a recruited central location test (CLT). A CLT usually involves the need for a probabilistic sample plan or a category of respondent with a low incidence—they cannot be conveniently located by other approaches. In this type of study, respondents are screened ahead of time and invited to a location at a preset time for the actual interview. These locations may include an office, church, school, private facility, hotel, or even a mall research facility.

In-store intercepts are sometimes done to personally interview survey respondents. These studies are usually accomplished in a retail establishment central to the project's objectives (such as in a tire store for discussion of tire purchases).

Executive interviewing is the industrial equivalent of door-to-door interviewing. This type of interviewing requires very skilled interviewers who are well versed on the subject matter of the project. Consequently, this type of research is very expensive.

Telephone Interviews

Some of the same considerations involved with the development and management of a group of personal interviewers applies to telephone interviewers. However, greater control of a telephone interviewing staff can be maintained, particularly if the work is accomplished from a central telephone location. The entire interviewing effort can be monitored by a trained supervisor. On-the-spot questions can be answered and field editing can be accomplished to allow for quick correction of any problems with the data-gathering instrument. Computer-assisted interviewing systems have greatly automated telephone survey research and allow for better supervision, sample administration, and quality control. Currently, telephone interviewing is one of the most widely utilized types of survey communication, due to the time and financial advantages of the method. Callbacks can be made much more easily, and many people will talk on the phone rather than open their door to talk with a stranger. In addition, telephone interviewing can execute a study design that requires a probability sample that would be too costly to do in a door-to-door manner.

Mail Surveys

Mail surveys eliminate the problems of selecting, training, and supervising interviewers. They are convenient, efficient, and inexpensive. However, they create some of their own problems such as lack of response and coverage, inability to control the sample responding, time lags in response, inability to handle lengthy or complex material, and potential for misinterpretation of questions.[1]

The procedure for mail-survey administration is the same for questionnaire development, pretesting, finalization, and production. However, the mail survey eliminates the field-service worker. In place of the personal or telephone interview, there is a mailing or series of mailings of the questionnaire. Postcard reminders, incentives, tokens, and follow-up questionnaires can be sent at appropriate times to encourage return of questionnaires.

Internet Surveys

Internet surveys can take various forms and target different groups of respondents. One of the most common uses of Internet surveys is to gather data from existing customers or clients.

The Internet is increasingly being used as a means of conducting business research. **Internet surveys** can take various forms and target different groups of respondents. One of the most common uses of Internet surveys is to gather data from existing customers or clients. Most companies systematically gather email addresses from customers for their files and then use these email addresses to deliver Internet surveys they design themselves, or the email addresses are provided to a business research company that does Internet surveys. These surveys might cover topics such as purchase and service satisfaction, sales and service personnel evaluations, and future buying and shopping intentions. Typically, socioeconomic data (age, gender, income, education, geographic location, and occupation) is also collected to develop profiles of customers. This data can later be analyzed to determine differences in levels of satisfaction by customer type, gender, and location, and can be used to profile prospects for future business efforts.

A second commonly used type of Internet survey is one that is linked to the company's website. This could be a pop-up link or a permanent link on the website. This enables the company to gather information from website visitors who may or may not be customers of the company—basically anyone who visits the website and decides to complete the survey. Such surveys can determine how the visitor learned about the website and the company's products or services, and might also be used to collect additional data about the visitor such as email and mailing address, telephone numbers, and socioeconomic data. These types of surveys might also ask questions about

Georgejmclittle/Shutterstock.com

the website itself in terms of layout, finding needed information, and ease of using the website navigation tools.

A third type is an email-delivered message that asks the recipient to click on a link to take a survey. The email addresses can be purchased or they might be developed by the company by going to various websites to collect email addresses of those targeted in the survey. A typical email is shown below:

Dear IT Resource Manager,

Would you please help us? We are conducting a survey of university IT resource managers to get their input on monitoring employee and student uses of a university's IT resources. Your cooperation in clicking on the link below and completing the short Internet survey will be greatly appreciated. Your choice to participate is strictly voluntary and your responses are confidential and anonymous. Please understand that there is no correlation between survey responses and e-mail addresses. You can withdraw from the survey at any time. You should understand that by agreeing to take this survey, as with all surveys, you are accepting any potential risks associated with taking surveys. This survey has been approved by the University's Human Subject Research Review Committee. Your responses will remain confidential and combined with other respondents. You will not receive any promotional material or other emails in connection with this survey. The survey should take about five to seven minutes to complete.

If you would like a summary of the results, you can send us a separate email to request the summary.

To participate in the survey, simply click on the link below.

Survey

Thanks for your help,

Dr. Robert Stevens
John Massey School of Business
Southeastern Oklahoma State University
1405 N. 4th Ave., PMB 4176
Durant, OK 74701

Note that this survey was approved by the University's Institutional Review Board. This is usually necessary for surveys done by university personnel and is based on a university's human subjects research policies. Also note that the recipient is given an approximate time for completing the survey, which may encourage them to participate.

THE INTERVIEWING RELATIONSHIP

Cooperation

The first step in the interviewing process requires the interviewer to obtain the cooperation of the potential respondent to be interviewed and then to develop rapport with the respondent. If the interview is on an informal, conversational basis, the respondent will be at ease, and he or she will be less hesitant to voice real opinions. An interviewer need not lose control of the situation in order to be conversational and informal. A balance should be sought between the stiff, formal inquisition, in which questions are grimly read and answers methodically checked, and the situation where the interviewer is too friendly

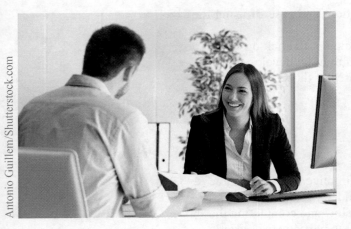

and is out of control. An interview in which twenty minutes is spent on the actual questions and twenty minutes more is devoted to irrelevancies and conversation is inefficient.

Rapport

The second step of the interviewer is to develop appropriate rapport with the respondent. Rapport is the term used to describe the personal relationship of confidence and understanding between the interviewer and the respondent; rapport provides the foundation for good interviewing. A prerequisite to good rapport is that the respondent knows where he or she stands in the interview. The interview is actually a new situation for most people and, when it begins, the respondent does not know what is expected or how far he or she can safely go in expressing opinions. Obviously, a respondent will react more favorably and openly in a situation he or she understands and accepts. The respondent should understand that the interview is confidential, that the interviewer is a friendly person ready to listen, that he or she can discuss the interview topics in detail, and that the information being provided is important. Throughout the interview, and especially in its early stages, the interviewer should make a careful effort to establish the tone of the interview in the respondent's mind. The respondent will then have a clear idea of where he or she stands, and what roles he or she and the interviewer have. The respondent should be made to understand that there are no right or wrong answers, that the interviewer is interested only in unbiased responses to the questions. Most people like to share their opinions. Good rapport, coupled with a well-designed data-gathering instrument, should serve the goal of making the interview a very positive experience for the respondent.

THE INTERVIEWING SITUATION

The Approach

The approach an interviewer takes in executing a survey is extremely important. In order for the sample to be representative, it is important that potential respondents are not lost or passed by because of something an interviewer might do or say to cause the potential respondent to refuse to participate or be excluded from the sample.

How To, How Not To

The method of approach will vary a great deal according to circumstances. As a general rule, the following scripted approach works well:

> Hello. I'm (name) from (agency). We're conducting a survey in this area on (subject), and I'd like your opinion.

Notice the introduction does not ask, "May I ask you some questions?"; "Are you busy?"; "Would you mind answering some questions?"; or "Could you spare a couple of minutes?" These are approaches that allow the respondent to say "No" easily and should be avoided.

Qualified Respondent

The interviewer should make sure that the respondent qualifies for the survey. If only certain types of people are specified for in the study, no compromise can be made.

In most surveys, only one member per household should be interviewed. Including more than one interview per household will bias the survey. The exception, of course, is when the study itself seeks to collect data from multiple members of the same household, such as hearing from both husband and wife regarding a purchase decision.

Time Factor

The respondent should not be misled about how long an interview might take. An accurate answer should be given if asked, or in long interviews it is helpful to state the time required before an interview begins. However, the interviewer need not call attention to time or the length of the interview unless the respondent asks or appears to be in a hurry. For most respondents, time passes very quickly while they are engaged in responding to a survey.

Declines, "Too Busy"

Should a respondent initially decline to be interviewed, the interviewer should not give up too easily. He or she should be patient, calm, and pleasantly conversational. Often a potential respondent who has initially refused will then agree to participate. If a person is completely opposed to being interviewed, the interviewer should go on to find another respondent.

In some cases, the selected respondent *is* actually too busy or is getting ready to go out so that an interview at that time is impossible. The interviewer should give a general introduction and try to stimulate the respondent's interest to the extent that he or she will be willing to be interviewed at a later time. The interviewer may need to suggest several alternative times before a convenient time for the interview can be agreed upon. If the survey is being done by telephone, an excellent technique to obtain later cooperation is to offer the respondent the option of calling back on a toll-free 800 number at his or her convenience. Callback appointment times can be noted on the screening questionnaire.

Respondents may ask why they were selected. The interviewer should explain that they were selected as one of a very small number of people in the area to take part in the survey. The respondent should be told there are no right or wrong answers; the interviewer is only interested in candid opinions. The respondent should be told that responses are confidential and that his or her identity will not be disclosed since responses will be grouped or tabulated as part of a total with hundreds of other interviews.

THE ACTUAL INTERVIEW

If at all possible, the respondent should be interviewed alone. The presence of other people may influence the respondent's answers. Occasionally a respondent might be accompanied by a friend who might begin to answer the questions with or for the respondent. The interviewer should remind the friend that he or she is interested in only the opinions of the respondent.

The Questionnaire

The interviewer should be completely familiar with the designed questionnaire and all survey materials before conducting an interview. Practice interviews should be conducted to assure that the interviewer will not be awkward with his or her first respondents.

The interviewer should know and follow instructions that are actually printed on the questionnaire or CRT screen in all capital letters or enclosed in parentheses. They will indicate:

- skip patterns (tell which questions to ask next when a specific answer to a question is given)
- when to read or not read possible answer sets
- when only one answer may be recorded or when multiple answers are acceptable

Legibility

This issue arises when interviewers are unable to input responses directly into the computer. Legibility is of paramount importance in filling out such questionnaires. Often a lot of time is wasted in the tabulation process by trying to decipher just what was written.

The interviewer should always take time at the end of the interview to scan the work and rewrite any words that may be difficult to read by someone else. Each interview should be checked to see that it is entirely legible and understandable.

The interviewer should always use a lead pencil with sufficiently dark lead to be easily read. Do not use colored pencils or any form of ink; a number 2 lead pencil is preferable. Some forms to be scanned require blanks to be filled in with a number 2 pencil.

Asking the Questions

Each question on a questionnaire has been designed for a specific purpose. If an interviewer were to record or put the questions into his or her own words, a bias would be introduced and the interviews would no longer be like those of fellow interviewers who are asking the questions as stated on the questionnaire.

In a case where a respondent does not seem to understand the question, the interviewer should repeat the question to the respondent slowly, but again, not explain it in his or her own words. If the respondent cannot answer or refuses to answer a question, the circumstances should be noted in the margin and the interviewer should go on to the next question.

Do Not Lead the Respondent

The interviewer must not lead the respondent. By this we mean that the interviewer should not ask the respondent anything that would direct the respondent to answer the way he or she thinks the interviewer would like. The interviewer should never suggest a word, phrasing, or idea to the respondent. An example of leading would be:

> **Respondent:** It tasted good.
> **Interviewer:** By good, do you mean fresh?
> **Respondent:** Yes.

The interviewer's correct clarification to a "It tasted good" response should be "What do you mean by 'good'?"

Do Not Be Negative

It is human nature to ask a question in a negative way. By this we mean that instead of asking, "What else do you remember?" as he or she should, the interviewer may ask inappropriately, "Don't you remember anything else?" or "Can't you remember anything else?" By asking a question in a negative way, the interviewer might put the respondent on the defensive, and continued negative questioning can lead to irritation and termination. In addition, the normal reply to a negative probe is a negative response. . . . No.

Record the Response Verbatim

Not only should the questions be asked verbatim; the interviewer is to record the answers verbatim. The interviewer will usually be able to keep up with the respondent. If the answer rushes on, the interviewer may have to repeat each of the respondent's words as he or she writes. The respondent usually slows down when this is done. Or, the interviewer may have to say, "You were saying something about. . . ." The respondent will usually go back and cover the point again.

Another way of slowing down the respondent is by explaining that his or her answer is very important and the interviewer wants to be sure to get every word down.

The exact words of the respondent capture more of the flavor of the response and the respondent than through the use of pet phrases and words. The interviewer must not edit or rephrase the respondent's answer. Responses are recorded in the first person, exactly as the respondent states the answer.

"X" or Circle, Not a Check

Unless otherwise specified by specific survey instructions, closed-end responses should be noted with an "X." An "X" has been proven to be more legible than a check.

If the instructions indicate that the interviewer is to circle a specified number on the questionnaire to indicate a respondent's answer to a question, it should be neatly circled and should not extend around a second word or number. When a questionnaire uses a grid format for responses, care should be taken to circle the answer in the column number corresponding to the question number.

Interviewer Attitude

The interviewer must remain completely neutral. A respondent's answers can easily be biased by the interviewer interjecting improper voice inflections, biasing comments, or making facial gestures.

The respondent should not be rushed. Some people just do not think or converse as rapidly as others. It should be recognized that the respondent is being asked for an opinion, without prior preparation, about which he or she has had very little time to think.

When interviewing, the interviewer does not have to have an expressionless face. He or she should develop the habit of encouraging the respondent to talk, without leading, and then listen carefully to what is said. There are many ways to indicate that the interviewer is following the respondent's remarks. Sometimes the nod of the head is sufficient; sometimes unbiased remarks such as "I see what you mean," "I understand," or "That's interesting," will keep the respondent expressing ideas and thinking further about the topic without leading or biasing the data.

CLOSURE

After completing the interview, the respondent should be thanked. Before the interviewer leaves a respondent, he or she should review responses to all questions to be certain that they have been answered correctly and the answers are clear, meaningful, and legible. The interviewer should then leave as quickly and pleasantly as possible.

Classification, Demographic, and Statistical Information

Generally, questionnaires include some classification questions such as income, age, education level, occupation, number of children in household, and the like. Most people answer such questions willingly. Refusals will be rare if these questions are asked properly in an unapologetic fashion. Respondents may also be told that the answers are tabulated by a computer and that no one answer will be looked at individually.

Validation

A **validation questionnaire** should be prepared for every project. This questionnaire should include the original screening questions plus standard questions on method of recruitment, acquaintance with the interviews, and participation in other studies. Validation should be completed within one to two days of the end of fielding the real survey. This important quality check on the fieldwork ensures that the interview has actually taken place. Ten to 15 percent of all respondents who were reportedly interviewed are recontacted to verify their participation. If a respondent cannot answer the verification questions satisfactorily, then the interview that he or she allegedly completed is declared invalid and those results are not included in the aggregated tabulations. If more than one invalid survey is attributed to a specific interviewer, all of that interviewer's work is discarded.

Validation questionnaire should include the original screening questions plus standard questions on method of recruitment, acquaintance with the interviews, and participation in other studies.

FIELDING A RESEARCH PROJECT

Security of the Survey

The questionnaires, the responses, and all materials used in conjunction with the survey are confidential and should be returned to the supervisor at the completion of interviewing. Respondents generally are not told for whom the study is being conducted. The interviewer should not discuss interviews with family, friends, other interviewers, or anyone else. Confidentiality of the client and survey content and results is of utmost importance.

Briefings

Briefings, or training sessions, will be held before each project is initiated. The entire job will be discussed, giving both the supervisor and the interviewers an opportunity to carefully study job specifications and instructions and to ask any questions pertaining to the job. Field instructions will be reviewed and practice interviews will also be conducted to familiarize interviewers with the questionnaire. Individuals will be assigned quotas or specific duties involved with the job.

Supervisor Assistance

Each research project must have adequate supervision. If a question or problem arises, the interviewer should ask the job supervisor—and not another interviewer—for assistance. Once called to the supervisor's attention, any questions or problems can be remedied for all interviewers on the job or can be referred to the client for resolution.

Do Not Interview Friends or Acquaintances

A friend or acquaintance of the interviewer should never be interviewed. He or she might answer the questions in a manner that he or she thought would please the interviewer, rather than give a candid response.

Adhere to the Study Specifications

The specifications of a study have been set forth for very definite reasons, and they must be adhered to, to the letter. Therefore, if the interviewing method is personal, the interviewer cannot interview a respondent on the telephone; if the interviewer is to contact only one person in the household, he or she cannot interview other family members; if the interviewer is to interview one person at a time, he or she cannot interview a group of respondents. The interviewer cannot interview the same respondent on multiple studies at the same interview. By doing any of these things, the interviewer would not be following the specifications, and the interviews would be rendered useless.

Follow All Study Procedures and Instructions

It is very important that each interview be conducted in the same manner by all interviewers. Instructions about showing exhibit cards, posters, or keeping products concealed must be obeyed the same way in all interviews. Detailed field instructions are designed to reiterate to supervisors and interviewers the technical aspect of executing the specific study, and are usually provided for each project. These instructions come in many forms. A simple study may require an administrative guide, an interviewer's guide, a tally sheet, and sample questionnaire. More complicated tests may require quota sheets, test plans, preparation instructions, product-handling procedures, exhibits, concept statements, and sorting boards.

The administrative guide is designed for the field supervisor of the study. It provides useful background information, a start and end date, quotas, respondent qualifications, procedures for conducting the study, personnel requirements, briefing instructions, and many other special instructions.

The interviewer guide is provided for each interviewer. The interviewer guide usually has some of the same information as the administrative guide, as well as specific step-by-step, question-by-question instructions on how to administer the survey questionnaire.

Accurate Record Keeping

It is the interviewer's responsibility to keep accurate records of all information required by the supervisor or the survey's client. If the addition of columns of numbers is required, it is the interviewer's responsibility that the addition be correct. Information collected through use of a tally sheet is often just as important as information collected in the actual interview.

Complete Assignments on Time

An interviewer is responsible for completing assignments on time. Should unforeseen circumstances arise, or if the interviewer anticipates that the assignment will not be completed within the specified time, the supervisor should be notified immediately.

Work Efficiency

Two factors can affect the efficiency of work performance: speed and quality. Conducting interviews at a reasonable speed is important. However, speed for the sake of numbers should never sacrifice quality. On the other hand, gaining desired information from the respondent is critical and can be done without spending undue time on any one area or by undue conversation with the respondent.

Probing

Many questions, particularly in in-depth interviews, are open-ended and require the interviewer to coax the answers from the respondent. Getting as much information as possible from open-ended questions often requires skillful **probing**. The interviewer should never assume anything about what the respondent is implying, but he or she should probe to get clear and complete answers to all parts of the question in the respondent's own words. The two basic purposes of probing are to clarify and develop additional information.

Probing two basic purposes of probing in an interview are to clarify and develop additional information.

Clarify

The interviewer should get as much information as possible from open-ended questions. An answer that tells something specific is much more valuable than getting several answers that are vague. The interviewer's objective should be to **clarify** why the respondent gave a particular answer to one of the questions. The more concrete and specific these reasons are, the more valuable the information becomes. For example, a respondent is talking about a car that he or she believes would be economical. What does he or she mean by "economical"? The respondent means that it is not very expensive to buy, that it gets good gas mileage, that it is not very expensive to maintain, that it has a high trade-in value, or something else. It is up to the interviewer to find out precisely what the respondent means by "economical."

Clarify an answer that tells something specific is much more valuable than getting several answers that are vague. The interviewer's objective should be to clarify why the respondent gave a particular answer to one of the questions.

The following is an example of how to probe for clarity.

Respondent: It's not my kind of movie.

Interviewer: Why do you say that?

Respondent: It doesn't look interesting.

Interviewer: What do you mean by "interesting?"

Respondent: The thread of the picture seems difficult to follow and the action is slow and drawn out. I enjoy fast-paced, action-packed movies.

Develop Additional Information

An interviewer must often get respondents to expand on an answer. "It would be true to life" or "It makes you think" and other general answers should be probed by saying "Why do you say that?" or "Tell me more about that." Many of the best probes are on key words, and the interviewer may repeat the key words from the respondent's answer as a question: "True to life?" or "Makes you think?"

The following is an example of probing for additional information.

Respondent: They showed a bowl of soup.

Interviewer: What kind of soup was it?

Respondent: It looked like vegetable soup.

Interviewer: What else did they show?

Respondent: A little boy eating the soup and smiling because he liked it.

Interviewer: What did they say about the soup?

Respondent: They said this soup makes a warm and nutritious meal in itself.

Technical Aspects of Probing

1. When key words are probed, the word in the respondent's answer being probed should be underlined, such as, "I thought the soup looked tasty."
2. Probing questions asked that are not tied to key words should be indicated by prefacing those questions with a "p" with a circle around it, signifying an interviewer probe.
3. Answers should always be recorded verbatim in the respondent's own words. The interviewer should not edit, try to improve his or her English, or put things in complete sentences for him or her. Abbreviations may be used when possible as long as they are obvious to anyone who might see them. If they are not, go back after the interview and write them out.
4. The interviewer should begin writing the minute the respondent begins to speak. Responses are much more easily recorded if started before the respondent gets underway.
5. If necessary, the interviewer may ask the respondent to stop for a minute, or to repeat something he or she missed.
6. The interviewer should never lead the respondent. Legitimate probes must be distinguished from leading questions. A leading question would be "Was it a bowl of vegetable soup?" or "Do you remember the little boy that was in the ad?" Anything that suggests something specific about the subject is inadmissible.

Summary of Probing Questions

Get specifics. Ask "what else" only after probing the original response. Do not accept an adjective or a thought—find out why the respondent feels that way. Get the respondents to expand on their answers. Details, whether positive or negative about the subject, are very important. Figure 10.1 illustrates words to clarify and questions to help probe and clarify.

Sequencing of Contact Methods

It is not unusual in survey research to use multiple mediums in a sequence to ensure a higher rate of response. For example, a research project might use the following sequence:

1. Select respondents, obtain their phone number, mailing address, e-mail address.
2. Contact respondents by mail or e-mail telling them they have been selected for the study, asking them to go to a website or call an 800 number to arrange a time for a phone interview, or tell them a questionnaire will be mailed soon.
3. Phone interview conducted or questionnaire mailed or e-mailed.
4. Phone, mail, or e-mail follow-up to ask for completion of survey if response not received.

Words to Clarify			
All right	Different	Good/Bad	Rich
Appealing	Difficult	Homemade	Satisfying/Satisfied
Appearance	Dislike	Tastes	Service
Attractive	Easy/Hard	Interesting	Shape
Better/Best	Effective	Lighting	Size
Cheap	Expensive	Like	Smell/Odor
Cleanliness	Feel/Soft/Hard/Stiff	Many	Smooth
Color	Few	Material	Spicy/Spicier
Comfortable	Fine	Neat	Stayed in Place
Consistency	Fit	Nice	Better
Convenient	Flavor	Okay	Sweet/Sweeter
Cost	Food	Price	Taste/Flavor
Crisp/Crunchy	Frequently	Protection	Texture
Décor	Fresh	Quality	Variety
Design	Funny	Quick	Worse/Worst

Questions to Help You Clarify	Probe Phrases
Why do you feel that _____ ?	What else can you tell me?
What do you mean by _____ ?	What other reasons do you have?
Would you explain that more fully?	What else can you remember?
Would you be more specific?	Your ideas and opinions are so helpful; can you tell me more?
Where does that occur?	
When did you notice _____ ?	What (specific wording in question)?
How is it?	
What makes it _____ ?	
What about _____ ?	
In what way is it _____ ?	

Final Probe
Are there any other ideas and opinions/brands/types/reasons?
TELL RESPONDENTS YOU ARE WRITING THEIR RESPONSES DOWN. THIS WILL ELIMINATE LONG UNCOMFORTABLE PAUSES.

FIGURE 10.1. Clarifying and Probing

ERRORS IN DATA COLLECTION

The accuracy of any data provided in a research project depends on several interrelated things. First of all, there must have been clearly articulated research objectives. Second, correct design must have been accomplished. Third, correct sampling techniques and procedures must have been used. Fourth, the data must have been collected well, and finally,

FIGURE 10.2 Sources of Research Error

the data must be analyzed correctly. Mistakes or errors at any point can negate excellent design sampling, survey technique, and questionnaire design. Figure 10.2 illustrates the relationship between sampling and nonsampling error.

There are many types of errors generally classified as sampling and nonsampling errors. Sampling error was discussed in Chapter 9. However, nonsampling error, which results from some systematic bias being introduced during the research process, can be a bigger problem than sampling error. Nonsampling errors are not a result of sampling. They include mistakes that come from sampling frame errors, nonresponse errors, and data errors.[2] Nonsampling errors commonly arise from errors in design, logic, interpretation, field service, or presentation.

Nonsampling errors are a numerous breed. They are pervasive in nature and are highly arbitrary. Nonsampling errors, unlike sampling errors, do not decrease with sample size. In fact, they tend to increase as sample size increases. While sampling errors can be estimated, the direction, magnitude, and impact of nonsampling errors are generally unknown. As a result of this, nonsampling errors are frequently the most significant errors that arise during a research project. Their reduction is not dependent on increasing sample size, but on improving methods and procedures dealing with the handling of the data itself.

TYPES OF NONSAMPLING ERRORS

There are three basic types of nonsampling errors: sampling frame error, nonresponse error, and data error. Sampling frame errors occur when certain parts of the survey population are not represented or are overrepresented in the study. This could result if part of the population of interest was not included or if some portions of the population are overrepresented. Nonresponse errors result when there is a systematic difference between those who respond and those who do not respond to a survey. Data errors occur because the information gathered is inaccurate or because mistakes are made while the data is being processed. Quite often nonsampling errors are made without the researcher being aware of them. This makes them potentially harmful to the outcome of the project. An understanding of these types of errors will help the researcher prevent or correct them.

Sampling Frame Errors

Sampling frame errors generally consist of noncoverage and overcoverage errors. Noncoverage errors occur when some elements of the original population are not included in the sample. The bias from this type of error is the difference in characteristics, attributes, and opinions between those who are included and those who are not included. This is a very troublesome problem in business research because researchers do not know if there are significant and strategic differences between the ones who did not respond and the ones who did, when there is no information on the noncovered potential respondents. Noncoverage is basically a problem with the sampling frame. The sampling frame is simply a listing of all the possible members of the population being studied. All of the basic survey methods depend on a listing of the members of the population under study. Telephone directories are not complete frames of a city's population because not every household has a number. Furthermore, of those that do, many are unlisted, and many people are in transition at any given time. Mail surveys have the same noncoverage problems, because there is rarely a list that exactly includes the total population under study.

The noncoverage of sample members is as important as the noncoverage that results from not including all possible respondents in the sample frame. This occurs when the listed sample units are not contacted and happens with both personal and telephone surveys. Quite often this situation arises when interviewers do not follow instructions or do not make the appropriate callbacks.

The most effective ways to limit the extent of noncoverage error is to recognize its existence and to take conventional measures. These measures are: (1) improve the sample frame; (2) establish clear instructions concerning who to interview, when to interview, and where to interview; (3) specify callback requirements; and (4) when possible, verify or monitor interviews.

Overcoverage errors occur when there is duplication or overrepresentation of certain categories of sampling units in the sampling frame. In many cases, noncoverage of certain portions of the sample frame leads to overcoverage of other portions. Overcoverage can also occur when certain sample units are listed more than once. This leads to double counting and study bias.

Nonresponse Errors

Nonresponse errors occur when some of the elements of the population selected to be part of the sample do not respond. This happens most frequently in Internet and mail surveys, but can also occur in telephone surveys and personal interviews. The people originally chosen to be interviewed might not respond because they are not at home or because they refuse to participate. Incorrect email addresses are a continuing problem for Internet surveys.

"Not at homes" result because the potential respondent is not at home when the interviewer calls. This source of nonresponse error tends to be on the increase. Included in the "not at home" category of respondents are those who are literally not at home and those who cannot be located. This includes those who use their answering machines or caller ID to screen their calls while they are out for the day, gone on an extended trip, or even those who have recently moved. There is some evidence that the "not at home" categories of respondents tend to have different characteristics than those who are more easily located. Dual-career households tend to aggravate the problem. Care must be taken to account for the "not at home" factor or survey results will be incomplete and biased. The segments less likely to be home will be underrepresented and the results skewed toward the more frequently at home respondents.

Refusals occur when some respondents decline to participate or terminate prematurely after beginning the survey. The actual rate of refusal will depend on the nature of the respondent, the subject of the research, the ability of the interviewer, the length and design of the questionnaire, and the personal situation of the respondent. Mail surveys are particularly susceptible to the refusal nonresponse error. Personal, telephone, and Internet interviews are also plagued with refusal nonresponse. Overall, the refusal rate appears to be increasing. More and more people are being interviewed and the novelty of being surveyed is wearing off. Because of fraud and crime, people are leery of having interviewers come into their homes. The use of the phone for telemarketing sales pitches disguised as surveys has also made legitimate surveys more difficult to complete.

Fortunately, there are many effective methods of reducing nonresponse problems. Some of the most common ones are:

1. Sell the respondent on the importance of his or her opinion and the value of the research.
2. Notify the respondent in advance and make an appointment for a callback at a mutually agreeable time.
3. Ensure confidentiality.
4. Maintain contact with a callback or a follow-up mailing.
5. Include return postage and envelopes for mail surveys.
6. Use tokens or money incentives.
7. Provide a toll-free number so the respondent can call back at his or her convenience.

Careful use of these techniques will increase the response rate of surveys and help avoid the problems associated with nonresponse error.

Data Errors

Data error consists of interviewer errors, measurement errors, and processing errors.

Data errors consist of interviewer errors, measurement errors, and processing errors. Usually these errors occur because inaccurate information is gathered from the respondent or the wrong information is recorded. This can result from measurement instrument bias resulting from a poorly designed questionnaire. In some cases, processing error is also introduced during the editing, coding, tabulating, and processing of the data. Interviewer bias occurs due to interaction between the interviewer and the respondent. Respondents may overstate or understate certain behaviors, either consciously or unconsciously. In some ways, these types of errors are the most harmful because, unlike nonobservational errors, researchers have no idea when and how observational errors might arise. Careful training, supervision, monitoring, and editing are required to minimize this type of error. A final type of data error that should be mentioned is cheating. Cheating is the deliberate falsification of information by the interviewer. To avoid this problem, adequate control and supervision must be exercised.

Research Project Tip

If your research project involves descriptive or causal research, you must describe in detail how you will obtain the desired information from the field. That is, you must describe the experimental design and the details of its implementation for causal research (see Chapter 5), or how the descriptive research will be carried out. Use the following checklist to ensure you have a plan for taking the descriptive research questionnaire to the field:

1. **Budgets: has money been appropriated for the following?**
   ___Wages of interviewers, supervisors, and general office support
   ___Telephone charges
   ___Postage/shipping
   ___Production of questionnaire and other forms
   ___Supplies
2. **Guidelines for interviewers: have the following been done?**
   ___An introduction been written
   ___Interviewers know how much time the interview will take when asked by respondent

    ___Provision has been made on the interview form for second callback appointment

    ___Interviewer is thoroughly familiar with questionnaire

    ___Interviewer has been trained as to the proper way to ask questions and probe for responses

    ___Interviewer records answers verbatim in legible handwriting

    ___Interviewer uses proper attitude in conducting interview

3. **Validation**

    ___Validation questionnaire has been designed

    ___Validation questionnaire has been used

4. **Administrative Guide: the field supervisor has a guide that includes the following:**

    ___Background information on the purpose and objective of the research

    ___Start and end dates

    ___Quotas for interviewers

    ___Respondent qualifications

    ___Procedures for conducting the study

    ___Personnel requirements

    ___Briefing instructions

5. **Interviewing—Probing**

    ___Interviewers know when and how to probe to clarify or obtain additional information

6. **Nonsampling Errors: Have the following nonsampling errors been addressed through preplanned procedures to prevent or overcome the problems?**

    ___Sampling frame errors

    ___Noncoverage

    ___Overcoverage

    ___Nonresponse errors

    ___Not at home

    ___Refusals

    ___Data errors

    ___Interviewing errors

SUMMARY

Once a data-gathering instrument is designed and the appropriate sample frame and size selected, it is time to field the instrument and execute the data-gathering process. To accomplish this smoothly and with a minimum of error, preplanning is a necessity. Proper budgeting and personnel recruitment lead the list of planning activities for the well-executed field-service effort. Interviewers should be trained, briefed, and well supervised to obtain optimum results.

The interviewing relationship requires special attention to ensure proper rapport and understanding between the interviewer and respondent. Specific guidelines should be followed by interviewers depending on the type of interview being conducted.

General rules of interviewing must be maintained at all times. They include: ensuring security of the survey, providing proper training and briefing sessions, having close supervision, adhering to specific study specifications, following all study procedures and instructions, keeping accurate records, completing assignments on time, working efficiently, probing appropriately, and achieving clarity.

KEY TERMS

Clarify (p. 183)
Data error (p. 188)
Internet surveys (p. 176)
Nonresponse error (p. 187)

Probing (p. 183)
Sampling frame error (p. 187)
Validation questionnaire (p. 181)

DISCUSSION QUESTIONS

1. Why is it important to focus on reducing total error in a research project and not just on sampling error? What else, besides sample size, are potential contributors to total error?

2. Discuss the correct way to probe during interviewing.

3. Discuss the three types of nonsampling errors.

ENDNOTES

1. Don A. Dillman, *Mail and Internet Surveys* (New York: John Wiley and Sons, 2000).

2. Technically, sampling frame error could be thought of as one subcategory of sampling error. However, we will follow convention and describe it here as a nonsampling error, and leave sample error to be that random error described in Chapter 7.

Data Analysis and Reporting

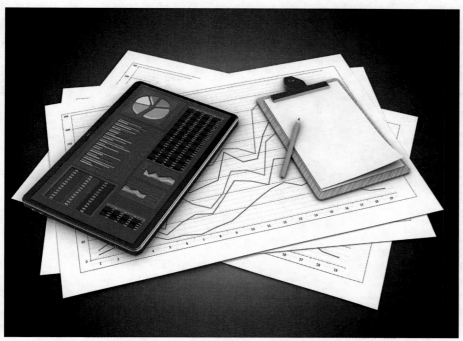

Mmaxer/Shutterstock.com

Analyzing and Interpreting Data for Decisions

Alexander Lukatsky/Shutterstock.com

Learning Objectives

Upon completing this chapter, you should understand:

- The relationship between data analysis and decision making.
- The importance of planning the data analysis procedures to be used on the collected data.
- How frequency distributions, measures of central tendency, and dispersion help in summarizing and understanding data.
- The usefulness of cross tabulations in data analysis to understand underlying differences in responses.

CLOUDS SET

Vik Y/Shutterstock.com

Hamlet:	Do you see yonder cloud that's almost in shape of a camel?
Polonius:	By the mass, and 'tis like a camel indeed.
Hamlet:	Methinks it is like a weasel.
Polonius:	It is backed like a weasel.
Hamlet:	Or like a whale?
Polonius:	Very like a whale.

-*Hamlet*, Act III, Scene ii

Data, like cloud formations, can be made to appear to support any number of conjectures. The fertile mind of the analyst can "see" conclusions to the data that may be more the creation of the imagination than an objective reading of the information generated by the research. This gives pause to the researcher or analyst, because it implies that, while there may be an ultimate truth, the analyst's personal agenda, perceptual inclinations, experience, and even personality can influence the interpretation of the research study's results. Nevertheless, we must use all the means at our disposal to arrive at the most objective, concise, but also thorough analysis possible of the data generated by the research. However, the same observation of objective data may be subject to multiple interpretations. Consider the following apocryphal story:

> An American shoe company sent three researchers to a Pacific island to see if the company could sell its shoes there. Upon returning they made a presentation to management. The first researcher summed up the findings this way. "The people there don't wear shoes. There is no market." The second researcher said: "The people there don't wear shoes. There is a tremendous market!" The third researcher reported: "The people there don't wear shoes. However, they have bad feet and could benefit from wearing shoes. We would need to redesign our shoes, however, because they have smaller feet. We would have to educate the people about the benefits of wearing shoes. We would need to gain the tribal chief's cooperation. The people don't have any money, but they grow great pineapples. I've estimated the sales potential over a three-year period and all of our costs including selling the pineapples to a European supermarket chain, and concluded that we could make a 30% return on our money. I say we should pursue the opportunity."[1]

Here the three analyses reported the same results, but with different implications. The term "**data analysis**" covers a huge number of techniques, statistical programs, and processes that can be applied to the results generated by the data-collection instrument(s) used in our research. These can range from interpreting respondents' reactions to projective research (see Chapter 5), or the conclusions drawn from conducting focus groups (see Chapter 6), to sophisticated multivariate statistical techniques used to manipulate large databases. It is beyond the scope of this book to address these extremes of the data analysis continuum. The reader interested in such analytical processes should read material that specifically addresses those topics.[2] The discussion in this chapter will be limited to data analysis basics that will permit the researcher or analyst to successfully draw useful information out of the types of data generated via a descriptive research survey format.

FROM DATA TO DECISIONS

The manipulation and analysis of data generated by research becomes a value-added management activity when it takes place within a series of tasks leading to management decisions and, ultimately, to a market's reaction to those decisions. Figure 11.1 suggests that the output of the data analysis process is to always lead to better decision making than could have been done without having conducted the research. This is consistent with the philosophy about the value of research presented throughout this book.[3] An example may help to elucidate the process shown in Figure 11.1.

Data refers to facts or information that is used as the basis of decision making.

Data analysis the process of breaking down facts or information to get meaning from the data.

Research ----------> Analysis ----------> Decision Making ----------> Evaluation

Tools	Tools	Tools	Tools
Surveys	Univariate and Multivariate Techniques:	Models and Simulations	Data-Based Management
Experiments			
Observations	• Cross Tabs		
	• Factor Analysis	Management Judgement	
Etc.	• ANOVA		
	• Etc.		

FIGURE 11.1 Overview of the Data Analysis and Management Decision-Making Relationship

Note: Results are data bits that, along with other new data bits from research, become information that leads to implications or that suggests new research.

Worthington Foods, now owned by Kellogg, a company that markets egg substitutes (such as Scramblers and Better 'N' Eggs) conducted survey research which, in part, sought answers to these research objectives:

1. **Why do people control their cholesterol?**
2. **How did people who use egg substitutes first hear about them?**
3. **What is the trial-to-usage ratio for those cholesterol controllers who have tried a brand of egg substitute?**

A phone survey of a demographic cross section of the adult U.S. population was conducted (2,000 respondents). Once respondents passed a set of screening questions identifying them as cholesterol controllers, they were asked to respond to these and other relevant questions:

1. **What is the primary reason you are controlling your cholesterol intake? (check one response)**
2. **Which of the following brands of egg substitutes have you ever tried? Which do you currently use?**
3. **From which of the following sources did you first hear about egg substitutes?**

The following is a sampling of the data bits generated from these questions:

1. Reason for Controlling Cholesterol

On doctor's orders	36%
Family history of cholesterol problem	11%
Concerned about future levels	53%

2. Percentage of all cholesterol controllers trying and using egg substitutes brands:

	Tried	Currently Use
Egg Beaters	72%	25%
Scramblers	12%	07%
Second Natures	04%	01%
Eggs Supreme	01%	—

3. Source of "first heard" for egg substitute triers:

TV ad	13%
Physician	10%
Friend or Relative	26%
Magazine ad	24%
Hospital	02%
Saw Product in Store	07%

Each of the numbers listed in these sample tables represents a data bit. Obviously, even a short phone survey can generate thousands of these bits of data. Although interesting by themselves, they become of even greater value when combined with each other to generate "information." For example, if we know the number of people who have tried a particular egg substitute brand (a data bit) and which of these same people currently use that brand (another data bit), we can determine that brand's retention ratio, the percentage who have tried and still use, or the brands rejection ratio, the percentage who tried and no longer use (that is, information pieces).

Moreover, when multiple pieces of information are combined, some important implications can be drawn. Consider, for example, what is learned when information is combined about the primary reason for controlling cholesterol with usage or nonusage of egg substitutes:

Egg Substitute		
Reason for controlling cholesterol	Users	Nonusers
On doctor's orders	61%	32%
Family history	12%	11%
Concerned about future levels	27%	57%
Total	100%	100%

Here, the implication can be drawn that users of egg substitutes are much more likely to be under physicians' orders to control cholesterol than are nonusers. Looking at the data from another angle, of all the cholesterol controllers under physicians' orders to control cholesterol, the vast majority are users of egg substitutes (74% of all those under physicians' orders to control cholesterol are users of egg substitute brands).

Egg Substitute			
Reason for controlling cholesterol	Users	Nonusers	Total
On doctor's orders	74%	26%	100%
Family history	20%	80%	100%
Concerned about future levels	31%	69%	100%

Another related implication comes from combining information about how respondents first heard about egg substitutes with their retention or rejection information.

% of Egg Substitute Triers			
First heard of egg substitutes from:	Rejectors	Continuing to Use	Total
TV ad	58%	42%	100%
Magazine ad	45%	55%	100%
Friend or relative	38%	62%	100%
Physician	18%	82%	100%

The implication from this table is that those who first hear about egg substitutes from a physician are more likely to continue using them after trial than those who first hear of them from other sources.

Combining these and other implications about usage and information sources leads to decision alternatives regarding the allocation of resources among TV media, magazine ads, coupons, in-store promotions, and calling on physicians. When the company conducting this research did a subsequent cost-benefit analysis of promoting directly to physicians, they determined that it was to their advantage to begin to pursue that course of action.

This illustration shows how data bits are combined into pieces of information, which are combined into implications, which suggest decision alternatives, which lead to decisions. In this case, the decision to make physicians aware of the egg substitute brand and give their high-cholesterol patients a coupon for a free package of that brand was based on research findings that demonstrated that getting trial usage from that source was much more likely to result in continued usage than if trial were gained from other sources. Monitoring the results of this change in the allocation of promotional resources showed that the efforts with physicians were very cost effective in increasing sales. Thus, these decisions led to results that became data bits that ultimately resulted in future decisions (continued promotion to physicians).

This example also demonstrates that data analysis goes beyond merely determining answers to research questions. The analytical aspects of this case did not stop with reporting answers to the original three research objectives, but rather sought to reveal the *association* that might exist between the three questions. That is, the *implications* drawn between the information pieces were what added real, significant value to the research findings. The research analyst is acting as more than a reporter of findings; he or she is seeking to know the answer to such provoking questions as:

What does it mean that *this* (why they control cholesterol) and *this* (a difference in retention rate) are both true simultaneously? and

What does it matter that the researcher has discovered this association? Answer: It suggests physicians could play an important gatekeeping role in generating product trial for people who may prove to be brand-loyal heavy users. Not reported in this example, but true for the research, was the discovery of a direct correlation between egg substitute usage rate and physician involvement.

Therefore, the researcher or analyst's job is only half over once the research is finished. The real value-added activities come with the data-analysis tasks performed on the gathered data.

We will now discuss the means by which such data analysis can be conducted.

DATA SUMMARY METHODS

Developing a Plan of Analysis

For the purposes of this discussion we will assume that the researcher or analyst has successfully coded and entered data into the computer and now desires printouts that can be analyzed and interpreted.

Summary statistics measures used to summarize data by percentages or representative values.

The first step in generating summary data to be analyzed is to prepare a **plan of analysis**. Actually, the genesis of such a plan began with the discussion in Chapter 1 concerning how to state research questions and hypotheses, and continued in the Chapter 5 discussions of dummy tables. Therefore, the heart of a plan of data analysis consists of:

How to obtain answers to research questions.
How to test hypotheses to determine if they are supported by the data or must be rejected.
The execution of the dummy tables that were used early in the research design process to alert the researcher to the type and form the descriptive survey data should take.

However, as demonstrated by the egg substitute research example at the beginning of this chapter, it may be necessary to go beyond obtaining answers to the research questions, testing existing hypotheses, and filling out dummy tables. In that example, a new hypothesis was generated during the data analysis. The new hypothesis was that retention rates of egg substitute usage would vary by reason for controlling cholesterol and by source of first mention of egg substitutes. Such a hypothesis could very well have been generated at the time the research purpose and objectives were stated at the very start of the research process. However, it is inevitable that some hypotheses or specific tabulations or analytical outputs will be initiated during the data-analysis process and not before.

Frequency Distributions

It is common for researchers to generate a set of **frequency distributions** which indicate how respondents answered the survey questions. For example:

Q: What is the primary reason you are controlling your cholesterol intake?

	Number	Percentage
On doctor's orders	651	36%
Family history	199	11%
Future concern	959	53%
	1,809	100%

Note that of the 2,000 respondents surveyed, only 1,809 answered this question. The remaining 191 were omitted for the usual reasons (spoiled questionnaire, refusal to answer and the like). The percentage is best computed as 100 percent for those respondents who did answer the question, rather than based on the full 2,000 respondents. However, the researcher may wish to know why the 191 subjects were not included. If many could not easily choose a primary reason (they were controlling cholesterol for two or three reasons), or were controlling cholesterol for reasons not given as a response option (because their spouse was controlling and prepared meals with reduced cholesterol), then the researcher would want to know this so she or he could revise the question in the future to make provision for such problems. Hopefully, exploratory research done before the survey would reveal most or all of the response categories needed. Also, offering a fourth option:

Other [Record]: _____

is an expensive, but effective, means of learning of other reasons respondents control cholesterol. Nevertheless, if the analyst is primarily concerned with how the target population is distributed among these three reasons, then the percentages should be computed based on the 1,809 respondents instead of 2,000.

If the question had been phrased differently a different-looking frequency distribution might result:

Q: Why are you controlling your cholesterol intake? [Check all that apply]

	Mentions	
	Number	Percentage
On doctor's orders	702	39%
Family history	295	16%
Future concern	1,120	62%
	2,117	117%

Here it is obvious we have multiple reasons given by some of the 1,809 respondents, and the percentages are computed based on the number of respondents instead of number of responses. The percentages may be interpreted as follows: "39 percent of the respondents mentioned that they controlled their cholesterol because of a physician's orders; 16 percent mentioned controlling. . . ." We might be interested in asking this question both ways, with "check all that apply" asked first, followed by the "primary reason" question. Researchers should be cautioned to carefully consider why they are asking such questions and how they plan to analyze the results before assuming automatically that it would be best to always ask both questions. Time is valuable and only a limited amount of it will be given by respondents. If the researcher uses it up by asking these two questions it means he or she will not be able to ask some other important question within the time frame.

Before leaving percentages as a topic, two important aspects of their use should be mentioned:

1. Percents cannot be averaged unless the percentage is weighted by the size of the sample responding to the question. For example, consider the following frequency distribution:

Usage Rate:	Egg Beaters		Scramblers	
	Number of users	Percent	Number of users	Percent
High	250	50%	75	37.5%
Medium	100	20%	100	50%
Low	150	30%	25	12.5%
	500	100%	200	100%

It would be incorrect to say that an average of 35 percent of users of these two brands are medium users (i.e., 20% + 50% = 70% ÷ 2 = 35%) when actually medium users represent 28.6 percent of the two brands' usage rate (i.e., 100 + 100 = 200 ÷ 700 = 28.6%).

2. Do not refer only to percentages when the base of their computation is very small. For example, while the following percentages may be accurate, be careful not to misrepresent the data by referring to just the percentages:

	Male Respondents	
Reason for controlling cholesterol	Number	Percentage
On doctor's orders	7	70%
Family history	2	20%
Future concern	1	10%
	10	100%

Nicoleta Ionescu/Shutterstock.com

3. Dealing with "don't know," "no opinion" responses is a matter of analyst judgment. Usually it is best to include them as a legitimate answer to knowledge or attitude-type questions and record the response rate such as:

Q: Which do you believe would be higher priced, Egg Beaters or Scramblers?

Egg Beaters	65%
Scramblers	30%
Don't know	4%
No opinion	1%
	100%

Researchers should be aware that it is standard operating procedure for business research firms using phone or personal interviewers to push for responses other than "don't know" or "no opinion" when asking a knowledge or attitude question, and recording a "don't know" response only when, after unsuccessful prodding, the respondent insists on maintaining that answer. Therefore, the "don't know" and "no opinion" responses will almost always be underrepresented in the final data. While in many cases that is desirable, in some cases it may grossly distort the truth.

As an illustration of such a danger, consider results generated by research which asked triers of multiple brands of egg substitutes which brand had a higher fat content. The results (simplified here for discussion purposes) were as follows:

Percent Mentioned as High Fat	
Brand A	17%
Brand B	13%
Don't know	70%
	100%

This distribution actually was a test of the researcher's hypothesis that the low involvement of people in purchasing a product such as an egg substitute brand would be reflected in their lack of knowledge about such attributes as fat levels for the brands they had purchased. Consequently, interviewers were instructed to record the first response of the subjects and not to use SOP to push for an answer other than "Don't know." The results supported the hypothesis and suggested that altering some product attributes would have a limited effect on brand demand. Therefore, researchers should consider how they wish to deal with the "Don't know" and "No opinion" response percentages.

Central Tendency and Dispersion Measures

Central tendency calculated measures that are used to summarize data by using a number to represent the shape or typical values of a data set such as the mean, median or mode.

Dispersion measures of the variation of values from a central tendency such as the range, quartiles of standard deviation.

As seen in the discussion in Chapter 6 on measurement, the measures of **central tendency** that can be used to describe the data depend upon the type of data we have generated (nominal, ordinal, interval, ratio). The frequency distribution discussion in the previous section is pertinent to each of these four types of data.

Additionally, Figure 11.2 displays the measures of central tendency and **dispersion** that can be computed for the data types.

Nominal	Mode
Ordinal	Mode, Median
Interval	Mode, Median, Mean,
Ratio	Mode, Median, Mean, Standard Deviation, Geometric and Harmonic Mean

Mode = The most frequently occurring response.
Median = The response that separates the top half of response frequencies from the bottom half.
Mean = The average of the responses computed by summing all responses and dividing by the number of responses.

FIGURE 11.2 Measures of Central Tendency and Dispersion

The most commonly used measures in Figure 11.2 and will be discussed in this section of the chapter.

When the question involves indicating the frequency with which something occurs (for example, the number of times a person eats at a fast food restaurant in a typical week) the frequency is multiplied by the number of respondents checking that answer, those numbers are summed, and the mean is computed by dividing that sum by the number of total respondents. For an example see Table 11.1.

Here, a judgment was made regarding how to code a range of responses. Since people are being asked to give an estimate of their behavior instead of requiring them to keep a diary or an accounting of their actual behavior, researchers are dealing with approximate responses instead of documented frequencies. Consequently, the coded midpoint of the range (two to three times per week coded as 2.5) is an estimate, and the mean of 1.85 times per week is also an approximation. Researchers should not forget this fact later when they are using this number in calculations and when drawing implications from such calculations.

It is important to assess the mean's ability to accurately reflect the sample respondents' responses by calculating a standard deviation for the responses.

TABLE 11.1 Calculation of the Mean

(1) Number of times eat at fast food restaurants/week	(2) Number of Respondents	(1) x (2)
Less than once a week (coded as .5)	100	50
Once or twice a week (coded as 1.5)	250	375
Two or three times a week (coded as 2.5)	175	437.5
More than three times a week (coded as 4)	50	200
TOTAL	575	1062.5
Mean = 1.85 times per week (1062.5 ÷ 575)		

Standard Deviation: Representing the degree of the spread of responses among the response categories, it tells us the range of answers that includes roughly 70 percent of the sampled respondents.[4]

So, for example, if the mean is 1.85 times/week and the standard deviation is .32, then roughly 70 percent of respondents (and hence the population universe) eats at fast food restaurants between 1.53 and 2.17 times per week (1.85 − .32 = 1.53; 1.85 + .32 = 2.17). Obviously, the smaller the standard deviation is, the closer are the actual responses to the mean. If the standard deviation is large relative to the range of responses, then the mean is not a very good measure to use in understanding the data. For example, if in the illustration above the standard deviation is 1.70, it is almost half of the range (4 times/wk minus .5 time/wk = 3.5). The mean of 1.85 is relatively meaningless, since answers in this case are spread widely throughout the range of responses, and few people are actually near the mean. This could be an important observation when dealing with a highly segmented population. Consider Figure 11.3, which illustrates this idea.

FIGURE 11.3 Segmented Populations

In this case the market in question consists of five market segments. Graphically depicted is a mean which is the computation of the responses from the segment members, but, as seen here, there is no segment of respondents which actually is at the mean. The mean in this hypothetical example represents no one and is therefore highly misrepresentative of the data. Consequently, considering the standard deviation along with the mean as a measure of central tendency helps inform the analyst of the dispersion of the data and what precautions to take when reporting the results.

CROSS-TABULATION

It is almost certainly true that virtually all sets of marketing data will reveal only a fraction of the possible significant findings if viewed only in terms of frequency distributions and measures of central tendency and dispersion. As seen in the egg substitute market data, more is revealed about the underlying relationship between variables of interest when two or more variables are considered simultaneously. Cross-tabulation, probably the most often-used analytical technique in business research, involves examination of one variable "crossed" by one or more other variables. In the egg substitute example trial-to-usage or retention rates were examined for egg substitutes crossed by reasons for controlling cholesterol. Several observations about the use of **cross-tabulations** will help the analyst achieve maximum benefit from the use of this analytical tool.

Cross tabulations an analysis technique that is used to compare two or more variables by "crossing" one variable by another like product preference by age.

Setting Up Cross-Tabulation Tables

We usually think of a cross-tabulation table as looking at two or possibly three variables simultaneously. This is most often the case when a firm conducts the research project itself, including processing the data and using some software program such as SPSS or Mini-Tab to run each cross-tabbed table. If the researcher has contracted with an independent business research firm to do the survey (send out and receive the mail questionnaires or do the phoning of respondents), they will likely be doing the data processing, including setting up the cross-tabs per the researcher's instructions. If they are responsible for the data collection and processing, then they will probably include as part of the contracted price what will be referred to as an 18-point or 20-point (or some other number) banner (see Figure 11.4 as an example).

This means they will provide a set of computer printout pages that are 18 or 20 columns wide for every question in the survey. Each question in the survey would appear down the side of a page, called the stub. For example, in a series of Likert-scaled attitude questions, demographic questions, and other types of questions, each question would have a separate printout as shown in Figure 11.4.

The appeal of banners is obvious—they provide a simple way to look at survey questions crossed by the most important variables the researcher is interested in exploring (gender and region in this example).

Page 1 I like the taste of the egg substitute brand I usually eat.	Grand Total	Gender		Region				Etc.
		M	F	S	N	E	W	
Strongly Agree 5								
Agree 4								
Neither Agree nor Disagree 3								
Disagree 2								
Strongly Disagree 1								
Page 2 Household Income	Grand Total	Gender		Region				Etc.
		M	F	S	N	E	W	
More than $40 K								
$35,0001 – $40,000								
$25,001 – $35,000								
$15,000 – $25,000								
< $15 K								
Page 3 Control Cholesterol	Grand Total	Gender		Region				Etc.
		M	F	S	N	E	W	
Yes								
No								

FIGURE 11.4 Sample Printouts

An 18-point banner means any combination of column headings that total 18 can be used. It is usual practice to devote the left-most column to Grand Total, which in effect gives the frequency distribution for each question. So, this column on Page 1 of the example in Figure 11.4 indicates the total number and percentage of people who answered Strongly Agree, Agree, etc., for that question. The remaining 17 columns can be divided in any combination of columns desired. In Figure 11.4 a set of two columns is devoted to gender, followed by four columns for region of the country. How are the column headings selected? In a single cross-tabulated table such as education level by income the independent variable would normally be placed across the top and the dependent variable down the side (see Figure 11.5).

Income	Grand Total	Education Level						
		<HS	HS	Some College	College Grad	Some Grad	Grad Degree	Etc.
$25 K+								
$20–25 K								
$15–20 K								
< $15 K								

FIGURE 11.5 Single Cross-Tabulations

We are maintaining that income depends upon education, so income is the dependent variable and education is the independent variable. An easy way to identify the independent and dependent variables in any situation is to ask the question:

Does *A* depend upon *B*?
A = Dependent variable
B = Independent variable

So, if the researcher is wondering about the relationship between age and attitude toward pop music, it makes sense to ask:

Does *your attitude toward pop music* depend upon *your age*?

The converse question:

Does *your age* depend upon *your attitude toward pop music*?

is obviously illogical—I cannot expect that my attitude will influence what my age is.

It is customary to have the banner headings consist of independent variables that the research purpose, questions, and hypotheses suggest are most likely to be influencing the dependent measures of interest (such as attitudes, consumption rate, likelihood of purchase, and membership or nonmembership). However, this is not an inviolate rule since the researcher might want to examine some categories of dependent variables for numerous questions in the survey. The researcher might want to see how heavy users, light users, and nonusers differ from each other in terms of their attitudes, demographics, behaviors, and the like, and would therefore use those three categories of a dependent variable (rate of consumption) as a set of three columns in a banner. If it is decided to include some dependent variables as banner points it is suggested that two banners be used—one 18- or 20-point banner with all independent variables and a second 18- or 20-point banner with dependent variables. This will help prevent confusion of what the data are revealing, as will be shown shortly.

Another common practice in setting up a banner heading or single cross-tabbed table is to consistently move from low to high moving from left to right in the banner, and from high to low moving down the stub. Therefore, a banner heading for income would look like this:

< $15K   **$15–20K**   **$20–25K**   **$25K+**

and a stub heading for income would look like this:

Income
$25K +
$20–25K
$15–20K
< $15K

An easy way to remember this structure is to envision a graph, which is set up the same way:

If the variable is not a quantifiable number but is rather one of an expressed intensity of feeling, the same rule holds, such as in Figure 11.6 (that is, more positive as you move left to right or bottom to top).

Agreement with Statement	Attitude Toward Product		
	Unfavorable	Neutral	Favorable
Strongly Agree			
Agree			
Neither			
Disagree			
Strongly Disagree			

FIGURE 11.6 Cross-Tabulations of Nonquantifiable Values

Choosing Variables for Cross-Tabulations

It might be tempting to ask the data processors to cross everything by everything so that a cross-tabled table for every combination of two questions in the survey is available. That way, no matter what the issue, one or more tables are available to help the researcher determine the relationship between the variables of interest. Such a temptation should be resisted because it both fails to recognize all the valuable thinking about the project prior to this point, and it also generates a surprising number of tables (50 variables generates 1,225 two-way cross-tab tables, 100 variables generates 4,950 two-way tables). Having a request for everything crossed by everything delivered as a four-foot stack of computer printouts is a sure way to inhibit the start of an analysis of the data! Considerable thought has already been given to the variables of interest as delineated in the research questions, hypotheses, and dummy tables. In fact, a cross-tabbed table is merely inserting data into a dummy table, so the plan of analysis primarily consists of determining which variables (questionnaire questions) should be simultaneously examined for possible relationships to get answers to questions, test hypotheses, or fill in dummy tables. While, as previously mentioned, the researcher will think of relationships he or she wishes to examine during the analysis and not before, there is also a point at which the researcher must get on with the implications and alternative decision suggestions, which is the purpose of the research and its analysis. It is easy to become distracted by the almost infinite number of possible relationships such that one avoids drawing the conclusions necessary to move through the process shown in Figure 11.1. Finding some balance between focusing only on the original objectives of the research and adding to those objectives as the analysis progresses must be achieved if conclusions are to be reported in a timely fashion.

Interpreting Cross-Tabulations

To this point, tables have been set up and a determination made concerning some finite number of relationships between variables to explore. It is now necessary to discuss some important considerations involved with their interpretations. First, if the tables have been set up as suggested, it is possible to analyze the pattern of percentages from left to right to see if there is a positive or negative relationship between the independent and dependent variables. If the percentages increase moving left to right, there is a positive relationship between the variables. If the percentages decrease, then the relationship is negative. For example, in Table 11.2 there is a positive relationship between willingness to pay more to get the favorite brand of egg substitutes and consumption rate.

Note that in this case it is merely being observed that a positive relationship exists between a willingness to pay more to get the favorite brand and consumption rate, without trying to make a claim that one variable causes the other. In fact, causal relationships cannot be determined from cross-tabulated data, even if the demonstrated relationship is statistically significant (to be discussed shortly). That is true even if computing a correlation coefficient that determined a very strong positive relationship between two intervally scaled variables. While too involved to discuss in depth here, the reader should understand that evidence of a positive relationship between variables does not provide evidence that the variables should be thought of as causally related. This is not necessarily a major problem in the analysis, however, since it may in many cases be sufficient for managers to know that a relationship exists to choose among alternative decisions (see discussion in Chapter 3). Evidence of causality does not necessarily alter the conclusions drawn nor the resulting decision. Knowing

TABLE 11.2 Two-Way Cross Tabulations

I will pay up to 25¢ more to get my favorite brand of egg substitute.	Egg Substitute Consumption Rate					
	Low		Medium		High	
	#	%	#	%	#	%
Strongly Agree or Agree	113	34%	239	54%	308	67%
Neither Agree nor Disagree	107	33%	108	24%	101	22%
Strongly Disagree or Disagree	108	33%	98	22%	54	11%
TOTAL	328	100%	445	100%	463	100%

that high consumers of our brand of egg substitutes believe it is worth paying more to get our brand has managerial significance apart from the issue of whether consumption rate causes attitude or attitude causes consumption. One additional conclusion that might come from such an observation is that it is necessary to look more closely at the way the variables are related. This leads to the next issue in analyzing data via cross-tabulations.

Three-Way Cross-Tabulation

Researchers who see a positive relationship between two variables of interest, such as shown above, might wonder if there is a third variable that is possibly related to both of these two variables and that may actually explain more about the existence of this relationship. In this example, the researcher might wonder if household income explains both attitude (willingness to pay more to get their brand) and usage rate (low, medium, high). These questions can be explored by conducting a three-way cross-tabulation (see Table 11.3).

TABLE 11.3 Three-Way Cross Tabulations

I will pay up to 25¢ more to get my favorite brand of egg substitute.	Income											
	Low Consumption Rate						High Consumption Rate					
	Low		Medium		High		Low		Medium		High	
	#	%	#	%	#	%	#	%	#	%	#	%
Agree	84	30	62	32	20	32	29	60	177	71	288	72
Neither Agree nor Disagree	98	35	54	28	21	34	9	19	54	22	80	20
Disagree	98	35	78	40	21	32	10	21	20	8	33	8
TOTAL	280	100	194	100	62	98	48	100	251	101	401	100

It appears that both agreement with the statement (see percentage of agreement varies by consumption rate) and consumption rate (see column totals for number or respondents) vary with income, which mitigates the conclusion that agreement is related to consumption rate (i.e., there is a stronger relationship between income and agreement than consumption rate and agreement, or, the relationship between consumption rate and agreement depends upon income). These observations reveal an important caveat to analysts using cross-tabulations as their primary analytical tool—sometimes cross-tabulations may in fact be showing a spurious relationship between variables. A spurious relationship disappears when another variable enters the analysis. Figure 11.7 graphically illustrates this.

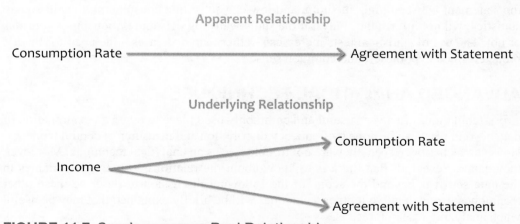

FIGURE 11.7 Spurious versus Real Relationships

How can the researcher avoid basing conclusions, and ultimately decisions, on spurious relationships? The only real answer is that the savvy analyst must maintain a certain skepticism about what she or he can legitimately conclude from the data and come to an implication only after carefully examining the data from several angles. There is no single procedure or tool of analysis which will avoid all erroneous conclusions. A healthy dose of skepticism is the analyst's best defense against future regret and recrimination. As Thomas Huxley said: "Skepticism is the highest of duties, blind faith the one unpardonable sin."

One sure way to fall prey to spurious relationships and at the same time become distracted from the objectives of the analysis is to indiscriminately generate cross-tabulations and begin to examine them for "meaningful relationships." The danger is that the analyst might encounter some table where there is a strong relationship between two variables that he or she would not ordinarily examine or predict to have such a relationship. A fertile imagination then takes hold, and very plausible-sounding explanations are devised for what is, in reality, a spurious and meaningless association between variables. This leads to the sort of fanciful conclusions that Hamlet and Polonius engaged in as quoted at the beginning of the chapter. The analyst's best friend in this case is the theories (research questions, hypotheses, relationships of interest) that originated at the beginning of the research. Analysts would do well to remember that logic should drive data, not data drive logic (let hypotheses, which are based on logical expectations, be tested by the data; do not let a blind empiricism of indiscriminate data analysis determine what is logical). This is not to say that data that is not consistent with presuppositions should be ignored. Rather, it argues that our theories of how consumers behave and the market operates are altered only after multiple findings consistently and persuasively suggest our old theories are wrong and new ones must be developed to explain the findings.

Statistical Significance in Cross-Tabulation

Analysts of cross-tabulated data do not have to wonder whether they are looking at relationships that might or might not be statistically significant. A statistical test called *chi-square* will reveal whether the differences noted in the table are real or could be merely due to chance. Readers interested in how chi-squares are calculated are referred to relevant works on the subject.[5] For our purposes here, most software programs such as SPSS that perform cross-tabulations will print chi-square statistics indicating whether the relationship between the table's variables is **statistically significant** or could have occurred by chance due to sampling variations. It should be noted here that chi-square tests require data that are categorical rather than continuous (that is, low, medium, high consumers instead of one, two, three, four, five, etc., times per week), the numbers analyzed must be counts and not percentages, and there must be at least five or more counts in each cell. (Other requirements are necessary, but these are the ones of primary interest to readers of this book.) While useful in helping to determine if the observed relationship is statistically significant (such as, there really is a difference in the rate of agreement with the statement between high, medium, and low egg substitute consumers), the chi-square statistics will not inform the analyst if the statistically significant relationship is spurious or not. The use of statistical tests increases—rather than decreases—the need for theory, predetermined hypotheses, and common sense.

Statistical significance the likelihood or probability that observed results could have occurred by chance.

ADVANCED ANALYTICAL TECHNIQUES

Cross-tabulations are a very useful and commonly used place to begin an examination of data beyond what can be done by frequency distribution and measures of central tendency. However, as has been seen, they are not trouble free as an analytical technique. Moreover, they cannot reveal all that there is to know about the relationship between variables in the data set. It is beyond the scope of the following discussion to describe these other techniques in any depth, but other techniques will be briefly explained that may be useful when analyzing research results.

Correlation

Correlations establish a relationship between any two intervally scaled variables. Variables can be negatively and positively correlated. Correlation scores range from +1.00 to –1.00 with 1.00 (or –1.00) indicating a perfect relationship and 0 indicating no relationship at all. Generally (depending on sample size), two variables are said to be slightly correlated when the correlation scores are between .21 and .35. Moderate degrees of correlation are generally associated with scores of .36 through .55. High degrees of correlation would be .56 through .75. Extremely high degrees of correlation would be associated with the scores .76 through .99. When two variables are positively correlated, it means that when one variable tends to increase in value (importance, preference, and the like), the other will likewise tend to increase. When two variables are said to be negatively (or inversely) correlated, it means that when one variable increases in value, the other decreases and vice versa. An example: The purchase selection factor of the importance of product quality is inversely correlated to the importance of cost savings. This would mean that as the quality of the product increased, the importance of cost savings to the consumer would decrease.

Correlation a measure of the association or the relatedness of two or more variables like income and age.

SUMMARY

Up to the point of data analysis the research that has been conducted to address a management problem has merely generated costs, with no return. It is only with the advent of data analysis that research begins to generate a return against those costs. Therefore, it is critically important to the success of the project that the researcher or analyst use all appropriate means of extracting valuable insights from the data. While a tool box of sophisticated statistical programs may be necessary to get the most from a data set, it is also true that many of the research objectives and hypotheses that drove the research can be addressed with techniques as simple as cross-tabulation. Another valuable tool of data analysis is the analyst's reluctance to draw implications and make decisional recommendations until he or she is convinced, by looking at the data from a variety of perspectives, that the information truly suggests the validity of those implications and recommendations.

KEY TERMS

Central tendency (p. 200)
Correlation (p. 209)
Cross tabulations (p. 202)
Data (p. 194)
Data analysis (p. 194)

Dispersion (p. 200)
Frequency distribution (p. 198)
Plan of analysis (p. 198)
Statistical significance (p. 208)
Summary statistics (p. 197)

DISCUSSION QUESTIONS

1. Discuss how the process of analyzing data leads to solving management problems.
2. What is a plan of analysis and why is it important to have a plan before beginning the analysis of research data?

3. In your own words, describe how to analyze a cross-tabulated table.

ENDNOTES

1. Adapted from Philip Kotler, Marketing Management 8th ed. (Englewood Cliffs, NJ: Prentice-Hall), 1994, p. 24
2. Some reference works for those readers interested in a more in-depth discussion of analysis include: For analysis of qualitative research see Matthew B. Miles and A. Michael Huberman, Qualitative Data Analysis, Thousand Oaks, CA: Sage, 1994; Norman K. Denzin and Yvonna S. Lincoln, eds., Handbook of Qualitative Research, Thousand Oaks, CA: Sage, 1994; Harry F. Wolcott, Writing Up Qualitative Research, Thousand Oaks, CA: Sage, 1990. For statistical analysis, including multivariate statistical techniques see Sam Kash Kachigan, Statistical Analysis (New York: Radius

Press), 1986; Joseph F. Hair, Ralph E. Anderson, Ronald L. Tatham, and William C. Black, Multivariate Data Analysis, 4th ed. (Englewood Cliffs, NJ: Prentice-Hall), 1995. Harvey J. Brightman, Statistics in Plain English (Cincinnati: South-Western Publishing Co.), 1986.

3. It should be noted, however, that there is definitely a place for research findings which may not lead to an immediate decision, but which educate decision makers in a more general way. Well-informed, knowledgeable decision makers are valuable by-products of the analysis of decision-oriented research information. Therefore, researchers would not fail to report findings which may not in themselves suggest a decision, but which serve to edify management in important ways about the company's markets, customers, or significant trends in the environment.

4. We will assume that the researcher/analyst has a computer printout which shows both the mean and standard deviation (and standard error of the mean) for the intervally scaled questions in the survey. Readers who desire more information on how to compute and interpret standard deviations and other descriptive or inferential statistics are referred to any of the standard statistical texts such as the Kachigan or Brightman books listed in Footnote 2.

5. See for example, pp. 342–356 of the Kachigan book listed in Footnote 2.

Analyzing Qualitative and Big Data

Mikko Lemola/Shutterstock.com

Learning Objectives

Upon completing this chapter, you should understand:

- The types of decisions that use qualitative methods.
- The questions researchers should ask themselves during qualitative data analysis.
- The steps in analyzing qualitative data.
- Big data and its interpretation.

Phvovir/Shutterstock.com

Often managers don't associate "analysis" and "qualitative research" because qualitative research usually doesn't involve number crunching statistics. However, in its most basic form, analysis means examination or investigation. Analysis breaks down some complex whole into its fundamental parts, while interpretation asks what something means. Qualitative research is about examining the features of a market through detailed research that explores the background or context for decision making.

As discussed in Chapter 4, qualitative research has roots in a variety of disciplines, including anthropology, sociology, psychology, linguistics, communication, economics, and semiotics. It is concerned with how the social world is interpreted, understood, experienced, and produced. According to John W. Creswell (1998), qualitative research is "an inquiry process of understanding based on distinct methodological traditions of inquiry that explore a social or human problem. The researcher builds a complex, holistic picture, analyzes words, reports detailed views of informants, and conducts the study in a natural setting" (p. 99).[1] Business managers who analyze qualitative data gain valuable insights when consumers reveal how they feel about the purchase decisions they make and why they behave as they do in the market.

CHARACTERISTICS

Qualitative data data that may not be represented by numbers but rather themes or patterns of verbal or written responses such as recorded focus group interviews.

As previously outlined in Chapter 4, **qualitative data** differs from quantitative information in three main ways. First, qualitative research examines consumer buying behavior in great detail to answer questions regarding *why* consumers buy goods and services. Second, qualitative research occurs in continuous series or iterations (think version 2.0). Third, qualitative analysis uses inductive reasoning methods: Ideas or theories arise from the results of the analysis, compared to quantitative research, which looks for information that validates or refutes a hypothesis.

Qualitative research is about investigating the features of a market through in-depth research that explores the background and context for decision making. This provides managers a better understanding of the market, why a person skips the crowds at retail stores on Black Friday to shop online on Cyber Monday or why some Super Bowl commercials make us laugh and strengthen our loyalty to that brand while others bring about social media outrage and bans. Managers essentially do market research to identify how and why things happen. If the manager only needs to know what occurred, or how often, then quantitative research would meet the researcher's needs. But to understand the meaning that people assign to their experiences often requires research practices that acutely examine the consumer's perceptions, interpretations, motivations, and actions. Specifically, this research is successfully used in market segmentation, marketing strategy development, new product development, product line extensions, product line and brand improvement, product positioning, product differentiation, marketing promotion effectiveness, sales analysis, buyer decision analysis, and measurement of perceptions, motivations, and attitudes.

Theoretical Approaches and Methods

To gain market insight, managers use various approaches to collect qualitative data. The ethnographic, netnographic, grounded theory, and case study methods detailed in Chapter 4 include: observation, in-depth interviews, focus groups, immersion groups, and projective

TABLE 12.1 Qualitative Research Approach

Dimension	Ethnography	Netnography (Online Ethnography)	Grounded Theory	Case Study
Research Purpose	To describe the cultural characteristic of a group of people and to describe cultural science.	To adapt ethnographic methods to the study of online communities and cultures.	To inductively generate a grounded theory describing and explaining a phenomenon.	To describe one or more cases in depth and address the research questions and issues.
Disciplinary Origin	Anthropology.	Anthropology.	Sociology.	Multidisciplinary roots, including business.
Common Methods for Data Collection	Participant observations, interviews with informants.	Online interactions (observations, interviews, focus groups, structural network analysis and ethnography).	Observations, in-depth interviews, focus groups, and collection of artifacts and texts.	Multiple methods are used (e.g., interviews, observations, documents).
Data Analysis Approach	Holistic description and search for cultural themes in data.	Complete description and search for social themes in data.	Begin with open coding, then axial coding, and end with selective coding.	Holistic description and search for themes shedding light on the case. May also include cross-case analysis.

techniques. Knowledge of the various approaches to qualitative research is vital in determining how to define the research problem and review the literature. Key characteristics of four approaches are summarized in Table 12.1.

ANALYSIS AND INTERPRETATION

Qualitative data analysis involves the identification, examination, and interpretation of **patterns or themes** in textual data and determines how these patterns and themes help answer the research questions at hand.

Qualitative analysis is (NSF):

- Not guided by universal rules
- Is a very fluid process that is highly dependent on the evaluator and the context of the study
- Likely to change and adapt as the study evolves and the data emerges.[2]

Researchers should take note that qualitative data analysis is an ongoing and recurring process that takes place throughout the data-collection phase and carries over to the data-entry and analysis stages. Though the steps listed below are sequential, to some extent they do not always (and sometimes should not) occur apart from one another. Further, it is important for the researcher to keep some guiding questions in mind to reflect back on the purpose, research questions, and potential of the study. Figure 12.1 lists examples of questions researchers should ask themselves throughout the analysis process.

Themes or patterns reoccurring ideas/responses that come from respondents from which data is collected such as comments about the size of an exhibit.

While examining your qualitative data it is imperative that you continuously ask yourself the following types of questions:

- What patterns or widespread themes appear around particular items in the data?
  - How do these patterns (or absence of) help to make clear the overall study questions(s)?
- Are there any variations from these patterns?
  - If yes, what factors could clarify these uncommon responses?
- What interesting anecdotes surface from the data?
  - How can these stories help to make clear the overall study question(s)?
- Do any of the patterns or developing themes suggest that further data need to be collected?
  - Do any of the questions need to be modified?
- Do the emerging patterns reinforce the findings of other corresponding qualitative analyses that have been performed?

This figure was adapted from the National Science Foundation's (1997) analyzing qualitative data.

FIGURE 12.1 Questions to Ask During the Qualitative Analysis Process

The steps outlined in Table 12.2 provide an adaptable guide for analyzing qualitative data:

TABLE 12.2 Steps in Analyzing Qualitative Data

Step 1	Process and Record Data Immediately
Step 2	Begin Analyzing as Data Is Being Collected
Step 3	Data Reduction
Step 4	Identifying Meaningful Patterns and Themes
Step 5	Conclusion Drawing and Verification

Interview transcripts, field notes, and observations offer a description of the research study, but they do not provide explanations. It is the researcher or business manager who has to make sense of the information that has been gathered by studying and interpreting it.

Analysis Tip   Qualitative data analysis requires that the researcher moves the focus from what is stated by participants, what the researcher has observed them doing, or what the researcher has read in a text (the level of description) to exploring and explaining what is "underlying" or to "distill essence, meaning, norms, orders, patterns, rules, structures, and so on (the level of theories).[3] (Rapley, 2011, 276)

In qualitative research, data analysis often will start during, or immediately after, the first data are collected and continue throughout the study. This first round of data analysis may also further guide subsequent data collection. For example, the structure of the discussion in a focus group may be slightly modified in consideration of emerging findings, where further explanation may be needed.

Step 1: Process and Record Data Immediately

As soon as data is gathered the researcher must promptly process the information and document the method with thorough notes. These notes could include:

- Aspects that stuck out to the researcher
- Time and date details
- Highlights from the interaction
- Other observations.

Documenting the interaction immediately will help to ensure that the researcher's thoughts, reactions, and recount are as accurate as possible.

It is useful to make a reflection sheet template that you complete after each interaction so that it is consistent across all data collection points.	*Analysis Tip*

Step 2: Begin Analyzing as Data Is Being Collected

Qualitative data analysis should start the instant a researcher begins collecting the first piece of information. A researcher should then begin examining the data and perceptively processing it for patterns or themes that were exposed. This should occur at an early point in the process so that the researcher is able to focus on these patterns or themes as they occur in later data collections.

Step 3: Data Reduction

While qualitative analyses commonly yield a large amount of data, sometimes information collected does not add meaning or value. Once data has been collected, a researcher will need to carry out a data reduction process in order to identify and focus on what is meaningful. It is the job of the evaluator to examine the raw data and decide what is important and transform the data into a basic format that can be understood in the framework of the research questions (Krathwohl; Miles and Huberman).[4,5]

Data reduction begins to occur simultaneously during the first two steps. A researcher starts the process of reducing data by simply not recording each solitary thing that happens in the data collection. Instead, researchers will record only what they felt was most meaningful, usable, and significant. From the beginning, the researcher is also reducing data by keeping an eye out for themes and specific patterns. However, the process of data reduction must stretch beyond the data-collection stage.

When a researcher is trying to determine what is meaningful data, it is helpful to refer back to the research questions.	*Analysis Tip*

Step 4: Identifying Meaningful Patterns or Themes and Drawing Conclusions

Before qualitative data can be analyzed it must first be grouped into the meaningful patterns or themes observed by the researcher. The process of categorizing information is often referred to as coding the data. However, this process does not involve assigning numerical codes as one does in quantitative analysis. Coding qualitative data helps to bring meaning to the words before the researcher identifies themes and patterns and organizes them into categories.

This process is generally conducted in two primary ways:

- Content analysis
- Thematic analysis

The type of analysis is highly dependent on the nature of the research questions and the types of data collected. Sometimes a study will use one type of analysis and, other times, a study might use both types.

Content analysis is carried out by:

1. Coding the data for certain words or content
2. Identifying their patterns
3. Interpreting their meanings.

This type of coding is done by going through all of the text and labeling words, phrases, and sections of text (either using words or symbols) that relate to the research questions of interest. After the data is coded the researcher can sort and examine the data by code to look for patterns.

Thematic analysis is the grouping of data into themes that will help answer the research questions. These themes might directly evolve from the research questions before the data collection begins, or naturally emerge from the data as the research is conducted (Pope).[6]

The process of thematic content analysis involves identifying themes and grouping the data so that the meaning of the themes can be analyzed and connected back to the research questions. This process involves finding themes in the transcripts and trying to confirm them by searching through the data and repeating the process to identify additional themes in the categories (Pope).[7]

To do this, once the interviews have been transcribed, the researcher reads each transcript and makes notes in the margins of words, theories, or short phrases that summarize what is being said in the text. This process is known as open coding. The goal of open coding is to provide a summary statement or word for each thing that is discussed in the transcript. Table 12.3 is an example of the initial coding framework used in the data generated from an interview with a child in a study to determine how the influence of food Business affects children's dietary preferences and choices.

Thematic analysis the grouping of data into themes that will help answer the research questions.

TABLE 12.3 An Example of an Initial Coding Framework

Interview Transcript	Initial Coding Framework
Interviewer: "Can you tell me about what you like to eat?"	
Child: "I like chips, but I like chocolate the most. I like apples, strawberries, and grapes. Oh and pizza, I really like pepperoni pizza."	• Food Preferences
Interviewer: "What do you like about those things?"	
Child: "Well, apples and fruit taste good and I think they are healthy. We eat those at McDonald's and in school now and my friends like them, so we eat them together. I really like chocolate though it is my favorite. I think it has sugar and it is bad for you so I just eat a little, tiny bit."	• Food Preferences • Taste • Healthy/Unhealthy • Location • Friends

TABLE 12.4 An Example of an Initial Coding Framework

Final Coding Framework	Initial Coding Framework
1. Consumer-related benefit	• Taste • Convenient • Quality • Free-range/Fair-trade • Location • Endorsed • New • Extra • Family/friends • Fun
2. Health benefit	• Healthy • Health professional • Weight • Digestion • 5 a day
3. Specific nutrients or ingredients	• Wholegrain/multigrain • Fruit/vegetable • Other
4. Minimization/elimination of nutrients	• Fat/cholesterol • Preservatives • Light/lite • Reduced • Other

In the second stage, the researcher amasses all of the words and phrases from all of the interviews onto a new document. Next, the researcher will go through the pages and cross out all duplications in order to reduce the number of categories (Burnard).[8] Once the shorter list of categories has been compiled, the researcher can further refine it by grouping together the theoretical ideas developed during the research. Table 12.4 provides an example of what the final reduced list might look like.

Next, the researcher will go through the transcripts and pull out data that fit under a particular category. Finally, all of the sections of data are entered under each category, and from that list the researcher can report the findings of the study. To draw reasonable conclusions, the researcher will need to:

■ Take a step back and interpret what all of the findings mean
■ Determine how the findings help answer the research questions
■ Draw implications from the findings (Krathwohl; Miles and Huberman)[9,10]

Regardless of what format the researchers choose to display the information, it should enable them to arrange and think about the data in new ways and assist in identifying patterns and relationships across themes (Miles and Huberman).[11] The display can be a graphic, table, matrix, or textual display.

The process previously outlined can be done by hand, or it can be managed by a computer program. There are several computer-assisted qualitative data analysis software (CAQDAS) packages available that help the researcher to sort, organize large amounts of data, store, note and retrieve text, locate words and phrases, formulate diagrams, and extract quotes (Seale).[12] However, the programs do not analyze the data—they are simply instruments that help make the handling of data easier for the researcher. A brief list of software to perform qualitative analysis is displayed in Table 12.5.

TABLE 12.5 Brief List of CAQDAS

Software	Web Site	Description
ATLAS.ti	www.atlasti.com/	A popular software for both Windows and Mac platforms
NVivo	www.qsrinternational.com/	Navigable software for both Windows and Mac platforms
HyperRESEARCH	www.researchware.com/	HyperRESEARCH and Hyper-TRANSCRIBE are available for Windows and Mac platforms
Qualrus	www.qualrus.com/	Uses intelligent computational strategies

Analysis Tip	The following web site provides information to assist in making an informed decision among software packages: www.surrey.ac.uk/sociology/research/researchcentres/caqdas/support/choosing/

Verification a process used to verify the observations/statements made by an analyst by having the same observations/statements reviewed by another researcher.

Step 5: Verification

Interpreting the study findings in a qualitative data analysis is a process that some argue is more subjective than quantitative data analysis. Because of this argument, there is an ongoing debate as to whether qualitative researchers should have their analyses validated by a third party.

There are two main ways of having data analyses verified by others:

- Respondent/Participant validation
  - Asking the participants to validate or refute the researcher's interpretation of the data analyses
- Peer review (such as inter-rater reliability)
  - Another appropriately experienced qualitative researcher independently reviews the data analysis and emerging themes

Big data large quantities of information collected by an organization on constituents such as the number, types, and amounts of transactions from customers of a large retail store. Such data is usually beyond the capability of some data software and requires specially designed software to provide analysis of the data.

While the debate regarding the validity of qualitative research continues, there is no conclusive answer. Researchers must revisit the data (multiple times) to ensure rigor of the process and thorough analysis of conclusions drawn from the study.

Writing Tip	Writing is key to establishing what the researcher knows (and doesn't know) and in assisting the researcher in making conceptual leaps. A researcher should begin transforming his or her thoughts onto paper throughout the process of the study. The process of writing not only helps the researcher explain and justify ideas, but also develop them.

BIG DATA

The term "**big data**" is a relative term in the sense that any data that exceeds the capability of commonly used hardware and software tools can be considered to fit the definition (Franks).[13] Thus, the term "big data" can be applied to the large volume of baseball data that had to be analyzed by hand at the turn of the 20th century (Schwartz) or the millions of postings on a company's Facebook page.[14]

everything possible/Shutterstock.com

The **three V's of big data** affect data analysis: volume, velocity, and variety (Chartier).[15] In terms of volume, there are virtually unlimited amounts of sports statistics and social media postings. For example, it is estimated that Google processes an amount of data that equals all the words ever spoken by humankind every 250 days (Chartier).[16] Data also comes much faster as technology improves. Just imagine the number of automated credit card transactions or email messages that take place every day. Finally, data is provided in a variety of forms we were previously able to capture. Everything from smart phone apps to YouTube provide data that will require analysis techniques if it is to be of any value to researchers and practitioners.

As the data that marketers are able to collect grows, two primary issues need to be addressed: how to analyze the data and the ethics involved in sorting through the data without violating the privacy of the participants.

One problem in analyzing big data is that it is not easily categorized into primary or secondary data. Instead, as we collect primary data for market research, we may well get a great deal of what some researchers refer to as "data exhaust" (George, Hass, and Pentland).[17] This is ambient data that is collected along with the primary data. While it may have little value for the project under consideration, it can be combined with other data to create customer insights (George, Hass, and Pentland).[18] For example, cell phone tracking that looks for shopping behavior may also reveal traffic patterns. Placing Radio Frequency Identification (RFID) tags on casino chips can help casinos know which games a customer plays and can also tell the casino where the player is when not gaming (buffet, bar, shopping) (Franks).[19]

Another problem with analyzing big data is the lack of structure that characterizes some of the data (Franks; George, Hass, and Pentland).[20,21] Conventional data is transactional. That is, it lends itself to commonly used statistical tools such as baseball statistics, which are just numbers. It is much more difficult to accurately analyze the thousands of postings of text on an individual website or Facebook page. Techniques such as text mining that examine text and assign meanings to each word or phrase are used to analyze this type of data. Types of text mining techniques include natural language processing, sentiment analysis, and pattern recognition (Franks).[22] Many of these processes are available in prepackaged software.

Three V's of big data volume, velocity, and variety, each of these affect the timing and type of analysis to be used.

Although these techniques for analyzing text may help market researchers determine correlation patterns, it is doubtful they can lead to explanations of causality. For that, researchers will need to develop new theories of causality and then test these theories based on the data (George, Hass, and Pentland).[23] A major goal of market research is to link theory with practice so that data can be put to practical use by the businesses and not-for-profits that rely on the research.

Despite the complexity of big data, there is a movement to simplify the analysis. As noted in Chapter 9, if we collect a large enough amount of data, we get false positives. That is, everything is significant and p values become meaningless. Attempts to develop new software to solve this problem may only make the problem worse. It is believed by many that a better way to analyze this data is with basic Bayesian statistics and stepwise regression models. Predictive analysis techniques are used to develop algorithms and models for taking existing data and predicting future behavior such as which consumers in our data base are most likely to respond to a promotion offering discounts.

The second issue concerning big data is privacy. As noted in Chapter 2, market research ethics are grounded in informed consent and anonymity. Informed consent is endangered in big data analysis when others, with whom you associate, consent to disclose information about their behavior. For example, if several of your Facebook friends do disclose information to a market researcher, the researcher may then make assumptions about your behavior based solely on the idea that you must be like your friends. The result is that assumptions are made about your behavior and consumption patterns without your consent (Barocas and Nissenbaum).[24]

Additionally, market researchers may promise anonymity, but by that they mean anonymous records. Most research firms know your computer or phone's IP address and can distinguish it from others. Researchers can also associate that IP address with previous interactions and purchase behavior. An organization may not share data outside of itself, but there is little true anonymity within the individual firm's database (Barocas and Nissenbaum).[25] At present, there is no clear solution to this problem as individuals create more and more information about themselves; it is an issue that will need new and creative solutions by market researchers.

SUMMARY

While there are a range of approaches to the analysis of qualitative data, they all have a shared focus on moving from the level of description and summary to investigating and explaining the fundamental patterns, processes, and structures. Researchers look at the collected data to come up with theories and answers to societal questions or concerns. Generally, researchers will apply coding to identify themes, patterns, and ideas. They may also include some statistics that explain what the data is showing along with narrative analysis that centers on grammar, word usage, and underlying messages.

KEY TERMS

Big Data (p. 218)
Thematic analysis (p. 216)
Themes or patterns (p. 213)

Three V's of big data (p. 219)
Qualitative data (p. 212)
Verification (p. 218)

DISCUSSION QUESTIONS

1. What is meant when the text states that qualitative research is an ongoing process? How does this relate to the questions researchers should ask themselves throughout the study? Explain your answer.

2. The text discusses several types of business decisions that use qualitative methods. Pick one and discuss how this type of analysis would be useful to a Business manager.

3. Pair up with another student in the course and ask each other the following questions: What types of green products or services do you buy? What do you like about those things? Next, apply the process of thematic analysis to the interviews and create a final coding framework.

4. Why is looking for exceptions in the data important?
5. Why is writing part of the process of analysis? Discuss its importance.
6. What does the term "big data" mean?
7. What are the two primary issues related to big data?

ENDNOTES

1. Creswell, J.W. (1998). Qualitative inquiry and research design: Choosing among five traditions. London: Sage.
2. NSF-National Science Foundation (1997). Chapter 4: Analyzing qualitative data (User-friendly handbook for mixed method evaluations). Retrieved from http://www.nsf.gov/pubs/1997 /nsf97153/chap_4.htm.
3. Rapley, T. (2011). Some pragmatics of qualitative research analysis. In D. Silverman (Ed.), Qualitative research (273–290). Sage.
4. Krathwohl, D.R. (1998) Methods of educational and social science research: An integrated approach (2nd ed.). Waveland Press Inc., Illinois.
5. Miles, M.B, & Huberman, A.M. (1994). Qualitative data analysis (2nd ed.). Newbury Park, CA: Sage.
6. Pope, C., Ziebland, S., & Mays, N. (1999). Qualitative Research in Health Care. Second Edition. London: BMJ Publishing Group. Chapter 8. Analysing Qualitative Data. Retrieved from http://www.bmjpg.com/qrhc /chapter8.html.
7. Pope, C., Ziebland, S., & Mays, N. (1999). Qualitative Research in Health Care. Second Edition. London: BMJ Publishing Group. Chapter 8. Analysing Qualitative Data. Retrieved from http://www.bmjpg.com/qrhc /chapter8 .html.
8. Burnard, P. (2006). A pragmatic approach to qualitative data analysis. In Newell, R. & Burnard, P. (Eds.), Research for evidence based practice (97–107). Oxford: Blackwell Publishing.
9. Krathwohl, D.R. (1998) Methods of educational and social science research: An integrated approach (2nd ed.). Waveland Press Inc., Illinois.
10. Miles, M.B, & Huberman, A.M. (1994). Qualitative data analysis (2nd ed.). Newbury Park, CA: Sage.
11. Miles, M.B, & Huberman, A.M. (1994). Qualitative data analysis (2nd ed.). Newbury Park, CA: Sage.
12. Seale, C. (2000). Analysing your data. In Silverman, D. (Ed.) Doing qualitative research (154–174). London: Sage.
13. Franks, B. (2012). Taming the big data tidal wave: Finding opportunities in huge data streams with advanced analytics. Hoboken, NJ: John Wiley & Sons.
14. Schwartz, A. (2004). The numbers game. New York: St. Martin's Press.
15. Chartier, T. (2014). Big data: How data analysis is transforming the world. Chantilly, VA: The Great Courses.
16. Chartier, T. (2014). Big data: How data analysis is transforming the world. Chantilly, VA: The Great Courses.
17. George, G., Hass, M.R., & Pentland, A. (2014) Big data and management. Academy of Management Journal, 57(2), 321–326.
18. George, G., Hass, M.R., & Pentland, A. (2014) Big data and management. Academy of Management Journal, 57(2), 321–326.
19. Franks, B. (2012). Taming the big data tidal wave: Finding opportunities in huge data streams with advanced analytics. Hoboken, NJ: John Wiley & Sons.
20. Franks, B. (2012). Taming the big data tidal wave: Finding opportunities in huge data streams with advanced analytics. Hoboken, NJ: John Wiley & Sons.
21. George, G., Hass, M.R., & Pentland, A. (2014) Big data and management. Academy of Management Journal, 57(2), 321–326.
22. Franks, B. (2012). Taming the big data tidal wave: Finding opportunities in huge data streams with advanced analytics. Hoboken, NJ: John Wiley & Sons.
23. George, G., Hass, M.R., & Pentland, A. (2014) Big data and management. Academy of Management Journal, 57(2), 321–326.
24. Barocas, S., & Nissenbaum, H. (2014). Big data's end run around procedural privacy protections. Communications of the ACM, 57 (11), 31–33.
25. Barocas, S., & Nissenbaum, H. (2014). Big data's end run around procedural privacy protections. Communications of the ACM, 57 (11), 31–33.

Advanced Data Analysis

Chapter Outline

ImageFlow/Shutterstock.com

Learning Objectives

Upon completing this chapter, you should understand:

- The difference between statistically significant differences and managerially significant differences.
- What it means to say we are testing hypotheses.
- How to explain the difference between a null and alternative hypothesis.
- How to explain the different types of error that may occur when we test hypotheses.
- How to explain the purpose of ANOVA and the two commonly used forms.
- How to describe the different types of bivariate association.
- How to describe various multivariate techniques and how they are used.

Jeanette Dietl/Shutterstock.com

Once you have collected data through descriptive or causal research, and have run descriptive statistics and cross tabulations, you may wish to conduct some of the statistical analyses described in this chapter. But first we will discuss how marketing researchers approach the use of statistical tests in analyzing data.

BUSINESS RESEARCH AND STATISTICAL ANALYSIS

Business research, as we well know by now, is conducted to help reduce the uncertainty in decision making. If we could be certain of making the correct decision without conducting research, why would we ever want to do research? Business research in such cases would not reduce uncertainty because there would be no uncertainty. You would always know which decision would be best. However, we all know that managers are often unsure which decisional alternative is best. Consequently, we conduct research to help determine which alternative should be selected, given what we discover is the nature of the market from conducting the research.

Statistical significance the observed differences or association between or among a set of variables is too great to have occurred by chance a certain proportion of times.

Managerial significance a statistically significant difference does not mean that the findings have a managerial significance in that management should take note of the findings and act on the findings. Managerial significance indicates that the results have important meaning to managers and would indicate that some action on their part is justified.

Statistical analysis the process of collecting, exploring, and describing data to derive meaningful information.

Statistics help us to better understand the significance of marketplace characteristics. We should distinguish between statistical and managerial differences, however:

Statistically significant differences: when a difference (such as between two market segments, attitudes, or likelihood of purchase between two products) is big enough that it is unlikely to have occurred due to chance.

Managerially significant differences: when any observed difference in findings is considered significant enough to influence management decisions. For example, some statistically significant differences are considered inconsequential to management, while some that do not cross a certain statistical threshold to be considered statistically significant may influence management decisions.

Business researchers run statistical analyses on the data they have collected in order to be able to reduce the uncertainty of management decisions by identifying those measured variables that are managerially significant and also statistically significantly different from one another. For example, **statistical analysis** of business research data may reveal that a market consists of five consumer segments that differ from one another in ways significant to business managers making targeting and positioning decisions. Without the use of statistical analysis, we would not have been able to identify or define these segments or the important differences among them—differences upon which business decisions will be based.

We arrive at this point because of the research decisions we previously made. Before we begin a discussion of the kinds of statistical analytical procedures of value to researchers, let us briefly review how we arrived at this point of the research process. Readers will remember that we devoted considerable time and effort to the development of a statement of management problem or opportunity; identification of the research purpose (which required stating the decision alternatives and criteria); and the research objectives (research questions and hypotheses), which have driven all of our subsequent research decisions. Our research design, data-collection methods, measurement tools and methods, and data-collection instruments were all selected and developed as the most effective and efficient means possible of answering our research questions and testing our hypotheses, which allow us to achieve our research purpose and thereby solve our management problem or capitalize on our management opportunity. The statistical process we use at the analysis stage is merely another step along this same path, leading from management problem to data to decisions to problem solution. We emphasize this interconnectedness of the steps because it is easy for the novice researcher to become so overwhelmed by the variety and complexity of the statistical procedures that he or she fails to keep the big picture in mind. We are analyzing data for a reason—to allow us to choose the best among the decisional alternatives that help solve our problem. Statistical analysis merely aids in that choice. Our discussion of statistics in this chapter is no substitute for the kind of coverage one gets in a statistics course, but rather covers the main topics of interest to business researchers seeking to reduce the uncertainty of management decision making.

HYPOTHESIS TESTING

As we noted in Chapter 1, hypotheses are speculations regarding specific findings of the research. When researchers refer to **hypothesis testing**, they are referring to any means used, such as the use of cross-tabulated tables (see Chapter 11), to determine if the hypotheses we stated at the early stages of the research are supported by the evidence. For example, H: First-time home buyers spend more time researching how to determine construction quality than people buying for the second or third time. When researchers speak of hypothesis testing they are referring to a particular process and set of statistical tools used to determine the probability of observing a particular result from the research if the stated hypothesis were actually true. This formal statistical process—hypotheses testing—is what we are describing.

We have hypotheses because we *suspect* our results will reveal some characteristic of the population under study. If we already *knew* the results would be a particular way we would not need to do the research. So, we approach the testing of an hypothesis the same way we do research in general: We are not out to prove (or disprove) anything, but rather seek to discover, test, and learn the "truth." We are testing our hypotheses to determine whether they should be accepted as statements accurately portraying the population's characteristics, or rejected because the observed difference is likely due to sampling error and there really is no difference as we hypothesized.

The underlying rationale for testing the hypothesis is that we will make different decisions based upon whether the results of the statistical tests lead us to conclude the hypothesis is supported or not. For example, if our hypothesis is that there is no difference between males and females in their preference for product design A or B, and that hypothesis is rejected (the results indicate the preferences for males versus females are real and unlikely due to chance), then we would make different decisions on which product design to introduce and how to target our marketing programs for the product.

Hypothesis testing involves five steps:[1]

1. The hypotheses are stated, with decisions identified for the outcome of the hypothesis test.
2. Determine the costs related to the two types of errors arising from your decisions.
3. Select the significance level (the alpha) you will use to determine whether to reject or fail to reject (FTR) the **null hypothesis**.
4. Collect the data and conduct the appropriate statistical tests.
5. Compare the results to your null hypothesis and make your decision.

The following example illustrates how business researchers could use these steps to help business managers make better decisions. Assume you work for a company that manufactures light bulbs. Your R & D (research and development) department has developed a new light bulb (named the Longlast bulb) that they claim lasts much longer than traditional bulbs, but could sell for only a 50 percent premium over traditional bulbs. The business manager believes this bulb could have a competitive advantage in the market, but to attract consumers

Hypothesis testing a process used in scientific research to test assumptions about a population parameter or value which may or may not be true.

Null hypothesis a statement about a population parameter or value that is made specifically to test whether or not a statement is true. It is usually expressed as a negative statement of no difference or no association between or among variables. The null hypothesis is tested and is either accepted or rejected.

Ruslan Grumble/Shutterstock.com

the company will need to provide a money-back guarantee for the minimum life expectancy of the bulb—if it does not last at least thirty-six months the consumer gets a full refund. The company needs to know if such a guarantee makes economic sense, since they have decided that if the average life of the bulb does not exceed thirty-six months they will not go to market the bulb (not enough of a competitive advantage). The decision, then, is to either market the bulb with the guarantee or not market the bulb.

Step 1: Stating the Hypotheses and Decisions

Hypotheses are stated in two forms:

Null hypothesis is stated in terms that indicate you expect to find no difference or no effect.
Alternative hypothesis states that you expect to find a difference or effect.

In our Longlast light bulb case these hypotheses and the resulting decisions would be:

Null hypothesis: The unknown mean (average) life of our Longlast bulb population is less than or equal to thirty-six months.
Decision NH: If we accept (or more appropriately fail to reject) the null hypothesis we will not market the bulb.
Alternative hypothesis: The unknown mean life of our Longlast bulb population is greater than thirty-six months.
Decision AH: If we accept the alternative hypothesis we will market the bulb.

The statement of a null hypothesis is in keeping with the healthy skepticism mentioned in Chapter 11. That is, while our R & D people claim the Longlast bulb will last more than 36 months ("Oh, no problem. Piece of cake. Easily last more than 36 months," as they put it.), you retain a healthy dose of skepticism, and the null hypothesis reflects that skepticism. We assume the null hypothesis is true until evidence suggests otherwise. The alternative hypothesis says what you hope will be true, that the R & D claims are correct. These are competing hypotheses—only one can be true.

Step 2: Determine the Costs of Decision Errors

Since we are going to collect a sample of light bulbs and determine the average life of the light bulbs in the sample instead of testing every light bulb produced (which would not leave us any to market!), we are going to draw inferences from our research sample to the entire Longlast bulb population. These inferences can either be right or they can be wrong. Table 13.1 illustrates the possible combinations of inferences made about the null hypothesis.

Type 1 Error: We reject the null hypothesis when it is actually true.
Type 2 Error: We accept the null hypothesis when it is actually false.

When testing a hypothesis in any particular study we can make either a Type 1 error or a Type 2 error (or no error), but not both a Type 1 and Type 2 error. Table 13.2 shows how this table looks for our Longlast example.

TABLE 13.1 Possible Inferences about the Null Hypothesis

Based on the Sample Evidence We Decide to:	The Truth About the Population Parameter	
	Null Is True	Null Is False
Accept the Null (FTR the Null)	Correct Decision	Type 2 Error
Reject the Null	Type 1 Error	Correct Decision

Alternative hypothesis a statement that is accepted if the null hypothesis is rejected. It is usually stated in a positive format such as one value is significantly larger than another value or one value is significantly associated with another value.

TABLE 13.2 Longlast Example

Based Upon the Sample Evidence	The Truth about the Longlast Bulb				
	36 months or less		Over 36 months		
Not market the bulb	Correct Decision	1	2	Type 2 Error	
Market the bulb	Type 1 Error	3	4	Correct Decision	

We all know (or at least suspect, if we have not had personal experience) that making the wrong business decisions incurs costs. In the Longlast case both Type 1 and Type 2 errors are costly, but in different ways. If we decide to market the bulb because the average life of our sample (which we thought would also be true of the population) was longer than thirty-six months, but its life was actually shorter than thirty-six months (a Type 1 error), we will discover our error when people begin to return expired bulbs and get their money back in perhaps twenty-four or thirty months from when they were first marketed. Lots of Longlast bulbs have been sold in the past twenty-four to thirty months. The *Wall Street Journal* runs a front-page story of how we are flooded with returned bulbs and requests for refunds, consumer confidence in our other products begins to slip, we have trouble recruiting good business people who do not want to be associated with such a company, and other unpleasantness occurs.

A Type 2 error would occur when we decide not to market a bulb whose actual life is more than thirty-six months, but the lifetime of our sample was less than thirty-six months. We had a winner on our hands but did not capitalize on the opportunity. Depending on the number of people who would have been interested in our competitive advantage, we might have missed out on a golden opportunity.

Step 3: Setting a Significance Level

No one wants to have significant bad decisions on their career track record, but there always is the possibility that when we make decisions based on inferring from a sample to our population, we were wrong. In hypothesis testing, the significance level is the maximum risk you will accept of making a Type 1 error (marketing the light bulb when you should not have). It now becomes clear why Step 2 is so important:

> We must consider how significant the costs are to making a mistake by marketing the light bulb when we should not have in order to know how low to set our *maximum* risk of making such an error of judgment.
> or
> The greater the costs associated with a Type 1 error, the lower we should set our maximum risk.

Some guidelines help us determine how to set the **level of significance**:

1. If costs associated with a Type 1 error are high and a Type 2 error is not costly, set the level of significance (the chance of making a Type 1 error) very low—at .05 or below.
2. If costs associated with a Type 1 error are not very high, but making a Type 2 error is costly, set the level of significance much higher (perhaps at .25 or above).
3. If both Type 1 and Type 2 errors are costly, set the level of significance very low and increase the sample size, reducing the chance of a Type 2 error. (However, this does increase the costs of the research.)

Level of significance the numerical value placed on the likelihood that a value did not occur by chance when it actually did occur by chance and is usually expressed as a probability like .05. This means values this different would only occur 5% of the time or less if the null hypothesis is true.

In the Longlast light bulb case the potential costs associated with making a Type 1 error are of sufficient magnitude to justify setting the level of significance very low (say, .01). This means if you reject the null hypothesis (i.e., decide to market the light bulb), the chance that you made a Type 1 error (decided to market it when you should not have because the average life expectancy was actually less than thirty-six months) is only one chance in a hundred. In other words, you can be 99 percent confident that you made the right decision.

Step 4: Collect the Data and Conduct Statistical Tests

This is the step where the research is designed, data are collected, and the appropriate statistical tests are used to analyze the data. Our research design in this case would involve descriptive research since exploratory is not used to collect data per se, and our hypothesis does not involve cause-effect relationships. The research could run internal (within the company) tests of a sample of light bulbs, or we could conduct in-home tests, where consumers agree to try the product in typical consumer-usage situations. This approach provides researchers with information about the product's performance under actual market conditions, and the subsequent research that tests consumers' opinions, perceived benefits received, problems, future purchase intent, and the like provides valuable marketing targeting and positioning information.

In this case we will assume we select a random sample of 1,000 light bulbs (we use *probability* sampling since we are doing descriptive research) for an internal test and use a special testing technology that "speeds up" time so that we do not have to wait thirty-six months for the results of our test of the bulbs' lifetime. So, we run our test of 1,000 light bulbs and determine the average simulated lifetime of the bulbs in months. We discover the following:

Sample mean (written as $\bar{x}$) = 37.7 months
Standard deviation (written as s) = .42 months

We use a t test in this case to determine if the null hypothesis should be rejected or accepted (FTR) because we do not know the population's standard deviation. However, because the sample size is so large, the t value is the same as the Z value.

A t test is constructed as follows:

$$t = \frac{\text{Sample value} - \text{Hypothesized population value}}{\text{Standard deviation of the sample value}}$$

In the Longlast light bulb case the calculation would be:

$$t = \frac{37.7 - 36.0}{.42} 4.05$$

See Table 13.3 for the appropriate statistical tests for the different forms of hypotheses.

Step 5: Compare Results to the Null Hypothesis and Make a Decision

Looking at a t distribution table we see that the t value for n-1 degrees of freedom (999 in our case, but "infinity" on the table) and for an alpha (the level of significance, which was .01 in our case) in a "one-tail" test (on a normal curve, the area under the curve at only one end of the curve rather than both ends) was 2.326. Since our t value of 4.05 exceeded this 2.326 value, we can say we are *more than* 99 percent confident that our sample mean of 37.7 months is drawn from a population whose mean is more than 36. Or, in other words, the chances that our sample mean would be 37.7 when the actual population mean is 36 months is very, very unlikely (less than one in a hundred). Because the odds of the null hypothesis being true (that our population mean is 36 months or less) are so small, it is much more reasonable to assume that the reason our sample mean was 37.7 months is that the null hypothesis should be rejected and our alternative hypothesis should be accepted (that the population mean is greater than 36 months).

TABLE 13.3 Statistical Tests for Hypothesis Testing

Types of Hypotheses	Number of Subgroups or Samples	Scale of Data	Test	Requirements
Hypotheses about frequency distribution	1	Nominal	Chi-square X2	Random Sample
	2 or more	Nominal	Chi-square X2	Random, independent samples
	1	Ordinal	Kolmogorov-Smirnov	Random
Hypotheses about proportions (percentages)	1 (large sample)	Interval or ratio	Z-test for one proportion	Random sample of 30 or more
	2 (large sample)	Interval or ratio	Z-test for two proportions	Random sample of 30 or more
Hypotheses about means	1 (large sample)	Interval or ratio	Z-test for one mean	Random sample of 30 or more
	1 (small sample)	Interval or ratio	t-test for one mean	Random sample of less than 30
	2 (large sample)	Interval or ratio	Z-test for two means	Random sample of 30 or more
	3 or more (small sample)	Interval or ratio	One-way ANOVA (one independent variable)	Random sample

Source: Adapted from Carl McDaniel and Roger Gates, *Contemporary Marketing Research* (Cincinnati, OH: South-Western, 1999), pp. 516–517.

In Step 1 we established a decision rule that said if we reject the null hypothesis and accept the alternative hypothesis we will market the Longlast light bulb, so that is what we should do. Referring to Table 13.2, this decision means we either will make the correct decision (cell 4), or will be making a Type 1 error (cell 3). The actual chance that we are making a Type 1 error is called the *"p* value," which in this case would be the likelihood of getting a sample mean of 37.7 months if the null hypothesis were true. This is very remote (less than 1 chance in 100), which is very reassuring of the correctness of our decision.

While our null hypothesis was stated as a test of means (i.e., Was our sample's average of 37.7 months statistically significantly different from the hypothesized population's average of 36 months?), we could state hypotheses as frequency distribution, differences between subgroups (e.g., men versus women), or proportions (e.g., percentages of college educated versus noncollege graduates intending to buy our product). Table 13.3 shows the appropriate statistical tests for different forms of hypotheses. Once we set up the hypothesis and go through the steps outlined here, a statistical software program such as SPSS can be used to conduct the appropriate statistical tests. Otherwise, the same process (the five steps) are followed to arrive at a decision based on the business-research results. See Table 13.4 for a list of statistical software sites on the web.

Analysis of Variance (ANOVA)

The purpose of **analysis of variance (ANOVA)** is to determine if samples come from two or more populations with equal means. We could run multiple *t* tests, but this will inflate the overall Type I error rate. ANOVA does not inflate the Type I error, especially when we are comparing a number of groups. Basically, ANOVA determines the probability that

Analysis of variance (ANOVA) a statistical analysis technique designed to determine if 3 or mores values are significantly different and analyzes their variances. This is a useful techniques for model building and in experimental research.

TABLE 13.4 Statistical Software Sites on the Internet

Software	Web Site	Description
SPSS	www.ibm.com	A popular, comprehensive statistical package with links to other sites and data sets.
STATA	www.stata.com	STATA software for Windows, Apple.
UNISTAT	www.unistat.com	Comprehensive package compatible with Windows Excel. Data handling, analysis, and graphic presentation.
StatSoft	www.statsoft.com	Presents the STATISTICA range of statistical analysis products. Easy to use yet powerful statistical package.

differences in group means are due to sampling error and not Type I error. ANOVA is used when there is a true experimental design with random assignment of subjects to each group. Below is a discussion of the two of the most used ANOVA designs. The purpose is to familiarize the student with the design. The statistical analysis of ANOVA is beyond the scope of this text.

One-way ANOVA is based on one independent and one dependent variable. The researcher assumes that the populations from which the samples were drawn are normally distributed, have equal variances, and that the samples are randomly and independently drawn. The null hypothesis (H0) is that the means of all the groups are equal.

$H_0: \mu_1 = \mu_2 = \mu_3 \ldots = \mu_n.$

The alternative hypothesis is that they are not all the same;

$H_1:$ Not all μ_n are the same.

Two-way ANOVA examines: (1) two factors of interest on the dependent variable, and (2) the interaction between the different levels of the two factors. For example, our two factors of interest may be the percent of sugar in boxes of children's cereal and the line speed of the boxing process. The interaction between these two factors would involve attempting to understand if the level of sugar per box of cereal depended on the level of the line speed. The same assumptions apply to two-way ANOVA as to one-way ANOVA (populations are normally distributed, populations have equal variances, and independent random samples are drawn). Hypotheses for a two-way ANOVA are as follows:

For Factor A

$H_0: \mu_1 = \mu_2 = \mu_3 \ldots = \mu_n.$
$H_1:$ Not all μ_n are the same.

For Factor B

$H_0: \mu_1 = \mu_2 = \mu_3 \ldots = \mu_n.$
$H_1:$ Not all μ_n are the same.

For the interaction effect:

$H_0:$ the interaction of A and B equals zero
$H_1:$ the interaction of A and B is not equal to zero

Concluding Thoughts on Hypothesis Testing

Hypothesis testing is very decision oriented, as demonstrated in this discussion. In fact, the underlying reason for testing hypotheses is to get to the point (Step 5) where you can determine how confident you can be in choosing between two previously identified decision alternatives (in this case, to market or not to market the Longlast light bulb). Some other thoughts on hypothesis testing are:

1. As described in Chapter 5, we use exploratory research to *generate* hypotheses, we use descriptive or causal research to *test* hypotheses. While the exploratory research detective work may allow us to check out our hunches by looking at secondary data and doing exploratory communication or observation, and even provide us with enough information that we are willing to make a decision without further research, we cannot claim we have tested hypotheses by doing exploratory research. This is true even if we conduct an exploratory survey of thousands of people. The reason is that true hypothesis tests, as described here and listed in Table 13.3, all demand probability samples that are the province of descriptive and causal research. If we have not obtained our sample using a probability sampling approach (simple random, stratified, systematic, or cluster sampling methods), the plain fact is that we cannot conduct these hypotheses tests, no matter how large our sample. This is not to say that we cannot use exploratory survey results to make decisions. We simply cannot arrive at those decisions through statistical tests of our hypotheses.

2. There are two types of errors possible when conducting tests of hypotheses. We must determine their respective costs and then set the level of significance consistent with the costs of making a Type 1 error. In doing this we must understand that we do not want to automatically set the significance level very low (.05 or less) so we will not make a Type 1 error. The fear of making a Type 1 error is only justified when the costs of a Type 1 error are very high. Sometimes the costs of a Type 2 error (*not* marketing the Longlast bulb when we should have in our example) may be high as well and must be factored into our decision. As described in Step 3, when Type 2 error costs are high relative to Type 1 error costs, we should set our level of significance much higher (.25 or higher).

3. Doing causal research also may involve hypothesis testing. Although beyond the scope of our discussion, one typical statistical test used in determining the difference between experimental treatments is the ANOVA test (Analysis of Variance, see Table 13.3). For example, we can use an ANOVA test to determine if there is a statistically significant difference in the sales of a cereal brand that was tested in an experimental design with three coupon levels: 35¢, 50¢, and 75¢. ANOVA is not used exclusively with experimental data (it can be used with descriptive survey results), nor is it the only way to analyze experimental data, but it is a commonly used statistical test for experimental data.

MEASURES OF ASSOCIATION

Marketers frequently want to know how variables are associated with each other. For example, Levi's may want to know what types of people are interested in a more formal, dressy line of pants. Target may want to know the lifestyle characteristics of the women who visit their Web site so they can change its content to satisfy customer needs, and IBM may want to know which characteristics best describe their top salespeople. In such cases marketers are interested in using statistical analysis to determine the degree to which two or more variables are associated with each other. Our discussion of cross-tabulation in Chapter 11 was an example of looking for associations. In this chapter, we will examine other statistically measurable means of determining association among variables. We will examine bivariate (association between two variables) and multivariate (between three or more variables) techniques.

Bivariate Association

The association between two variables can be graphically described in a variety of ways (see Figure 13.1):

- *Nonmonotonic:* there is no discernable direction to the association or relationship between the two variables, but the relationship exists.

Bivariate association a measure of the relationship between two variables to determine if there is a relationship and if so, the strength of that relationship.

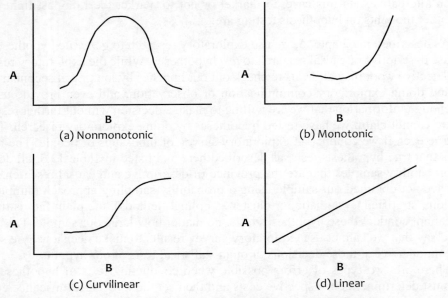

(a) Nonmonotonic

(b) Monotonic

(c) Curvilinear

(d) Linear

FIGURE 13.1 Graphic Representation of Bivariate Association

- *Monotonic:* there is a general direction to the association between the two variables.
- *Curvilinear:* the association between the variables can be described by a curved line.
- *Linear:* a straight line can be drawn to describe the relationship between the variables.

We will restrict our discussion to associations between variables that can be described as linear. Linear relationships may either be positive or negative in nature. In Figure 13.2(a) we see a positive relationship: as variable A increases (education) so does B (income). This association does not have to be perfect. There are examples of people with little education but very high income, and people with very high education but modest incomes (such as college instructors), but in general the relationship is positive.

In Figure 13.2(b) we see a negative relationship: as variable A increases (price), variable B declines (sales of cellular phones).

Marketers are very interested in determining the association between variables so they can use this information in making decisions. If buyer loyalty for a personal computer manufacturer as measured by repeat purchase behavior is associated with a buyer's satisfaction with the company's toll-free help line, and satisfaction with the help line is associated with the number of trained customer service agents, the company may decide to hire and train more customer service agents. If the association between two variables is strong, we can predict one variable by knowing the other one, but first we must be able to measure the degree of association. We will discuss the primary statistical procedures used for measuring association. Readers wishing for a more comprehensive discussion of these and other statistical measures of association should consult one of the standard works on the subject.[2]

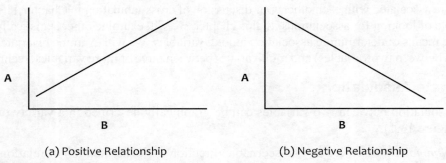

(a) Positive Relationship

(b) Negative Relationship

FIGURE 13.2 Relationship Between Variables

TABLE 13.5 Bivariate Measures of Association

Type of Data	Measures
Interval or ratio	Pearson product moment correlation
Ordinal	Spearman rank-order correlation
Nominal	Chi-square analysis

The choice of bivariate measures of association depends upon the scale of the data being analyzed. Table 13.5 describes several common measures.

Pearson Product Moment Correlation

The Pearson product moment correlation is used to measure the degree to which two variables are correlated or associated with each other when both of those variables are *metric* (that is, either intervally or ratio-scaled data). The output of running this statistical analysis on two variables is a single number called a correlation coefficient, which can range from -1.00 to $+1.00$. The closer the correlation coefficient is to -1.00 or $+1.00$, the stronger the association is between the variables. Two variables are perfectly inversely correlated when the coefficient is -1.00 and perfectly positively correlated when it is $+1.00$. A correlation coefficient of 0.00 indicates there is no statistical association between the two variables. Statistical software packages such as SPSS will compute both the Pearson product moment correlation coefficient (referred to as the r) and the statistical significance statistic (referred to as the p) for two sets of metric-scaled data. The r measures the strength of the association on the -1.00 to $+1.00$ scale, while the p indicates the likelihood that the association is due to chance (i.e., that the null hypothesis of no association between the two variables is supported).

A $p = .05$ says that the chance we would be seeing the strength of the r (the association or correlation between the two variables) as what we see it for our sample data, when in fact there is no association ($r = 0.00$) between the two variables is only 5 chances in 100. So, a p of .05 or lower would indicate that the degree of association between the variables as measured by the r is "real" and unlikely due to chance. Once we see that the p indicates that we are looking at a statistically significant association, we can look at the r to determine the strength of the association. Physicists expect to see perfect (or very near) correlations between the physical materials they study. Marketers, as behavioral scientists, realize that people are far from "perfect" and so the correlations we measure between variables related to the behavior of consumers are not going to be -1.00 or $+1.00$. Marketers measure and correlate such variables of interest as:

consumption rate	correlated with	satisfaction with product
attitude toward product	correlated with	intention to buy
household size	correlated with	frequency of usage

These, and many other correlations involving metric data of interest, are looking at correlations revealing various degrees of less-than-perfect association. Table 13.6 suggests some general rules of thumb for correlation coefficients and implied strength of association.

Spearman Rank-Order Correlation

Business researchers may find that they seek to know the association between two variables that are ordinally (i.e., rank ordered) rather than intervally or ratio scaled. In such cases we should use the Spearman rank-order correlation rather than the Pearson product moment correlation. For example, we might want to know if there is any association between the way people rank ordered brands of automobiles based on "sportiness" and "like to be seen driving." The resulting correlation coefficient, r_s, and the measure of statistical

TABLE 13.6 Correlation Coefficient and Strength of Association

Range of Correlation Coefficient	Strength of Association
Greater than .80	Very Strong
.61 to .80	Moderate to Strong
.41 to .60	Weak to Moderate
.21 to .40	Weak
.00 to .20	Nonexistent to Very Weak

significance are interpreted in the same way as we do for the Pearson product moment correlation. That is, a higher rs indicates higher degrees of association (or stronger inverse association if the coefficient is a negative value).

Chi-Square Analysis

As shown in Table 13.3, chi-square tests are run when we are conducting hypothesis tests for nominally scaled variables. Chi-square tests are run on cross-tabulated data when we want to determine if the frequencies we see in each cell of a cross-tabbed table fit an expected (hypothesized) pattern. Since the null hypothesis states that we expect not to find an association between the two variables, the chi-square tests tells us whether we should accept the null hypothesis or not. So, for example, if we want to know whether there is an association between the preferences of males versus females for new product concept A or B, our cross-tabulated data might look like this:

Preference for New Product Concept	Males	Females	Total
A	199	18	217
B	40	43	83
TOTAL	239	61	300

The decision we want to make is whether or not to target the two new products to consumers on the basis of gender. The question of the statistical analysis then becomes, "Is there a statistically significant difference in the preferences between males and females for the two new product concepts?" The null hypothesis for the chi-square test is then:

H_o: There is no relationship between gender and new product concept preference.

And our alternative hypothesis is:

H_a: There is a significant relationship between gender and new product concept preference.

When you enter the data in the cross-tabulated table (which must be in "counts" not percentages, and at least five or more counts must be in each cell of the table) into a statistical program such as SPSS, the program then calculates the probability you would find evidence in support of the null hypothesis if you repeatedly collected independent samples and got these results. So, if the chi-square test showed a .01 probability for the null hypothesis, the conclusion would be that you would get these results only 1 time in 100 occasions if the null hypothesis were true. That is highly unlikely, so the null is rejected and the alternative hypothesis is accepted: There is a relationship between gender and product concept preference. Chi-square does not tell the researcher the nature of the association (whether males prefer A and females B), only that the association exists by telling you the probability of seeing such results if the null hypothesis were true. Researchers would then need to study the association between the variables more closely to discern the nature of the association between the variables and ultimately, along with other research findings, what decisions should be made about marketing the new products.

Multivariate Association

Multivariate (multiple variable) association refers to the statistical methods that simultaneously analyze multiple measurements of attitudes, attributes, or behavior. Multivariate techniques are simply extensions of univariate (analysis of single variable distributions) and bivariate techniques (two variable methods such as cross-tabulations, correlations, and simple regression). For a research project to terminate prior to employing multivariate techniques assumes that the purpose of the research was only to identify the variables, or that the importance of the results for the decision information required would need no more than the establishment of the associations between two variables. Multivariate techniques serve to determine the relationships that exist between multiple sets of variables. Multivariate methodologies are clearly sometimes needed to examine the multiple constraints and relationships among pertinent variables to obtain a more complete, realistic understanding of the market environment for decision making.

Multivariate association measures of the relationship among more than two variables to determine if there is a relationship and if so, the strength of that relationship.

Description and Application of Multivariate Techniques. The satisfactory utilization of multivariate methods assumes a degree of understanding of the market dynamics or market behavior in order to conceptualize a realistic model. The identification of the variables whose relationships are to be measured is foundational to an incisive multivariate approach. The nature and number of variables to be examined will determine what type of multivariate method will be utilized.

The first commonly used method is known as *multiple regression.* Multiple regression allows for the prediction of the level or magnitude of a phenomenon such as market size or market share. Multiple regression has as its objective the identification of the optimum simultaneous relationship that exists between a dependent variable and those of the many independent variables. For example, frequency of listening to a particular radio station may well be a function of a number of marketing mix variables such as the type of programming, listener loyalty, community promotionals, billboard advertising, disc jockey personality, and tastefulness of the commercials.[3]

Another method is multiple discriminant analysis. *Multiple discriminant analysis* has as its objective the identification of key descriptors on which various predefined events will vary. It might be learned from a discriminate analysis that middle-income families who work in a downtown area and who have school-age children might be expected to be the first to move into a new, rural, totally planned community housing development.

Canonical correlation analysis allows for the establishment of a predictive model that can simultaneously forecast or explain several phenomena based on an understanding of their correlates. The canonical correlation analysis differs from multiple regression analysis in that there is more than one dependent variable. Whereas family income and family size might be used to predict the number of credit cards a family might have (by using a multiple regression technique), the canonical correlation analysis would also be able to predict the average monthly charges on all of their credit cards.[4]

One of the more popular of the multivariate techniques is *factor analysis.* Fred Kerlinger states that the factor analysis might be called the queen of analytic techniques because of its power and elegance. He describes factor analysis as a method for determining the number and nature of underlying variables among larger numbers of measures. It also serves to reduce large groups of complex variables to their underlying and predictive entities. Factor analytic techniques first gained prominence in psychological and psychiatric studies. For example, verbal ability, numerical ability, memory, abstract reasoning, and spatial reasoning have been found to underlie intelligence in some studies.[5]

The applications for factor analysis have been used extensively for behavioral and attitudinal studies used in the marketplace. For example, a recent study that measured a large group of variables related to job satisfaction and morale among a certain group of engineers revealed the ability to grow professionally was the most important factor in morale and job satisfaction. This was followed closely by self-esteem as it related closely to the type of firm they work for. The analysis revealed five central factors, which in general terms, fit closely to Maslow's hierarchy of organizational needs, except that the order of prominence for each of Maslow's needs was found to have a different sequence for the engineers surveyed. Factors identified by this technique, therefore, have served as a new dimension of segmentation that focuses on shared agreement among respondents as the differentiation among the segments.

Multidimensional scaling addresses the problem of identifying the dimensions upon which customers perceive or evaluate phenomena (products, brands, or companies). Multidimensional scaling techniques result in *perceptual maps* that describe the positioning of companies or brands that are compared relative to the position they occupy in the minds of customers according to key attributes. These maps allow the decision maker to examine underlying criteria or dimensions that people utilize to form perceptions about similarities between and preferences among various products, services, brands, or companies. The question of positioning, as viewed by multidimensional scaling (MDS) and perceptual mapping, deals with how a firm compares to its competitors on key attributes, what the ideal set of attributes sought by the customer might be, or what positioning or repositioning strategy should be developed for a specific sector of the marketplace.[6] A medium-sized bank might learn, for example, that the most effective way to compete for commercial loan business with larger, more prestigious banks with a wider range of services, is by focusing on the genuine concern communicated by loan supervisors as well as the expertise they develop in their knowledge of their client's subsector of industry (see Figure 13.3).

Cluster analysis allows for the classification or segmentation of a large group of variables into homogeneous subgroups based on similarities on a profile of information.

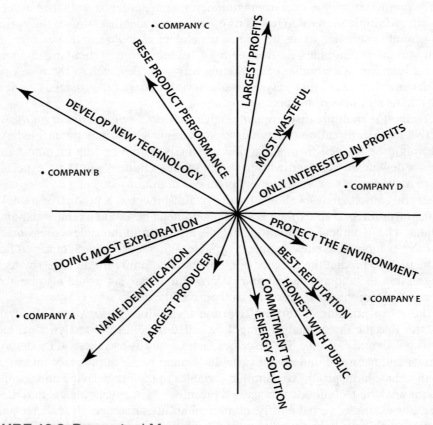

FIGURE 13.3 Perceptual Map

Cluster analysis enables the description of topologies or profiles according to attitudes toward preferences, appeals, and the like that might also include psychographic data. For example, this analysis might be used to describe psychographic profiles and interest in new transactional services among savings and loan customers.

The last major technique to be explained is *conjoint analysis.* Conjoint analysis, also known as trade-off analysis, is used for evaluating judgmental data where choices between attributes are involved. It is more commonly used in measuring the trade-off values of purchase selection factor attributes. Specifically, conjoint analysis is concerned with the joint effect of two or more independent variables on the ordering of a dependent variable. In essence, this method allows a determination of how consumers value various levels of purchase criteria and the extent to which they might tend to forego a high level of one attribute in order to obtain a high level of another. For example, the trade-off values of holding power, scent, nonstickiness, brand name, and price for hair spray might be cause for a conjoint evaluation.[7]

SUMMARY

Business researchers use statistical analysis of association to know how to interpret data describing the relationship between two or more variables. Ultimately, as suggested in Chapter 11, such analysis of data needs to provide us with answers to our research questions and lead us to choices among our decision alternatives. Statistical analysis gives us a window with which we can view the results of our research and see which decisions would be best. It is very important that we use the appropriate statistical-analytical procedures, or the window we are looking out of can give us a distorted view of reality, and our decisions based on that distorted view could be ill-chosen.

KEY TERMS

Alternative hypothesis (p. 226)
Analysis of variance (ANOVA) (p. 229)
Bivariate association (p. 231)
Hypothesis testing (p. 225)
Level of significance (p. 227)

Managerial significance (p. 224)
Multivariate association (p. 235)
Null hypothesis (p. 225)
Statistical analysis (p. 224)
Statistical significance (p. 224)

DISCUSSION QUESTIONS

1. Which is more important, statistically significant differences or managerially significant differences? Explain.
2. What do we mean when we say we are testing the hypotheses of our research?
3. Explain why we state hypotheses as "null hypotheses."
4. Does rejecting a null hypothesis mean the results have no real meaning for the researcher? Explain.
5. What is the difference between univariate and multivariate analysis?
6. Explain decision error. What are the costs associated with each type of error?
7. Why are multiple *t* tests not appropriate for determining the differences in means across a number of populations? What statistical method can be used to solve this problem?
8. Describe the different types of bivariate association.
9. Discuss the uses of various multivariate techniques.

ENDNOTES

1. Much of this discussion of hypothesis testing is adapted from Harvey J. Brightman's *Statistics in Plain English* (Cincinnati, OH: South-Western Publishing Co., 1986), pp. 160–173.
2. See Paul Newbold, *Statistics for Business and Economics* (Englewood Cliffs, NJ: Prentice-Hall, 1991).
3. Fred N. Kerlinger, *Foundations of Behavioral Research, Third Edition* (New York: Holt, Rinehart and Winston, 1986).
4. Joseph F. Hair, Rolph E. Anderson, Ronald L. Tatham, and William C. Black, *Multivariate Data Analysis, Fourth Edition* (Englewood Cliffs, NJ: Prentice-Hall, 1995).
5. *Foundations of Behavioral Research.*
6. David A. Aaker and George S. Day, *Marketing Research: Private and Public Sector Dimensions* (New York: John Wiley and Sons, Inc., 1980).
7. *Multivariate Data Analysis.*

The Research Report

Chapter Outline

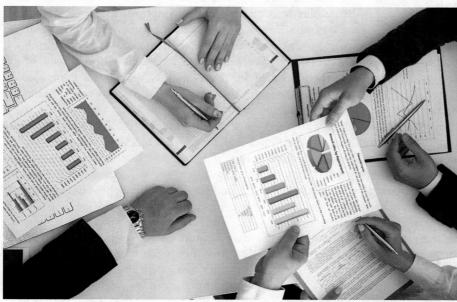

Hanna Kuprevich/Shutterstock.com

Learning Objectives

Upon completing this chapter, you should understand:

- The importance of a clearly written report and the make up of the audience in communicating the findings of the research.
- The basic components of a written report.
- How the use of charts and graphs can improve the communication value of the results of the study.
- The need for preparing and troubleshooting oral reports.

chuanpis/Shutterstock.com

INTRODUCTION

This chapter discusses the essentials of preparing the research report. The basic purpose of the **research report** is to communicate the results, conclusions, and recommendations of the research project. (If a project encompasses several phases or a long period of time, progress reports are normally sent to the purchaser or user of the research to inform them of the progress to date on a given project.) The key word in the preceding statement of purpose is communicate. The report must be an effective tool of communication not only to accurately present the findings and conclusions, but also to stimulate the reader to some managerial action. The research project was predicated on the need for information to aid in the decision-making process. Now the cycle has been completed and the report must address that decision and recommend a course of action in view of the research findings. The user or purchaser of the information must decide whether or not to heed the advice given in the recommendation of the report, but the actions recommended by the researcher must be communicated.

Research report a written or oral (or both) presentation of the findings of a research project to the specific audiences for whom the research was requested or to other interested parties.

As with any other instance in which you wish to communicate effectively, the marketing researcher should understand the target audience—its objectives for studying the research report, its tendencies for selective perception (selectively choosing to see what they want to see and ignoring what they do not), the time they will devote to the report, etc. Marketers and marketing researchers are trained to look at what they do through the eyes of the "target market," and it is particularly important that those skills be applied to the development of the research report.

In writing the report, the marketing researcher should keep two audiences in mind: the decision makers who commissioned the research in an effort to reduce the uncertainty of their decisions, and those people, unacquainted with the genesis of the research, who will pick up the report sometime in the future and want to use the findings to help them better understand something about the market. The report should serve as a guide to those interested in immediately implementing the recommendations cited in the report, but it must also be an archival document, able to "tell its story" to someone unacquainted with the study's background (i.e., management problem or opportunity initiating the need for research, the research purpose, etc.). It is possible that sometime in the future, decision makers may feel the need to duplicate the study in order to track market trends or changes in the decisional environment. In such cases a report originally written with an eye toward it becoming an archival document would contain all the information needed to duplicate the study in the absence of the original researchers and decision makers.

REPORT FORMAT

While there is no standardized reporting format used in all research reports, the following outline gives the elements commonly included. Each of these elements of the report will be discussed, using an actual research report written by one of the authors as an example (with changes in individual and company names to respect confidentiality).

A. Title Page
B. Tables of Contents
C. Introduction & Research Objectives
D. Research Methodology
E. Executive Summary
F. Findings
G. Conclusions and Recommendations
H. Supporting Documentation (Appendices)

Title Page

The title page (see Figure A.1) should tell the reader four things: (1) the subject of the study, (2) who it was prepared for, (3) who it was prepared by, and (4) the date of the study. This title page may also bear the logo of the preparing organization, if applicable. If the report has been revised, this revision should be noted on the title page.

Table of Contents

A good rule to follow for including a table of contents, charts, and illustrations is to base the decision on the length of the report (see Figure A.2). If the report is only ten to twelve pages in length, then a table of contents is not necessary. For longer reports, a table of contents, charts list, and illustrations list are usually included to enable the readers to locate the sections or illustrations in the report which they want to refer to at a given time. The table of contents should be detailed enough to serve as a guide to locating specific sections in the report. Thus, subheadings should be listed if the sections are long and contain many different subsections. This is especially true of the "findings" section.

Introduction and Research Objectives

The introduction to the report should refer the reader to the basic purpose of the research and the specific objectives that were agreed upon in the research proposal (see Figure A.3). In most cases it is advisable to list the statements of management problem, research purpose (including decision alternatives and criteria), along with your research objectives and hypotheses. This material should represent your latest thinking on these topics. If the research study (particularly the exploratory research) has caused you to change the objectives or list new hypotheses not identified in the original research proposal (see Chapter 1), these changes should be noted here (e.g., state both original and new objectives).

Research Methodology

This section should include a brief summary of the research methods (see Figure A.4). Remember the audience for the report—executives are not (or at least, rarely) interested in the small details of how the research was conducted. This description should be limited to mention of the primary means of data collection (e.g., focus groups followed by a telephone survey, or the series of experiments conducted, etc.); who were the respondents, how many were contacted and where they were located; the type of instrument used to collect the information (e.g., structured or unstructured surveys or interview guides); and a general discussion of the analysis process.

Executive Summary

The **executive summary** of the report presents the highlights of the research report in a straightforward and precise manner (see Figure A.5). This summary is usually organized by topics investigated or by questions that must be answered before a decision is made.

This may be the only section read by some executives, so enough detailed statements of major issues must be given to arm them with the basic facts that emerged in the study. It should be strong enough to permit the reader to get the essence of the findings without assuming that careful reading of the entire report will be made by *every* reader.

The summary should take the form of a detailed abstract in describing purpose, methodology, and findings. Usually two to three pages is the maximum length for a good summary. It is best to photocopy the executive summary on colored paper so it can easily be located by the busy executive who may ignore the rest of the report.

Executive summary the executive summary is usually a key component of the final report and summarizes the most important findings and recommendations of the research. As the name implies, it is written for the executives who may not take the time or have an interest in digesting the entire report.

Findings

This section of the report contains the detailed findings of the study (see Figure A.6). A great deal of detail is given in this section with supporting graphs and charts included as both references and sources of support for the statements that are made in the narrative of this section. This section is normally the largest section of the report and should be organized in a logical way. A topically organized format lends itself to both ease of preparation and reading. The major topics related to each research objective are presented so that the reader is taken in a step-by-step progression through all of the findings of the study. This also ensures that all the objectives are covered in the write-up of the findings.

Conclusions and Recommendations

As mentioned earlier, the culmination of the research deals with the statements given in reference to the decisions to be made based on the results of the research (see Figure A.7). This material could be given in the summary but it will have more impact on the readers if it is separated into a new section. The researcher's role is not just to present the facts, but to draw conclusions on the basis of the findings and to make recommendations on the basis of the conclusions. The reader should be presented a set of conclusions and recommendations for managerial action. While no researcher can force a manager to act on a set of recommendations, he or she should know enough about the decision and the data collected to recommend a course of action. That is what the researcher is being paid for! To simply "present the facts" and offer no recommendations is to lose the advantage gained by having someone who is not responsible for making the decision to at least suggest *some* alternative actions. The decision maker still has to "drive the car," but the one who just reads the "road map" can surely offer some suggestions about which direction to go! (Actual recommendations were removed in the banking study in the example in Figure A.7).

Supporting Documentation (Appendices)

The **appendices** can be used to present copies of questionnaires used in the study, more detailed secondary data, or any other type of data or material that might be helpful to the user of the report (see Figure A.8). In one study of a new outdoor recreational concept, articles on innovative recreational concepts that had been previously introduced were given. This is only one example of how appendices can be used. The researcher should avoid any attempt to "pad" or build up the size of a report through the use of appendices. This only takes away from the communicative force of the body of the report. However, detailed statistical analysis or even computer printouts can be included in an appendix. It is also possible to provide this material in a separate volume for those who will make a detailed study of the report.

Presentation

Copies of such reports may be used for years and binding ads protection to the contents. In general, a good rule of thumb to use when considering what to say and where to say it in the **written report** is to ask this question: "If someone totally unfamiliar with this research project were to take this report out of a file a month from now, would the report be complete enough to give them enough information to make decisions in this area?" Supply a sufficient number of copies for everyone attending the oral presentation of findings, plus at least two copies for the files of the primary recipient of the report and two copies for the researcher's file.

GUIDELINES FOR THE WRITTEN REPORT

There are two methods used to present statistical data: **tables and graphs**. Both of these methods are commonly used in research reports. The type of data or the emphasis the researcher wishes to put on a given set of data determines which method to use.

Appendices a report usually includes several appendices that contain the data gathering instrument, detailed findings, quotations, and in some cases, more detailed statistical information that some managers may be interested in.

Written report a written document following a specific format to describe the procedures, findings, and recommendations of research person or team. This document may become a reference tool for the current issues/problems being addressed as well as future research.

Tables and graphs tools used to display data/findings for the research and present a summary of the data and give a visual image of the research. Computerized software is usually used to generate and display the information.

Zern Liew/Shutterstock.com

Tables

A statistical table is a method of presenting and arranging data that have been broken down by one or more systems of classification. Analytical tables are designed to aid in a formal analysis of interrelationships between variables. A reference table is designed to be a repository of statistical data. The distinction between these two types of data is their intended use and not their construction. Table 14.1 is an example of an analytical table and Table 14.2 is an example of a reference table.

Table 14.1 was prepared to analyze differences in preferences based on the age of the respondents—an analytical table. Table 14.2 was prepared to report to the reader the number of respondents of each sex that were interviewed—a reference table.

Care should be taken in preparing tables to include proper headings, notes about discrepancies (percentages that add to more or slightly less than 100, for example), and sources of data. This helps the reader interpret the data contained in the tables and avoids obvious questions such as "Why don't the figures total 100 percent?"

Graphs

Many types of graphs can aid in presenting data. Three of the most commonly used are bar charts, pie charts, and line charts. These three add a visual magnitude to the presentation of the data. Graphics software packages offer a wide variety of options and are easy to use in creating a report with more visual impact.

A bar chart is easily constructed and can be readily interpreted even by those not familiar with charts. They are especially useful in showing differences between groups. Consider, for example, how much more clear and impactful the bar chart shown in Figure 14.1 is for communicating the findings of the data presented in Table 11.2. Here

TABLE 14.1 Preferences for Motel-Related Restaurants by Age of Traveler*

	Prefer Motel Restaurants		Prefer Non-motel Restaurants		
	Number	Percent	Number	Percent	Totals by Age
Under 25	7	5.5	130	45.3	137
25–34	13	10.3	62	21.6	75
35–44	29	23.0	38	13.2	67
45–54	33	26.2	35	12.2	68
Over 55	44	34.9	22	7.7	66
Total	126	99.9**	287	100.0	413

Source: Survey data.

*Preference was defined as where they would eat if they were traveling and staying at a motel with a restaurant.

**Does not add up to 100 percent due to rounding.

TABLE 14.2 Sex of Travelers

	Number	Percent
Male	294	71.1
Female	119	28.9
Total	413	100.0

it is possible to visually represent in a clear and convincing fashion our interpretation of the relationship between the variables. Recall that in our Chapter 11 discussion we used Table 11.2 to identify a possible relationship between consumption rates and agreement to pay more to get your favorite brand of egg substitutes. The use of graphics to tell your analytical story can not only communicate your message more effectively, but also may leave more lasting recollection of the point you are making compared to use of tables full of numbers.

A pie chart is a useful graph in marketing studies especially when showing market share or market segments. Figure 14.2 presents a sample pie chart. Adding color to highlight certain sections increases visual impact in pie charts. This permits identifying different shares held by different competitors also.

Figures 14.3 and 14.4 are line charts that are especially useful in showing trends in data and comparing trends for different products, customers, and market areas.

General Advice

Some general advice for preparing the written report is:

1. The written report represents you and your work. Make certain it leaves the impression you desire people to have about you as a professional by ensuring the report is well written, with proper grammar, no errors, correctly labeled tables, page numbers in table of contents matches text, and so on. Be obsessive about getting every detail correct and people will believe the report was written by the kind of true professional you are striving to become.

FIGURE 14.1 Bar Chart of Table 11.2 Data

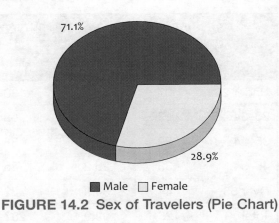

FIGURE 14.2 Sex of Travelers (Pie Chart)

FIGURE 14.3 Sales by Year

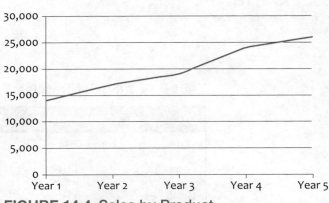

FIGURE 14.4 Sales by Product

2. Do not organize the report by the stages of the research (e.g., a heading of "Literature Review Results, Case Analysis Results," etc.). The decision makers reading the report do not want you to tell them what you discovered in each phase of the research (e.g., "In the literature review we found . . .," "In the in-depth interviews we discovered . . ."). They want you to put all the pieces together and discuss the overall findings, conclusions, and recommendations. Therefore, organize the report by key decisional areas and combine all the findings from all sources and all stages of the research in your discussion of that key decisional area. For example, if part of the research objectives related to making decisions about packaging, you might title this section of the report "Packaging Decisions" and report findings on industry trends discovered in your literature search, what inventory-management personnel of your key customer accounts said in in-depth interviews, the results of a descriptive-research sample survey of customers, and the findings of an experiment testing the sales of two different package designs in this section, along with your conclusions and recommendations for packaging decisions.

3. Write for your audience. Some managers are interested in knowing that you used factor analysis to determine the underlying attributes people use to evaluate coffee brands, other managers perceive your telling them this is "showing off," irrelevant, and evidence that you are not part of the team.

4. Do not discuss exploratory reports using statistics (e.g., "42 percent of focus group participants liked this idea"). It is best to avoid heavy use of statistics even when reporting the results of a large sample size exploratory survey. It is better, for example, to report a finding as "about a third of the males said they would be willing to try the product," rather than:

Would you be interested in trying this product?

	Males	Females
Yes	31%	27%
No	60%	70%
Not Sure	9%	3%

Reporting the results of an exploratory survey in the same way you would for a descriptive research study will result in the reader of the report attributing the same degree of precision and confidence in the exploratory as he or she did to descriptive research. Remember, the purpose of exploratory is to provide insights and ideas, and not measure frequencies and covariation with calculable amounts of precision and confidence intervals as in the case with descriptive research. Make sure the reader of the report understands how the type of research you conducted is reflected in the way you report the findings, and correct someone (tactfully) when he or she misstates a finding by suggesting it is something it was never intended to be (e.g., a statistic instead of a general observation).

5. Do not perform mathematical calculations on interval scaled data that can only be legitimately performed on ratio data. For example, let's say you were comparing your new brand of car wax to the market leader and asked people to indicate from their observation how shiny each wax made a car's hood look on the following scale:

Very shiny	Shiny	Neutral	Not very shiny	Not at all shiny
☐	☐	☐	☐	☐
5	4	3	2	1

Your wax is neither 27 percent nor 300 percent shinier than your competitor's product because you cannot use an interval scale to compute a ratio such as was done here.

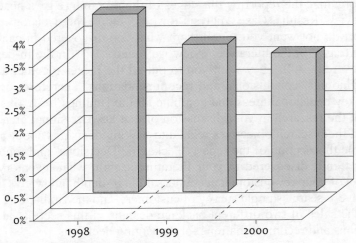

FIGURE 14.5 Bar Chart of Table 9.2 Data

6. Do not manipulate your graphs to mislead a reader in his or her interpretation of the research findings. Consider, for example, the impression left by the bar chart in Figure 14.5. The impression is that there has been a significant downward trend in the percentage of sales dollars allocated to advertising, when actually the decline is less than one percentage point of sales. This misrepresentation would be even more egregious if actual advertising dollars had risen or remained the same from 1998 to 2000. Intentionally misleading the reader of your report is not only unethical, it brings all of your findings, conclusions, and recommendations into question. Do not do it.

7. Unless you are divinely inspired, do not think your first draft of the report will be your last. Allow enough time before the report is due to make several drafts. Have someone with good editing skills edit your work (expect to pay them for this job). Have someone unfamiliar with the research study read the report. If someone without a background in this particular project can read and understand why you needed to do the research, what you did, what you found, and sees the conclusions and recommendations as legitimate outcomes of the findings, then you probably have written a report that will actually influence decision making.

8. Quote respondents verbatim at appropriate points to "put a face on" your statistics. These quotes may be from statements made in the exploratory research phase, such as in a focus group, or from an open-ended question in a descriptive survey. For example, you may have just reported that only 13 percent of people found the graphics in a print ad attractive. You then might include some verbatim statements to illustrate the problem with the ad:

   "I give up. What is it supposed to be?"

   "Looks like one of those Rorschach tests."

   "I'd tell you what I think I see but my mother would wash my mouth out with soap."

   "You can't be serious!"

   Judicious use of concrete examples to illustrate abstract points makes your findings more memorable.

9. If 12 out of 17 people responded yes to a question, do not report the results as Yes = 70.59 percent. Inevitably someone will ask for the sample size and when you tell them you will at best look idiotic if not untrustworthy. Do not give results an aura of precision they do not deserve.

10. Make liberal use of headings and subheadings to aid the reader's navigation through the report.

11. Use headings that communicate findings of interest to the decision makers. "Consumers Demand Quality" is better than "Findings Regarding the Importance of Quality."

12. Do all the other things you know you are supposed to do (e.g., use active instead of passive voice, say "we" instead of "I," use present tense as much as possible, begin paragraphs with topic-revealing sentences, avoid researcher jargon, use short words (e.g., "now" instead of "currently"), avoid clichés, do not use six words when two will do, etc.). Refer to one of the standard works on how to write well.[1]

ORAL REPORTS

Another effective way to present the results of a study is in an **oral report**. The authors do not recommend this as a substitute for a written report, but as a supplement to the written document. The written report should be seen as an archival document, and not just a cryptic written presentation for those people thoroughly familiar with the project. If the oral presentation is effectively done, it becomes a communication tool to reinforce what is given in the written report. In many cases it becomes a technique to communicate results to key executives who might not otherwise have interest or access to those who have been collecting data outside the organization.

With today's audiovisual technology, no researcher should fail to use these aids in an oral presentation. Plenty of evidence suggests that we remember more of what we see and hear than of what we read only. Slides and transparencies can be prepared at modest costs for most research budgets and greatly add to the impact of the presentation. Again, computerized presentation graphics are easy to use and enable the researcher to customize the graphics used in the oral presentation by including company logo, industry symbols, etc. Short excerpts from videotaped focus group sessions can be very effective in demonstrating with a specific example the broader finding and conclusions that tape segment is intended to illustrate. Remember, people are more likely to recall and use in formulating their own conclusions those bits of information presented in graphic or visual form rather than as tables or numbers. The following is some general advice for preparing and presenting an oral report:

1. There is increasing use of computerized presentation software such as PowerPoint, Aldus Persuasion, Astound, Harvard Graphics, Freelance Graphics, and Presentations when making oral presentations. The use of such programs may be expected by your audience, and use of "low-tech" presentation material such as overhead transparencies or flip charts may, unfortunately, label you as unsophisticated, inexperienced, or hopelessly behind the times. Check to see what is the common practice for presentations to this audience. If you use a computer software presentation package, ensure that you will be able to run your presentation software, even if it means bringing your own hardware.

2. Do not assume optimal conditions and equipment for your presentation. In fact, do not assume anything except that you will get to the room and none of your requests will have been met. Get there far enough ahead of the scheduled presentation that you can rearrange the seating, set up the screen and projector/computer that you brought in case your request for equipment was not met, ensure everything operates as it should, etc.

3. Practice your presentation at least three times before making it in front of the audience. Know your material in great detail. Be comfortable with your material. Plan your presentation to take up only about two-thirds of the allotted time. Know where you need to be in your presentation by specific points in time (e.g., each fifteen minutes). If you are behind schedule, skip less important material rather than rushing through everything.

Oral report an oral presentation of the research project highlighting the research objective, findings and recommendations of the research person or team and usually accompanies the written report.

4. Make sure you present your findings in an order that is consistent with the way people draw connections between pieces of information and construct meaning for information. Have your presentation "tell the story" that you have identified in the findings.

5. When appropriate, use visual aids (e.g., product packages, story boards, etc.) to help the audience better relate to the research and findings. A good idea, for example, is to at different points in the presentation play a few minutes of videotape from a focus group session to demonstrate how actual consumers feel about the topic. This could also be done when discussing descriptive research results when a few consumers on the videotape express in a more visceral way what the emotionless data are revealing.

6. As with the written report, use charts and graphs whenever that method of displaying the results communicates the findings more effectively than tables.

7. Provide the audience with an outline of the presentation and paper copies of the key visuals (graphs, tables, conclusions, recommendations, etc.).

8. Do all the other things common sense tells you you should do in a presentation (e.g., tell them what you are going to tell them, tell them, tell them what you told them; face the audience when describing a visual; make eye contact; do not make extravagant gestures, but do not seem stiff either; do not play with your pointer; make text on your visuals large enough to read by the person farthest away from you; do not read from a script; make sure everyone hears a question from the audience before answering it; etc.).

SUMMARY

This chapter has presented a brief overview of the steps involved in preparing a research report. The research report is not only a communication tool, but is also a source document for future reference. The preparation of the report provides the researcher with the major vehicle to communicate findings to management and to display the results of the work that went into completing the project.

KEY TERMS

Appendices (p. 242)
Executive summary (p. 241)
Oral report (p. 247)

Research report (p. 240)
Tables and graphs (p. 242)
Written report (p. 242)

DISCUSSION QUESTIONS

1. What are the objectives you want to achieve when writing a research report and making a presentation of research results?

2. What are the researcher's responsibilities in writing conclusions and recommendations?

3. Describe how "thinking like a marketer" will influence how you write the report and make the presentation.

ENDNOTE

1. Kenneth Roman and Joel Raphaelson, *Writing That Works* (New York: Harper and Row, 1981); William Strunk, Jr. and E. B. White, *The Elements of Style*, Third Edition (New York: Macmillan, 1979); William Zinsser, *On Writing Well*, Third Edition (New York: Harper and Row, 1985); Tim J. Saben, *Practical Business Communications* (Burr Ridge, IL: Irwin/Mirror Press, 1994); David Morris and Satish Chandra, *Guidelines for Writing a Research Report* (Chicago: American Marketing Association, 1993).

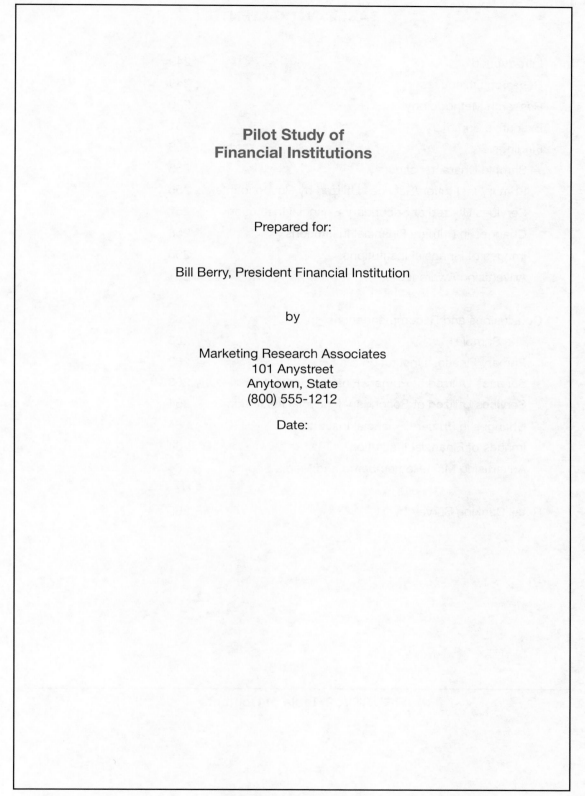

**Pilot Study of
Financial Institutions**

Prepared for:

Bill Berry, President Financial Institution

by

Marketing Research Associates
101 Anystreet
Anytown, State
(800) 555-1212

Date:

FIGURE A.1 Title Page

TABLE OF CONTENTS

FIGURE A.2 Table of Contents

INTRODUCTION

The following study was conducted to assist local financial institutions with the planning necessary to determine future courses of action in response to changing market conditions. This involves developing a database from which conclusions can be drawn about positioning strategy, market share goals, and promotional strategy. The purpose of this present study was to analyze the retail banking market in the City area. The study analyzed market share by primary financial institutions, services utilized by primary and secondary institutions, images of financial institutions, and advertising awareness.

RESEARCH OBJECTIVES

The specific research objectives of this study were as follows:

I. Determine the market share for primary institutions for the major financial institutions in the area.
II. Evaluate the utilization of various services at both primary and secondary institutions.
III. Identify the level of satisfaction with primary institutions and the reasons for any dissatisfaction.
IV. Determine changes in primary institutions by respondents and the reasons for any changes.
V. Assess respondents' image of various financial institutions on a series of image characteristics.
VI. Measure advertising awareness and media exposure of respondents.
VII. Analyze responses by socioeconomic characteristics such as age, sex, income, and education.

FIGURE A.3 Introduction and Research Objectives

RESEARCH METHODOLOGY

To accomplish these objectives, telephone interviews were conducted with 299 area residents who used the services of local financial institutions. Respondents were randomly selected from the City area telephone book to assure a representative sample was used as the basis of data analysis.

The respondents were surveyed using a structured questionnaire designed to respond to the project's specific research objectives. The questionnaire was thoroughly pretested before being administered to improve the quality of the measuring instrument. The resulting data were edited, entered into computer files, and processed by a statistical-analysis program to provide a comprehensive set of tables and cross-tabulations for the study. The tables included number of respondents and percentages by response to each question, and chi-square analysis of the cross-tabulations of the data by primary financial institution to identify differences in response patterns to the questions contained in the questionnaire.

FIGURE A.4 Research Methodology

EXECUTIVE SUMMARY

• A survey of 299 City area respondents was completed during the months of April and May. The survey involved the use of a structured questionnaire administered by telephone to randomly selected area residents who had an account with a local financial institution. The questionnaire was pretested to assure the completeness and accuracy of responses. A typical respondent could be described as follows: married; male; between the ages of 35-44; lived in the area for 6-12 years; median income of between $35,000-$49,999; attended or graduated college.

• Each respondent was asked to identify his or her primary financial institution. City Bank was by far the most frequently mentioned financial institution (47 percent), followed by The First National Bank (14 percent) and Public Bank (11 percent).

• The services utilized most frequently at the primary financial institution were checking accounts, savings accounts, ATMs, and investment instruments. Fifty-one percent of the respondents had done business at their primary institution for six or more years and 52 percent were highly satisfied with their primary financial institution.

• Thirty-eight percent of the respondents reported having an account at a secondary institution. The most frequently utilized services were savings (18 percent), checking (14 percent), and investment instruments (13 percent). The majority of the respondents have done business with their secondary financial institution for over six years. The high proportion of respondents with secondary institutions may indicate a preference for multiple financial relationships or a lack of cross-selling by primary institutions.

• Sixty-two (20.7 percent) of the respondents stated they had changed their primary financial institution since living in the area, and of this group 62.9 percent had done so in the last five years. This indicates the volatility of the market with major changes (Public and The First National) during that time period. Based on this study and supplemental sources on deposits, it appears that City Bank and The First National Bank have both gained market share at the expense of Public Bank. Most respondents who reported switching financial institutions changed from one bank to another bank.

• Respondents were also asked to respond to 17 image characteristics to measure the image of several different institutions. City Bank was the most frequently mentioned institution on every item except "the one you would never recommend." City Bank was followed most closely by The First National Bank, while Public Bank was a distant third.

• The main reason respondents gave for switching primary financial institutions was poor service. This theme was echoed in responses to another question on dissatisfaction with their current primary institution. Poor service was named by 55 percent of the respondents who expressed dissatisfaction with their current primary financial institution. Keeping current customers satisfied with the service received appears to be a safeguard against dissatisfaction and ultimate switching from one financial institution to another.

• Respondents appear to see City Bank, the First National Bank, and to some extent Public Bank as well-managed, progressive, innovative, customer-oriented institutions with a strong financial base, local, and involved in community activities. They were viewed as providing the best service, leaders among local financial institutions with friendly, knowledgeable employees—the one they would recommend to others and best for people like themselves.

FIGURE A.5 Executive Summary

EXECUTIVE SUMMARY (continued)

• Respondents were also asked questions to determine advertising awareness and media exposure for financial-institution advertising. When the three financial institutions with the most active promotional campaigns (The First National Bank, Public Bank, and Premier Homestead) were compared, 29 percent remembered seeing or hearing an ad for the First National Bank, 22 percent remembered Public Bank, and 17 percent remembered Premier Homestead. Media exposure for these campaigns was: (1) saw/heard TV ad—43 percent; (2) heard radio ad—27 percent; and (3) saw newspaper ad—16 percent. All other media accounted for only 14 percent.

FIGURE A.5 Executive Summary (continued)

FINDINGS

This section presents the findings of the study. The first part shows the characteristics of the respondents who participated in the project. This is followed by a question-by-question analysis of the results of the study.

Sample Characteristics

FIGURE E-1: LENGTH OF TIME RESPONDENTS HAVE LIVED IN AREA

Length of Time	Frequency	Percent
0-2 years	40	13
3-5 years	67	23
6-12 years	52	17
13-20 years	41	14
Over 20 years	92	31
Don't Know/Refused	7	2
Total	299	100

FIGURE E-2: MARITAL STATUS OF RESPONDENTS

Marital Status	Frequency	Percent
Single with No Children	74	26
Married with No Children	50	17
Married with Children at Home	86	30
Single with Children at Home	12	4
Married with No Children at Home	53	18
Single with No Children at Home	11	4
Refused	4	1
Total	290	100

FIGURE E-3: AGE CATEGORY OF RESPONDENTS

Age Category	Frequency	Percent
18-24	44	15
25-34	84	29
35-44	55	19
45-54	44	15
55-64	28	10
65 and older	20	7
Refused	13	5
Total	288	100

FIGURE A.6 Findings

FINDINGS (continued)

FIGURE E-4: TOTAL FAMILY INCOME OF RESPONDENTS

Total Family Income	Frequency	Percent
Under $15,000	22	7
$15,000-24,999	44	15
$25,000-34,999	48	16
$35,000-49,999	49	17
$50,000-64,999	33	11
$65,000-79,999	7	2
$80,000-94,999	–	–
$95,000-110,000	–	–
Over $110,000	8	3
Don't Know/Refused	88	29
Total	299	100

FIGURE E-5: EDUCATIONAL LEVEL OF RESPONDENTS

Educational Level	Frequency	Percent
High School Graduate	52	17
High School Graduate with Some College	88	30
College Graduate	102	34
College Graduate with Some Graduate School	15	5
Graduate Degree Holder	18	6
Don't Know/Refused	24	8
Total	299	100

FIGURE E-6: SEX OF RESPONDENTS

Sex	Frequency	Percent
Male	150	52
Female	140	48
Total	290	100

FIGURE E-7: AVERAGE MONTHLY BALANCE IN CHECKING ACCOUNT OF RESPONDENTS

Monthly Balance	Frequency	Percent
Under $250	24	8
$250-500	43	14
$501-1,000	63	21
$1,001-2,000	27	9
Over $2,000	51	17
Don't Know/Refused	91	31
Total	299	100

FIGURE A.6 Findings (continued)

FINDINGS (continued)

FIGURE E-8: AMOUNT RESPONDENTS HAVE INVESTED IN CDS, MONEY MARKET DEPOSIT ACCOUNTS, INDIVIDUAL RETIREMENT ACCOUNTS, OR OTHER HIGH-YIELD INVESTMENTS

Amount Invested	Frequency	Percent
None	82	28
Under $10,000	41	14
$10,001-25,000	38	13
$25,001-75,000	27	9
Over $75,000	7	2
Don't Know/Refused	103	34
Total	298	100

FIGURE E-9: TYPICAL MONTHLY BALANCE FOR NONCHECKING SAVINGS ACCOUNT OF RESPONDENTS

Monthly Balance	Frequency	Percent
None	32	11
Under $2,500	38	13
$2,501-5,000	37	12
$5,001-7,500	32	11
$7,501-10,000	19	6
Over $10,000	37	12
Don't Know/Refused	104	35
Total	299	100

Primary Institution/Services Utilized by Respondents

Each respondent was asked to identify his or her Primary Financial Institution. The results revealed the following statistics.

FIGURE E-10: RESPONDENTS' PRIMARY FINANCIAL INSTITUTION

Financial Institutions	Frequency	Percent
City Bank	136	47
First Bank	25	9
The First National Bank	39	14
Premier Homestead	13	4
City Homestead	19	7
Public Bank	33	11
Other	24	8
Total	299	100

Of the 289 customers interviewed, 136 or 47 percent stated that City Bank was their primary financial institution. The First National Bank was the primary financial institution for 39 or 14 percent of the respondents. Of those surveyed, Public Bank was preferred by 11 percent or 33 of the respondents as their primary financial institution. The following figure shows the services utilized by respondents at their primary financial institutions.

FIGURE A.6 Findings (continued)

FINDINGS (continued)

FIGURE E-11: SERVICES UTILIZED BY RESPONDENTS AT PRIMARY FINANCIAL INSTITUTION

Services	Frequency	Percent
Automatic Teller Machine	162	54
Personal Loan	48	16
Automobile Loan	47	16
Home (Mortgage) Loans	28	9
Telephone Bill Paying Service	7	2
VISA/MasterCard Service	85	28
Safe Deposit Box	58	19
Checking Account	286	96
Savings Account	229	77
Trust Account	11	4
Money Market Deposit Account	23	8
CDs and Investment Instrument	116	39
Individual Retirement Accounts (IRAs)	54	18
Overdraft Protection	69	23
Educational Loan	17	6
Other	14	5

Of those surveyed, 286 or 96 percent have a checking account with their primary financial institution. A savings account was the second largest service utilized by 229 respondents or 77 percent. The automatic teller machine was used by 162 respondents or 54 percent. CDs and other investment instruments were used by 116 or 39 percent of those surveyed at their primary financial institution. Only 7 or 2 percent of those surveyed used the telephone bill paying service at their primary financial institution. Another infrequently used service by respondents is the trust account, used by 11 or 4 percent.

FIGURE E-12: LENGTH OF TIME RESPONDENTS HAVE DONE BUSINESS WITH THEIR
PRIMARY FINANCIAL INSTITUTION

Length of Time	Frequency	Percent
Less than 1 Year	34	12
1-2 years	30	10
3-5 years	79	27
6-12 years	82	28
Over 12 years	67	23
Total	292	100

Of those surveyed, 28 percent or 82 respondents have done business with their financial institution for 6 to 12 years. Seventy-nine respondents or 27 percent have done business with their primary financial institution for 3 to 5 years. Of those surveyed, 51 percent have done business with their primary financial institution for 6 or more years.

FIGURE A.6 Findings (continued)

Services Utilized at Secondary Financial Institution

Of those respondents interviewed, 112 or 38 percent have accounts at a secondary financial institution. The following figure outlines the services used by the respondents at their secondary financial institution.

FIGURE E-13: SERVICES UTILIZED BY RESPONDENTS AT SECONDARY FINANCIAL INSTITUTION

Services	Frequency	Percent
Automatic Teller Machine	8	3
Personal Loan	11	4
Automobile Loan	17	6
Home (Mortgage) Loans	25	8
Telephone Bill Paying Service	1	–
VISA/MasterCard Service	15	5
Safe Deposit Box	5	2
Checking Account	42	14
Savings Account	53	18
Trust Account	3	1
Money Market Deposit Account	3	1
CDs and Investment Instrument	38	13
Individual Retirement Accounts (IRAs)	17	6
Overdraft Protection	1	-
Educational Loan	6	2
Other	2	1

Those respondents who have a secondary financial institution use a savings account as the primary service (53 respondents or 18 percent). A checking account as a service at a secondary financial institution was used by 42 of the respondents or 14 percent. Of those surveyed, 38 or 13 percent utilized CDs and investment instruments at their secondary financial institution. The services utilized least by respondents at their secondary financial institution were telephone bill paying service, overdraft protection, and trust accounts.

FIGURE E-14: LENGTH OF TIME RESPONDENTS HAVE DONE BUSINESS WITH THEIR SECONDARY FINANCIAL INSTITUTION

Length of Time	Frequency	Percent
Less Than 1 Year	5	4
1-2 Years	14	12
2-5 Years	28	25
6-12 Years	32	28
Over 12 Years	36	31
Total	115	100

FIGURE A.6 Findings (continued)

Of those surveyed who have secondary financial institutions, the majority (59 percent) have done business with their secondary institution for over six years. This indicates that either respondents prefer to have more than one financial institution or that primary institutions are not doing a good job of cross-selling their services.

Changes in Primary Financial Institutions

Respondents were asked if they had changed primary financial institutions while living in this area. Of those surveyed, 62 or 21 percent had changed primary financial institutions. The following figure shows how long ago the change was made.

FIGURE E-15: HOW LONG AGO RESPONDENTS CHANGED PRIMARY FINANCIAL INSTITUTIONS WHILE LIVING IN THIS AREA

How Long Ago Change Was Made	Frequency	Percent
Less Than 1 year	13	21
1-2 Years	8	13
3-5 Years	18	29
6-12 Years	10	16
Over 12 Years	13	21
Total	62	100

Of those surveyed who changed primary financial institutions while living in this area, 18 or 29 percent made that change three to five years ago. This indicates a great deal of volatility in the customer base of financial institutions in the area. In the last five years, 63 percent have changed their primary financial institution.

The following figure states what type of change was made when respondents changed primary financial institution.

FIGURE E-16: TYPE OF FINANCIAL INSTITUTION CHANGE MADE BY RESPONDENTS

Categories	Frequency	Percent
A Bank to a Savings and Loan	3	5
A Bank to a Credit Union	2	3
A Savings and Loan to a Bank	5	8
A Savings and Loan to a Credit Union	–	–
A Credit Union to a Bank	–	–
A Credit Union to a Savings and Loan	–	–
A Bank to Another Bank	50	84
Total	60	100

Of those surveyed who changed primary financial institutions while living in this area, 84 percent or 50 respondents changed from one bank to another bank. The other types

FIGURE A.6 Findings (continued)

of changes made were from a savings and loan to a bank with five respondents or 8 percent making this type of change, 5 percent of the respondents changed from a bank to a savings and loan, and 3 percent changed from a bank to a credit union.

The following figure will outline the main reason respondents changed primary financial institutions while living in this area.

FIGURE E-17: MAIN REASON RESPONDENTS CHANGED PRIMARY FINANCIAL INSTITUTIONS

Reason for Change	Frequency	Percent
Poor Service at Old	22	34
Better Location at New	14	22
Unsure of Stability/Felt Safer at New	9	14
Interest Rates Higher at New	5	8
Other	14	22
Total	64	100

According to those surveyed, the most frequent reason to change primary financial institutions was poor service. Twenty-two percent of respondents also stated that a better location was the reason they changed. Of those surveyed who have changed primary financial institutions, 14 percent changed because they were unsure of the stability of their current bank and felt safer at another institution, 8 percent changed to get a higher interest rate, and 22 percent stated some other reason for their decision to change primary financial institutions.

The following figure will look at respondents' level of satisfaction with their current primary financial institution. Respondents were asked to rank their financial institution on a scale of 1 to 5, where 1 is strongly dissatisfied and 5 is very satisfied.

FIGURE E-18: RESPONDENTS' SATISFACTION WITH THEIR PRIMARY FINANCIAL INSTITUTION

Categories		Frequency	Percent
Strongly Dissatisfied	–1	2	1
	–2	9	3
	–3	31	11
	–4	97	33
Very Satisfied	–5	152	52
Total		291	100

The overall level of satisfaction with the primary financial institution of respondents was fairly high. Of those surveyed, 52 percent or 152 respondents were very satisfied with their primary financial institution. A satisfaction rating of "4" was given to primary financial institutions by 97 respondents or 33 percent. Of those surveyed, 31 or 11 percent gave their primary financial institution a satisfaction level of "3." Only 2 respondents or 1 percent were strongly dissatisfied with their primary financial institution with a rating of "1" and 9 respondents or 3 percent gave a rating of "2."

Respondents that rated their overall level of satisfaction with their primary financial institution as "Strongly Dissatisfied –1 or –2" were asked to specify why they were dissatisfied. The findings are in Figure E-19. This figure reinforces the earlier findings that poor service causes dissatisfaction and eventual departure from a particular financial institution.

FIGURE A.6 Findings (continued)

FIGURE E-19: RESPONDENTS' REASON FOR DISSATISFACTION WITH PRIMARY
FINANCIAL INSTITUTION

Categories	Frequency	Percent
Poor Service	6	55
Bad Location	–	–
Unsure of Stability	5	45
Interest Rates are Low	–	–
Other	–	–
Total	11	100

Of those surveyed, only 11 expressed dissatisfaction with their primary financial institution. The main reason cited for dissatisfaction was "Poor Service," indicated by 55 percent of the respondents. Respondents' second major reason for dissatisfaction was "Unsure of Stability," indicated by 5 respondents or 45 percent.

Images of Financial Institutions

Respondents were asked to express their initial impression or opinion about financial institutions in the area. Those surveyed were asked to mention what financial institution came to mind when the interviewer mentioned each factor about financial institutions. The results are listed in the following figure (on the next page).

Of those responding, Figure E-20 shows the percentage of respondents that chose each of the banks for the various factors. In all the categories, City Bank was the number one choice, except on the question that asked respondents to name the "One financial institution they would never recommend." The respondents' perceptions on City Bank were highest when asked to name the financial institution "Most involved in community leadership and activities," with 66 percent of those surveyed choosing City Bank. When respondents were asked to name the financial institution with the "Best reputation for being successful, reliable, and honest," "Best managed," and "The leader among local financial institutions," City Bank was clearly the favorite choice.

FIGURE E-20: RESPONDENTS' PERCEPTION OF LOCAL FINANCIAL INSTITUTIONS

Factor	City Bank	First Bank	First Nat.	Premier Home	City Home	Public Bank	Other
Best managed	51%	6%	20%	4%	2%	12%	5%
Friendliest, most personal service	47	8	16	6	5	12	6
Most customer-oriented	46	10	19	5	3	12	5
Most progressive and up-to-date	39	5	33	5	2	13	3
Best for investment-oriented customers	38	8	30	6	4	10	4
Most innovative in the market	43	5	32	4	1	12	3

FIGURE A.6 Findings (continued)

The financial institution most involved in community leadership and activities	66	6	14	2	2	6	4
Strongest financial base	37	7	31	5	2	14	4
Best reputation for being successful, reliable, and honest	53	8	16	4	2	12	5
The one you would recommend	45	9	21	4	2	13	6
The one you would never recommend	10	21	6	9	30	12	12
Has the best advertising	59	5	17	4	2	12	1
The leader among local financial institutions	49	7	26	3	1	10	4
Has the best service	43	9	21	5	3	12	7
Makes fewest errors on accounts	43	10	18	5	6	11	7
Friendliest, most knowledgeable employees	44	10	17	7	5	11	6
Is the best place for people like you	46	9	21	5	2	11	6

City Bank was the dominant choice in several other categories as well. When respondents were asked which financial institution has the "Friendliest, most personalized service"; the "Most customer-oriented"; "Most innovative in the market"; "Has the best service"; and "Makes fewest errors on accounts," City Bank has the highest percentages in each of these categories.

In several of the categories City Bank and The First National Bank were the 2 obvious favorites. When respondents were asked to name the financial institution that is the "Most progressive and up-to-date," 39 percent chose City Bank and 33 percent chose The First National Bank. When asked to name the financial institution with the "Strongest financial base," 37 percent chose City Bank and 31 percent chose The First National Bank.

Advertising Awareness

Respondents were asked if they remembered recently seeing or hearing advertising for any of the local financial institutions. The following figure states which financial institutions were remembered by respondents for advertisements.

FIGURE E-21: RESPONDENTS' RECOLLECTION OF RECENT ADVERTISEMENTS BY LOCAL FINANCIAL INSTITUTIONS

Financial Institution	Frequency	Percent
Public Bank	47	22
The First National Bank	61	29
Premier Homestead	37	17
All Others	67	32
Total	212	100

FIGURE A.6 Findings (continued)

Sixty-one respondents (29 percent) remembered recently seeing or hearing advertisements for The First National Bank. Of those surveyed, 67 or 32 percent remembered advertising for "All others," which would include any of the financial institutions in the area except the ones mentioned above (Public Bank, the First National, and Premier Homestead).

The following figure outlines the media source remembered by respondents as advertising for a local financial institution.

FIGURE E-22: MEDIA SOURCE REMEMBERED BY RESPONDENTS IN ADVERTISEMENTS FOR A LOCAL FINANCIAL INSTITUTION

Media Source	Frequency	Percent
Heard TV Advertising	98	43
Heard Radio Advertising	62	27
Saw a Newspaper Ad/Article	36	16
Saw a New Sign Going Up	8	3
Billboards	21	9
Someone Told Me About It	3	1
Other	2	1
Total	230	100

Ninety-eight respondents (43 percent) cited TV as the media source remembered for advertisements for a financial institution. Radio was the second largest media source remembered, cited by 62 respondents or 27 percent. Advertising through the paper was remembered by 16 percent of the respondents.

FIGURE A.6 Findings (continued)

CONCLUSIONS AND RECOMMENDATIONS

The Sample

The sample consisted of interviews with residents in the City area who had an account with a local financial institution. Of the 299 area residents who were surveyed, 52 percent were male and 48 percent were female. A typical respondent is described as a married male between the ages of 35-44, who has lived in this area for 6 to 12 years, with a median income of between $35,000 and $49,999, and has attended or graduated from college.

Primary Financial Institution

Of the 299 residents who were surveyed, 47 percent named City Bank as their primary financial institution, followed by The First National Bank, named by 14 percent of the respondents.

FIGURE E-23: PRIMARY FINANCIAL INSTITUTION

Financial Institution	Frequency	Percent
City Bank	136	47
First Bank	25	9
The First National Bank	39	14
Premier Homestead	13	4
City Homestead	19	7
Public Bank	33	11
Other	24	8
Total	289	100

Services Utilized at Primary Financial Institutions

Once the primary financial institution of respondents was established, respondents were asked which services they utilized at their primary financial institution. The following figure lists those services used most by residents who were surveyed.

FIGURE E-24: SERVICES UTILIZED AT PRIMARY INSTITUTION

Services	Frequency	Percent
Checking Account	286	96
Savings Account	229	77
Automatic Teller Machine	162	54
CDs and Investment Instruments	116	39
VISA/MasterCard Service	85	28

Of those surveyed, 96 percent utilize a checking account at their primary financial institution, and 77 percent utilize a savings account. Fifty-one percent of the respondents have done business with their primary financial institution for six or more years.

FIGURE A.7 Conclusions and Recommendations

Services Utilized at Secondary Financial Institution

Of those respondents with secondary financial institutions, 59 percent have done business with their financial institution for six or more years.

FIGURE E-25: SERVICES UTILIZED AT SECONDARY INSTITUTION

Services	Frequency	Percent
Savings Account	53	18
Checking Account	42	14
VISA/MasterCard Service	36	13
Home (Mortgage) Loan	25	8

Of those respondents with secondary financial institutions, 59 percent have done business with their financial institution for six or more years.

Changes in Primary Financial Institution

Of those surveyed, 21 percent had changed primary financial institution while living in this area. Respondents were asked what type of change they made, and 84 percent changed from one bank to another. The main reason respondents changed primary financial institutions while living in this area was due to poor service.

This finding coincides with respondents' level of satisfaction or dissatisfaction with their primary financial institution. Fifty-two percent of those surveyed were very satisfied with their primary financial institution, while 4 percent of those surveyed were strongly dissatisfied. Those respondents who stated they were dissatisfied were then asked why they were dissatisfied. Fifty-five percent of those stated their main reason for dissatisfaction was poor service.

Images of Financial Institution

Respondents were asked to express their initial impression about financial institutions in the area to determine the image of several local financial institutions. The overall favorite in all of the categories (except for "the financial institution you would never recommend"), was City Bank. Some of the characteristics respondents were asked about were: which local financial institution is well managed, progressive, innovative, customer-oriented, with a strong financial base, and involved in the community. The local institution mentioned first by the majority of the respondents was City Bank. The First National Bank was the respondents' second most frequently mentioned, and Public Bank came in a distant third.

Advertising Most Remembered and Media Source

To determine advertising awareness and media exposure for local financial institutions, respondents were asked to identify financial institutions for which they recalled seeing or hearing advertising. When The First National Bank, Public Bank, and Premier Homestead (the three local financial institutions with the most active promotional campaigns) were compared, 29 percent remembered seeing or hearing an ad for The First National Bank, 22 percent remembered Public Bank, and 17 percent remembered Premier Homestead. Those who did recall seeing or hearing ads for financial institutions were also asked to identify the media sources where they saw or heard the ads. The media source most frequently remembered was TV (43 percent), radio ads (27 percent), and newspaper ads (16 percent).

FIGURE A.7 Conclusions and Recommendations (continued)

Retail Banking Survey

[1-3] Hello. Am I speaking with the man/lady of the house? (IF NO, ASK TO SPEAK TO THAT PERSON.)

Hello, I'm _____. We're conducting a marketing research project with area residents. This study deals with financial institutions and we need your help in this project. Your answers will be confidential and used only in combination with the responses of other people.

1a. Do you, or does a member of your household, work for a bank, savings and loan, credit union, advertising, public relations, or market research firm?
___ YES (Terminate)
___ NO

1b. Do you have a checking or savings account with a local financial institution?
___ YES
___ NO (Terminate)

[4] 2. How long have you lived in this area?
___ 0-2 Years[1]
___ 3-5 Years[2]
___ 6-12 Years[3]
___ 13-20 Years[4]
___ Over 20 Years[5]

[5] 3. What is the name of your primary financial institution?
___ City Bank[1]
___ First Bank[2]
___ The First National Bank[3]
___ Premier Home Bank[4]
___ City Home Bank[5]
___ Public Bank[6]
___ Other[7]

4. What services are you currently utilizing at your primary financial institution? (READ)
[6]   ___ Automatic Teller Machine
[7]   ___ Personal Loans
[8]   ___ Automobile Loans
[9]   ___ Home (Mortgage) Loans
[10]   ___ Telephone Bill Paying Service
[11]   ___ VISA/MasterCard Services
[12]   ___ Safe Deposit Box
[13]   ___ Checking Account
[14]   ___ Savings Account
[15]   ___ Trust Account
[16]   ___ Money Market Deposit Account
[17]   ___ CDs and Investment Instrument
[18]   ___ Individual Retirement Accounts (IRAs)
[19]   ___ Overdraft Protection
[20]   ___ Educational Loans
[21]   ___ Other

[22] 5. How long have you done business with your primary financial institution?
___ Less than 1 year[1] ___ 1-2 years[2] ___ 3-5 years[3] ___ 6-12 years[4] ___ Over 12 years[5]

[23] 6. Do you also have accounts at other institutions?
___ YES [1] ___ NO [2]

7. What services do you currently utilize at this institution?

FIGURE A.8 Supporting Documentation

[24] ___ Automatic Teller Machine
[25] ___ Personal Loans
[26] ___ Automobile Loans
[27] ___ Home (Mortgage) Loans
[28] ___ Telephone Bill Paying Service
[29] ___ VISA/MasterCard Services
[30] ___ Safe Deposit Box
[31] ___ Checking Account
[32] ___ Savings Account
[33] ___ Trust Account
[34] ___ Money Market Deposit Account
[35] ___ CDs and Investment Instrument
[36] ___ Individual Retirement Accounts (IRAs)
[37] ___ Overdraft Protection
[38] ___ Educational Loans
[39] ___ Other

[40] 8. (If secondary financial institutions) How long have you done business with your secondary financial institution? ___
___ Less than 1 year[1] ___ 1-2 years[2] ___ 3-5 years[3] ___ 6-12 years[4] ___ Over 12 years[5]

[41] 9. Have you changed your primary financial institution while living in this area?
___ YES1 ___ NO2 (Skip to question 13)

[42] 10. ___ How long ago did you make that change?
___ Less than 1 year[1] ___ 1-2 years[2] ___ 3-5 years[3] ___ 6-12 years[4] ___ Over 12 years[5]

[43] 11. Did you change from:
___ A bank to a savings and loan[1]
___ A bank to a credit union[2]
___ A savings and loan to a bank[3]
___ A savings and loan to a credit union[4]
___ A credit union to a bank[5]
___ A credit union to a savings and loan[6]

[44] 12. What was the main reason you changed financial institutions?
___ Poor service at old[1]
___ Better location of new[2]
___ Unsure of stability of old/felt safer at new institution[3]
___ Interest rates higher at new[4]
Other, specify[5] _____

[45] 13. On a scale of one to five, where "one" is strongly dissatisfied and "five" is very satisfied, how would you rate your satisfaction with your primary financial institution?
Strongly dissatisfied 1 2 3 4 5 Very satisfied

[46] If dissatisfied (1 or 2), ask Why are you dissatisfied?
___ Poor service at old[1]
___ Better location of new[2]
___ Unsure of stability of old/felt safer at new institution[3]
___ Interest rates higher at new[4]
Other, specify[5] _____

14. Now I would like you to think for a moment about financial institutions in this area. As I mention several factors about financial institutions, please tell me which one comes to mind first for each factor. It does not matter if you have ever done business with them or not. This is simply your initial impression or opinion.

FIGURE A.8 Supporting Documentation (continued)

	City Bank	First Bank	First Nat.	Premier Home	City Home	Public Bank	Other
[47]a. Best managed	1	2	3	4	5	6	7
[48]b. Friendliest, most personalized service	1	2	3	4	5	6	7
[49]c. Most customer-oriented	1	2	3	4	5	6	7
[50]d. Most progressive and up to date	1	2	3	4	5	6	7
[51]e. Best for investment-oriented customers	1	2	3	4	5	6	7
[52]f. The most innovative in the marketplace	1	2	3	4	5	6	7
[53]g. The financial institution most involved in community leadership	1	2	3	4	5	6	7
[54]h. Strongest financial base	1	2	3	4	5	6	7
[55]i. Best reputation for being successful	1	2	3	4	5	6	7
[56]j. The one you would recommend	1	2	3	4	5	6	7
[57]k. The one you would never recommend	1	2	3	4	5	6	7
[58]l. Has the best advertising	1	2	3	4	5	6	7
[59]m. The leader among local financial institutions	1	2	3	4	5	6	7
[60]n. Has the best service	1	2	3	4	5	6	7
[61]o. Makes fewest errors on accounts	1	2	3	4	5	6	7
[62]p. Friendliest, most knowledgeable employees	1	2	3	4	5	6	7
[63]q. Is the best place for people like you	1	2	3	4	5	6	7

FIGURE A.8 Supporting Documentation (continued)

15. Do you remember recently seeing or hearing advertising for local financial institutions? If yes, which ones?

[64] ___ Yes, Public

[65] ___ Yes, First National

[66] ___ Yes, Premier

[67] ___ Yes, Other

[68] ___ No (Skip to question 17)

16. On what media did you hear the advertising? (Mark all that apply)

[69] ___ Heard TV advertising

[70] ___ Heard radio advertising

[71] ___ Saw a newspaper ad/article

[72] ___ Saw new sign going up

[73] ___ Billboards

[74] ___ Someone told me about it

[75] ___ Other

[76] 17. Now just a few more questions about you. Are you:

___ Single with no children[1]

___ Married with no children[2]

___ Married with children at home[3]

___ Single with children at home[4]

___ Married with no children at home[5]

___ Single with no children at home[6]

___ Refused[7]

[77] 18. Which age category do you fit into?

___18-24[1] ___25-34[2] ___35-44[3] ___45-54[4] ___56-64[5] ___65 and older[6] ___Refused[7]

[78] 19. What is the category that includes your total family income? (READ)

___ Under 15,000[1] ___$15,000 to $24,999[2] ___$25,000 to $34,999[3] ___$35,000 to $49,999[4] ___$50,000 to $64,999[5]

___$65,000 to $79,999[6] ___$80,000 to $94,999[7] ___$95,000 to $110,999[8] ___ Over $110,000[9] ___ Don't know/refused[10]

[79] 20. Are you: (READ)

___ A high school graduate[1]

___ A high school graduate with some college[2]

___ A college graduate[3]

___ A college graduate with some graduate school[4]

___ A graduate degree holder[5]

___ Refused[6]

[80] 21. Sex: (Do not ask unless necessary)

___ Male[1] ___ Female[2]

[81] 22. Which of the following most closely approximates your average monthly balance in your checking account(s)? (READ)

___ Under $250[1]

___ $251–$500[2]

___ $501–$1,000[3]

___ $1,001–$2,000[4]

___ Over 2,000[5]

___ Refused[6]

[82] 23. Which is the approximate amount you have invested in CDs, money market deposit accounts, Individual Retirement Accounts, or other types of high-yield investments with financial institutions? (READ)

___ None[1]

___ Under $10,000[2]

___ $10,001–25,000[3]

FIGURE A.8 Supporting Documentation (continued)

___ $25,001–75,000[4]
___ Over $75,000[5]
___ Refused[6]

[83] 24. Finally, what would be a typical monthly balance for your non-checking savings accounts? (READ)
___ None[1]
___ Under $2,500[2]
___ $2,501–5,000[3]
___ $5,001–7,500[4]
___ $7,501–$10,000[5]
___ Over $10,000[6]
___ Refused[7]

Thank you very much for your time and cooperation.

FIGURE A.8 Supporting Documentation (continued)

Sample Proposals

Affordable Care Act Requirements Employee Satisfaction Proposal

Problem Statement

I have experienced many changes, positive and negative, as a result of the introduction of the Affordable Care Act. The Affordable Care Act has impacted the healthcare facility where I work, both its patients and financial services department. I have also witnessed changes within my own employer and other employers and how those changes have affected my family and friends. I am interested in researching the effects that the Affordable Care Act has had on my company as an employer, and specifically what changes they have made in order to accommodate the Affordable Care Act requirements in order to limit adverse effects on their employees and ultimately on profitability. Employee benefits are reviewed and changed every fiscal, and management is receiving mixed feedback from employees regarding the previous changes.

Literature Review

According to "ObamaCare Employer Mandate" (n.d), the requirement of the Affordable Care Act (ACA) for employers with greater than 50 employees to provide health insurance to their employees and dependents was delayed from its original planned start in 2014 until 2015/2016. This "mandate" would result in a fee for employers who did not comply. With this delay in consequences, the effects of the required changes on employers and employees may not yet have occurred. Antos and Capretta (2016) (as cited from "Labor Market Effects" 2014) note that "the law's likely effects on labor markets in February 2014. The agency concluded that the ACA's 'largest impacts will probably occur after 2016, once its major provisions have taken full effect and overall economic output nears its maximum sustainable level.'"

According to Burtless (2015) it is not yet clear what effects the higher costs to employers have had on hiring or employment, however does state that "in the case of minimum-wage workers there is considerable evidence that most employer costs associated with health insurance are passed along to workers in the form of lower money wages."

Both Burless (2015) and Antos & Capretta (2016) mention that it is hard to determine exactly what has caused negative changes for employees since the ACA was signed. Whether it was the ACA changes or the effects of what they call the "worst downturn since the Great Depression" referring to increased unemployment and low payroll employment.

Even with the requirements of the ACA for employers to offer insurance at an affordable rate, some employees still seek insurance options elsewhere based on lack of affordability, and are not required to take the insurance offered by their employer ("ObamaCare Employer Mandate," n.d.).

One impact of the requirement for employers to provide coverage for full-time employees is a reduction in the amount of full-time employees. According to "Impact of ObamaCare . . ." (n.d.),

"As an effect of the new employer mandate some larger firms who have to provide insurance for employees come 2015/2016 are cutting back employee hours to part-time to avoid paying for their health coverage. Other employers have moved workers from part-time to full-time to embrace the law."

Palmer (n.d.) also notes that:

"Data from the Federal Reserve Bank in Dallas shows that 84% of manufacturing firms report increased healthcare costs this year. Over 25% of these companies say they have fewer employees than before, and 16% said they hired more part-time workers. Furthermore, 17% said they outsource more work, and 20% say they have cut wages. We see some businesses cutting back hours to keep some employees part-time so they do not have to provide health insurance. These companies have weighed the costs and found that it just doesn't make good business sense to spend the money on the staffing if they must also spend more on insurance."

I have personally noted a change in some employers to hiring more part-time employees to fill what was a full-time position or utilizing staffing agencies to employ temporary workers. Palmer (n.d) implies a link between this shift and the ACA requirements. Antos & Capretta (2016) state that "The new *Health Affairs* studies do not find evidence that the ACA has caused a shift from full-time to part-time employment or major changes in the labor market behavior of low-income adults thus far." However, they go on to argue that according to the COB reports, some employers may have delayed changes as a result of the postponed employer mandate penalties.

Burtless (2015) acknowledges that there is a part of the population of part-time employees who would rather be full-time, however that we cannot be certain that the lack of full-time availability can be blamed on the ACA with unemployment high as well: "My guess is that the number of workers who involuntarily hold part-time jobs has remained high because of the weakness of the economic recovery rather than the effect of the ACA. It is not easy to devise a statistical test that allows us to confirm this suspicion, however." This article by Burtless however was written in 2015, which was the first year that the penalty was being enforced on employers, which could also be a factor in the lack of affects. Gorenstein (2016) quotes Bowen Garrett (Garrett & Kaestner, 2014) "'We still need to know more about whether that's really an effect of the ACA of it that is due to economic recovery. That could be causing some of these shifts.'" He also makes the point that it may be too soon to see a shift caused by the ACA requirements of employers to offer healthcare considering that the fines were not enforced on employers until a year ago, 2015.

Thomspon (2015) points out that temporary/contract workers are the employees of the staffing agency, therefore "it's easy to see how some employers figured they could avoid health care costs by outsourcing individuals to agencies." Another cost reducer pointed out by "FAQ: How Obamacare . . ." (2013) is the shift by companies to revoke coverage options for spouses or dependents completely or offering incentives to not cover them under their plan, or even bonuses to not utilize their insurance all together.

Palmer (n.d.) suggests that the rise in healthcare costs will continue to cause employees to leave their jobs after "realizing they're paying more for health insurance by having a job than they would be without having a job". Shubham, Stueland & Ungerman (2011) notes that "overall, employees value cash compensation several times more than health coverage" and that some younger employees also prefer career advancement opportunities to health insurance offerings. "FAQ: How Obamacare . . ." (2013) also predicts that the cost of healthcare will increase, and employers will shift that increase in cost onto the employees, causing more out of pocket cots for employees, both monthly and based on their plan coverage.

Palmer (n.d.) indicates that in order to keep claims low and "possibly decrease overall healthcare spending", some employers will increase their "employee wellness programs" or other incentives for employees to maintain a healthy lifestyle. "FAQ: How Obamacare . . ." (2013) also indicates that employers are trying to reduce their costs by "trying to make them think more about health-related expenses and behavior." They use an example of an employer offering incentives for price comparison and healthy lifestyle choices, but also utilizing the "discriminatory measures" allowed by the ACA and penalizing unhealthy lifestyle choices, using the example of smoking. Shubham, Stueland & Ungerman predicted in their 2011 article that once employers become more aware of the law, they will "make drastic changes" to their health care offerings including seeking alternatives to "traditional" employer sponsored insurance (ESI), including the possibility of dropping it altogether. Their research raises the question of whether or not employees who stay with their employers if they ceased offering ESI. Shubham, Stueland & Ungerman (2011) point out that even if an employer drops ESI, they will likely make up for it in some other aspect to their employees using vacation time, retirement, or health-management programs as examples.

Gorenstein (2016) concludes his article suggesting more research to analyze what is going on with what he calls the "vulnerable workers at the margins." I think Shubham, Stueland & Ungerman (2011) said it best, concluding that "In this new world, employers must quickly examine the implications of health care reform on their benefit and workforce strategies, as well as the opportunities and risks that reform generates." Most existing research focuses on the predicted shift from employers offering full-time work to part-time to avoid penalties from the ACA while also protecting their bottom line. I found it difficult to find any reports from the perspective of an employee. I also found little discussion of the effects of the penalties for individuals to go uninsured, those who chose not to enroll in their company's offered insurance.

Research Objectives

The purpose of this research is to discover the changes that my employer has had to make in order to accommodate the Affordable Care Act requirements. Specifically I intend to identify how the changes have affected our current employees to predict how to proceed with any future changes to have a positive effect on current and prospective employees.

Importance/Benefits

Change is constant in any business, and can have a positive or negative impact on many aspects of a company if it is not mitigated with attention to detail and planning. It is important that as any employer adopts change, they do so in a manner to maintain employee satisfaction and retention, while simultaneously focusing on profitability. High levels of employee turnover and increased levels of the overall cost of employees' (wages and benefits for example) can combine to have a negative impact on profitability.

Research Design

Exploration: Qualitative. I will expand my knowledge by interviewing Human Resource Managers and/or Executive level managers in order to develop an understanding of what changes were implemented to accommodate the Affordable Care Act within the company, with the purpose of developing an online survey to be distributed to all employees.

Questionnaire Design. An online, self-administered questionnaire distributed via my company's internal email system will be the most cost effective and anonymous way to gather opinions from employees on how the implemented changes have effected their experience as an employee. The survey will be made available for a 7 day time frame to allow all employees an opportunity to complete it with varying schedules. The questions will be based off of the information gathered through the interview mentioned in the previous paragraph, and prompted responses will be based on satisfaction levels on a scale from 1 to 5, one being completely dissatisfied, 5 being completely satisfied with a section at the end for any additional comments.

Logistics. I recommend using SurveyMonkey to distribute the questionnaire, as the employees have experience with this format, and it has proven to result in a simple and quick process for surveys in the past.

Pilot Test. I will test the questionnaire by distributing it first directly by email to a sample of employees with an additional comment section at the bottom for feedback about the survey format to allow any changes to be made to the questions prior to distributed company wide.

Evaluation of Nonresponse Bias. A census of names will be gathered following the end of the questionnaire's response window of the employees who did not respond to the questionnaire. These nonresponders will be interviewed over the phone and their responses to the questions or their reason for not taking the survey will be included in the final data interpretation.

Data Analysis

The questionnaire responses will be reviewed and organized based on the level of satisfaction reported for each question (change). This data will be organized into a chart for a visual representation of changes versus employee experience. The open ended question (comment section) responses will be interpreted and reported separately as pertaining to the purpose of the research. Identification of the least and most satisfied results will allow the HR Manager to see a representation of the changes that have been made to accommodate the ACA requirements, and the effects they have had on their employees in order to better understand how to approach decisions regarding changes for the upcoming fiscal year, what features to keep the same and where to look for alternatives.

Budget

Questionnaire Design. The development of a customized online survey will use a Survey-Monkey account. This will be an electronic survey therefore no print materials will be required for distribution.

Cost Summary:

Interview	$1,500.00
Travel Costs	$1,000.00
Questionnaire Development	$500.00
Survey Monkey Account	$200.00
Secure FTP site	$300.00
Final Report	$800.00
Total Costs	$4,300.00

REFERENCES

Antos, J., & Capretta, J. (2016, Feb. 3). The ACA and Its Employment Effects. Retrieved October 30, 2016 from http://healthaffairs.org/blog/2016/02/03/the-aca-and-its-employment-effects/

Burtless, G. (2015, March 20). Employment Impacts of the Affordable Care Act. Retrieved October 30, 2016, from https://www.brookings.edu/blog/health360/2015/03/20/employment-impacts-of-the-affordable-care-act/

The Congressional Budget Office (COB). Labor Market Effects of the Affordable Care Act: Updated Estimates. (2014, Feb.). Retrieved October 30, 2016 from http://www.cbo.gov/sites/default/files/cbofiles/attachments/45010-breakout-AppendixC.pdf

Garrett, B. & Kaestner, R. (2014, Sept. 14). Little Evidence of the ACA Increasing Part-Time Work So Far. Retrieved on November 6, 2016 from http://www.urban.org/sites/default/files/alfresco/publication-pdfs/413217-Little-Evidence-of-the-ACA-Increasing-Part-Time-Work-So-Far.PDF

Gorenstein, D. (2016, Jan. 6). The Effect of Obamacare on Employment. Retrieved November 6, 2016 from http://www.marketplace.org/2016/01/06/health-care/effect-obamacare-employment

Impact of ObamaCare on Jobs: Does ObamaCare Kill Jobs? Retrieved October 30, 2016, from http://obamacarefacts.com/impact-of-obamacare-on-jobs/

(2013, Oct. 11) FAQ: How Obamacare Affects Employers and How They're Responding. Retrieved on November 6, 2016 from http://www.npr.org/2013/10/11/231103865/faq-how -obamacare-affects-employers-and-how-they-re-responding

ObamaCare Employer Mandate. Retrieved October 30, 2016 from http://obamacarefacts.com/obamacare-employer-mandate/

Palmer, P. Effects of the Affordable Care Act on Employers. Retrieved October 30, 2016, from https://billadvocates .com/effects-affordable-care-act-employers/

Shubham, S., Stueland, J., & Ungerman, D. (2011, June). How US Health Care Reform Will Affect Employee Benefits. Retrieved on November 6, 2016 from http://www.mckinsey.com /industries/healthcare-systems-and-services/our-insights /how-us-health-care-reform-will-affect-employee-benefits

Thompson, W. (2015, Feb. 24). Impact of the Affordable Care Act on the Staffing Industry. Retrieved on October 30, 2016 from http://www.akkencloud.com/impact-affordable-care-act -staffing-industry/

Online Accounting Education: Employer Perceptions and Expectations

Problem Statement

Accounting education is changing due to the internet and the popularity and availability of online learning. With the growing availability of technologies, levels of technological understanding and a faster-paced world, online learning is more available now than ever before. And with that availability comes the opportunity for students to choose online learning and attain an education completely online. The advantages of online learning are the availability, flexibility and opportunities for individuals who have other obligations that may prevent them from attending a university full-time in a face-to-face environment. Along with the changes in education, accreditation standards have adapted to govern the assessment of learning for online courses. Independent organizations specialize in quality online learning initiatives, standards and training. Educators are learning and adapting to this change and utilizing standards established through research to attain effective teaching both in the classroom, online and through hybrid classes.

This research will look at the attitudes and intentions of employers in the accounting profession in relation to online learning. Accounting education is unique in that many who attain an accounting degree also attain a certification through a national exam. Also, in many states, the certification exam requires more college credit hours than a bachelor's degree. With these additional requirements, the online accounting degree is enhanced with national standards applicable to both traditional and online learning. However, potential employers of accountants may have differing opinions of online accounting education despite the leveling that the standardized exam and requirements beyond a traditional bachelor's degree may provide. This research will also look at the employers' perceptions of attaining the 150 hours and the skills needed to succeed in accounting in the context of online accounting education.

Literature Review

The issue of online learning needs to be understood by those making the hiring decisions. Many believe that with online learning, the qualities necessary to succeed are lost. Research indicates that the key issues that should be addressed and understood by those delivering online education and by those potentially hiring online graduates are the learning value of distance education courses, the design of effective courses, assessment issues, teacher training and resources needed and student issues (Salimi, 2007). While accounting educators are focusing on the accreditation requirements and effective online learning techniques, the workforce needs to begin to understand how the academic adaptations impact online learning and see this is a paradigm shift of learning not just an easier way to attain an education.

For those concerned with the level of learning of an online accounting degree, the Certified Public Accountant (CPA) exam is the most common leveling of accounting degrees. Whether a student has earned an online degree or a face-to-face degree, the national exam is a rigorous exam designed to allow only those who have attained a certain level of knowledge to hold the distinction of the CPA license. Many states require up to 150 hours of college credit for CPAs. The 150-hour requirement recommendations are for technical, communication and analytical skills. In addition, the American Institute of CPAs (AICPA) recommends that CPA candidates have the ability to work well with others (150 Hour Requirement, 2017). They recommend that hours be obtained through a graduate degree but do not specify if online or face-to-face is recommended. Recommended skills at the graduate level are communication, presentation, and interpersonal relations and integration of technical skills. All of which can be obtained in an online graduate program with sufficient technologies and trained professors.

The State Board Report (July, 2016) by the National Association of State Boards of Accountancy (NASBA) showed that pass rates for the CPA exams improved with schools with 1) investments in students and programs and 2) AACSB accreditation. In this research, no indication of face-to-face or online learning played a role in the pass rate for the students. Changes resulting from AACSB accreditation related to improved pass rates were increase in accounting faculty, reduction in concentrations, addition of entry exams and graduate exit tests (State Board Report, 2016). While the Association to Advance Collegiate Schools of Business (AACSB) accreditation does certainly have high standards that improve the quality of the coursework and the quality of the professors and the university, there is no requirement for face-to-face learning for this accreditation and many online and hybrid programs are available with this accreditation (Best Business Schools, 2017).

A study by Bunker and Harris (2014) found that students from predominantly online accounting programs significantly underperform on overall CPA Exam pass rates and average CPA Exam scores compared to both AACSB-accredited business schools and traditional, non-AACSB-accredited business schools. However, they did not do a comparison of programs both online and face-to-face who did have AACSB accreditation. Further indicating that an understanding of AACSB accreditation and the impact it has on the quality of learning, both face-to-face and online is essential for employers to understand the impact online learning has as well as an understanding of the accreditation standards required by universities.

Lindquist (2012), discussed research conducted with the big four accounting firms and the differences in hiring accounting graduates from a for-profit and a not-for-profit school. In these discussions, managers and partners said they have not hired a graduate from a for-profit institution. Lindquist continued the research by looking at the objective measures of program certification and performance of graduates on the CPA exam in comparing these two types of schools. Once again, the program certification of AACSB continued to show preference for hiring due to the faculty and curricula design required for such a designation rather than a comparison of face-to-face and online programs both with AACSB accreditation.

Quality Matters (QM) is a self-supporting organization which offers certification and faculty training programs based on a research directed at improving online education. Benton and White (2010) researched this national standard to determine if online education in a graduate accounting course met the quality standards established by QM. Student evaluations and GPA both raised as a result of implementing the QM standards to this accounting course.

Other research by Scofield and Walsh (2009), asked students completing an online accounting course what recommendations they have for students. From their research, the authors identified two categories of advice: input themes and action to take themes. The majority of the suggestions relate to good time management skills necessary to be successful in an online accounting course, but did not indicate that they were at a disadvantage by taking an online course in accounting.

In 2007, Seibold did a study of the perceptions of employers of online education in general. He found that participants in this study did not think online coursework is equivalent to traditionally acquired coursework. In general, lack of interactivity and community were lacking which resulted in a perceived lack of teamwork and networking. The participants did however indicate that other skills were developed in online learning such as self-motivation and technology skills and because of this finding recommended hybrid learning environments. This research specifically addressed the change in perceptions of employers from four years ago to the time of their research and then five years into the future. With the rapid change in technology, employer perceptions and knowledge should be researched and discussed frequently.

Grossman and Johnson (2015) did a study of employer perceptions of online accounting degrees. Their research specifically focused on an experimental study of educational environment, institutional reputation, employer type, undergraduate coursework mix and graduate coursework mix. They found that the reputation of the university does not significantly affect willingness to hire. They also found that the Big 4 firms are equally willing to hire online accounting graduates as most other accounting firms. In addition, they found that in coursework, employers favor applicants who complete their work on campus and a graduate degree online or vice versa rather than completing both degrees online.

Burke and Slavin (2000) discuss in the CPA Journal that accounting education is moving to distance learning both for educating nonaccounting graduates and for promoting lifelong learning to their current employees. In their paper, they present several examples of large accounting firms using technology to incorporate learning into their organizations with real-time interaction, cost savings and the ability to learn virtually. With reliable technology, rehearsed presenters and high quality programs, many firms believe this is the way to fulfil the shortage of accountants by educating their workforce and providing continuing education for currently employed accountants.

With the significant changes to CPEs to online formats, the status quo of accounting education may also soon change to the acceptance of online learning. Currently, many State Boards of Accounting accept online accounting courses as sufficient for meeting the requirements to sit for the CPA exam. For example, Oklahoma accepts online accounting courses but Texas requires 30 hours of accounting with 15 of those earned in a physical attendance format (thiswaytocpa.org, 2017). The AICPA recommends that candidates contact their state of residence to determine how many hours and the requirements of those hours to sit for the certification exams.

While not all accountants hold a certification, many do and those that do are required to earn Continuing Professional Education (CPE) throughout their career. CPEs are offered online and the big accounting firms are providing CPEs for their CPAs already in online formats through learning management systems and quality standards (Burke and Slavin, 2000). Other corporations are using online learning for training (Adler, 2001; Burke and Slavin, 2000). While final approval of online CPE is at the state level, the National Association of State Boards of Accountancy (NASBA), already sponsors and approves many online CPE courses (nasba.org).

CPAacademy.org was founded in 2012 and offers many CPE credits online that are NASBA approved. The president of CPAacademy.org, Scott Zarret, recently did a presentation on the future of CPEs and the impact technology has had and will have on the accounting profession. His prediction, based on Ohio State University and KPMG news, is that the status quo will change to not only online, but free learning through venues such as Massive Open Online Courses (MOOCs) which will navigate the future for CPEs in the accounting profession (Zarret, 2016). With these changes in accounting education at the corporate level, the perception of these same employers of an online undergraduate degree in accounting will provide information to help understand the future of accounting education.

Research Objectives

The purpose of this research is to ascertain the attitudes and intentions of accountants and managers who hire accountants with online accounting degrees. In addition, this research will attempt to ascertain employers' expectations for accountants to complete the 150 hour requirements in the context of online accounting education and what skills should be attained throughout the accountant's education.

Importance/Benefits

Understanding the attitudes and intentions of potential employers will enable educators and students to design and explain online accounting education. With the tools of accreditation, assessment and national standards, educators can work to help potential employers understand the impact online learning has on accounting education.

By first understanding current perceptions, online accounting program leaders can work to educate the workforce on the ways online education is adapting to the needs of society.

Research Design

Qualitative: A series of interviews with corporate managers, human resource managers, bank managers, CPAs and CPA firm partners will enable the refinement and better understanding of the questions developed from the literature review. In addition, the interviews will provide meaningful information related to the research topic.

Questionnaire Design: An online, self-administered questionnaire will be distributed to human resource managers and accounting managers through a nationwide database. Two groups are identified with 1,500 from each group chosen as a recipient of the survey: Decision makers in CPA firms and Decision makers in accounting departments. The recipients are selected from a nationwide pool of finance professionals. The purchased list will include first/last name, job title, business name, postal address, phone number and email address.

The survey will define online, face-to-face and hybrid learning and then will ask a series of questions related to hiring accountants and hiring CPAs. The survey will also ask questions to gather information related to the knowledge of accreditation, transcripts and online learning. Many questions will be based on a 7-point Likert scale, but some will be fill in the blank and ranking of criteria. For questions with continuous responses, MANOVA will be utilized for statistical analysis.

Logistics: The survey will be designed and analyzed using Survey Monkey software and will be delivered in an email with instructions and explanations given by university professors.

Data Analysis

The interview responses will be written up and organized according to the research topics discussed. In addition, all responses will be sorted and analyzed according to relationships and attributes and will be written in a narrative representation. The questionnaire responses will be analyzed for statistical significance based on the Likert scale responses and the ranking of criteria.

Budget

No print materials are needed due to the use of the online Survey Monkey tool. The purchased email list will cost $250 per thousand names or $750 total. No other direct costs are involved in this research project.

REFERENCES

150 Hour Requirement for Obtaining a CPA License. Retrieved February 8, 2017 from http://www.aicpa.org/BecomeACPA /Licensure/Requirements/Pages/defulat.aspx

Adler, J. (2001). Long-distance Learning. Crain's Chicago Business. Volume 24, Issue 10.

Bento, R. & White, L. (2010). Quality Measures that Matter. Issues in Information Science and Information Technology, Volume 7, pp. 61–72.

Best Business Schools. The Association to Advance Collegiate Schools of Business (AACSB). Retrieved May 20, 2017 from http://bestbizschools.aacsb.edu/undergraduate/programs.

Bunker, R. & Harris, D. (2014). Online Accounting Degrees: An Empirical Investigation of CPA Exam Success Rates. Journal of Business and Accounting: Volume 7, Number 1, pp. 86–93.

Burke, J. & Slavin, N. (2000). Just-in-time Accounting Education. CPA Journal, Volume 70, Issue 4, pp 46–51.

Grossman, A. & Johnson, L. (2015). Employer Perceptions of Online Accounting Degrees. Issues in Accounting Education; Volume 31, Number 1, pp. 91–109.

Lindquist, Tim M. (2012, April). Online Accounting Degrees: Research on the Quality of For-Profit and Not-For-Profit Programs. The CPA Journal, 66–71.

National Accounting Standards Board (NASB). CPE Requirements. Retrieved February 27, 2017 from https://www.nasbaregistry.org/cpe-requirements.

Salimi, A. (2007). The Promise and Challenges for Distance Education in Accounting. Strategic Finance, January, Volume 88, Issue 7, pp. 19–20;53.

Scofield, Barbara and Walsh, Robert (2009) "Student Advice for Online MBA Accounting Courses," *Kentucky Journal of Excellence in College Teaching and Learning*: Vol. 7, Article 3.

Seibold, K. N. (2007). Employers' perceptions of online education. (Doctoral dissertation, Oklahoma State University, Oklahoma, USA). Retrieved February 27, 2017, from *http://digital.library.okstate.edu/etd/umi-okstate-2378.pdf*.

thiswaytothecpa.org. (2017). State and Territory Requirements. Retrieved May 20, 2017 from https://www.thiswaytocpa.com/exam-licensure/state-requirements/TX/.

Zarret, S. (2016). Online Education: Global Trends and the Impact on CPAs. Retrieved February 27, 2017 from https://www.cpaacademy.org/archived_show/a0DC000000ndibdMAA.

Social Media Use in the Workplace CVR Energy Exposure to Risk

Problem Statement

As popularity and use of Social Media continue to rise, CVR Energy is concerned about personal use in the workplace. To what extent do employees use company computers, cell phones, wi-fi, and internet to access personal social media? These devices are connected to the company intranet and have access to company databases and records. This could unnecessarily expose the company to viruses and hackers and are a primary concern. Employee productivity and increased system traffic are related secondary concerns.

Literature Review

"Social networks are typical characterizations of human behavior to fulfill the need to communicate and connect with people they know, meet new people who share a common interest, collaborate, participate and share information and knowledge as well as gain new knowledge." (Yeshambel, Belete, & Mulualem, 2016).

As social media becomes more prevalent in society the question is asked, how does this affect security and productivity within businesses? (Diercksen, DiPlacido, Harvey, & Bosco, 2013) (Siegel, 2014) Ample research has been conducted regarding these topics. Conclusions vary regarding effect on productivity. (Olmstead, Lampe, & Ellison, 2016) Some studies have concluded that employee productivity increases as the brain is given a rest or at most effects are negligible. (Drønen, 2014) (Williams, 2009) Other studies argue that "each social media user costs their company $4452.00 every year" (Hawan, 2013).

Security of company systems is another valid concern for organizations. Social media can be a very effective on-ramp for malware attacks. Other threats include network breaches, intellectual property theft, and leakage of sensitive business information and hijacking of Websites. These types of attacks could devastate a company's reputation and profits.

Various studies have concluded 50–100% of respondent's access social sites daily in the workplace. (Munene & Nyaribo, 2013) (Herlle & Astray-Caneda, 2013) These staggering statistics are a cause of concern for businesses. To combat this issue companies have responded with formalized company policies regarding social media or use of software blocking such sites. This is imperative to protect the company from productivity loss and security risks if excessive social media use is discovered.

Research Objectives

*Facebook, Twitter, LinkedIn, YouTube, Instagram, Tumblr, Pinterest, Google+. . .*The list of social media sites available today is seemingly endless. These popular sites are a breeding ground for hackers and mischief.

The purpose of this research is to determine the amount of time and types of Social Media accessed via company devices within the workday. This information will be used to evaluate company exposure to security risks and employee productivity effects.

Importance/Benefits

As a publicly traded entity it is imperative that company information is properly secured. The company database contains employee information as well as other proprietary elements crucial to the success of the organization.

Research Design

Exploration: Qualitative. An interview of individuals within the IT department will be conducted to expand knowledge of the company databases, internet, and intranet. This interview will also further my understanding of Social Media sites that are likely to expose the company to the most risks.

Questionnaire Design. A self-administered, anonymous survey of company employees at all CVR sites.

Logistics. The survey will be distributed in hardcopy paper form to each employee via department supervisor. The completed form can be returned and deposited within any of several lockboxes. A lockbox will be placed in every clock house and break room.

Pilot Test. A small number of employees will be selected to test the questionnaire. Upon completion of Pilot Testing the questionnaire will be revised and submitted to CVR management for final approval.

Evaluation of Nonresponse Bias. 20 employees will be randomly selected who elected not to respond. These employees will be confidentially interviewed. The nonresponder answers will be compared statistically with those of the responders.

Data Analysis

A final report will be submitted to CVR Management. Statistical analysis of reported social media sites visited, time spent per day on personal sites, respondent perceived impact on performance, and company devices used to access sites.

Results: Deliverables

1. Development and production of questionnaire
2. Final report of findings.

Budget

Questionnaire Design. The Questionnaire will be printed on 4¼" by 5½" cards to fit four (4) surveys per 8½" by 11" page. The CVR Energy logo will be printed in the upper left hand corner of each survey.

Cost Summary

Interviews	$500.00
Questionnaire development	$1250.00
Equipment/Supplies	$750.00
Final Report	$1500.00
Total costs	$4480.00

REFERENCES

Herlle, Myrian, and Astray-Caneda, Vivian. "The Impact of Social Media in the Workplace." (2013). Retrieved from: http://digitalcommons.fiu.edu/cgi/viewcontent.cgi?article=1205&context=sferc

Yeshambel, Tilahun, Belete, Mengistu, and Mulualem, Yelkal. "Impact of Online Social Networking on Employees Productivity at Work Place in University of Gondar – A Case Study." *International Journal of Computer Applications* Volume 135, No. 3 (2016 Feb.) Retrieved from: http://www.ijcaonline.org/research/volume135/number3/yeshambel-2016-ijca-907844.pdf

Aguenza, B., Amer Hani Al-Kassem, and Ahmad Puad Mat Som. "Social Media and Productivity in the Workplace: Challenges and Constraints." *Interdisciplinary Journal of Research in Business* 2.2 (2012): 22. Retrieved from: http://www.idjrb.com/articlepdf/article223.pdf

Hawan, Erica D. "Social Media Hurts Productivity." (2013 Aug.) Retrieved from: http://ericadhawan.com/social-media-hurts-productivity/

Drønen, Sverre Ole. "How Private Social Media Use at Work Affects Work Performance." *ScienceNordic* (2014 Nov.) Retrieved from: http://sciencenordic.com/how-private-social-media-use-work-affects-work-performance

Munene, Assa Gakui and Nyaribo, Yeliffe Misuko. "Effect of Social Media Pertication in the Workplace on Employee Productivity." International Journal of Advances in Management and Economics Volume 2, Issue 2 (2013) Retrieved from: http://www.managementjournal.info/download1.php?f=17022013.pdf

Siegel, Barbara. "Social Media in the Workplace: Does it Impact Productivity?" (2014 Mar.) Retrieved from: http://www.lakeforestmba.edu/blog/social-media-workplace-impact-productivity/

Williams, Ray. "Social Media: Does it Help or Hinder Productivity?" (2009 Nov.) Retrieved from: https://www.psychologytoday.com/blog/wired-success/200911/social-media-does-it-help-or-hinder-productivity

Olmstead, Kenneth, Lampe, Cliff, and Ellison, Nicole B. "Social Media and the Workplace." Pew Research Center. (2016 Jun.) Retrieved from: http://www.pewinternet.org/2016/06/22/social-media-and-the-workplace/

Diercksen, Michael, DiPlacido, Matthew, Harvey, Diane, and Bosco, Susan. "The Effects of Social Media in Today's Workplace." Roger Williams University. (2013) Retrieved from: http://www.nedsi.org/proc/2013/proc/p121102007.pdf

Sample Questionnaires

To: All Employees

Subject: Survey for all Employees

In an effort to better understand how the changes to our company benefits packages have affected our employees, we are seeking your input. We would like to know your opinions regarding our employee benefits so that we are able to make future changes as beneficial as possible for everyone. Your participation in this survey will help to make sure that all bases are covered and ensure that we are providing the best options to meet your needs.

Please take this opportunity to complete this anonymous survey by selecting the link below. It should take no longer than 10-15 minutes of your time. The survey will open Wednesday, December 7th and close at the close of business on Wednesday, December 13th, so please complete it at your first opportunity.

https://www.surveymonkey.com/EXAMPLE

Thank you for your cooperation,

Emily Godfrey

1. Are you currently enrolled in the health insurance offered by your employer?
❑ Yes   ❑ No

2. Do you currently have any dependents enrolled in the health insurance plan offered by your employer?
❑ Yes   ❑ No

3. Has the cost of your coverage changed over the last 12 months?
❑ Yes   ❑ No   ❑ I am not enrolled

4. How has the cost of your coverage changed in the last 12 months?
❑ Less expensive   ❑ About the same   ❑ More expensive   ❑ I don't know

5. What features, if any, of your insurance have changed in price over the last 12 months?
_____

6. How would you rate the cost of the insurance options available through your employer?
❑ Unaffordable   ❑ Expensive   ❑ Average   ❑Affordable
❑ I don't know the costs

7. Have coverage options been reduced over the last 12 months?
❑ Yes   ❑ No   ❑ I don't know

8. If so, what options were revoked that you would prefer to still be offered?
_____

9. Do you have health insurance available to you from another provider?
❑ Yes   ❑ No

10. If so, where?
_____

11. How does your employer's health insurance plan compare to other plans you have priced out?

❏ Less expensive ❏ Comparable ❏ More expensive

12. What other health insurance prices have you researched, if any?

_____

13. Has your employer offered you incentives to maintain a healthier lifestyle?

❏ Yes ❏ No

14. What types of incentives do you prefer?

_____

15. Has your employer enforced penalties for any lifestyle choices?

❏ Yes ❏ No

16. What have you been penalized for?

_____

17. Have any of the changes made by your company to the health insurance benefits over the last 12 months affected your decision to stay or consider leaving your current position?

❏ Not at all ❏ Somewhat ❏ I am actively looking for a new job

18. What could your employer change to make you more satisfied with your healthcare benefits package?

_____

19. Would you rather another benefit be offered by your employer in place of health insurance?

❏ Yes ❏ No

20. If so, what benefits would you prefer in place of health insurance?

_____

21. Do you have any feedback regarding your current health care benefits options and how they can be improved over the next 12 months or before your next enrollment period?

_____

For clarity, the Online Learning Consortium has recently updated its e-learning definitions as follows.

Classroom Course (face-to-face): Course activity is organized around scheduled class meetings.

Blended (also called Hybrid) Classroom Course: Online activity is mixed with classroom meetings, replacing a significant percentage of, but not all required face-to-face instructional activities.

Online Course: All course activity is done online; there are no required face-to-face sessions within the course and no requirements for on-campus activity.

Survey topics:

1. In the last 3 years, how many accountants have you hired? (fill in blank)

2. How many accountants do you expect to hire in the next 3 years? (fill in blank)

3. What are the top 3 characteristics you look for in a candidate? (fill in blank)
   1)
   2)
   3)

4. a. If I am hiring an accountant, having a CPA certificate influences my decision to hire them.
   (Likert scale)
   b. If so, in what ways? (comment)

5. Are current employees encouraged and/or compensated to get a certification such as a CPA license? (yes or no)

6. a. Are current employees encouraged and/or compensated to attain a Master degree? (yes or no)
   b. Is the requirement that the master degree relates to their assigned duties/position? (yes or no)

7. Do you ask for undergraduate transcripts of applicants? (yes or no)
   If yes, how do you use these? (check all that apply)

   GPA (overall)
   GPA (in accounting)
   Delivery method
   Courses taken
   Time to complete

8. How do you evaluate the transcripts (please choose all that apply)

   GPA in accounting courses
   GPA overall
   Courses taken
   Hours earned
   Time to complete degree
   If any, what criteria do you use (GPA requirement, hours earned, etc.)? (open ended)

9. The reputation of the university where the applicant earned their degree affects my decision (Likert scale).

10. The accreditation of the university where the applicant earned their degree affects my decision (Likert scale).

11. An accounting degree from an online program would affect my decision to hire (Likert scale)

12. A percentage of **accounting** classes taken online would impact my decision to hire (Likert scale)

13. A percentage of **business** classes taken online would impact my decision to hire (Likert scale)

14. What percentage of online classes would you be comfortable with in a bachelor's degree in accounting?

    | 0-20% | 21-40% | 41-60% | 61-80% | 81-100% |

15. What percentage of online classes would you be comfortable with in a master's degree?

    | 0-20% | 21-40% | 41-60% | 61-80% | 81-100% |

16. How do you determine if courses are online or face-to-face? (check all that apply)

    Ask applicant
    Review transcript
    Contact University

17. An MBA from an online program would affect my decision to hire (Likert scale)
    Comments: Why or why not?

A Quality Matters Certified Course is an online or blended course that has met QM Standards for a QM Rubric in an Official Course Review. Once certified, organizations can display the QM Certification Mark to demonstrate their commitment to quality and continuous improvement.

18. Quality matters certification or something similar for each of the online courses taken would change my opinion of online courses. (Likert scale)

19. Of the following, please rank your concern, if any, for online courses:
    a. Learning value of distance education courses
    b. Design of effective courses
    c. Assessment issues
    d. Teacher training
    e. Resources utilized
    f. Student issues (Salimi, 2007)
    g. Integrity of online courses
    h. Opportunities for live interaction
    i. Accreditation
    j. Career preparation (Bunker and Harris, 2014)
    k. No concern

20. What is the best way for an accounting student to fulfill 150 hour requirement so that they can sit for the CPA exam? (choose one)

    Double major
    Minor
    Master's degree
    No preference

21. If you chose minor or double major, do you have a suggestion for a subject? (fill in blank)

22. If you chose Master's degree, which would you suggest? (choose one)

    MBA
    Master of Accounting
    Other (fill in blank)

23. How do you offer continuing education at your place of employment? (choose all that apply)

   Online
   Face-to-face
   Self-Study

24. Do you foresee a demand for accountants in your firm? (yes or no)

   5 years? (yes or no)
   10 years? (yes or no)

25. Supply and demand for accounts would change my view of online education. (Likert scale).

26. Please list the skill expectations you have of an applicant for an accounting position:

Demographics

Age
- 1 - Below 25
- 2 - 26-35
- 3 – 36-45
- 4 – 46-55
- 6 – Above 55

What is the highest level of education you have completed?
- Graduated high school
- Attended college but did not complete degree
- Completed associate's degree
- Completed bachelor's degree
- Completed master's degree
- Completed doctorate degree
- Do you hold any certifications such as CPA, CMA, CIA, etc? If yes, which ones? (fill in blank)

Gender
- Male
- Female

What is your current position at your place of employment? (check all that apply)
- Staff
- Management
- Human Resources
- Accounting department
- Owner

What best describes your industry?
- Public accounting
- Service
- Merchandising
- Manufacturing
- Other (fill in blank)

In what state(s) do you hire accountants? (fill in blank)

Employee Survey

CVR Energy is conducting an employee survey to better understand use and attitudes regarding social media. Your responses will be confidential and combined with others within the organization. Please deposit your completed survey in one of the various lockboxes located in facility clock houses and break-rooms.

1. What is your current job classification within the organization?
    a) operations
    b) professional/technical
    c) administrative
    d) managerial

2. Do you have a personal computer in your home?
    a) Yes
    b) No

3. Do you have access to internet in your home?
    a) Yes
    b) No

4. Do you have a personal cell phone?
    a) Yes
    b) No

5. Do you have company desktop/laptop computer?
    a) Yes
    b) No

6. Do you have a company cell phone?
    a. Yes
    b. No

7. Do you participate in social media? (Facebook, Twitter, LinkedIn, Instagram, etc . . .)
    a) Yes
    b) No

8. What social media accounts do you use? Circle all that apply.
    a) Facebook   b) Twitter   c) YouTube
    d) Instagram   e) LinkedIn   f) Tumblr
    g) Google+   h) Pinterest   i) Vine
    j) Other_____

9. How many Facebook "Friends" do you have?
    a) I do not use Facebook
    b) 0-100
    c) 101-200
    d) 201-300
    e) 300+

10. How many Twitter followers do you have?
    a) I do not use Twitter
    b) 0-100
    c) 101-200
    d) 201-300
    e) 300+

11. What is your estimated total time spent using/browsing social media on a day to day basis?
    a) I do not use social media
    b) 0-2 hours daily
    c) 2-3 hours daily
    d) 4-5 hours daily
    e) 6+ hours daily

12. How often do you log into your social media accounts at work?
    a) Never
    b) Seldom (Monthly)
    c) Occasionally (Weekly)
    d) Frequently (Daily)

13. Do you use company provided Wi-Fi on your personal devices at work?
    a. Yes
    b. No

14. Do you access social media sites using company Wi-Fi and/or internet?
    a) Yes
    b) No

15. Do you use company devices (laptops, cell phones, etc . . .) to access social media sites at home?
    a) Yes
    b) No

16. Have your personal e-mail or social media accounts ever been hacked or received a virus?
    a. Yes
    b. No

17. Do you feel that others within the organization abuse internet/Wi-Fi privileges at work?
    a) Yes
    b) No

18. Do you lock your company phone and/or computer when it is not in use?
    a) Yes
    b) No

19. In general do you see social media as a problem within the workplace?
    a) Yes
    b) No

20. How secure do you feel your personal information is when accessing social media sites?
    a) Very Secure
    b) Somewhat Secure
    c) Not Secure

Glossary

Alternative hypothesis a statement that is accepted if the null hypothesis is rejected. It is usually stated in a positive format such as one value is significantly larger than another value or one value is significantly associated with another value.

Analysis of selected cases case analysis involves the study of a specific situation similar to the current research problem. It is particularly valuable for complex research problems.

Analysis of variance (ANOVA) a statistical analysis technique designed to determine if three or more values are significantly different and analyzes their variances. This is a useful techniques for model building and in experimental research.

Appendices a report usually includes several appendices that contain the data gathering instrument, detailed findings, quotations, and in some cases, more detailed statistical information that some managers may be interested in.

Applied business research used to answer a specific question that has direct application to a particular business.

Attitudes refer to a person's feelings, convictions, or beliefs for an object, idea, or individual.

Autonomy people's freedom to make their own decisions and to choose the activities they wish to engage in and which activities to avoid.

Awareness and knowledge referring to what subjects do or do not know about an object of investigation.

Basic business research Business research that is exploratory in nature, and is not directly applicable to a specific business problem. Instead, basic research expands our knowledge and understanding of an issue.

Behaviors actual actions taken by respondents.

Big data large quantities of information collected by an organization on constituents such as the number, types, and amounts of transactions from customers of a large retail store. Such data is usually beyond the capability of some data software and requires specially designed software to provide analysis of the data.

Bivariate association a measure of the relationship between two variables to determine if there is a relationship and if so, the strength of that relationship.

Business research the function that links the business to information and knowledge that can be used for determining, implementing, and evaluating the opportunities and goals for a firm.

Causal research research that determines if one variable (the *independent variable*) causes a change in another variable (the *dependent variable*).

Central tendency calculated measures that are used to summarize data by using a number to represent the shape or typical values of a data set such as the mean, median or mode.

Clarify an answer that tells something specific is much more valuable than getting several answers that are vague. The interviewer's objective should be to clarify why the respondent gave a particular answer to one of the questions.

Cluster sample the population is divided into mutually exclusive subgroups, and the next step involves the selection of a random sample of subgroups rather than a random sample from each subgroup.

Communication includes various direct approaches of asking questions of respondents either by personal interview, telephone survey, electronic survey, or mail questionnaire

Comparative rating scale also known as a *constant-sum scale*, this scale requires respondents to divide a fixed number of points, usually a 100, among items according to their importance to the respondent.

Computer survey computer is utilized in telephone (CATI) interviewing, personal interviews conducted at shopping malls, or at a central location.

Confidentiality data collected in the research process is not to be shared in any way that it can be identified with any particular individual.

Construct abstract constructions (hence, the name) that are of interest to researchers. Some examples of constructs of interest to business researchers are customer satisfaction, heavy users, channel conflict, brand loyalty, and marketing orientation.

Construct validity involves the desire to measure or infer the presence of abstract characteristics for which no empirical validation seems possible.

Content validity is the extent to which it provides adequate coverage of the topic under study.

Control group a randomly selected group of units in the experiment that does not receive a treatment and thus serves as a benchmark for comparing the effects of treatments.

Convenience sample any process that quickly and easily selects sample elements.

Correlation a measure of the association or the relatedness of two or more variables like income and age.

Cross tabulations an analysis technique that is used to compare two or more variables by "crossing" one variable by another like product preference by age.

Cross-sectional analysis research that involves a sampling of a population of interest at one point in time. Also revered to as a *sample survey*.

Data refers to facts or information that is used as the basis of decision making.

Data analysis the process of breaking down facts or information to get meaning from the data.

Data error consist of interviewer errors, measurement errors, and processing errors.

Debrief debrief informs the study subjects of the results and conclusions on the research.

Deception occurs when study subjects are lead to believe something the researcher knows is not true.

Demographic and socioeconomic data information such as age, education, occupation, marital status, sex, income, ethnic identification, and social status.

Descriptive research research that *describes* something. It is much more structured than exploratory research and assumes more prior knowledge of the research problem.

Dichotomous questions give two choices: either yes or no, or a choice of two opposite alternatives.

Disguise how evident the purpose of the question or questionnaire is.

Dispersion measures of the variation of values from a central tendency such as the range, quartiles of standard deviation.

Distributive justice deals with the equitable determination of rewards.

Ethics the set of values and standards we use to make decisions about right and wrong.

Ethnography the researcher experiences life events along with the study participants—asking questions, observing, and recording their own feelings as they share the experience.

Executive summary the executive summary is usually a key component of the final report and summarizes the most important findings and recommendations of the research. As the name implies, it is written for the executives who may not take the time or have an interest in digesting the entire report.

Experimental design the researcher not only measures variables, as in other research designs, but also attempts to control some or all of the conditions under which the data are collected.

Exploratory research research that is undertaken when a problem is not well understood and there is no prior research available. Exploratory research is often used to better develop an understanding of the problem to aid in future research projects.

External secondary data data that originates outside the confines of the organization.

External validity concerned with whether the results are generalizable to other subjects, stores, or areas.

Field experiments experiments that are carried out in a natural setting with a minimum of artificial elements in the experiment.

Focus group a small number of people (usually eight to twelve), convened to address topics introduced by a group moderator.

Focus group interviewing consists of a small group of people (usually eight to twelve) assembled for the purpose of discussing in an unstructured, spontaneous manner topics introduced by a group moderator.

Frequency distribution a set of data that has been organized based on certain criteria such as number of occurrences or percentage of occurrences.

Grounded theory based on the concept that people act in response to environmental clues. The theory evolves during the research process.

Hypothesis testing a process used in scientific research to test assumptions about a population parameter or value which may or may not be true.

In-depth interview interviewing subjects with experience, expertise or position that gives them a unique perspective on the subject of interest.

Informed consent the researcher fully discloses the purposes and procedures involved in the research and obtains an affirmative acceptance from the subject before the research begins.

Institutional review board (IRB) The purpose of an IRB is to approve, monitor, and review any research that involves humans.

Intentions refer to the anticipated future behaviors of an individual.

Interactive justice (also known as interactional justice) involves the communication used in the relationship. Communication should be clear, understood by all, and the dignity of the individual respected.

Internal secondary data sources of information or information found within the organization initiating the research process.

Internal validity has to do with whether the independent variables that were manipulated caused the changes in the dependent variable, or whether other factors involved also influenced the dependent variable.

International organization for standardization a voluntary organization representing 163 countries, ISO develops common standards of measurement and quality to facilitate world trade.

Internet surveys can take various forms and target different groups of respondents. One of the most common uses of Internet surveys is to gather data from existing customers or clients.

Interval scale a scale with two features: (1) a unit of measurement, and (2) an arbitrary origin. The arbitrary origin of the interval scale means there is no natural origin or zero point from which the scale derives.

Itemized rating scales the points on the scale are itemized, with a description of the scale point provided.

Judgment sample a subjective approach to sampling, the knowledge and experience of a professional researcher can create a very representative sample.

Justice principle refers to the fairness of processes and rewards when dealing with others.

Laboratory experiments experiments conducted under artificial conditions, such as testing television ads in a movie theater rather than in buyers' homes.

Level of significance the numerical value placed on the likelihood that a value did not occur by chance when it actually did occur by chance and is usually expressed as a probability like .05. This means values this different would only occur 5% of the time or less if the null hypothesis is true.

Likert scale determine the strength of someone's attitude, positive or negative, toward an object by summing their scores for each of the item statements.

Literature review an investigation of previous research related to the research issues under study.

Longitudinal study research that monitors behavior over time and identifies behavioral or attitudinal changes.

Mail surveys commonly used in either ad hoc (one time) or mail panel research.

Managerial significance a statistically significant difference does not mean that the findings have a managerial significance in that management should take note of the findings and act on the findings. Managerial significance indicates that the results have important meaning to managers and would indicate that some action on their part is justified.

Moral philosophy (also known as virtue ethics) this school of thought posits that ethical decisions are based on one's moral virtue.

Motivations inner states that direct our behavior toward a goal.

Multichotomous questions provide several alternatives to respondents.

Multivariate association measures of the relationship among more than two variables to determine if there is a relationship and if so, the strength of that relationship.

Netnography ethnography that studies the consumer behavior of online communities.

Nominal scale the lowest level of measurement. It measures difference in kind (male, female, member, nonmember, and the like).

Nonprobability sampling sampling techniques that do not involve the selection of sample elements by chance.

Nonresponse error occur when some of the elements of the population selected to be part of the sample do not respond.

Nonsampling error is introduced into the research results from any source other than sampling.

Null hypothesis a statement about a population parameter or value that is made specifically to test whether or not a statement is true. It is usually expressed as a negative statement of no difference or no association between or among variables. The null hypothesis is tested and is either accepted or rejected.

Observation methods involves the process of physically or mechanically recording some specific aspect of a consumer's activity or behavior.

Open-ended questions provide an unlimited range of replies the respondent can make.

Operational definition indicates what observable attributes of the construct will be measured and the process that will be used to attach numbers to those attributes so as to represent the quantity of the attributes.

Opportunity a chance to improve overall performance.

Oral report an oral presentation of the research project highlighting the research objective, findings and recommendations of the research person or team and usually accompanies the written report.

Ordinal scale goes a step further than the nominal scale to introduce a direction of difference.

Personal interviewing face-to-face method is employed when the survey is too long to conduct over the telephone or there might be material to show the respondent.

Plan of analysis specifications of how the data will be broken down and the analytical techniques to be used to process the data.

Population or universe often this universe is called a target population because of the importance of focusing on exactly who the study objects are and where they are located.

Predictive or pragmatic validity the success of measures used for estimating purposes.

Primary data data that is collected explicitly for the research study at hand. Data that is not available in a secondary form that must be collected to address the specific needs of our research.

Principle of beneficence beneficence refers to the benefits of a study as opposed to its risks.

Privacy researchers must identify themselves when conducting a study, avoid any unwanted intrusion, and set interviews at mutually convenient times. Researchers must also follow all state and Federal privacy laws.

Probability sampling samples where each element has a known chance to be included in the sample.

Probing two basic purposes of probing in an interview are to clarify and develop additional information.

Problem anything that stands in the way of achieving an objective.

Procedural justice involves the "rules of the game" and if they are followed.

Projective techniques a form of research that is effective in discovering the hidden (latent) motives and attitudes of the research subjects. It is also useful when dealing with sensitive subjects.

Psychographics and lifestyle data this type of data is concerned with people's personality traits, what interests them, how they live, and their values.

Qualitative data data that may not be represented by numbers but rather themes or patterns of verbal or written responses such as recorded focus group interviews.

Qualitative research a type of exploratory research used to examine a problem involving underlying attitudes, opinions, and motivations in order to develop a hypothesis for future research.

Questionnaire the main type of data-gathering instrument in descriptive-research designs.

Questionnaire design for simplicity of format the sequence for developing a questionnaire is given on a step-by-step basis, rarely is a questionnaire constructed in such a routine way.

Quota sample takes great pains to obtain a representative sample by dividing the population and assigning appropriate quotas based on prior knowledge and understanding of the characteristics of the population.

Rank-order scale the respondent puts objects in an order of some variable under study (such as an order of liking, preference, intention to buy, or quality) generating ordinal data.

Ratio scale This scale has a natural origin. Zero means a complete absence of the property being measured. Properties measured on a ratio scale include weight, height, distance, speed, and sales.

Relativism ethical decisions based on the people around the decision maker or the specific context in which the decision maker finds him- or herself.

Reliability A reliable measure is one that consistently generates the same result over repeated measures.

Research design the road map for the researcher, indicating the route the researcher will take in collecting the information to ultimately solve the management problem or evaluate an opportunity under consideration.

Research report a written or oral (or both) presentation of the findings of a research project to the specific audiences for whom the research was requested or to other interested parties.

Rights principle this principle holds that a decision is ethical when it is the same decision most people would make based on universal morals (i.e., morals held by all people such as respect for life). This leads to the concept that an ethical decision is correct if it can be applied to all similar situations.

Sample bias is introduced into a sample when the sample varies in some systematic way from the larger population.

Sample size the size of the sample will be a function of the accuracy of the sample.

Sampling consists of obtaining information from a portion of a larger group or population.

Sampling error occurs when the sample does not perfectly represent the population under study.

Sampling frame a listing of the members of the target population that can be used to create and draw the sample.

Sampling frame error generally consist of noncoverage and over coverage errors. Noncoverage errors occur when some elements of the original population are not included in the sample.

Scales can be considered a multichotomous question, it deserves separate consideration.

Secondary data data that have already been collected for purposes other than the current research project.

Semantic differential scale a seven-point scale using pairs of adjectives or phrases that are opposite in meaning.

Simple random sample a technique that allows each element of the population an *equal* and *known* chance of being selected as part of the sample.

Stapel scale used as a substitute for the semantic differential when it is difficult to construct pairs of bipolar adjectives.

Statistical analysis the process of collecting, exploring, and describing data to derive meaningful information.

Statistical significance the likelihood or probability that observed results could have occurred by chance.

Stratified sample characterized by the fact that the total population is (1) divided into mutually exclusive subgroups (strata) (different age or income groups and the like) and that (2) a simple random sample is then chosen from each subgroup.

Structure the degree to which the question and the responses are standardized at some point in the data-collection process.

Structured-disguised questions maintain the advantages of structuring while attempting to add the advantage of disguise in eliminating possible bias from the respondent's knowledge of the purpose of the survey.

Structured-undisguised questions every respondent is posed the same questions in the same sequence, with the same opportunity of response.

Substantive significance refers to the strength of a relationship or the magnitude of a difference between two values.

Summary statistics measures used to summarize data by percentages or representative values.

Systematic sample every element has a known but not equal chance of being selected.

Tables and graphs tools used to display data/findings for the research and present a summary of the data and give a visual image of the research. Computerized software is usually used to generate and display the information.

Telephone interviewing usually employed when the study design requires speedy collection of information from a large, geographically dispersed population that would be too costly to do in person.

Test marketing a set of experimental or quasi-experimental (field) studies that are intended to determine the rate of market acceptance for (usually) a new product.

Thematic analysis the grouping of data into themes that will help answer the research questions.

Themes or patterns reoccurring ideas/responses that come from respondents from which data is collected such as comments about the size of an exhibit.

Three V's of big data volume, velocity, and variety, each of these affect the timing and type of analysis to be used.

Unstructured-undisguised questions often used in motivation research to determine the whys of an individual's behavior.

Utilitarianism (also known as teleology) the greatest good for the greatest number of people.

Validation questionnaire should include the original screening questions plus standard questions on method of recruitment, acquaintance with the interviews, and participation in other studies.

Validity the extent to which differences found among respondents using a measuring tool reflect *true* differences among respondents.

Verification a process used to verify the observations/statements made by an analyst by having the same observations/statements reviewed by another researcher.

Written report a written document following a specific format to describe the procedures, findings, and recommendations of research person or team. This document may become a reference tool for the current issues/problems being addressed as well as future research.

Index